W9-CRN-760

ESSENTIALS OF REAL ESTATE ECONOMICS

FIFTH EDITION

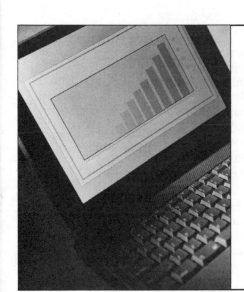

Dennis J. McKenzie

MBA, MA Economics, and Realtor®
College of The Redwoods

Richard M. Betts

MAI, SRA, ASA (Real Estate)
Property Analyst

THOMSON
SOUTH-WESTERN

Australia • Canada • Mexico • Singapore • Spain • United Kingdom • United States

THOMSON
★
SOUTH-WESTERN

Essentials of Real Estate Economics   Fifth Edition
Dennis J. McKenzie   Richard M. Betts

VP/Editorial Director:
Jack W. Calhoun

VP/Editor-in-Chief:
Dave Shaut

Executive Editor:
Scott Person

Associate Acquisitions Editor:
Sara Glassmeyer

Sr. Marketing Manager:
Mark Linton

Sr. Production Editor:
Cliff Kallemeyn

Sr. Technology Project Editor:
Matthew McKinney

Manufacturing Coordinator:
Charlene Taylor

Art Director:
Linda Helcher

Project Manager
Arlin Kauffman, LEAP

Production House:
Cadmus Inc.

Printer:
West Group
Eagan, MN

COPYRIGHT © 2006
Thomson South-Western, a part of
The Thomson Corporation. Thomson,
the Star logo, and South-Western
are trademarks used herein under
license.

Printed in the United States of
America
1 2 3 4 5 08 07 06 05

ISBN 0-324-18744-0

ALL RIGHTS RESERVED.
No part of this work covered by the
copyright hereon may be reproduced or used in any form or by
any means—graphic, electronic, or
mechanical, including photocopying, recording, taping, Web distribution or information storage and
retrieval systems, or in any other
manner—without the written permission of the publisher.

For permission to use material from
this text or product, submit a
request online at
http://www.thomsonrights.com.

Library of Congress Control Number:
2005930548

For more information about our
products, contact us at:

Thomson Learning Academic
Resource Center

1-800-423-0563

Thomson Higher Education
5191 Natorp Boulevard
Mason, OH 45040
USA

Asia (including India)
Thomson Learning
5 Shenton Way
#01-01 UIC Building
Singapore 068808

Australia/New Zealand
Thomson Learning Australia
102 Dodds Street
Southbank, Victoria 3006
Australia

Canada
Thomson Nelson
1120 Birchmount Road
Toronto, Ontario
M1K 5G4
Canada

Latin America
Thomson Learning
Seneca, 53
Colonia Polanco
11560 Mexico
D.F.Mexico

UK/Europe/Middle East/Africa
Thomson Learning
High Holborn House
50/51 Bedford Row
London WC1R 4LR
United Kingdom

Spain (including Portugal)
Thomson Paraninfo
Calle Magallanes, 25
28015 Madrid, Spain

BRIEF CONTENTS

CONTENTS

CHAPTER 3
Government's Role in the Economy   36

CHAPTER 11
Rural and Recreational Real Estate Markets

PART THREE
Major Influences On Real Estate Development

CHAPTER 12
The Economics of Real Property Taxation

CHAPTER 13
Land-Use Controls   306

PART FOUR
REAL ESTATE INVESTMENT
THE ECONOMICS OF THE PARCEL

ANSWERS TO REVIEWING YOUR UNDERSTANDING QUESTIONS   453

INDEX   458

PREFACE

This fifth edition is a complete update of the fourth edition. The format of the book has been retained, but many new topics have been added. This edition contains an appendix for each chapter called "Case & Point," covering diverse topics such as Adam Smith's life, graphic presentation of demand and supply curves, the pros and cons of allowing homeowners to deduct mortgage interest, the Laffer curve, housing, and detailed demographic stats for California counties and cities. Other Case & Point topics include discussions of whether government should be involved in neighborhood preservation, and the question of whether gated communities are a form of American apartheid. These hot-button topics will pique readers' interest. The sections on cash flow analysis and federal income tax rules for real estate investments have been completely updated. All other material has been reviewed and revised where needed. In short, this new edition presents the current information needed for a successful course in real estate economics for real estate agents, appraisers, and investors.

As noted in the earlier edition, this book is an outgrowth of years of teaching real estate economics at California community colleges and private schools. The material is structured in convenient blocks to allow all instructors to adapt the book to various formats. The publisher is developing a new Instructor's Manual for this edition which will include Lecture Notes, Quizzes, Examinations, a PowerPoint presentation, as well as Transparency Masters.

This book emphasizes the factors that cause real estate value to change. To present this complex subject in a practical manner, we have heeded Thoreau's plea to "simplify." The text is intended for real estate students who have little or no background in formal economics. Thus, the approach is direct and practical.

It is not possible to acknowledge all the assistance we have received from our students, colleagues, and friends. We hope we have successfully communicated the insights that they have provided. In addition, we dedicate this fifth edition to our mentors and role models: Dr. Russell Connett, Professor Emeritus of Real Estate, Humboldt

State University; Dr. John Grobey, Professor Emeritus of Economics, Humboldt State University; Emeritus and the late Dr. Paul Wendt, Professor of Real Estate, University of California, Berkeley.

Dennis J. McKenzie

Richard M. Betts

PART ONE
BASIC ECONOMIC BACKGROUND FOR REAL ESTATE ANALYSIS

CHAPTER 1
INTRODUCTION TO REAL ESTATE ECONOMICS

A s you begin reading this textbook, you probably have certain questions in mind: What is economics? What is *real estate economics*? Why should you study real estate economics? What topics are covered in this book? How is the material organized? This introductory chapter answers these questions so you will know what to expect from this textbook.

What Is Economics?

Economics is a social science that is concerned with how individuals and societies choose to use scarce resources to produce, distribute, and consume goods and services. The demand for goods and services frequently exceeds the supply, and how these scarce resources are allocated is the main interest of economists.

The study of economics can be broken into two main categories: macroeconomics and microeconomics. *Macroeconomics* is the study of the national economy and its various segments, such as national income, output, employment, and growth. *Microeconomics* is concerned with the individual units within the general economy, such as business firms and households. Whether the focus is macro or micro, the role of the economist is to analyze how resources are currently being utilized. The economist may offer suggestions for change and forecasts of trends.

What is Real Estate?

Real estate is defined as land, that which is affixed to the land, that which is appurtenant to the land, and that which is immovable by law. The ownership of real estate carries certain rights, known as the *bundle of rights*. The bundle includes the right to use, possess, exclude, and dispose. These rights are not absolute; they can be legally modified by private restrictions and government regulations and laws. In short, real estate or real property is land and improvements and the rights associated with the ownership of same.

What is Real Estate Economics?

Real estate economics is about people and how their actions affect real estate values. A formal definition would be: *Real estate economics is a study that uses economic principles, both macro and micro, to analyze the impact that national, regional, community, and neighborhood trends have on real estate values.*

In our society, our desire for goods and services frequently exceeds the supply available. This scarcity gives rise to the idea of economic value. Real estate economics focuses on the economic principles that affect real estate values.

What Real Estate Economics is Not

Real estate economics is neither the study of general economics nor a course in the practice of real estate. Rather, real estate economics is the link between general economic theory and applied real estate practice. A course in general economics concentrates on how society attempts to use limited resources to satisfy the wants of its people. However, such a course does not examine how this affects local real estate markets. On the other hand, a course in real estate practice concentrates on the specific techniques needed to complete a real estate transaction but spends little time discussing the economic influences that determine whether a home purchase or other real estate investment will be profitable over the years.

Real estate economics draws principles from both general economics and real estate practice and then combines them in order to study changes in real estate activity. The main thrust of real estate economics is to help real estate students anticipate future trends and what impact these trends will have on local real estate values.

Figure 1.1 illustrates the relationships among general economics, real estate economics, and real estate practice.

Figure 1.1 The field of real estate economics draws principles from both general economics and real estate practice.

Why Study Real Estate Economics?

Real estate economics helps people understand what causes fluctuations in real estate activity and how these changes can affect local real estate markets. Investors and licensed agents make real estate decisions that influence the shape, form, and value of property in a given community. Real estate decisions made today will be reflected in real estate values in the cities and neighborhoods of tomorrow; a course in real estate economics aids people in understanding what impact today's real estate actions will have on future real estate values. In California, for instance, real estate economics is considered so important that state law requires that a course in real estate economics, or its equivalent, be completed before a person can become a licensed real estate broker.

A General Overview

It is suggested that you study this brief introduction to the text, as well as the Table of Contents, in order to gain a sense of the relation of each chapter to the overall thrust of this book.

This textbook is divided into four parts, starting with general economic principles and moving on to applied real estate economics. Part One, "Basic Economic Background for Real Estate Analysis," contains five chapters, which review the major principles of economics and discuss why these principles are important to real estate students. After outlining the basic economic principles of the U.S. economy, Part One explores the role of government and foreign interests in the economy, devotes a chapter to monetary policy, and discusses the economic characteristics of real estate markets.

Part Two, "Understanding Real Estate Markets," devotes six chapters to regional, community, and neighborhood real estate analysis. The objective is to discuss why local and regional economies change and how these changes are reflected in the real estate market.

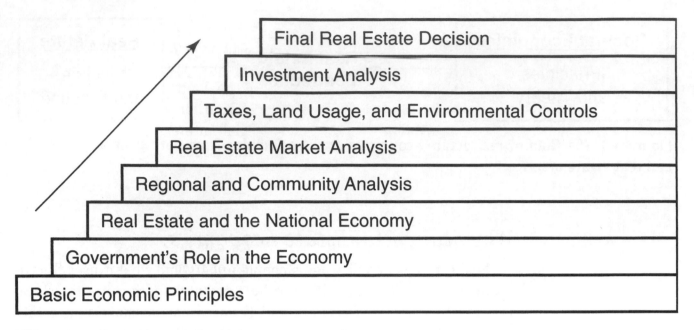

Figure 1.2 The stairway of real estate economics.

Part Three, "Major Influences on Real Estate Development," presents one chapter on each of four topics: real property taxation, land-use controls, real estate development procedures, and required government reports. These subjects are controversial issues in the field of real estate.

In Part Four, "Real Estate Investment: The Economics of the Parcel," four chapters bring together all the material previously presented in order to demonstrate how the principles of real estate economics can be used to analyze a specific property. Topics include investment principles, cash flow analysis, income tax aspects of real estate, and forecasting trends.

Figure 1.2 illustrates how this textbook advances from one level of understanding to the next. The steps outlined form the basis for sound real estate decision making.

Chapter Outlines

Each chapter in this textbook begins with a short preview of the material and a list of objectives that you should be able to achieve upon completion of the chapter. After each section within a chapter, there is a series of brief questions to check your understanding of the material in that section. You should work methodically through each chapter, taking time to review each section for any points you have not understood.

At the end of each chapter, starting with Chapter 2, there is a brief summary and a list of the important terms and concepts found in that chapter, plus 25 multiple-choice questions. Answers are given at the back of the book. Once again, you can test your understanding of what you have read by studying the chapter summary, reviewing the terms and concepts, and answering the multiple-choice questions. This material is a valuable aid in preparing for examinations. Finally, a number of figures and other special interest inserts have been included in each chapter to clarify some issues and provide variety in your reading.

A Final Word

The study of real estate economics can be approached from the mathematical view, called *econometrics*, or from the nonmathematical perspective, using verbal descriptions. Econometrics combines economics, mathematics, and statistics to express economic relationships in terms of mathematical equations. The verbal approach uses words rather than equations to describe economic relationships.

This textbook uses the verbal approach wherever possible, and special emphasis has been placed on a streamlined and summarized approach to explaining economic concepts. Students who wish to pursue economic principles in more detail are encouraged to contact their local college and obtain information about course offerings in economics.

CHAPTER 2
REVIEW OF THE ECONOMIC PRINCIPLES OF CAPITALISM

PREVIEW

This chapter reviews the basic economic principles of capitalism. Section 2.1 examines the purpose of an economic system and the characteristics of a pure capitalist economy. Section 2.2 describes the factors needed to produce goods and services and includes a model showing the flow of goods, services, and income in a capitalistic economy. Section 2.3 deals with the importance of a market and how prices and output are established in a competitive market. The Case & Point at the end of the chapter sketches the life of Adam Smith. When you have completed this chapter, you will be able to:

1. Describe why every society must have an economic system.

2. List the basic characteristics of pure capitalism.

3. List the factors of production that enable our economy to produce goods and services.

4. Describe how prices are established in a competitive market.

2.1 Basic Economic Concepts

Economics Revisited

As stated in Chapter 1, economics is *a social science concerned with how individuals and societies choose to use scarce resources to produce, distribute, and consume goods and services*. A science that is concerned with human behavior is frequently called a social or behavioral science. Therefore, economics is a social or behavioral science that studies how people allocate scarce resources in order to satisfy their need for food, clothing, housing, and recreation.

The desire for material goods and services usually exceeds the supply available, and economics attempts to determine how scarce goods and services can be distributed efficiently. For example, imagine how many people would like to live on a 10- to 15-acre ranch within an easy 20 minute commute of their jobs in a large city. When such a mini-ranch becomes available, who gets it? Who decides which person(s) gets the land and the opportunity to enjoy a rural setting and who must continue to live in the congested city? Should names be drawn out of a hat? Should it go to the highest bidder? Should the land be subdivided? Should the government make it into a park? As you can see, this is a problem involving scarcity. There is simply not enough land to satisfy all of the people who wish to live on miniranches.

Choice and Opportunity Cost—No Free Lunch

A key concept in economics is choice and opportunity cost. Resources are scarce, and individuals and societies must choose among competing uses of limited resources. Once a choice is made, that which is given up or not selected is the trade-off, or *opportunity cost*, that one must pay for a particular choice. For example, if a person works in a large city but chooses to live in a quiet suburban area, the trade-off or opportunity cost of living in the suburbs is the expense, time, and frustration of a long daily commute. In short, every choice incurs a cost; there is no free lunch. It is the role of the economist to examine alternate solutions to scarcity problems, pointing out the advantages and opportunity cost of each solution.

Economics Is an Inexact Science

As a social science, economics is concerned with human behavior, not with mere physical objects. A chemist can predict with great accuracy what will occur when certain chemicals are mixed. But an economist cannot always predict accurately what will occur when certain economic ingredients are mixed. For example, if a country is in a recession, reducing income taxes should stimulate the economy because people and businesses will have extra dollars to spend. But a tax cut will not immediately stimulate the economy if people and businesses decide to save rather than spend their newfound dollars. The key point is that people can change their behavior patterns, and these changes add uncertainty to economic predictions. However, by constantly studying human behavior and upgrading their analytical tools, economists are continually attempting to improve the accuracy of their forecasts.

Economic Solutions May Contain Value Judgments

Frequently, economists can agree on the nature of an economic problem but, because of data interpretation and their own personal beliefs, can differ as to the best solutions. For example, if a nation is suffering rapid inflation an excessive, caused by (price increases) demand for goods, beyond the increase in supply that businesses can achieve, most economists would agree that inflation should be reduced. But what actions should be taken to stop inflation? Should the government increase taxes to cut consumer spending? If so, whose taxes should be increased? Or should the government cut back on its own spending? If so, which government programs—welfare, defense, highways, low-income housing—should be cut?

Students should not become bewildered by disagreements among economists. Disagreements among experts exist in most fields of study. How can two equally qualified real estate experts arrive at different conclusions as to the ideal use for the same parcel of land? Is there not just one ideal land use? Or does the interpretation of an ideal land use depend on the circumstances, interests, and experiences of the person proposing the solution?

As trained social scientists, economists attempt to minimize the number of personal value judgments that enter into their analyses, but students should recognize that some bias does exist. When disagreements arise among experts, students should carefully listen to all sides and then form their own opinions.

Different Economic Systems

What will be produced? How will it be produced? For whom will it be produced? These are the economic questions that every society must answer, and economists have agreed that there are three general types of answers to these questions. If the society chooses to continue doing things as they have been done before, we call its system a *traditional economy*. A child follows the parent's trade, a farmer uses age-old methods, social stratification remains fixed— these are the hallmarks of a traditional economy like that of medieval Europe and is found today in some underdeveloped countries. If the great majority of decisions about production and distribution are made by private individuals in competitive markets, the system is called a *market economy*, or *capitalism*. If it is the government that makes most of the economic decisions in society, the system is a *command economy*, more commonly known as *socialism* or *communism* (see Figure 2.1).

Although some of the underdeveloped world still has a traditional economy, our concern will be with the market and command solutions to the basic questions of production and distribution. The major distinction between these two systems is the role of the government. In a "pure" market—or capitalist—society, the government provides only defense needs and a judicial system that will protect the rights of individuals and foster competitive markets. Private individuals own the property and resources of the society. They produce goods and services and distribute them according to supply and demand using a competitive market system. It is the ability to pay, not the need to have, that determines who gets what in this system. In a "pure" command—or socialist—society, the government owns the major resources as a trustee for the people. The government produces and distributes goods and services according to its interpretation of its citizens' needs.

In the real world, there is no such thing as pure capitalism or pure socialism. Although in recent years there has been a worldwide decline in socialism, all large economies have some mixture of the two systems. The United States is primarily a capitalistic country, but its economy has many features of the command system: Just look at the

Figure 2.1 Span of economic systems.

uses the government makes of tax dollars. Whether citizens like it or not, the U.S. government builds missiles, supports various social services, builds roads, and gives food to developing nations. On the other hand, countries with more socialistic economies allow their farmers to have private plots of land, encourage some individuals to own and operate businesses, follow public buying patterns to determine what consumer goods to produce, and create profit incentives for some categories of workers.

Basic Principles of Pure Capitalism

The present economic system of the United States has its roots in the principles and theories of pure capitalism. Therefore, it is important to understand certain key elements known as the principles of capitalism.

Principles of Capitalism

1. *Private Property*: The right of the individual to own, control, and dispose of property.

2. *Private Enterprise*: The major resources and businesses are owned and controlled by private citizens, who have freedom of choice in the use of these resources.

3. *Competitive Markets*: Markets in which numerous buyers and sellers are pitted against one another as they bargain for the exchange of goods and services. No one buyer or seller has enough power to manipulate prices. Ultimately, the bargaining process results in goods and services being allocated at the lowest possible price.

4. *Profit Motive*: The desire for personal gain motivates individuals to take risks and form businesses to produce the goods and services demanded by society. Failure to produce what society wants at the correct price will cause personal bankruptcy, whereas success will generate profit and personal wealth.

5. *Laissez-faire* (hands off): A philosophy that the government should not interfere in the basic economic affairs of private citizens.

How Pure Capitalism Answers the Questions What, How, *and* for Whom

In a pure capitalistic economy, how does society answer the critical questions of what, how, and for whom to produce? The answers are determined by the interaction of supply and demand—what Adam Smith, the famous capitalist, called the "invisible hand." What to produce is determined by businesses as they produce goods and services to satisfy the demands of buyers. Do you remember the Pontiac Aztec? General Motors built it, but there was insufficient demand and the Aztec went out of production after a year. On the other hand, illegal drugs continue to be produced and distributed in spite of government efforts to prevent the flow of these harmful substances. Why? Because demand drives up prices and high prices in turn stimulate the supply, even if the supplier runs the risk of imprisonment and/or death from gang wars.

The question of how to produce is answered by the lowest possible production cost. To remain competitive, a manufacturer or service provider must constantly seek ways of producing at lower costs. According to pure capitalistic theory, these lower costs should ultimately result in lower consumer prices.

For whom shall the items be produced? Who gets the goods and services, and who must do without? According to the theory of capitalism, goods and services will go to those who have something of value to exchange. Usually the medium of exchange is money. In short, goods and services go to those who can pay for them.

Modern Mixed Capitalism in the United States

It should be clear from your understanding of American economic society that the United States does not have a pure form of capitalism. Economists refer to the American economy as a *mixed capitalistic system*. Although most goods and services are produced by private enterprise, the government plays an important role either directly or indirectly in controlling the economy.

The government in a mixed capitalistic system attempts to correct what it and the majority of its citizens consider to be the faults of pure capitalism. Especially since the Great Depression of the 1930s, the government has played a major role in attempting to maintain full employment, create general economic stability, and promote a reasonable level of economic growth. Other governmental interventions in the economy involve regulation of business, income redistribution, and welfare programs.

THEORIES AND
THEORETICIANS

FAMOUS CAPITALIST ADAM SMITH (1723–1790)

From the Warren J. Samuels Portrait Collection, Duke University.

In 1776, in addition to the American Revolution, another event took place that would have a profound effect on the world: Adam Smith wrote *The Wealth of Nations*. This book described an economic system based on the concept of private ownership and free competitive markets without government interference. Smith used the term *laissez-faire* (hands off) to describe the government's role.

Smith stressed that an economy free of government, where individuals were motivated by profit and self-interest, would unknowingly provide for the efficient allocation of resources.

Modern-day capitalistic theories spring from the ideas set forth by Adam Smith in 1776. See the Case & Point at the end of this chapter for more details on the life of Adam Smith.

As befits a democratic society, we hear voices of gloom on the right and doom on the left preaching, respectively, the adoption of a less or more active governmental role in preserving the fundamental essence of the American system.

THEORIES AND THEORETICIANS

FAMOUS SOCIALIST KARL MARX (1818–1883)

From the Warren J. Samuels Portrait Collection, Duke University.

In 1867, another important book was published that would also have a profound effect on the world. Karl Marx, an impoverished philosopher living in England, wrote a book entitled *Das Kapital* (Capital).

In his book, Marx predicted that capitalism was doomed to fail because capitalists motivated by profits would force workers to take less money, thus lowering wages to the subsistence level. In time, a few rich capitalists would have all the wealth, while the workers would be living in misery. Workers would then arise, overthrow the capitalists, and seize the wealth on behalf of the workers.

Marx believed that this revolution would lead to a new, classless society. All would willingly work according to their abilities and receive goods according to their needs. Some modern-day socialism and much of today's communism stem from the ideas of Karl Marx.

In the field of real estate you might hear voices asking for less regulation over land use. A few minutes later the same voices are demanding that the government do something to lower interest rates to make housing more affordable! Today there are many spokespersons for the current system of economic compromise. This mixed capitalistic system has evolved over many decades, and the voters have made it abundantly clear that neither pure capitalism nor pure socialism is acceptable.

Before taking a closer look at the American economy to see how goods and services are produced, how income is generated, and the importance of land, review the questions below.

REVIEWING YOUR UNDERSTANDING

Basic Economic Concepts

1. What is the definition of economics?

2. What does an economic system attempt to do?

3. What is government's role under capitalism? Under socialism?

4. Explain the following: private property, private enterprise, competitive markets, profit motive, and laissez-faire.

2.2 Economic Principles in Action

This section provides a simplified model of the U.S. economy that illustrates how goods, services, and income flow through the economic system.

Factors of Production

According to economists, there are four essential resources, called *factors of production*, that are needed to produce goods and services: land, labor, capital, and entrepreneurship.

Factors of Production

1. *Land* refers to all natural resources—trees, minerals, and water——as well as the surface of the earth. The land provides the raw materials needed to manufacture goods, grow food, and provide shelter.

2. *Labor* is the human effort needed to transform raw materials into finished products or to perform services.

3. *Capital* is any manufactured instrument used to increase production, such as machinery, tools, and buildings. Although *money capital* is needed to purchase *capital equipment*, money itself cannot extract resources or produce goods and services. The role of money capital in the real estate market is discussed later.

4. *Entrepreneurship* is the assembling of the other factors of production in a systematic manner to produce goods or services. This activity is performed by the owner, or entrepreneur, and is commonly known as "going into business."

These four elements come together to produce and distribute goods and services in the U.S. economy.

Rent, Wages, Interest, Profit, and Income

In a capitalistic economy, private individuals own the factors of production, and they insist upon payment for the use of their "property." Owners of land receive *rent* for the use of their land. Workers sell their labor for *wages*. Lenders of money *receive interest* from borrowers who want to purchase capital equipment. And successful entrepreneurs earn *profits* from the operation of their businesses. (Unsuccessful entrepreneurs, of course, incur losses or go out of business.)

Rents, wages, interest, and profits constitute *income*. If you are like most people, you spend a major portion of your income buying goods and services. Thus, *our economy has a circular flow*. Business buys land, labor, and capital from individuals, and individuals use this income to buy goods and services from business.

The Circular Flow of the Economy

Figure 2.2 illustrates the circular flow of the U.S. economy. The role played by government and foreigners will be discussed in the next chapter. For now, assume that the government and foreigners do not participate in the economy.

The solid inner lines in Figure 2.2 show the flow of resources and goods. The outer dotted lines show the flow of income. As you see, the individual is both buyer and seller. He or she sells land, labor, or Capital in the resource market and buys goods and services in the product market. Businesses buy land, labor, and capital in the resource market and sell goods and services in the product market. check your understanding of this circular flow by answering the following questions.

Figure 2.2 The circular flow of the economy, simplified model, excluding government's role and imports and exports.

REVIEWING YOUR UNDERSTANDING

Economic Principles in Action—Circular Flow of the Economy

What will happen to this circular flow if the following occurs:

1. Business experiences a decline in sales and decides to cut back on production. Will the economy expand or contract? Will employment rise or decline? Will household income increase or decrease?

2. What will happen to this flow if the reverse takes place and high profits motivate business to expand its output? You should be able to trace the changes through each section of Figure 2.2.

2.3 Markets and Prices

This section defines the term *market* and describes how prices and output are established in competitive markets. Special emphasis is placed on the factors that cause prices and output to change.

What Determines Prices and Output?

What determines the rent charged for land? The interest rate charged for capital? The wage level charged by labor? The price of goods and services? The amount of goods produced? In the U.S. economy, most of these questions are answered in the marketplace. A *market* is defined as *a place where buyers and sellers meet to bargain and exchange items of value at negotiated prices*.

The characteristics of a market can influence the level of output and the prices paid for goods and services. Markets can be broken down into two broad categories: markets with *perfect competition* and markets with *imperfect competition*.

Perfect versus Imperfect Markets

When conditions of perfect competition prevail in a market, there are many buyers and sellers bidding against each other for available goods and services. No one buyer or seller can exert influence over the market or control prices. The goods or services being offered are similar enough so that the buyer will select the lowest-priced offering. The bargaining between buyers and sellers establishes prices.

If either the buyer or the seller exercises some control over the market, then conditions of imperfect competition prevail. If there are several sellers and one buyer, a lower price will result. If there are several buyers and one seller, a higher price will result. Consider the previous example of the miniranch in the suburbs: If there is just one property for sale and demand is strong, the many prospective suburbanites will drive the price up by bidding against each other. But if 500 miniranches suddenly came on the market, the price of most miniranches in the area should level off or fall.

Demand and Supply—The Classic Answer to Price Determination

The U.S. economy has become so complex that it is difficult to find examples of perfect competition, but people tend to understand the market forces that influence prices more clearly by viewing them under conditions of perfect competition. Therefore, the following discussion assumes a perfectly competitive market. Later, the principles discussed below will be modified to analyze prices in the imperfect real estate market.

Prices in a market economy are determined by the interaction of buyers and sellers as they compete against one another for goods and services in the marketplace. *The total quantity that buyers are willing to buy at a given time at certain prices is called demand. The total quantity that sellers are willing to sell at a given time at certain prices is called supply.*

Demand

People must be careful not to confuse desire or need with demand. Demand is desire or need coupled with the ability and the willingness to spend. For example, Family A wants a $500,000 home but cannot afford it. Family B wants the same home and can afford it, but does not want to make the necessary high monthly payments. Family C wants the house, can afford it, and will make high monthly payments. Only Family C exercises real demand for this house. Families A and B are lookers, not buyers. Some economists use the term *demand* for desire or need, and when ability to pay is joined to desire or need, they use the term *effective demand*. Regardless of which term is used, it is effective demand, not wishful desire or need, that is the key to understanding demand in the marketplace.

The Law of Demand

As stated earlier, economists do tend to agree on some things. One of these common points is the existence of a few economic laws. An important law is the *law of demand*, which states: *The lower the price, the more consumers will buy. The higher the price, the less they will buy.*

At lower prices, consumers will buy more goods because they can afford more and because a lower price may entice them to buy more after their initial purchase. For example, you may buy one can of Brand A for $1.00, but to entice you to buy more, the grocer may lower the price to two cans for $1.75. At higher prices, consumers will buy fewer goods because they cannot afford as much and because each additional unit purchased will give less satisfaction than the original unit.

Changes or Shifts in Demand

Changing circumstances may change demand by causing an increase or decrease in the number of available buyers. Some of the causes of a change or shift in demand are listed below:

1. *An increase or decrease in population.* Demand rises or falls with population: As the number of people increases, demand increases; as the number of people declines, demand declines. More people increase the demand for housing, whereas fewer people decrease the demand for housing.

2. *An increase or decrease in per capita income.* Demand also rises and falls with the level of per capita income: The higher the level of income, the greater the demand; the lower the level of income, the smaller the demand.

3. *Changes in consumer taste and substitute products.* If consumers favor smaller cars over large SUVs, demand for the former grows and demand for the latter diminishes. The same is true in housing: If city dwellers create a trend to move to the suburbs, then the demand for city apartments will decline and demand for suburban homes will grow.

4. *The amount of credit available.* Easy credit tends to increase demand, whereas tight credit tends to reduce it. Of course, you must pay back later what you borrow now, and this will affect future demand.

5. *The effect of advertising.* The well-written newspaper ad or the catchy TV commercial can create desires that may eventually lead to purchases and increased demand.

Supply

Demand represents the buyer's side of the market. Supply represents the seller's side of the market. *The total quantity that sellers are willing to sell at a particular time and at a certain price is called supply.*

The Law of Supply

The *law of supply* states: *Producers will offer more products and services for sale as prices increase and fewer as prices decrease.* Higher prices may mean higher profits, so businesses increase output. As prices decline, profits usually decline, and businesses cut back on output.

Changes or Shifts in Supply

Supply, like demand, reflects changing circumstances. Some of the causes of a change or shift in supply are:

1. *Changes in the cost of the factors of production.* If land, labor, or capital becomes more expensive, some producers will be unable to make a profit and may have to drop out of business, thereby reducing the supply. If the factors of production become cheaper, perhaps because of better technology or global access, some producers might seek a profit by moving into that particular business, thereby increasing supply.

2. *A change in demand for one product can cause a change in supply of another product.* For example, if people decided to live in tents instead of houses, you could expect to see a cutback in the supply of homes and an increase in the supply of tents.

3. *Business anticipation of future prices and profits can change the amount of goods supplied.* Sellers will increase output if they think future prices and profits will increase; they will decrease output or even go out of business if they think future prices and profits will decrease.

Supply and Demand Together Determine Output and Price Levels

If all the sellers and buyers of goods and services were to come together, there would eventually be an auctionlike agreement among them, which would determine the selling (buying) price of the goods and services. If sellers were to insist on prices that are too high, some buyers would refuse to purchase. Not wanting excess goods on hand, sellers would then lower prices until they sold the merchandise. If prices were too low, sellers would not be able to make a profit. They would stop production, and the buyers, not wanting to do without the products, would gradually increase their bids until sellers were enticed back into production.

After much movement back and forth, prices settle at the point where the quantity that buyers are willing to purchase equals the quantity that sellers are willing to sell. This is called the *equilibrium point*; here buyers and sellers are matched, and the goods and services for sale in the market are sold. Rents, wages, interest rates, and prices of goods and services in a perfectly competitive market are established by this interaction of supply and demand.

But in a dynamic economy, things never stay the same for very long. The changes noted previously cause both supply and demand to shift, and these shifts change the equilibrium point. For example, if supply remains the same while demand increases, would you expect prices to increase or decrease? Would supply remain at the same point or would it change in response to the increase in demand? Prices would of course increase: More buyers are after fewer goods. Suppliers would then increase production and the quantity supplied to take advantage of the higher prices. Then the increase in demand and supply would create a new equilibrium point to clear out the market.

And what would happen if demand remained constant while supply increased? Prices would go down as sellers tried to liquidate their stocks, but this trend might force some sellers out of business. Soon the supply would decrease to reach a new equilibrium point with demand.

The Flow of the Economy—Revisited

Figure 2.3 shows the flow of the economy again, but this time it includes supply and demand. You can see that the individuals and households in the resource market represent supply; they are the sellers of land, labor, and capital. How much business must pay, and how much individuals and households receive as income, depend on the price and quantity as established by supply and demand. In the product market, the roles are reversed. Business is now the supplier, selling goods and services to individuals and households.

Impact of International Trade

Up to this point the overview of a pure capitalistic economy has illustrated a closed economy, ignoring the impact of foreign imports and exports. In reality most economies are somewhat open, allowing

Figure 2.3 The circular flow of the economy.

some imports and exports. This flow of imports and exports can directly affect domestic incomes and prices.

International Trade Concepts

1. *Free Trade*: Restrictions, quotas, and tariffs are removed, and all goods and services can flow between countries without restriction in an open competitive market.

2. *Principle of Comparative Advantage*: Assuming free trade, this principle states that the entire world's standard of living will be increased if each nation specializes in producing those goods and services for which it has the lowest comparative cost.

3. *Balance of Payments*: A record of all transactions of the citizens of one nation with another or with all other countries.

4. *Balance of Trade*: A record of the merchandise (goods, not services) transferred between one nation and another or all other nations. An unfavorable balance of trade means that imports exceed exports. A favorable balance of trade means exports exceed imports.

5. *Rate of Exchange*: The rate or price at which the currency of one nation can be converted into the currency of another. Example: dollars for pounds, euros, or yen. A "strong dollar" means that a dollar buys more foreign currency. A "weak dollar" means that a dollar buys less foreign currency. A weakness in one currency means an automatic strength in another currency. If the dollar is down, the yen is up, and so on.

International Trade: Is Self-Sufficiency Better?

International trade between countries has an important impact on domestic economies. The flow of imports and exports can directly affect domestic incomes and prices.

Many people think that a nation is better off economically if it can become self-sufficient by producing all of its own goods and services. However, economic theory states that a nation that attempts to become self-sufficient will do so at a higher cost to its citizens than if the nation had entered into free-trade agreements with other nations. Example: The climate of Costa Rica is ideal for growing coffee, whereas the United States has the resources and capacity to produce computer software. If the United States wishes to become self-sufficient and grow its own coffee, it can do so only by creating massive hothouses at tremendous cost. This in turn will drive up the price of coffee for U.S. citizens. In the process, resources will be drawn away from the production of computer software, reducing output and raising the price of computer software. Therefore, it makes more sense for Costa Rica to concentrate on coffee and the United States to concentrate on computer software and for each to trade. The result will be higher quality coffee and computer software at lower prices for both Americans and Costa Ricans.

The theory of free trade makes economic sense, but political and other forces within nations tend to restrict international trade in an effort to protect special interest groups. Here are two examples: (1) The oil-producing export countries (OPEC) form cartels to regulate the production of oil and prices, and (2) the United States establishes tariffs and quotas to protect some domestic industries from foreign competition. This prevents U.S. citizens from purchasing foreign imports at the lowest prices. If free trade were allowed, the price of all goods and services would be lower. Will low-priced foreign goods cause some Americans to lose their jobs? Yes, in the short run, inefficient American companies and their employees will be displaced as low-priced foreign goods displace higher priced domestic goods. However, in time and/or with training, the locally displaced resources would flow into industries in which America has a comparative advantage, and these industries will expand and absorb the displaced resources.

Some people support self-sufficiency on the grounds that national defense requires a country to be able to stand alone and not depend on other countries for vital products. Other people counter this argument by stating that no nation can become truly self-sufficient in all products and that any attempt to do so would result in an inefficient and weak national defense.

In today's world each country attempts to maximize its own welfare by cooperating with other nations on some occasions and not cooperating at other times. The result is an international economy that is constantly in flux as political and economic events cause alliances to shift. This in turn causes national economies to shake and roll as international events unfold. These unfolding international events cause national and local real estate markets to feel the impact. For example, the lower value of the dollar versus other foreign currencies should attract many foreign investors to what seem to them to be bargain prices for U.S. real estate. This investment by foreigners stimulates the U.S. real estate market, driving up prices and adding to U.S. profits and commissions.

Question:	What should happen to this process when the value of the dollar rises?
Answer:	Investments by foreigners should slow down because prices of U.S. real estate will appear too high. This is because the foreign investor must put up excessive amounts of foreign currency to convert to the high-valued dollars needed to purchase U.S. real estate.

The result should be a drop in demand and a drop in real estate prices, profits, and commissions.

The Economic Theory Sounds Good, But . . .

Thus far, this chapter has stressed the interaction of supply and demand in perfectly competitive markets and in a pure capitalistic system. But the real world is not so simple. Many of the markets in the United States are imperfect, either because of trade restrictions or because the buyer or the seller is in a superior position and can influence price and output. The automatic corrections that take place in a perfectly competitive market do not always work in imperfect markets. Furthermore, the U.S. mixed capitalistic system grants a role to the government that also disturbs the pure capitalistic concept of supply and demand.

Nevertheless, the study of a "perfect" system creates an understanding of the basic mechanics of capitalism. Although the United States has imperfect markets and some government control of resources, it must be stressed that the main economic philosophy in the United States is still capitalism. Individuals do have the right to own property, run businesses, compete, and earn profits. But these rights are not absolute: The principles of pure capitalism have been modified to reflect social as well as private rights. This point is discussed in the next chapter, which examines the role of the government in the economy.

REVIEWING YOUR UNDERSTANDING

Markets and Prices

1. In the short run, if supply stays the same but demand decreases, what will happen to price? In the long run, to the amount supplied?

2. If the demand remains the same but supply increases, what will happen to price? To the amount supplied?

3. If the main industry in your town goes out of business, what short-term effect will this have on the price of homes?

CHAPTER SUMMARY

Economics is a social science that examines how people use and allocate scarce resources. There are several ways of solving the problems of what will be produced, how it will be produced, and for whom it will be produced. A capitalistic economy leaves the decisions to private individuals operating in competitive markets. Command or socialistic systems look toward government for the decision making. The United States operates under a mixed capitalistic system, using both government and private enterprise to make economic decisions.

All economies need four elements, known collectively as the factors of production, in order to produce goods and services: land, labor, capital, and entrepreneurship. In a capitalistic economy, these factors are privately owned and must be paid for in order to be used. The payment for land is called rent, for labor it is called wages, for capital it is called interest, and for entrepreneurship it is called profit. When rent, wages, interest, and profits are received, they are called income. Income is earned by individuals when they sell the factors of production. The earned income is then spent to purchase goods and services produced by these same factors of production. Thus, the U.S. economy has a circular flow, of which imports and exports from international trade are a part.

The prices paid in a competitive economy are determined in markets through the interaction of supply and demand. Demand is the total quantity that buyers are willing to purchase at a given set of prices, in a particular market, at a particular time. The law of demand states that the lower the price, the more consumers will buy; the higher the price, the less they will buy.

Supply is the total quantity that sellers are willing to sell in a particular market, at a particular time, at given prices. The law of supply states that producers will offer more products for sale as prices increase and fewer as prices decrease. The law of supply is based on the profit motive.

It is the interaction of supply and demand that determines the prices paid and the quantity produced in a competitive economy. Certain influences cause either supply or demand to change. When this occurs, prices and output also change. Understanding how market changes influence price and output is essential for real estate investors.

IMPORTANT TERMS AND CONCEPTS

Balance of payments	*Factors of production*
Balance of trade	*Flow of the economy*
Capitalism—pure and mixed	*Free trade*
Change in demand	*Law of demand*
Change in supply	*Law of supply*
Command economy	*Market*
Comparative advantage	*Opportunity cost*
Demand	*Rate of exchange*
Economics	*Rent, wages, interest, profits*
Equilibrium point	*Supply*

REVIEWING YOUR UNDERSTANDING

1. A social science concerned with how people produce, distribute, and consume goods and services is:
   a. history
   b. economics
   c. geography
   d. political science

2. Famous capitalist who wrote *The Wealth of Nations*:
   a. Karl Marx
   b. John Stuart Mill
   c. Thomas Jefferson
   d. Adam Smith

3. The major economic decisions are made by a government committee, but minor economic decisions are left to private individuals. This describes:
   a. pure socialism
   b. mixed socialism
   c. mixed capitalism
   d. pure capitalism

4. All of the following are principles of pure capitalism, *except*:
    a. private property
    b. laissez-faire
    c. public ownership of basic resources
    d. open and competitive markets for goods and services

5. The payment for entrepreneurship is called:
    a. profit
    b. wages
    c. interest
    d. rent

6. In the circular flow of the U.S. economy, individuals go to the resource markets as sellers and to the product markets as buyers.
    a. true
    b. false

7. According to the *Law of Demand*, the higher the price of homes, the more likely that:
    a. the number of homes built will increase
    b. people will buy new homes
    c. the number of home sales will decline
    d. the number of homes built will decline

8. In a purely competitive real estate market, if demand by renters for apartments increases, while the number of apartment units available for rent decreases, apartment rents should:
    a. increase
    b. decrease
    c. remain in equilibrium
    d. become static

9. Under pure capitalism, goods and services are produced primarily for people who:
    a. need them
    b. desire them
    c. wish for them
    d. effectively demand them

10. In international trade, the price that the currency of one nation brings in terms of the currency of another nation is known as:
    a. balance of payments
    b. rate of exchange
    c. balance of trade
    d. principle of comparative advantage

11. "No free lunch" is best explained by the concept of:
    a. diminishing returns
    b. opportunity costs
    c. highest and best use
    d. excess demand

12. Solutions to economic problems may be:
    a. influenced by value judgments
    b. considered an absolutely precise answer
    c. reproduced uniformly with computers in a lab
    d. uniformly considered correct by all citizens

13. If individuals and societies make economic choices based on the way things have always been done, the economy is considered:
    a. communistic
    b. capitalistic
    c. socialistic
    d. traditional

14. According to the theory of pure capitalism, how goods and services are produced is determined by:
    a. buyer's demand
    b. the lowest possible production cost
    c. who has the most money to spend
    d. government committees

15. Which economist predicted that capitalism was doomed to fail because profit motivation would lower wages to a subsistence level, leading workers to overthrow the capitalistic system?
    a. Karl Marx
    b. John Stuart Mill
    c. John Maynard Keynes
    d. Adam Smith

16. A command economy is commonly called:
    a. traditionalism
    b. capitalism
    c. socialism
    d. opportunism

17. Regarding the circular flow of the economy, which of the following is true?
    a. Individuals and households sell goods and services and receive income.
    b. Business supplies resources and receives wages.
    c. The product market is where the factors of production are exchanged.
    d. In the resource market, land, labor, and capital are exchanged for income.

18. A place in which buyers and sellers meet to bargain and exchange items of value at negotiated prices is called:
    a. a market
    b. an economy
    c. gross domestic product
    d. derived demand

19. A change or shift in supply is caused by a change in:
    a. the cost of the factors of production
    b. population
    c. consumer tastes
    d. the amount of advertising

20. In a given real estate market, if the demand for commercial office space declines and the supply of office space also declines at the same ratio, market rent per square foot should:
    a. increase
    b. decrease
    c. remain the same
    d. shift to the right

21. That point at which supply and demand are matched at a price that will clear the market is called:
    a. open
    b. equilibrium
    c. comparative advantage
    d. surplus

22. The total quantity that buyers are willing to buy at a given time at certain prices is called:
    a. supply
    b. demand
    c. equilibrium
    d. perfect competition

23. A summary of all transactions between the citizens of one nation and the citizens of all other countries is called:
    a. free trade
    b. rate of exchange
    c. balance of trade
    d. balance of payments

24. In the short run, the lower the value of the U.S. dollar versus the Japanese yen, the:
    a. more attractive are American products for the Japanese
    b. less likely Japanese investors will buy U.S. real estate
    c. more likely U.S. citizens will purchase Japanese products
    d. more likely the price of U.S. exports will rise in the Japanese market

25. Economic theory states that the United States can become self-sufficient, with no need for international trade, if the United States is willing to:
    a. drive up the price of domestic consumer goods and services
    b. limit the economic choices of U.S. citizens
    c. cancel all trade agreements
    d. do all of the above

CASE & POINT

Adam Smith, Economic Philosopher

Adam Smith was born in 1723 in the town of Kirkcaldy, on the east coast of Scotland. His father, a lawyer, died before his birth. His mother, a local woman named Margaret Douglas, married Adam Smith's father in 1720.

After attending the local school, Adam Smith entered the University of Glasgow in 1737 at the age of 14. Unlike today's standards, entering college at 12 to 14 years of age was quite common in the 1700s. While studying at the university, Smith was greatly influenced by Francis Hutcheson, a professor of moral philosophy. This influence would be reflected in Smith's future literary works. After completing his studies at the university, Smith studied for six years at Balliol College in Oxford, England.

When his studies at Oxford were completed, Smith returned to Scotland, where a few years later he began to give a series of public lectures on rhetoric, civil law, and what was called belles-lettres. These lectures were well attended, and Smith began to gain fame. In 1751, at the age of 27, Smith was appointed professor of moral philosophy at the University of Glasgow, the position previously held by his mentor, Hutcheson, who had retired several years earlier.

Smith remained at the University of Glasgow for 12 years, during which he wrote the first of his books, *The Theory of Moral Sentiments* (1759). In this book Smith presented a theory on why people behave ethically. The book was an instant success, giving Smith fame not only in Scotland but throughout Europe.

In 1764, Smith was enticed to resign from the University of Glasgow and to tutor the young Duke of Buccleuch while they went on a grand tour of Europe. The tour lasted until 1766, during which Smith spent time in Paris and became friends with famous people such as Voltaire, Dupont de Nemours, and Francis Quesnay, the famous French economist. In addition, one of Smith's closest friends in Scotland was the famous philosopher David Hume.

Upon completing this grand tour in 1766, Smith returned to his hometown of Kirkcaldy and began writing his most famous book, *An Inquiry into the Nature and Causes of the Wealth of Nations*. Smith lived in Kirkcaldy until *The Wealth of Nations* was published in 1776. The book's main thesis was that the economic system common in Britain and Europe at the time, called mercantilism, which stressed the need to store up wealth in the government treasury, was doomed to fail and that a better economic system was needed. Smith then went on to outline what we now consider some of the basic principles of a capitalistic system. Much of Smith's material was not original, but his ability to organize and explain the working of a capitalistic economy was outstanding for that time. Like his earlier work, *The Wealth of Nations* became an immediate bestseller, giving Smith even more fame during his lifetime.

In 1777, Smith moved to Edinburgh to become the Commissioner of Customs and Salt Duties for Scotland. This government position assured Smith of a lifetime job while he issued updated editions of his famous works.

Smith never married, although he is reputed to have fallen in love several times. He became ill and died July 17, 1790, and is buried in Canongate churchyard, Edinburgh. Unfortunately for the world, on his deathbed he instructed his friends to destroy his volumes of working papers. Today, there is very little of Smith's original work for scholars to view. His gravestone reads:

Here

are deposited

the remains of

ADAM SMITH

author

of the

Theory of Moral Sentiments

and

Wealth of Nations

&cc &cc &cc

He was born, 5th June, 1723

And he died, 17th July, 1790.

On the next pages are photographs of Adam Smith landmarks in Scotland.

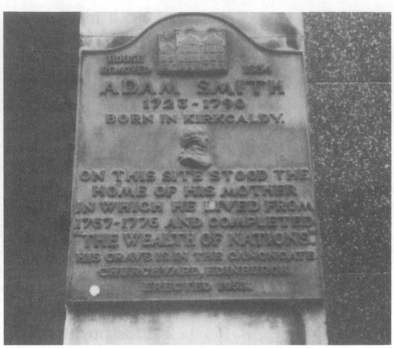

Bust in Adam Smith Theater, Kircaldy, Scotland.

Plaque denoting site where Adam Smith lived while writing *The Wealth of Nations* from 1766–1776, Kirkcaldy, Scotland.

Present use of site where Smith lived while writing *The Wealth of Nations* from 1766–1776, Kirkcaldy, Scotland.

House where Adam Smith lived at the time of his death in 1790, Edinburgh, Scotland.

Adam Smith's grave at Canongate Church, Edinburgh, Scotland.

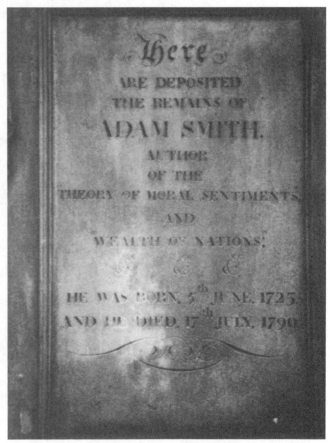

Epitaph on Adam Smith's gravestone, Canongate Church, Edinburgh, Scotland.

CHAPTER 3
GOVERNMENT'S ROLE IN THE ECONOMY

PREVIEW

This chapter summarizes the role played by government in the U.S. economy. Section 3.1 explains the major reasons why the government has joined business and consumers as a full partner in the operations of the economy. Section 3.2 shows how economists measure the performance of the economy using national income accounting and changes in business activity. Section 3.3 introduces fiscal and monetary policy, the tools used by the government to help fight the ills of inflation, recession, and unemployment. The Case & Point at the end of the chapter discusses the Laffer Curve. When you have completed this chapter, you will be able to:

1. Discuss why government's role in the U.S. economy has been expanding.

2. Define gross domestic product and label the phases of a business cycle.

3. Describe the trend in national real estate cycles.

4. Define and explain the two main tools used by the government to fight economic problems.

3.1 The Real World of Markets and Government

The pure capitalism of Adam Smith, which was discussed in the previous chapter, is not the capitalism that exists in the United States or in any other country. Many of the resources in the United States are manufactured and sold in *imperfect markets*.

Imperfect markets arise when a small group of buyers or sellers is able to influence directly the price and output of a good or service. This control may be in the form of an exclusive patent, ownership of a scarce commodity, or control of a transportation route. Control may also be obtained through extensive advertising or by other means.

A small group of sellers that can eliminate or dominate competitors can manipulate the market and generate abnormally high profits. On the other hand, when a small group of buyers can manipulate markets, profits may be driven so low that sellers fail to realize any return on their investments.

In the 1890s, to help balance the inequities created by imperfect markets, the U.S. government passed antitrust legislation and created regulatory agencies. The Sherman Antitrust Act, passed in 1890, forbade combinations that restricted competition between businesses. The Interstate Commerce Commission, created in 1897, regulated the practices of monopolistic sellers of interstate products. The trend from the 1890s to the 1970s was increased government regulation over business activities.

Beginning in the 1980s some deregulation occurred to reverse what many felt had been too strong a government role. Some argued that tight government regulations put a damper on businesses' ability to expand output and create jobs. The airline, trucking, and other transportation industries have been deregulated, as have many areas of the banking industry. Starting in the early 1990s, government regulations once again began to increase, for example, in the controversial areas of gun control and some reregulation of the banking and savings and loan industry. Whether more or less government regulation is good or bad is a debate that is rooted in both political and economic ideologies.

Government Intervention in the Economy

Government spending, regulatory agencies, welfare programs, zoning, planning, and environmental constraints are a few examples of current government intervention in economic affairs. Some of the

Special Interest Topic

Types of Imperfect Markets

Monopoly—A market in which there is only one seller.

Oligopoly—A market in which there are only a few sellers.

Monopolistic competition—A market in which a large number of sellers compete, but through advertising and promotion each attempts to convince consumers that one brand is better than another. If successful, the seller then can charge a slightly higher price for his or her product.

Monopsony—A market in which there is only one buyer.

Oligopsony—A market in which there are only a few buyers.

reasons given by those who favor regulations to justify why the government should become a full partner in the operations of the U.S. economy are:

1. Capitalism has a tendency to create imperfect markets; if they remain unchecked, a misallocation of resources can occur. Government intervention is needed to assure a reasonable degree of competition to prevent one economic group from dominating others.

2. Terror threats and international peacekeeping requires that government control some economic resources and personnel for defense needs.

3. Citizens have set certain social goals that can best be achieved by a nonprofit institution. Most of these goals include care for those who are unable to provide for themselves: the aged, the infirm, and the disadvantaged. If the government is to achieve these social goals, it needs more economic resources.

4. Citizens have requested that the government attempt to prevent economic instability. In other words, they have asked the government to fight inflation, recession, and unemployment. To do this, the government needs economic power.

5. Finally, some observers note that more and more voters are turning to the government for services once provided by private enterprise. To provide such services, the government must expand its economic activity.

On the other hand, antiregulators believe that the market is a more efficient allocator than government politicians and bureaucrats. They cite numerous unnecessary costs imposed on business by government regulations. If these wasted resources could be directed toward business expansion, more economic growth and jobs could be created. The pros and cons of government regulation are still another example of an economic topic that is deeply rooted in political philosophy.

Flow of the Economy—The Government Included

Figure 3.1 illustrates how the government fits into the flow of the economy. It is important to know how the government participates with individuals and businesses in the flow of money, goods, and services.

In Figure 3.1, note how individuals and households pay taxes to the government and in return receive government services. Businesses also pay taxes and receive government services. To provide the needed services demanded by individuals and businesses, the government must purchase factors of production from the resource market and goods and services from the product market. The money for these purchases comes mainly from the taxes paid by households and businesses (plus government borrowing, fines, and fees). Students should attempt to visualize this illustration as showing a continuous flow of money and goods, that is, a system that is always moving and always changing.

REVIEWING YOUR UNDERSTANDING

1. How does a monopoly differ from pure competition? Why are most monopolies regulated by the government?

2. If most real estate brokers charge the same commission rate, is the real estate business non-price competitive? How do real estate brokers compete?

3. Why does the government intervene in the economy? Does politics play a role?

4. If the government increases taxes, what impact will this have on the flow of the economy?

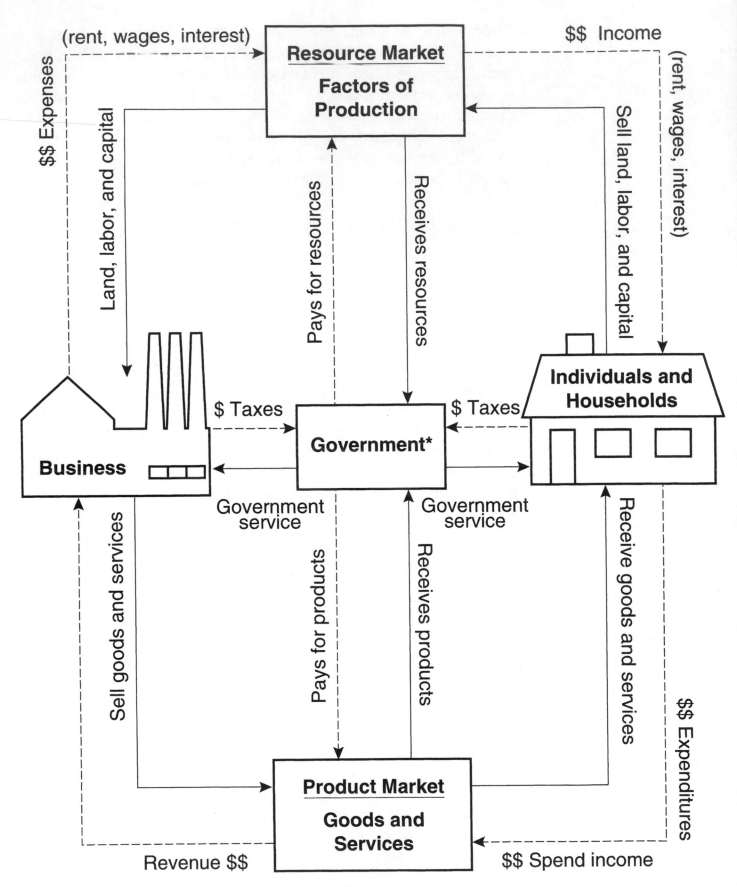

Figure 3.1 Simplified flow of the economy showing government's role.

3.2 Measuring the Performance of the Economy

J ust as a mechanic measures the condition of an automobile by checking various factors, the economist uses diagnostic tools to check the condition of the economy. When all the reports are in, the economist, like the mechanic, recommends any needed repairs. Unlike the mechanic, however, the economist may differ from his or her colleagues about what must be done to bring the economy back into good working order. As pointed out earlier, economics is not an exact science, and economic decisions frequently carry political overtones.

Local real estate markets are heavily influenced by economic changes in the immediate area. However, local economies are in turn influenced by the general trend of the national economy. Understanding the causes of changes in the national economy will help people to understand what impact these national changes will have on local communities.

National Income Accounting

One way to gauge the state of the national economy is to compare the output and income generated in the current year to that of past years. To do this, economists have developed several measurements, including the measurement called *gross domestic product*, frequently referred to as GDP and defined as *the total market value of all goods and services produced domestically in the United States during a given time, usually in one year*.

If you add up the final retail price of all goods and services produced in a year, the total dollar amount would be the GDP. The calculation of gross domestic product does not consider whether the business producing goods and services is foreign or domestically owned. If the goods and services were produced in the United States it counts toward GDP. Gross domestic product is compiled by the U.S. Department of Commerce and is reported on a monthly basis. When comparing GDP in one year with past years, one must be sure that the figures have been adjusted to omit the distortion of inflation. For example, if the GDP increases by 2 percent but prices have inflated by 6 percent, the real GDP has decreased by 4 percent. GDP adjusted for inflation is called *real GDP*.

Where Does GDP Go?

The gross domestic product of the United States is acquired by consumers, business, government, and foreign markets. Goods and services purchased by consumers are called *personal consumption expenditures*. Business buying is called *gross private domestic investment*. Government purchasing of GDP, simply called *government*, includes federal, state, and local government buying.

Other nations also purchase a portion of our GDP, which is called *exports*. The United States, in turn, purchases a portion of the GDP of foreign nations, and this is called *imports*. If the United States exports more than it imports, foreigners have purchased more GDP from us than we have purchased from them. This net amount is called *net export*.

In recent years, the U.S. purchase of imports has exceeded the sale of exports, so GDP showed a minus balance in this category. With the ongoing controversy regarding foreign trade, it should be noted that net exports only represent a small percentage of GDP. Table 3.1 shows the breakdown of GDP for selected years.

As shown in Table 3.1, GDP increased between 1990 and 2003. When adjusted for inflation, however, the increase is less than what the raw figures indicate.

If real GDP increases, the national economy is growing, and optimism and spending are adding to prosperity. However, it should be noted that increases in real GDP measure only the total growth in

Table 3.1 GDP Expenditures (billions)

Gross Domestic Product	1990	2000	2003
Current Dollars	5,522.2	9,963.1	11,004
Components			
Personal Consumption Expenditures			
Current Dollars	3,748.4	6,757.3	7,760.9
Gross Private Domestic Investment			
Current Dollars	799.57	1,832.7	1,665.8
Government Purchases of Goods and Services			
Current Dollars	1,043.2	1,743.7	2,075.5
Net Exports			
Current Dollars	−68.9	−370.7	−498.1

Source: U.S. Department of Commerce, Bureau of Economic Analysis, www.bea.gov

physical output and income. They do not measure the quality of life or the equality of the distribution of output and income. They also do not show if the GDP per *person* increased or declined.

Other Income Measurements

In an effort to study in detail the performance of the economy, economists have devised many other measurements. A few of the important measurements for real estate purposes are personal income, disposable personal income, and discretionary income.

Personal income is the total income earned by all individuals after business taxes have been paid out but before personal taxes are paid.

Disposable personal income is income after the payment of personal taxes. It is often called take-home pay. Disposable personal income is watched closely because it is an important measure of consumer purchasing power for all basic needs, including housing. If take-home pay increases faster than the rate of inflation, consumers may have more money to spend on various items, including housing.

Discretionary income is the amount of money people have after paying for necessities. Payments for basic housing, food, clothing, and transportation are subtracted from disposable personal income, leaving income that can be spent any way people wish.

An increase in discretionary income means that society is becoming more affluent and that people are in a position to spend more on luxuries. The successful operation of travel and leisure facilities, such as restaurants, theaters, motels, vacation homes, health clubs, and tourist attractions, is tied to adequate levels of discretionary income.

Keeping Up with National Income

Changes in GDP, personal income, disposable personal income, and discretionary income are important issues for real estate agents and investors. An increase in personal disposable income could mean that consumers are better able to qualify for mortgage loans or that tenants can afford higher rent levels.

An increase in discretionary income could mean that raw recreational land might be more in demand and that tourist-oriented real estate, such as ski facilities, could be developed. Increases in real GDP mean that industrial and commercial properties will be in demand as business activities expand.

Information about these changes can be found in such publications as *Business Week* or the *Wall Street Journal*. In addition, most

---

Interesting Controversies

Does GDP really stand for gross domestic pollution?

Environmentalists point out that economic growth represented by GDP does not take into consideration the pollution caused by the manufacturing of goods. They argue that a standard of living should include the quality of life, not just material possessions. Two dilemmas arise: how to increase economic growth without increasing pollution, and how to measure the quality of life.

Does an increase in GDP mean more goods and services per person?

One argument advanced by the advocates of zero population growth is that if real GDP remains the same while population declines, the standard of living will rise rapidly with a minimum increase in environmental damage. Looking at the equation below, what will happen if real GDP increases, but the U.S. population increases at a faster rate?

$$\frac{\text{RealGDP}}{\text{Population}} = \begin{array}{l}\text{Goods and}\\ \text{services}\\ \text{per capita}\\ \text{(standard}\\ \text{of living)}\end{array}$$

---

economic data can be obtained from the Bureau of Economic Analysis at www.bea.gov.

Foreign Ownership of U.S. Businesses and Real Estate

The amount of foreign ownership of U.S. businesses and real estate ebbs and flows with economic changes. Some reasons are:

1. The flight of capital out of politically unstable countries, followed by periods of relative calm.

2. The decline in value of the dollar relative to other currencies in some years, followed by a stronger dollar in other years. If the dollar is declining, U.S. prices to foreigners appear to be a bargain. If the dollar is rising, the opposite is true.

3. Politically, the U.S. Congress and the president have, for the most part, been unwilling to face the reality of the budget deficit by

cutting government spending or raising taxes. The easy short-run "fix" had been to increase government borrowing to cover the deficit. Heavy government borrowing tends to increase interest rates. Higher interest rates attract foreign capital and investment in the United States.

4. The United States represents a large homogeneous consumer market. U.S. residents spend a large percentage of their personal income: consumption is high and the savings rate is low. Foreign business interests wish to gain a foothold in this large consumer market. One way is to increase the shipment of foreign products to the United States. Another way is to purchase existing U.S. businesses that are currently serving the market.

Composition of Foreign Investment

Investors all over the world have acquired U.S. assets. Within the last decade the largest number of foreign investors have come from Canada, Britain, Japan, Western Europe, Asia, the Middle East, and Latin America. In California, Japanese, Koreans, and Chinese have been the dominant foreign investors.

With all the publicity regarding foreign ownership of U.S. businesses, it should be pointed out that Americans have been buying the assets of foreign countries for decades. Now that the trend is somewhat reversing, some people are uncomfortable.

3.3 **Changes in Economic Activity**

Since the Great Depression of the 1930s, real GDP has generally been on the rise, although this upward movement has fluctuated. The up-and-down movement in economic activity can result from a seasonal fluctuation, a business cycle, or a long-term secular trend.

Seasonal fluctuations are short-term changes in business and economic activity that occur within the year, resulting from either weather or custom. For example, housing construction declines in the winter months, retail sales increase at Christmas time, and travel increases in the summer.

Business cycles are the recurrent expansions and contractions in general business activity that take place over a period of about two to six years.

Long-term secular trends refer to economic changes that occur over an extended period of time, perhaps 50 years or more. Some examples of secular trends include a reduction in family size, a shorter work week, an increase in per capita income, and an increase in suburban housing.

As real estate investors observe economic change, it is important that they classify the change as seasonal, cyclical, or secular. If a person acquires real estate in a community that has severe seasonal changes, he or she must be prepared to support the investment when vacancies rise in the off-season. Apartments in college-dominated communities must generate enough income in nine months to help offset the loss of income in the summer recess. Ski resorts must generate enough extra income during the winter and spring to pay necessary expenses during the summer and fall.

Cyclical changes are especially important for a real estate investment. Business cycles cover economic activity changes that occur over a two- to six-year period, and this corresponds with the average length of time that many real estate investors keep an investment. Business cycles measure changes in employment, income, output, and prices (see Figure 3.2). All of these have a significant influence on the success of an investment, especially in its early years. Vacancy ratios and rental rates are closely tied to changes in employment, income, and prices.

Long-term secular changes are also important for real estate purposes. The time span of secular trends can run 50 or more years. Secular changes will be the major influence on long-term value changes.

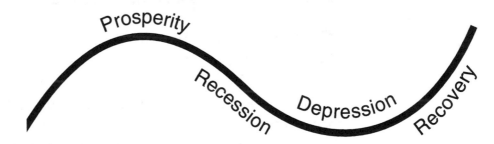

Figure 3.2 Changes of the business cycle and their effects.

Prosperity = boom times, high activity, high employment, increased income and prices. Recession = decline from high point, increased unemployment, real GDP decline. Depression = massive decline in sales, very high rate of unemployment. Recovery = bottoming out of depression or recession, increased employment and sales. In the real world, a business cycle is not as even as the diagram above. Many cycles go from recession to recovery without a depression. More time is usually spent in the recovery–prosperity phase than in the recession–depression phase.

Causes of Business Cycles

There are many theories about the cause of business cycles. Although economists are continually debating the merits of each theory, most agree that no single factor is the sole cause of business cycles. Instead, cycles are caused by a combination of the factors listed below, and the combination or "mix" varies with each swing in business activity.

Business cycles can be caused by the following:

1. *War and other international conflicts.*

2. *The introduction of innovations that create new industries.* Examples include radio in the 1920s, television in the 1950s, computers in the 1960s, and electronics in the 1980s, as well as software and digital technology in the 1990s and 2000s.

3. *Erratic spending patterns of consumers, businesses, and government.* There is a tendency for consumers, businesses, and government each to have periods of spending followed by periods of saving. This causes irregular supply and demand patterns.

4. *Changes in the amount of money and credit in circulation.* When money is plentiful and interest rates are low, spending tends to increase. When money is scarce and interest rates are high, spending tends to decline. In short, some economists believe that incorrect monetary policy causes business cycles.

5. *The psychological frame of mind of businesspeople and consumers.* If people are optimistic about the future, investment and spending will usually occur. If people are pessimistic, caution will prevail and business activity declines.

Forecasting Changes in Economic Activity

What a person does today is greatly influenced by what he or she thinks will occur tomorrow. One purchases real estate today on the basis of what one feels will happen to rents and property values in the future.

Economic forecasting is one way of reducing this inherent uncertainty. If investors can anticipate the direction of economic change, they will have a better idea of what lies ahead. Then they can decide whether they should take steps to protect their real estate investments from a shortage in income or an increase in expenses. In addition, economic forecasting can help investors decide whether now is the time to capitalize on a new investment opportunity.

Economic forecasting is an art, not a science. It is impossible to predict the future with absolute accuracy. Nevertheless, educated guesses are possible and are almost always better than blind plunges. Real estate students are encouraged to follow forecasts that are published by government agencies, financial institutions, economic research companies, and major universities. One can contact any of these institutions for monthly economic newsletters, or access the information online.

Real Estate Cycles

If we have national business cycles, do we also have national real estate cycles? Does real estate activity move through phases of prosperity, recession, depression, and recovery? Real estate markets clearly do have their ups and downs; however, the patterns are irregular.

A review of U.S. economic history shows that until the 1940s, real estate construction activity fluctuated severely, experiencing great booms and deep depressions. On the average, these cycles took approximately 18 years to move through the four phases of prosperity, recession, depression, and recovery. This 18-year cycle is known as the *long real estate cycle*.

Since the 1940s, economists have not been able to find clear signs of this long real estate cycle. Instead, they have located another, much shorter real estate cycle that takes perhaps three to six years to move through all four phases. This new cycle and its ups and downs is called the *short real estate cycle*.

Long-run trends in real estate activity appear to be influenced by gradual changes in population, age distribution, marriage rates, income levels, construction costs, taxes, and transportation patterns. Short-run trends in real estate markets are heavily influenced by the availability and cost of mortgage money and the current state of the national and local economy.

Most real estate purchases require the use of borrowed funds. If these funds are available at reasonable interest rates, real estate activity increases. If these mortgage funds are available at very high interest rates, real estate activity declines. Most drops in housing construction since World War II can be somewhat attributed to the availability and cost of mortgage money. In addition, in order to qualify for a real estate loan, people must have jobs and businesses must have profits. If the national or local economy is in a recession with high unemployment, the demand for real estate loans will decline.

Does this mean that the old long real estate cycle is dead? There is no definite answer, and economists are still debating the question. It is obvious that national real estate activity since 1945 has been closely tied to changes in the mortgage market and employment trends. More details on this important topic can be found in Chapter 4, "Money, Credit, and Real Estate."

REVIEWING YOUR UNDERSTANDING

1. If you knew that in the next five years the economy would experience prosperity with rapid inflation, would you invest in real estate today or would you wait for a couple of years? Why?

2. Assuming fixed interest rate loans, does unanticipated inflation benefit mortgage borrowers or mortgage lenders?

3. What influences long-run trends in real estate activity? Short-run trends?

3.4 Government Tools to Fight Economic Problems

One of the prime responsibilities of the federal government is to maintain economic stability by limiting the adverse effects of unemployment, inflation, and recession. This section discusses the major tools the federal government uses to fight declines in GDP and economic activity. The same tools can be used to fight inflation caused by excessive spending.

Fiscal Policy

Fiscal policy is the government's use of taxing and spending power to help counteract recession, unemployment, and inflation. When the economy is in a recession, an increase in government spending may create a demand for more land, labor, and capital. This generates more income for individuals in the form of rents, wages, and interest. Some of this added income will be saved, but much will be spent in the marketplace. This increase in spending should stimulate economic activity.

In addition to direct government spending, the economy can be stimulated if the government cuts taxes. A general tax cut will give consumers more disposable income and give businesses more after-tax profits. Some of this additional income and profit will be spent, thereby stimulating economic activity.

Government spending to fight recession should not be financed by an increase in taxes, because a tax increase would reduce private income at the very time an increase in spending is needed. Instead, the government frequently finances additional spending by going into debt. When government spending exceeds government income, it is called *deficit spending*.

When the U.S. economy is producing at full capacity and employment is high, it is in the prosperity phase of the business cycle. If consumers, business, and government continue to spend, pushing demand beyond the economy's ability to supply, then prices will rise, causing inflation.

Inflation is harmful because it drives up prices without increasing output. The uncertainty about price changes causes business and consumers to act hastily and to become dismayed, discouraged, and confused. This eventually causes major disruptions in all segments of the economy. The government can fight inflation by cutting back on government spending or increasing taxes. This will reduce disposable income and demand, thereby reducing the pressure on prices. The combination of reduced government spending and increased taxes can create a situation in which government income exceeds government spending, resulting in a *budget surplus*.

Monetary Policy

In addition to fiscal policy, the government can use monetary policy to counteract recession, unemployment, and inflation. The government uses monetary policy when it increases or decreases the supply of money in an effort to stabilize the economy.

During periods of recession, the government may increase the supply of money, which in the short run may lower interest rates and increase the availability of credit. With easier credit, the government hopes that consumers and businesses will borrow for expenditures and business expansion. This could generate employment and help fight the recession.

However, excessive long-run expansion of the money supply will eventually increase interest rates, as inflation causes lenders to "index" or increase their interest rate as a hedge against inflation.

**THEORIES AND
THEORETICIANS**

JOHN MAYNARD KEYNES (1883–1946)

From the Warren J. Samuels Portrait Collection, Duke University.

John Maynard Keynes, a British economist, is considered the founder of the "new economics." Keynes published his *General Theory of Employment, Interest, and Money* in 1936 and instantly started the "Keynesian Revolution."

Prior to Keynes, traditional economic theory held that there was a natural tendency for the economy to stabilize at full employment. Any unemployment would only be temporary since the economy would soon adjust itself to a full employment balance.

Keynes's work pointed out that, contrary to traditional theory, the economy could reach a balance at less than full employment, and unless steps were taken by the government to stimulate the economy, the unemployment would become permanent. Thus, Keynes shocked traditional capitalists by advocating government intervention into private economic affairs in order to preserve the capitalist system. Today, economists are debating whether Keynesian theory is relevant in today's globalized, market-driven economy.

In his private life, Keynes was a successful and shrewd business investor. He is reported to have made over $2 million (in 1930 dollars!) by speculating in bonds and international currency, devoting one-half hour of his time, before breakfast, to these private business ventures.

During periods of inflation, the government can use monetary policy to curb spending by reducing the supply of money and credit. A reduction in the supply of money will usually drive up interest rates. High interest rates discourage borrowing, which in turn will reduce

THEORIES AND THEORETICIANS

MILTON FRIEDMAN—FREE MARKET GIANT

University of Chicago

Milton Friedman, formerly of the University of Chicago, is one of America's foremost economists. A Nobel Prize winner in economics, Friedman is a free market advocate who believes that government's role should be limited to maintaining an environment where competition and free choice are allowed to flourish.

In Friedman's view, the free market is the most efficient allocator of social and economic well-being. Friedman stresses that the common person has fared better under capitalism, as opposed to communism, socialism, or fascism.

As a monetarist, Friedman points out that the money supply is a prime determinant of economic stability and that the Federal Reserve Board has caused chaos by constantly turning on and off the money machine. A steady increase of the money supply at a rate equal to the real growth of GDP is the best way to wring out inflation and maintain a stable economy, in Friedman's view.

spending. As spending declines, the pressure is taken off prices, and inflation may recede.

Monetary policy is carried out by a government agency called the Federal Reserve Board. Chapter 4 is devoted to the Federal Reserve System, money, and its effect on the real estate industry.

The Theory Sounds Good, but there are Some Problems

In theory, fiscal and monetary policy can fine-tune the economy to prevent recession and inflation. However, in the real world, fiscal and monetary tools run into some problems. Most of these problems fall into two broad categories: political and structural.

Fiscal and monetary policies are enacted by the government. The governmental process is essentially political because governmental representatives must be elected. Critics point out that either Congress, the president, or both will often delay appropriate fiscal measures that conflict with current political realities. In times of high prosperity, for example, fiscal theory suggests that taxes be increased and government spending be cut to create a budget surplus to help pay off previous budget deficits. But if an election is coming up, these actions may be delayed for fear that higher taxes or cutting someone's favorite government program might prove unpopular at the polls. Thus, budget deficits tend not to be reduced, but rather increased, even during a booming economy.

Moreover, the monetary policy of the Federal Reserve Board is not immune to political pressure, despite its theoretical independence. The Federal Reserve Board is a creature of Congress and, realistically, can be abolished or altered by an act of Congress. Thus, for better or worse, economics frequently must give way to politics.

The second major problem is structural. Neither fiscal nor monetary policies can be changed very rapidly. Fiscal policy must be enacted by Congress and approved by the president. The legislative process is long and drawn out. By the time the policy is enacted, it sometimes is too late to be effective.

Although monetary policy can be changed more quickly because the Federal Reserve Board does not have to contend with congressional red tape, monetary change, once enacted, takes a great deal of time to work its way into the economy. Indeed, it may be six months or more before changes in the money supply begin to influence economic decisions.

Special Interest Topics

Stagflation: Inflation During Recession

Traditional fiscal and monetary tools were designed to fight economic problems such as rising prices and overemployment during periods of excessive prosperity and declining prices and unemployment during periods of recession. But in the 1970s, a new economic phenomenon was identified—inflation during recession—and the term *stagflation* was coined to label it.

How do you fight stagflation? If you attempt to fight recession by increasing spending, you add to inflation. If you attempt to fight inflation by reducing spending, you prolong the recession. Stagflation disappeared in the 1980s, but economists are currently debating whether stagflation will return.

Automatic Stabilizers

Our economic system has some built-in stabilizers that tend to dampen large swings in the business cycle without waiting for governmental action. Two prime examples are the progressive income tax and unemployment insurance. During periods of prosperity, the amount of income taxes you pay could rise faster than your increase in wages. This reduces your ability to spend, while building up a surplus of money for the government. Also during prosperity, contributions to the unemployment insurance program increase, while unemployment claims fall, creating a larger surplus.

When the business cycle is heading for a recession, the process reverses itself. As your income declines, the amount of income tax you pay drops, leaving you with proportionately more money to spend. Also, those left unemployed by the recession can obtain money by filing unemployment claims.

Both of these processes move opposite to the business cycle and are called *automatic stabilizers*, meaning that they work without requiring direct government action.

Cyclical Versus Structural Unemployment

Cyclical unemployment is caused when the economy slips into a recession and jobs are lost because of this slowdown. Once the business cycle recovers, the jobs are regained.

Structural unemployment occurs when there are some fundamental changes in the economy that are not related to the normal ebb and surge of the business cycle. Recent examples include the elimination of defense jobs attributable to the end of the cold war, cuts in employment because of technological innovations, and certain U.S. jobs made obsolete by foreign competition resulting from globalization of the economy.

Structural unemployment does not recover as the economy grows. Thus, structurally unemployed workers must shift to tomorrow's new jobs or run the risk of being chronically unemployed.

How the Unemployment Rate Is Determined

The government uses two surveys to determine the unemployment rate. A monthly survey, called the *Household Survey*, asks a large statistical sample of individuals two main questions: (1) Are you employed? (2) If not, are you looking for work? From this the government publishes an unemployment rate. Then another monthly survey, called the *Payroll Survey*, asks businesses one main question: How many people work for you? From this an employment rate is calculated. The two Surveys are not always giving the same trend. In recoveries, the Household Survey can show more employment than the Payroll Survey, because the Payroll Survey initially misses new business starts and a faster recovery in the self-employed market. But as the recovery phase of the business cycle turns to the prosperity phase, the two surveys tend to join ranks.

REVIEWING YOUR UNDERSTANDING

Use fiscal and monetary tools to answer the following:

1. If the economy is in a recession, should the government increase or decrease taxes? Government spending? Money supply?

2. When should the government have deficit spending? Why? Should the government ever have a budget surplus (take in more taxes than it spends)? When?

CHAPTER SUMMARY

Today, the government is deeply involved in private economic affairs. Imperfect competition, international conflicts, nonprofit social goals, and a desire to maintain economic stability are some of the reasons why the government has become a full partner in the operations of the U.S. economy.

Economists have tools to measure the state of the economy. The most common measurement is gross domestic product (GDP), which measures the total value of goods and services produced domestically in a year. Other measurements include personal income, disposable personal income, and discretionary income. These measurements may be on a total or per capita basis.

The GDP does not stay level or change at a constant rate, but rather changes in irregular up-and-down movements. These fluctuations in economic activity are either seasonal, cyclical, or long-term secular trends. Most attention centers on business cycles, but to date no single theory is universally accepted as explaining the causes of business cycles.

In addition to business cycles, there are real estate cycles, which can be classified as either long or short. Since the 1940s, the short real estate cycle, caused by changes in the availability and cost of mortgage credit and in current business conditions, has been the most obvious. It is important for real estate investors to understand business and real estate cycles and to forecast their swings, because these cycles give a better idea of what lies in the future. Investors can then decide whether they should take steps to protect their investments.

Fiscal and monetary policies are the tools that the government uses to fight the problems of inflation, unemployment, and recession. Fiscal policy means the use of government spending and taxation to counteract economic ills. Monetary policy refers to changes in the supply of money to encourage or discourage consumer spending and business investments.

IMPORTANT TERMS AND CONCEPTS

Business cycles	*Long-term secular trend*
Discretionary income	*Monetary policy*
Disposable personal income	*Personal income*
Fiscal policy	*Real estate cycles*
Gross domestic product (GDP)	*Real GDP*
Imperfect markets	*Seasonal fluctuations*

REVIEWING YOUR UNDERSTANDING

1. A market in which there are only a few sellers is called a(n):
   a. monopoly
   b. oligopoly
   c. monopsony
   d. oligopsony

2. In the flow of the economy, government needs to generate money to pay for the benefits society demands from government. Government raises revenue by all of the following *except*:
   a. borrowing
   b. taxes
   c. fees
   d. labor

3. The total market value of all goods and services domestically produced in the U.S. economy in a given year is called:
   a. gross domestic product
   b. personal consumption expenditures
   c. net export
   d. gross private domestic investment

4. The slope downward from the peak of a business cycle is called:
   a. depression
   b. recovery
   c. recession
   d. prosperity

5. Which of the following best describes a cause of the rise in foreign ownership of U.S. businesses and real estate?
   a. very high value of the dollar
   b. disorganized U.S. consumer markets
   c. reduction in the U.S. budget deficit
   d. flight of capital seeking a safe haven

6. In the short run, real estate cycles tend to be most influenced by changes in:
   a. mortgage interest rates
   b. death rates
   c. age brackets
   d. cost of construction

7. The government's use of spending and taxing as a tool to control swings in the business cycle is called:
   a. automatic stabilizers
   b. fiscal policy
   c. monetary policy
   d. foreign policy

8. The government's use of money, credit, and interest rates as a tool to control swings in the business cycle is called:
   a. automatic stabilizers
   b. fiscal policy
   c. monetary policy
   d. foreign policy

9. During times of recession, the government can attempt to stimulate the economy by:
   a. decreasing government spending
   b. increasing taxes
   c. increasing interest rates
   d. increasing the supply of money

10. During times of rapid inflationary prosperity, the government can attempt to slow down the economy by:
    a. increasing government spending
    b. decreasing taxes
    c. decreasing interest rates
    d. decreasing the supply of money

11. A market consisting of a single buyer is called a:
    a. monopoly
    b. monopsony
    c. oligopsony
    d. oligopoly

12. Which of the following is a reason given to justify government intervention in private economic affairs?
    a. capitalism has a tendency to create imperfect markets
    b. citizens consistently vote for fewer government programs
    c. the market is the most efficient allocator of resources
    d. international peacekeeping is no longer needed

13. According to the circular flow of the economy, government:
    a. provides land, labor, and capital
    b. taxes businesses and households
    c. generates profits
    d. provides a vast array of consumer products

14. Per GDP measurements, net exports refer to:
    a. foreign currency
    b. balance of payments
    c. comparative advantage
    d. exports versus imports

15. Real GDP is GDP adjusted for:
    a. taxes
    b. government expenditures
    c. inflation
    d. unemployment

16. After-tax income (take-home pay) is called:
    a. personal income
    b. disposable personal income
    c. discretionary income
    d. taxable income

17. Fluctuations in economic activity, usually running from peak to peak in two to six years, are called:
    a. seasonal fluctuations
    b. secular trends
    c. business cycles
    d. GDP deflator

18. Unanticipated inflation tends to benefit buyers/borrowers:
    a. who wait to purchase real estate
    b. who acquire bonds
    c. with fixed interest rate loans
    d. with adjustable rate loans

19. According to fiscal theory, a tax decrease should:
    a. increase private spending
    b. decrease private savings
    c. fight inflation
    d. create unemployment

20. A famous economist, considered to be the founder of "new economics," who advocated using government fiscal policy to offset unemployment:
    a. Adam Smith
    b. Milton Friedman
    c. John Stuart Mill
    d. John Maynard Keynes

21. In the short run, a reduction in the supply of money should increase:
    a. taxes
    b. government spending
    c. interest rates
    d. real estate construction rates

22. When government revenues exceed government spending, there should be a budget:
    a. deficit
    b. balance
    c. decline
    d. surplus

23. The type of unemployment that recovers as the economy recovers is called:
    a. cyclical
    b. structural
    c. chronic
    d. stifled

24. Progressive income taxes and unemployment benefits are examples of the use of:
    a. monetary policy
    b. pure capitalistic theory
    c. automatic stabilizers
    d. Federal Reserve policies

25. Fiscal and monetary policies run into problems because of structural difficulties and:
    a. uniform applications
    b. political difficulties
    c. computer difficulties
    d. contractual applications

CASE & POINT

Laffer Curve

In the continuous debate over government taxation policy, economist Arthur Laffer points out that there is no economic theory, be it conservative or liberal, that states that a tax increase will stimulate the economy. According to Laffer, history indicates that tax revenue as a percentage of GDP is relatively constant regardless of the marginal tax rate.

Lowering tax rates would superficially appear to lower government revenues. However, lower tax rates do stimulate business activity and encourage more people to report income. This increases government tax revenue and makes up for revenue lost because of lower tax rates, Laffer reasons.

Higher tax rates would superficially appear to increase government revenue. However, high tax rates depress business activity and cause people to hide income or seek tax shelters or substitute non-tax leisure for taxable work, Laffer contends. This decreases tax revenue and offsets the increases the government hoped to collect when it enacted the high tax rates. Therefore, regardless of the higher tax rate, government tax revenue tends to remain rather constant. This is illustrated in Figure 3.3, the Laffer Curve.

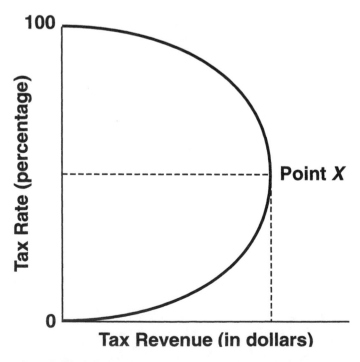

Figure 3.3 The Laffer Curve.

Many proponents of the Laffer Curve believe that current tax rates are set too high and are not at the most efficient point. Therefore, if the government lowered tax rates, government revenue would rise. They argue that this is the best way to attack the current government budget deficit.

0% tax rate = No tax revenue
100% tax rate = No tax revenue
Point *X* is where tax rates should be set to maximize tax revenue.

At 0% tax rates, Laffer reasons, government will not receive tax revenue, as no one will need to pay taxes. At 100% tax rates, government will not receive tax revenue, as no one will work just to pay taxes. At some point, where the curve reaches its apex (point *X*), tax rates will produce the maximum government revenue.

CHAPTER 4
MONEY, CREDIT, AND REAL ESTATE

PREVIEW

Money and credit have a critical effect on real estate activity. This chapter expands the explanation of economic principles and the role of the government by examining money's role in economic transactions. Section 4.1 discusses the functions of money and how it is created. It also examines the subject of inflation and its impact on the real estate market. Section 4.2 reviews the way that the Federal Reserve System controls the money supply in an effort to maintain economic growth and full employment without inflation. Section 4.3 emphasizes the impact that changes in the money supply have on real estate activity. The Case & Point at the end of the chapter discusses the savings and loan crisis of the 1980s and poses questions for the liberal home financing of the 2000s. When you have finished this chapter, you will be able to:

1. Explain what money is and describe how banks and other depository institutions create money.

2. Understand the purpose of the Federal Reserve System and describe three main tools it uses to regulate the flow of money and credit.

3. Discuss the impact that Federal Reserve policies have on real estate activity.

Understanding money and credit will allow a person to anticipate changes in the real estate market and to follow the relationship between current real estate market conditions and shifts in the money supply.

4.1 The Supply of Money

There is more to making money than just inking the printing presses. Most money in America is neither in coins nor bills; most money has been created by banks and other depository institutions in the form of demand deposits. This section explains the uses of money, the different types of money, and how money is created. Understanding the money supply is an important tool for understanding real estate economics.

What is Money?

1. *Money is a medium of exchange.* It allows people to exchange goods and services without the need to revert to a barter (or swap) system.

2. *Money is a measure of value.* It is used to compare the worth of unlike items. What is a home worth in relation to an automobile? What are the services of a physician worth as compared to the services of a plumber? Under a barter system, it might be said that 20 automobiles equal one home or two plumbers equal one doctor. Under the U.S. monetary system, each item is measured in dollars: an automobile, $20,000; a home, $400,000; a plumber, $70,000; a doctor, $140,000; and so on.

3. *Money is a store of value.* It is a way to save up wealth. If you choose not to buy goods and services immediately, you can store your right to spend later by saving money. But there are some risks. For example, what happens to your money during periods of inflation? Does it increase or decrease in value?

4. *Money is a standard of deferred payment.* It is used to describe what a debtor owes a creditor. If you buy now and pay later, the amount you owe is expressed in money.

What Makes "Good" Money?

Gold, silver, corn, cattle, and shells have been used as money at one time or another. Contrary to popular belief, money does not have to be a precious metal. Anything that is universally accepted by society can be used as money. In a practical sense, money should be *portable*, so it is easy to carry; *durable*, so it will not lose its value by wearing away; *divisible*, so it can be broken down into smaller units; and *stable*, so it will not radically change in value.

Money Today

Today, there are three types of money in the United States: *coins, paper currency*, and *checking accounts*. Pennies, nickels, dimes, quarters, half-dollars, and dollar coins make up the U.S. coin system. The metallic value of coins is less than their face value. If the value of the metal should exceed the value of the coin, people would tend to hoard the coins and then illegally melt them down in order to sell the metal. Coins account for approximately 2 percent of the total value of the U.S. money supply.

Paper currency ($1, $5, $10, and other bills) makes up approximately 25 percent of the total value of the U.S. money supply. These bills, issued by the Federal Reserve, are essentially promissory notes. Federal Reserve notes circulate as money and will continue to do so as long as people have faith in the strength of the government. Contrary to popular belief, U.S. paper money is no longer backed by gold stored in Fort Knox, Kentucky. The only thing backing U.S. currency is the strength of the government.

The rest of the U.S. money supply, approximately 73 percent, consists of checks drawn against checking accounts—bank money. *In economic terms, checking accounts are called demand deposits.* When you write a check, you are transferring a portion of your bank deposit to a third party. The bank must pay this money upon demand. No time delays are allowed; hence, the term *demand deposit*.

Credit Cards Are Not Money

Money and credit cards are frequently used interchangeably, but they are not the same. Money means currency and checks, a medium of exchange, or an assignment of assets from a buyer directly to a seller. Credit cards consist of a loan. A credit card company issues a line of credit to a borrower who then uses the line of credit to make a purchase. The business, who accepts the credit card, is paid by the credit card company for the goods and services given to the buyer. The credit card company then collects from the credit card user (buyer of the goods and services). Both money and credit cards are used to acquire goods and services and this leads some people to incorrectly think money and credit cards are the same thing. They are not. Economists frequently refer to credit cards as "near money." On the other hand, bank debit cards are money in the sense the funds are deducted directly out of the user's checking account. The checking account funds are transferred directly from the buyer to the seller, so no loan is involved.

Depository Institutions Create Money

Only the federal government may legally mint coins and print paper currency, but depository institutions such as commercial banks and savings banks can legally create demand deposits or checks. At one time, only commercial banks could issue checks and create money. But the Depository Institutions Deregulation and Monetary Control Act of 1980 plus other laws now allow various depository institutions, namely, savings and loan associations (now called savings banks) and

---

Currency and Portraits

Denomination	Face	Highest Federal Office Held
$1	Washington	1st President (1789–1797)
$2	Jefferson	3rd President (1801–1809)
$5	Lincoln	16th President (1861–1865)
$10	Hamilton	Sec. of the Treasury (1789–1895)
$20	Jackson	7th President (1829–1837)
$50	Grant	18th President (1869–1877)
$100	Franklin	Ambassador (1776–1785)
$500*	McKinley	25th President (1897–1901)
$1,000*	Cleveland	22nd & 24th President (1885–1889) and (1893–1897)
$5,000*	Madison	4th President (1809–1817)
$10,000*	Chase	Chief Justice (1864–1873)

*Printing of these bills was discontinued in 1945.

credit unions to also issue checks and create money. For simplicity, all depository institutions will simply be referred to as "banks."

Banks create money because of a concept known as *fractional reserve banking*. Federal law requires that the bank must set aside a reserve for each deposit received. These reserves cannot be used to meet withdrawals, but rather are used to give the Federal Reserve Board control over the money-creating ability of banks.

How Fractional Reserves Create Money

To see how banks actually create money, let us assume that federal law requires that 20 percent of each deposit in checking accounts must be kept as a reserve. The remaining 80 percent can be used to create a loan. (Actual reserve requirements are considerably less than 20 percent, and they vary with the size of the institution's deposits. Twenty percent is used here because it is easily divisible.)

Now let us assume that $1,000 is deposited in Bank A. Bank A will put $200 in reserve and loan out $800 to Mr. X. Mr. X will take the $800 and spend it. The receiver of this money will probably deposit the funds in Bank B. Bank B now has an $800 deposit, of which $160—20 percent—is kept in reserve and $640 is loaned out to Ms. Y. Ms. Y spends the $640, and the receiver deposits the money in Bank C. Bank C now has a $640 deposit, of which $128 is kept in reserve and $512 is loaned out. In theory, this process continues until all funds are exhausted. Table 4.1 illustrates this process.

A single $1,000 deposit under a 20 percent reserve requirement can expand to become a $5,000 deposit, $4,000 of which is loaned out. In essence, the banking system has created additional purchasing power (demand deposits). This has the same effect on spending as increasing the amount of coin and paper money.

In the real world, does this creation of bank money always occur at a constant, smooth rate? Not usually! Some banks differ in their reserve policy (choose to hold more reserves than required by law), and the amount of loans available from each deposit varies among banks. In addition, "leakage" occurs when people fail to deposit money in banks. Going back to Table 4.1, what would happen if the borrower of the $640 from Bank B buys merchandise, and the store owners put the $640 under their mattresses instead of depositing the money in Bank C?

Federal Deposit Insurance

With only a fraction of actual deposits in reserve, won't a bank or other savings institution fail if depositors panic and attempt a run on

Table 4.1 How Banks Create Money	*Banks*	*Deposits*	*Reserves*	*Loans*
	Bank A	$1,000.00	$200.00	$800.00
	Bank B	800.00	160.00	640.00
	Bank C	640.00	128.00	512.00
	Bank D	512.00	102.40	409.60
	Bank E	409.60	81.92	327.68
	All other banks together	1,638.40	327.68	1,310.72
	Totals	$5,000.00	$1,000.00	$4,000.00

the bank by trying to withdraw all their savings? Prior to the establishment of the Federal Deposit Insurance Corporation (FDIC) this was a distinct possibility. The FDIC is a federal agency, funded by banks and backed by the full faith of the U.S. government, that insures depositors up to $100,000. If a bank or savings and loan association fails, the FDIC will pay insured depositors up to $100,000 to cover their lost savings. The key here is insured savings. Some securities issued by banks and thrift institutions are not insured by the FDIC, and a subsequent institution failure could result in a total loss of money invested in these types of securities. See the Case & Point. "The Savings and Loan Crisis of the 1980s" at the end of this chapter.

Classifications of the Money Supply

For monitoring and analysis, the Federal Reserve classifies the money supply as follows: *M1* refers to coins, paper money, and demand deposits. *M2* is M1 plus items that can quickly be converted to money, such as small savings accounts, CDs, and money market accounts. *M3* is M2 plus large CDs of over $100,000.

Too Much Money Can Cause Inflation and Harm Real Estate Markets

As the money supply expands, interest rates tend to drop and credit becomes easier to obtain. This stimulates spending and increases the demand for resources, goods, and services. But a point is reached where additional increases in the money supply will stimulate demand beyond the ability of the economy to increase supply. The result will be inflation—a rise in general prices—too much money chasing too few goods.

DEMAND-PULL INFLATION

COST-PUSH INFLATION

Two Types of Inflation

Demand-Pull Type	*Cost-Push Type*
"Too much money chasing too few goods." Sellers are producing at full capacity and find it impossible to expand supply. Additional demand, fed by easy money and liberal fiscal policy, drives up prices. This type of inflation is curbed by reducing government spending and by reducing the money supply in order to slow down demand to the point where supply and demand are balanced.	Prices are pushed up because production costs (land, labor, and capital) are increasing. *Controversy*: Do strong labor unions force wages up, causing businesses to raise prices? Or do businesses raise prices, forcing unions to seek higher wages? Economists are still trying to find a solution to this type of inflation. Government wage and price controls have been used, but their success is debatable.

Inflation hurts people on fixed incomes, creditors, and workers who are unable to gain wage increases to offset inflation. Inflation also harms real estate markets. However, the federal government could gain during inflation, because inflation often pushes people into higher income tax brackets. This is, in effect, a "hidden" tax. To offset this problem, the income range subject to the federal income tax brackets are adjusted each year for inflation.

Real Estate Markets and Inflation

In periods of inflation, mortgage lenders are hurt because the money they receive from loan repayments is worth less than the money they originally loaned. Thus, to protect themselves during periods of rapid inflation, mortgage lenders increase interest rates. An increase in interest rates causes monthly payments to increase, thereby preventing some potential buyers from qualifying for loans. This reduces the demand for real estate.

Inflation can cause some depositors in thrift institutions, such as savings banks, to withdraw their funds and seek higher returns in other parts of the money market. This sometimes reduces the money available for mortgages.

During inflation, the cost of the components of construction (land, labor, and materials) rises. This increases the cost of construction and can price some people out of the housing market.

Increased prices also drive up the cost of purchasing the basic necessities of life. In effect, this reduces discretionary income—money for luxuries and leisure. A decline in discretionary income has harmful effects on the recreational and leisure real estate markets, such as vacation homes, motels, and tourist attractions.

Finally, inflation strikes at the core of decision making. Uncertainties about price changes cause businesses and consumers to act hastily, to become dismayed, discouraged, and confused. Ultimately, this causes major disruptions for all sectors of the economy.

The Importance of Controlling the Supply of Money

As discussed in the previous chapter, an increase or decrease in the money supply can be used to counteract fluctuations in the economy. However, there is always the danger that too great an increase in the supply of money can cause inflation, whereas not enough money can bring on a recession.

Section 4.2 discusses who controls the U.S. money supply and how it is done. Before you proceed, review your understanding of the following.

Special Interest Topic

Tangibles in Times of Uncertainty

During rapid inflation and/or political unrest some people abandon paper currency and seek refuge in tangibles, such as precious metals, art, antiques, and real estate. The key is to find some item that has a limited supply that cannot be easily expanded. As people swarm to these tangibles, their prices skyrocket. If the panic subsides, the price of the tangible levels off or declines.

This trend has occurred in some South American countries. There, runaway inflation drove many South Americans to acquire tangibles outside their own country, such as U.S. real estate.

Speculators capitalize on the trends by attempting to purchase on the low side and then ride the upswing and sell just before the market declines. If, on the other hand, prices continue to rise, the tangible may become a good long-term hedge against inflation.

In times of deflation or disinflation (inflation at a slower rate) the opposite tends to occur. People abandon tangibles and seek a refuge in paper money. The longer people hold paper money during deflation, the greater the purchasing power it commands.

REVIEWING YOUR UNDERSTANDING

The Supply of Money

1. How has the Federal Deposit Insurance Corporation (FDIC) strengthened our banking system?

2. If all banks keep 10 percent of deposits in reserve, what are the maximum deposits and loans that can be generated if a new $1,000 deposit is taken into the system?

3. If the economy is in a recession, and assuming you had the power, would you increase or decrease the percentage of reserves that banks must keep to back each deposit? Why?

4. How can too much money create inflation? What problems does this cause for real estate brokers?

4.2 The Federal Reserve System

The Federal Reserve System regulates most of the U.S. money supply. This section explains the tools available to the Federal Reserve and illustrates how these tools can counteract economic imbalances.

Purpose of the Federal Reserve System

The purpose of the Federal Reserve System (hereafter referred to as The Fed) is to regulate the supply of money and credit in order to achieve economic growth without inflation and unemployment. In short, The Fed views itself as a "money doctor," attempting to cure or prevent economic sickness by controlling the flow of money and credit.

The Fed was established by Congress in 1913. The system consists of 12 regional reserve banks and a seven-member Board of Governors located in Washington, D.C. (see Figure 4.1 and Figure 4.2). Each governor serves a 14-year term, in the hope that long-term appointments will insulate the governors against political pressures when making economic decisions.

Figure 4.1 The Federal Reserve System. (*Source*: The Federal Reserve.)

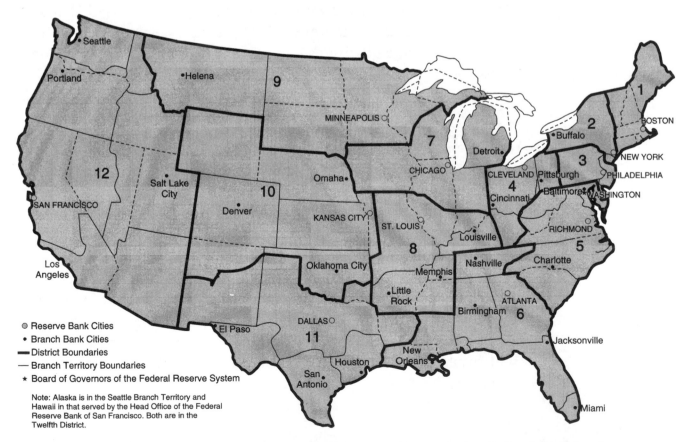

Figure 4.2 Federal Reserve map of the United States. (*Source*: The Federal Reserve.)

How the Federal Reserve Attempts to Control the Money Supply

Section 4.1 described how depository institutions create money by using fractional reserve banking. From your earlier reading, you will recall that the legal amount held in reserve by banks cannot be loaned out. Control over the legal percentage of reserves, therefore, would constitute control over the money supply: an increase in the percentage of reserves causes a decrease in the money supply, and a decrease in reserve percentages results in an increase in money and credit. This is exactly how The Fed operates. Using specific tools (frequently referred to as "weapons"), The Fed attempts to control the U.S. money supply by manipulating bank reserves.

Major Tools of the Federal Reserve

The Fed controls bank reserves by using the following major tools:

1. Changes in the reserve requirements

2. Open-market operations

3. Changes in the discount rate

Changes in the Reserve Requirements

All depository institutions are required to keep a certain percentage of each deposit as reserves. The percentages are established by law, but the Board of Governors of the Federal Reserve has the right to vary the percentages within a certain range. These reserves are kept at the regional Federal Reserve Bank. If The Fed believes that easy money and credit are feeding inflation, it can raise the reserve requirements, which will force banks to restrict their lending, as money must be diverted from loans to cover the shortage in reserves. This action is designed to decrease the amount of money in circulation, drive up interest rates, and eventually lessen inflation by slowing down spending.

What will happen if The Fed decreases the reserve requirements? Will this increase or decrease the money supply? Will this raise or lower interest rates? Trace the steps to check your understanding.

Open-Market Operations

As part of its money-management tools, The Fed is allowed to buy and sell government securities. The public (private citizens and financial institutions) also may buy and sell government securities as a form of investment. When The Fed buys government securities from the public, the seller of these securities (the public) receives The Fed's check, which the seller then deposits in a local bank. The local bank forwards the check to The Fed for payment. When The Fed receives its own check, it increases the reserves of the local bank by the amount of that check. The local bank now has more reserves than are required and therefore can grant more loans. *Thus, when The Fed buys government securities from the public, it increases the money supply by increasing bank reserves, which in turn will support more loans.*

What happens to the money supply when The Fed sells government securities to the public? The money supply tightens up, which increases interest rates and discourages borrowing. To help review your understanding, let us trace what happens when The Fed sells government securities.

When government securities are sold, an individual purchases them by writing a check on his or her local bank. The Fed receives the buyer's check and subtracts it from the reserve account of the local bank. The local bank now has fewer reserves and therefore must constrict its lending. *So when The Fed sells government securities, it decreases bank reserves, which in turn decreases the bank's ability to grant loans.*

Once again notice that the ultimate effect is a change in the money supply by manipulating bank reserves. But The Fed has still another important tool—changes in the discount rate.

Changes in the Discount Rate

When you need a loan, you frequently go to your bank. Where does a bank go when it needs a loan? One possible place is the Federal Reserve. The Fed is considered a banker's bank. When you borrow from your bank, you pay interest. When a bank borrows from The Fed, it is charged an interest rate known as the *discount rate*.

By decreasing the discount rate, The Fed can encourage banks to borrow. The borrowed funds increase the local bank's deposits and reserves, which allows for the expansion of loans. An increase in the discount rate discourages banks from borrowing, which will decrease the amount of money available for loans.

Federal Funds Rate

Although not technically listed as a major tool of The Fed, the *federal funds rate* is one of the most closely watched indicators as to the current thinking of the Federal Reserve people. What is the federal funds rate? When one bank is at a maximum loan to reserve requirement, it cannot grant additional loans to expand business until its reserves are increased. Or if the bank has granted too many loans relative to its existing reserves, it must by law either call in some loans or increase its reserves. One way to solve these problems is to borrow excess reserves from another bank that currently is not granting additional loans. The *federal funds rate*, then, is the rate of interest one bank charges another for the overnight use of excess reserves.

The federal funds rate should not be confused with the prime rate. The *prime rate* is the rate of interest a bank charges its large, better customers, such as major corporations. The federal funds rate is what one bank charges another bank for overnight use of excess reserves.

The Federal Reserve, in its effort to fight inflation or recession, increases or decreases the money supply to keep the federal funds rate in a certain trading range. If The Fed wishes to allow the economy to expand, it may allow the federal funds rate to drop below the trading range. This will encourage one bank to borrow the excess reserves of another and use the reserves to grant more loans, which should expand the economy. If The Fed wishes to slow the economy, it may tighten up the money supply and force the federal funds rate to rise. This discourages one bank from borrowing excess reserves from another bank, thereby discouraging the granting of additional loans. This will tend to keep the economy from expanding.

A Summary of the Major Federal Reserve Tools

Changes in the reserve requirement, open-market operations, and changes in the discount rate allow The Fed to control the supply of bank money. Of these tools, the most commonly used is that of open-market operations.

To increase the money supply, The Fed will either decrease the reserve requirement, buy government securities, decrease the discount rate, or use some combination of all three.

To decrease the money supply, The Fed will either increase the reserve requirements, sell government securities, increase the discount rate, or use some combination of all three.

In addition, The Fed will keep a close eye on the federal funds rate and attempt to raise or lower this rate, depending on The Fed's economic goals.

Special Interest Topic

U.S. Addiction to Foreign Capital

As noted earlier, politically the U.S. Congress and the president have been unwilling to face the reality of the large budget deficit by severely cutting government spending or drastically raising taxes, or some combination of the two. The easy short-run "fix" has been to increase government borrowing to cover the deficit. A substantial amount of this borrowing has come from foreign investors. Foreign purchases of U.S. government and private securities have moved the United States from a creditor nation to a debtor nation. This need for foreign capital gives rise to a couple of questions: Does the dependence on foreign capital reduce The Fed's ability to influence U.S. interest rates? If so, does this mean that The Fed's ability to use monetary techniques to help control the U.S. economy has been weakened? Although it is too soon to tell for sure, it appears that trends in the financial markets in Japan and Europe (both large buyers of U.S. bonds) have a strong influence on U.S. interest rates. This in turn makes The Fed's job more difficult. High or low interest rates in foreign markets help determine what U.S. interest rates must do to attract foreign investors to help finance the U.S. budget deficit. High interest rates could be counter to The Fed's wishes. For example, the U.S. economy could be in a slump. Monetary policy calls for lowering interest rates to stimulate production and jobs in such a situation. But lower interest rates would discourage foreign investors, thereby forcing Congress and the president to cut government spending or raise taxes. This would tend to depress the economy even further. On the other hand, if The Fed maintains high interest rates to attract foreign investors to cover the U.S. budget deficit, this will reduce the ability of U.S. companies and consumers to borrow for domestic economic expansion. This is just another example of the impact the globalization of financial markets has on domestic economies in today's world.

REVIEWING YOUR UNDERSTANDING

The Federal Reserve System

1. Why does the Federal Reserve System view itself as a "money doctor"?

2. Why are the governors of the Federal Reserve System appointed for 14 years? Who is the current chairperson of the Federal Reserve System?

3. If The Fed wishes to stimulate demand in an effort to fight a recession, would it increase or decrease bank reserves? What should it do regarding open-market operations? Regarding the discount rate?

4. What is the federal funds rate? Prime rate?

4.3 The Actions of the Federal Reserve Board and Their Effects on Real Estate Activity

This section explains how The Fed's attempts to regulate the money supply can influence the real estate market. This section also points out that the cyclical movement of the real estate market will not always be in perfect step with general economic trends.

Tight-Money Policies and Real Estate

The Fed institutes a restrictive monetary policy in order to combat inflation. Inflation itself is frequently caused by excessive private demand, government deficits, or a swollen money supply.

When The Fed fights inflation, it tightens up the money supply, which in turn causes interest rates to rise as government agencies and corporate borrowers bid against one another for the shrinking money supply. Higher interest rates can cause funds to flow out of depository institutions, as savers go elsewhere seeking higher rates of return. Depository institutions grant the biggest share of home mortgages. Thus, when banks and savings institutions lose funds, mortgage lending decreases, and the real estate market heads into a recession. The economic term for the outflow of funds from depository institutions into corporate and government notes is called *disintermediation*.

As a result, when The Fed tightens money to combat inflation, housing is one of the first economic sectors to feel the pinch. This frequently brings cries of "discrimination" from the real estate industry.

Does The Fed Discriminate Against Housing When It Tightens Money?

Does The Fed really discriminate against housing? In the purest sense, the answer is no. When The Fed decreases the money supply, it does not single out the real estate market and crimp only housing funds. Historically, real estate mortgages in tight-money markets are usually unattractive investments because they are long-term loans, which frequently bear low to moderate fixed interest rates.

During periods of prosperity and inflation, interest rates for other investments tend to rise. Some institutional lenders may refuse to lend on low-paying, long-term mortgages and instead are attracted to high-yield, short-term government notes and business loans. As the demand for funds continues to exceed the supply, interest rates on Treasury and federal agency instruments also increase, and disintermediation may take place. The Fed does not specifically discriminate against housing; rather, the structure of the mortgage market tends to defeat itself in tight-money situations.

Easy-Money Policies and Real Estate

During periods of economic slowdown, The Fed attempts to head off a recession by easing the money supply. An increase in money and credit, in time, may cause spending to increase, and this expansion will ideally bring an increase in employment.

As money and credit become more plentiful, interest rates tend to decline. These lower interest rates do not immediately attract business borrowers because the economic turndown still leaves a lingering feeling of pessimism. Meanwhile, private savings may increase as uncertainty causes people to become cautious and to restrict their spending.

Financial institutions find that savings are piling up. The Fed is making more money available, but few businesses are borrowing. So lenders look more favorably at real estate mortgages as an outlet for funds. As money moves back into the mortgage market, the demand for housing, which was previously suppressed by a lack of credit, begins to pick up, and the real estate market slowly recovers.

Recovery in the Real Estate Market Normally Precedes a Recovery in the National Economy

Because of the size and impact of the construction industry, an increase in home and other building helps to lead the economy out of a recession. As construction picks up, employment, income, and spending increase. This in turn generates even more activity, and the general business cycle heads for recovery.

However, if spending and demand rise beyond the equilibrium point, inflation will recur. If this happens, The Fed may tighten up the money supply, and the mortgage market will start to lose funds, causing real estate activity to decline.

The real estate market (cycle) in the short run may travel somewhat opposite to the general business cycle. When the general economy is at the top of a boom, real estate activity is usually already declining because of a tightening of credit. When the general economy starts to slow down, real estate activity may increase as funds flow back into the mortgage market.

Mortgage Market Reforms

With the introduction of adjustable rate mortgages, money market certificate accounts, and a vastly improved secondary mortgage market, depository institutions are becoming somewhat insulated against excessive disintermediation. Starting in the mid-1970s, both the general economy and the real estate market prospered simultaneously for the first time since World War II. However, some of these mortgage market reforms have driven up the cost of money for depository institutions, and the higher costs are being passed to mortgage borrowers in the form of higher interest rates and other costs.

REVIEWING YOUR UNDERSTANDING

The Actions of the Federal Reserve Board and Their Effects on Real Estate Activity

1. How do tight-money policies of the Federal Reserve System influence the real estate market?

2. What causes disintermediation from savings institutions? How does this affect real estate markets?

3. Why does a recovery in the real estate market usually precede a recovery in the national economy?

CHAPTER SUMMARY

Money acts as a medium of exchange, a measure of value, a store of value, and a standard for deferred payment. There are three types of U.S. money: coins, paper currency, and demand deposits (checking accounts). Demand deposits are by far the most important part of the U.S. money supply.

Although only the federal government may legally mint coins and print currency, U.S. banks and other depository institutions create checking account money. Banks create this money by fractional reserve banking.

The amount of money in circulation has a tremendous influence on the performance of the economy. Too much money and credit can create inflation, whereas too little can cause a recession. In an effort to control the flow of money and credit, Congress established the Federal Reserve System (frequently referred to as The Fed).

The Fed attempts to control the money supply by using three main tools: changes in the reserve requirements, open-market operations, and changes in the discount rate. All of these tools control the credit-creating ability of banks by manipulating the amount of money banks must keep as a reserve. If a bank's reserve requirement is high, the bank can lend less money. If a bank's reserve requirement is low, the bank can lend more money. The Fed also watches the federal funds rate.

If The Fed believes that there is too much inflation, it will attempt to tighten up the money supply. It does this by increasing the reserve requirements, raising the discount rate, or selling government securities in the open market. As the money supply tightens, one of the hardest-hit areas is the real estate market. Tight money and high interest rates make mortgage credit scarce and expensive. This makes it difficult to buy or build a home, and activity in the real estate market declines.

On the other hand, if the economy is heading for a recession, The Fed may increase the money supply. This encourages more spending and helps to slow the recession. An increase in the money supply is called an easy-money policy. During the early periods of easy money, activity in the real estate market picks up as interest rates decline and mortgage credit becomes more plentiful. Because of the size and impact of the construction industry, an increase in building helps to lead the economy out of a recession.

However, if spending and demand rise beyond our economy's ability to supply goods and services, inflation recurs. If this happens, The Fed may again tighten up the money supply so that funds flow out of the mortgage-lending institutions (disintermediation). This will cause a drop in real estate activity, and once again it becomes more difficult to buy and sell homes and other real estate. Understanding the impact that changes in the money supply have on local real estate activity is one of the most important concepts for successful real estate investing.

IMPORTANT TERMS AND CONCEPTS

Demand deposits	*Measure of value*
Discount rate	*Medium of exchange*
Disintermediation	*Open-market operations*
Easy-money policies	*Prime rate*
Federal funds rate	*Reserve requirements*
Federal Reserve System	*Store of value*
Fractional reserve banking	*Tight-money policies*
Inflation	

REVIEWING YOUR UNDERSTANDING

1. Which of the following *is not* considered a function of money?
   a. medium of exchange
   b. measure of value
   c. standard of deferred payment
   d. standard of tangible asset

2. The greatest percentage of the U.S. money supply is represented by:
   a. checks
   b. coins
   c. paper currency
   d. certificates of deposit

3. If the banking system is using a 10 percent reserve requirement, an initial $1,000 deposit can expand to a maximum of how much in new loans?
   a. $1,000
   b. $5,000

c. $9,000
d. $10,000

4. If the Federal Reserve wishes to expand the money supply it could:
   a. increase the reserve requirements
   b. raise the discount rate
   c. buy government bonds
   d. increase the federal funds rate

5. The rate of interest that one bank charges another for the overnight use of excess reserves is called:
   a. prime rate
   b. discount rate
   c. federal funds rate
   d. commercial rate

6. The flow of funds from depository institutions to the general money market is called:
   a. reintermediation
   b. disintermediation
   c. run on the bank
   d. recapitalization

7. Which of the following actions by The Fed tends to raise interest rates?
   a. selling government securities
   b. lowering the discount rate
   c. decreasing reserve requirements
   d. reducing the federal funds rate

8. The increase in the use of foreign capital tends to motivate Congress and the president to solve the U.S. budget deficit problem.
   a. true
   b. false

9. Which government agency insures savings accounts at approved depository institutions?
   a. Federal Reserve System
   b. Federal Home Loan Bank
   c. Federal Deposit Insurance Corporation
   d. Federal Trust Association

10. Which of the following is true?
    a. U.S. paper currency is not backed by gold.
    b. Inflation is always good for real estate because prices go up.
    c. Government deficits decrease the government's need to borrow.
    d. All economists agree that monetary policy is better than fiscal policy for controlling the economy.

11. Money has various functions. When money is used to describe what a debtor owes a creditor, this function of money is called a:
    a. medium of exchange
    b. measure of value
    c. standard of deferred payment
    d. store of value

12. Depository institutions create money as a result of a concept known as:
    a. fractional reserve banking
    b. demand deposits
    c. reintermediation
    d. capitalization

13. A decrease in the rate of inflation is called:
    a. deflation
    b. disinflation
    c. disintermediation
    d. disintegration

14. Rapid unanticipated inflation is most harmful to real estate:
    a. lenders who grant ARM loans
    b. lenders who grant fixed rate loans
    c. borrowers who have fixed rate loans
    d. purchasers who pay cash

15. For monitoring and analysis, the Federal Reserve classifies coins, paper money, and demand deposits as:
    a. M1
    b. M2
    c. M3
    d. M4

16. "Too much money chasing too few goods" is what kind of inflation?
    a. cost-push
    b. spiral-up
    c. twist-down
    d. demand-pull

17. The Federal Reserve System contains how many regional reserve banks?
    a. 5
    b. 7
    c. 12
    d. 14

18. The Federal Reserve's control over the economy is called:
    a. fiscal policy
    b. monetary policy
    c. fractional reserve policy
    d. market policy

19. When The Fed buys and sells government notes and bonds, it is called:
    a. change in reserve requirements
    b. change in discount requirements
    c. supply of money operations
    d. open-market operations

20. To decrease prevailing interest rates, The Fed:
    a. sells government notes
    b. lowers the discount rate
    c. increases reserve requirements
    d. increases the federal funds rate

21. Recovery in the real estate market frequently begins before a full recovery in the general economy.
    a. true
    b. false

22. When interest rates rise, the:
    a. demand for housing declines
    b. supply of housing increases
    c. demand for commercial real estate increases
    d. supply of commercial real estate increases

23. Historically, real estate mortgages in tight-money markets are attractive investments.
    a. true
    b. false

24. A decrease in mortgage interest rates tends to increase:
    a. home sales
    b. refinances
    c. home prices
    d. all of the above

25. Which mortgage market reform has insulated depository institutions from excessive disintermediation?
    a. adjustable rate mortgages
    b. money market certificate accounts
    c. an improved secondary mortgage market
    d. all of the above

CASE & POINT

The Savings and Loan Crisis of the 1980s: What Lessons Can Be Learned for The Liberal Real Estate Financing Programs of the 2000s?

Background

By the early 1980s excessive inflation during the previous decade had placed the savings and loan (S&L) industry in a financial bind. High interest rates were being paid by banks and money market funds to attract depositors, but savings and loans were prohibited by law from paying interest above a low passbook account rate. Thus, deposits were flowing out of S&Ls into other investments. In the meantime the savings and loan industry was saddled with a huge inventory of low fixed interest rate mortgages made in earlier years. The resale value of these loans was low because of the discount needed to increase the yield to the level demanded by investors. In short, the asset value of the entire industry was declining, and it looked like the real estate market, which was closely tied to the savings and loan industry, was heading for trouble.

The Proposed Solution

The proposed solution was to deregulate the savings and loan industry and allow its owners and managers to compete in the general marketplace, as did banks and other financial institutions. The thought was that this would stimulate the general economy and boost the real estate market. The following major events set this proposed solution in motion:

1. In 1980, Congress passed the Depository Institutions Deregulation and Monetary Control Act. This law, in phases, lifted interest rate ceilings for S&Ls and allowed the industry to issue checking accounts and certificates of deposits, grant commercial real estate and consumer loans, acquire stocks and bonds, and own and operate real estate development companies, mutual funds, and many other ventures. In short, they could operate similarly to commercial banks.

2. In 1981, Congress passed the Economic Reform Act to stimulate the economy, which was in a recession. One of the main provisions of this act was favorable accelerated depreciation for real estate investors. This in turn started a boom in new residential, commercial, and industrial development. The savings and loan industry was heavily involved in financing these projects. Many projects were built on speculation, without a buyer or tenant under contract. This was especially true in the rapidly expanding mountain states and the Southwest.

3. In 1982, Congress passed the Depository Institutions Act (Garn Bill), which continued the trend of deregulation. Another important feature of this law allowed real estate lenders to enforce due-on-transfer clauses, whereby lenders could call their existing low interest rate loans when a property was transferred to a new owner, rather than be stuck with a loan assumption at a low interest rate.

4. After much promotion, real estate lenders convinced the public to accept the concept of adjustable rate mortgages (ARMs). This helped to protect the value of the lender's portfolio by passing the risk of future inflation to the borrower and away from the lender. In addition, an increasingly sophisticated secondary market allowed lenders to package and resell their existing mortgages faster and avoid being saddled with unwanted inventory.

These events, plus others, placed savings and loan associations on an equal footing with other financial institutions and gave S&L owners and managers the economic freedom to go to the marketplace and generate profits.

What Happened?

Why did we have a savings and loan crisis? Why did Congress need to pass the "bailout" legislation known as the Financial Institutions Reform Recovery and Enforcement Act of 1989 (FIRREA)? Did deregulation fail? Did the free market theory fail to work?

These questions may never be answered fully, but here are some concepts to consider:

1. The collapse of oil prices led to the economic crash in the "oil patch" and mountain states (Texas, Louisiana, Oklahoma, Colorado, and Utah), which in turn led to massive real estate foreclosures and other business failures. After a decade of oil shortages, who in the late 1970s and early 1980s dreamed that we would have an oversupply of oil in the mid-1980s? Had oil prices remained stable,

might the savings and loan associations in these regions still be solvent?

2. Did deregulation really create a free market? Savings and loan managers were able to use government-insured deposits to invest in various ventures. Thus, a case can be made that there was not a free market. If government deposit insurance was not available, a depositor would scrutinize the financial background of the savings and loan association before depositing savings, just as a prudent investor would in any other nonguaranteed investment. With no government insurance, it is likely that savings depositors would have avoided the weak, poorly managed institutions, thereby depriving those institutions of the funds needed to make investments. Instead, depositors placed money with institutions, knowing that it did not matter if they were good or bad because the government would guarantee up to $100,000 worth of savings.

3. If the government intended to maintain the deposit insurance program, would it not have been prudent for the president and Congress to provide adequate funds for the inspection and examination of savings institutions? Instead, the budgets of the bank and savings and loan examiners reportedly were cut during the early and mid-1980s. This made it easier for crooked S&L owners and managers to loot the institutions. It also allowed incompetent, but not necessarily dishonest, managers to operate longer.

4. Did pressure from savings and loan association trade groups, along with their political action committee (PAC) fund contributions, generate political favors that added to the crisis?

5. It must be pointed out that many savings and loan associations were financially solid and profitable throughout this period. Apparently, deregulation and free market forces worked for these institutions.

As with many economic issues, there are no clear-cut answers to the questions posed by the S&L crisis. Economic historians will be debating its causes for many years to come. But in the end, the U.S. taxpayer footed most of the bill for this financial folly.

Liberal Housing Finance Programs of the 2000s: Another Crisis in the Making?

One method used to help pull the United States out of the post 9/11 recession was to lower interest rates and liberalize home financing terms. Traditional programs that required 10 to 20 percentage down payments faded, and instead no money down (100 percentage) financing programs, coupled with interest-only loans, increased in popularity. This allowed people who were not qualified to own a home under the traditional lending programs to become homeowners. These liberal financing programs also provide the fire to drive up home prices. Rising home prices can generate larger commissions for mortgage and real estate agents, while providing home sellers with large tax-free gains due to the liberalization of income tax laws passed in 1997.

So the question becomes, "Are we setting the stage for another real estate housing crisis down the road?" What if interest rates rise, the economy tanks, unemployment rises, and incomes drop? Will the demand for housing then decline, lowering home values and leaving many homeowners "upside down" or "underwater," meaning that they owe more than the home is worth? What if the homeowner then needs to sell and finds out that the lender is owed more than the home is worth? What will be the choices? Add money as a seller to close the sale? Walk away and let the lender foreclose? Ask the lender to forgive part of the loan to avoid foreclosure? What about the tax law that says if the lender forgives part of the loan, that part of the loan must then be declared by the borrower as taxable ordinary income, under the "debt forgiveness rule"? Will this become a crisis equal to the savings and loan crisis of the 1980s? Will the taxpayers be faced with footing the bill for another financial folly?

CHAPTER 5
IMPORTANT ECONOMIC FEATURES OF REAL ESTATE

PREVIEW

This chapter sketches the basic economic features of real estate. A more in-depth analysis of residential, commercial, industrial, and rural real estate markets will be presented in later chapters.

Section 5.1 discusses the major differences between a perfectly competitive market and typical real estate markets. Section 5.2 outlines how real estate markets react when the demand for real property changes. The Case & Point at the end of the chapter presents a graphic analysis of supply and demand in the real estate market.

Chapter 5 completes Part One, "Basic Economic Background for Real Estate Analysis." When you have completed this chapter, you will be able to:

1. List five reasons why a real estate market is considered to be imperfect.

2. Describe why real estate markets need the services of real estate professionals.

3. Discuss why the supply and use of land is considered fixed in the short run.

4. Describe how an increase or decrease in demand influences the value of real estate.

5.1 Economic Characteristics of Real Estate Markets

A market was previously defined as a place where buyers and sellers meet to exchange items of value. The character or makeup of a particular market influences the level of prices paid. In a perfectly competitive market, there are numerous buyers and sellers, each assumed to be knowledgeable and free to move in or out of the market at will. Neither party has control over the market. Because the products being sold are assumed to be alike, buyers will usually select the one offered at the lowest price. In such a perfect market, prices would be established purely by the principles of supply and demand.

In practice, most markets are imperfect. Some of the characteristics of a perfect market are either missing or distorted, preventing the principles of supply and demand from operating efficiently.

Are real estate markets perfectly competitive or are they imperfect? The answers may be found in Table 5.1, which compares the characteristics of a perfect market and a typical real estate market.

Table 5.1 shows that real estate markets are imperfect. Characteristics of an imperfect real estate market include the following: real estate buyers and sellers are frequently uninformed about real estate values and trends in the marketplace; the transfer of real property requires a legal and technical knowledge not possessed by the average citizen; each real estate parcel is separate and unique from all other parcels; and the location of the land cannot be moved to capitalize on better market conditions in other geographic areas.

Does This Mean That the Principles of Supply and Demand Do Not Work in Real Estate Markets?

No, the principles of supply and demand are still an important factor influencing the value of real estate. However, it is important to recognize that the principles operate differently in real estate markets. In a perfectly competitive market, supply and demand react quickly to changes in market conditions. *In real estate markets, supply is fixed in the short run and cannot respond quickly to changes in market conditions.*

The Supply of Land Is Fixed

One of the most fundamental principles of real estate economics is the recognition that the *total* amount of land is fixed. The land

Table 5.1 Perfect Markets Versus Typical Real Estate Markets

Characteristic	Perfect Market	Typical Real Estate Market
1. Number of buyers and sellers	Many participants; no monopoly, oligopoly, or monopolistic competition.	Few participants; seller controls during a "seller's market," and buyer controls during a "buyer's market."
2. Product knowledge and market exchange	Buyers and sellers are highly knowledgeable; the exchange takes place with ease.	Buyers and sellers are not always knowledgeable; the exchange is legalistic, complex, and expensive. However, information on the Internet may slowly change this lack of knowledge.
3. Standardized products	All products are alike and interchangeable; there is little difference between products of different sellers.	Each parcel of real estate is unique and separate from all others; no two are exactly alike.
4. Mobility	Products can be transported to capitalize on more lucrative markets.	The location is fixed; a real estate parcel cannot be moved to another, more profitable location; a real estate market is local, not regional or national.
5. Size and frequency of purchase	The item purchased is small and relatively inexpensive; it is purchased frequently.	Real estate is purchased infrequently (rarely more than four or five times in a lifetime); a home represents the largest single investment made by the average family.
6. Government's role	Government plays little if any role; laissez-faire prevails.	Government plays a dominant role in encouraging or discouraging real estate development through the use of fiscal and monetary tools and by use of other controls, such as zoning, environmental, and health codes.
7. Prices	Prices are established by the smooth action of supply and demand.	Prices are influenced by the interaction of supply and demand, but this interaction is not smooth; a lack of knowledge by either the buyer or seller can distort the prices paid.

surface cannot be increased or decreased according to the whims of demand. However, the *intensity of land use* can change, and in time this will increase or decrease the supply of real estate. For example, it may be impossible to increase the number of acres within a community, but you can increase the number of housing units per acre. If home construction increases, this will generate an increase in the supply of homes, but not necessarily an increase in the supply of land.

In the Short Run, Land Use Is Also Fixed

Any change in the intensity of land use takes time. If the demand for residential or other real estate projects was suddenly to increase, developers would need considerable time to acquire land and obtain permits and financing. The state and local permit process could take years and environmental groups and unhappy neighbors may sue to block further development.

Once a building is constructed, it tends to have a long life, regardless of the short-run changes in the real estate market. For example, if the demand for homes within a community declines, a builder with an unsold supply of houses will not demolish them simply because the demand for the homes has diminished. Instead, the homes will sit vacant on the market until they are sold. If they remain unsold, eventually the lender will foreclose and then sell the inventory at discount prices.

A Fixed Supply Means That Real Estate Prices Fluctuate with Demand

If the supply of real estate is fixed, in the short run current market prices and rents will be determined by local changes in demand. When the demand goes up, prices and rents rise as buyers and renters attempt to outbid one another for a fixed supply. When the demand goes down, prices and rents decline because a decrease in demand creates some vacancies, and owners and landlords attempt to fill these vacancies by lowering prices.

REVIEWING YOUR UNDERSTANDING

Economic Characteristics of Real Estate

1. Why is a real estate market classified as imperfect?

2. What is meant by the statement, "The supply of land is fixed, but in time the number of real estate uses can be increased"?

3. If in the short run the supply of real estate is fixed, what happens to prices and rents if demand increases? If demand decreases?

5.2 How the Real Estate Market Reacts to Changes in Demand

An increase in demand for real estate will generally have the following consequences:

1. An increase in demand will reduce existing real estate vacancies, be it in apartments or in the inventory of homes for sale.

2. This reduction in vacancies will be followed by an increase in rents and prices, assuming no rent controls, as more people continue to bid for the fixed supply.

3. As demand pushes rents and prices up, a point is reached at which investors and builders, motivated by profit potential, are drawn into the construction market.

4. Assuming favorable economic and governmental conditions, new construction takes place slowly, and the supply of real estate increases gradually.

5. As this new construction overtakes the increase in demand, vacancies begin to rise.

6. This increase in vacancies causes a fall in rents and prices. Price and rent declines may not be readily apparent, but instead show up as rent concessions or favorable seller-aided financing.

7. With lower rents and prices, the difference between building costs and sales prices begins to narrow, and profits disappear. This process is accelerated because increased construction activity forces up building costs, catching builder profits in a squeeze between rising costs and falling sales prices.

A decrease in the demand for real estate will generally have these consequences:

1. A decrease in demand causes an increase in vacancies in apartments and a larger number of unsold homes.

2. The increase in vacancies will cause rents and prices to decline.

3. With lower rents and prices, people can now obtain more spacious quarters at no increase in costs. This may absorb the vacancy. If not, the continued vacancy will eventually force

property owners to abandon their properties, go to foreclosure, or demolish the structures.

4. The real estate market will remain in this state until demand once again increases.[1]

What Causes Supply and Demand for Real Estate to Change?

Changes in real estate demand are caused by changes in population, income, availability of mortgage credit, personal lifestyles, and governmental actions. Long-run changes in supply result from changes in the rate of construction, conversion, demolition, and from governmental actions.

However, the cause of change can vary for each type of real estate market. The reasons for changes in the supply or demand for residential real estate are often different from the reasons for changes in commercial, industrial, or rural real estate. The specific causes for changes in supply and demand will be examined in detail in Chapter 9, "Housing Markets"; Chapter 10, "Commercial and Industrial Markets"; and Chapter 11, "Rural and Recreational Real Estate Markets."

Foreign Ownership of U.S. Real Estate[2]

In the 1980s, major segments of real estate shifted from being controlled by local developers, lenders, and agents to a global business with many foreigners playing a key role. Foreign investors initially acquired fully leased commercial properties with triple "A" tenants at excellent locations in major U.S. cities. By the mid-1980s, foreigners were perceived to be overpaying for the properties and driving up prices in the local real estate market. Some foreign investors either purchased or founded U.S.-based real estate companies to acquire and manage their properties. Later, foreign development companies created projects from the ground up rather than depend on existing buildings. Foreign investors are now considered market wise and are paying local market, rather than inflated, prices.

With the crash of commercial real estate market prices in the early to mid-1990s, many foreign investors took heavy losses on their U.S.

---

[1] *A Teacher's Guide for Real Estate Economics,* California Department of Real Estate, prepared by Dr. WilliamHippaka,, 1974, Sacramento, CA.
[2] Information based on Lawrence Bacow, "The Internationalization of the U.S. Real Estate Industry," Cambridge: Massachusetts Institute of Technology, 1989. For a copy and price, contact Director of Publications, MIT Center for Real Estate Development, Building W31□310Cambridge, MA 02139.

real estate. Using the accuracy of hindsight, it appears that many U.S. real estate owners sold at the peak of the market to foreign buyers, getting out just before the crash. By the mid-2000s, some foreign property owners had resold their buildings at a loss to U.S. interests.

The entire issue of foreign ownership of U.S. businesses and real estate has emotions running high. Here are some of the advantages and disadvantages frequently cited by persons on both sides of this issue.

Advantages of Foreign Ownership

1. Generates income for U.S. real estate owners who sell. This income is reinvested to stimulate the economy and provide additional employment.

2. Provides tax revenue to the government from the profits on the sale. This helps cover some of the budget deficit without raising tax rates or cutting government spending programs.

3. Generates commissions and fees for the real estate industry.

Disadvantages of Foreign Ownership

1. Makes the United States less self-sufficient and more dependent on foreigners. In short, constitutes a "selling of America."

2. Gives the U.S. government less incentive to solve the budget deficit problem by providing a short-run "quick fix" using foreign capital instead of reducing government spending or raising taxes.

3. High prices paid by foreigners keep local investors out of the real estate market.

No matter where a person stands on the issue of foreign ownership, it should be pointed out that U.S. citizens have been buying assets of foreign countries for decades. Americans supported free trade when they were buying into foreign countries; now that the reverse is true, some U.S. citizens are lobbying for restrictions.

The Role of the Real Estate Professional[3]

In perfectly competitive markets, there is no need for the services of a real estate professional or any other third party. Buyers

---

[3] *A Teacher's Guide for Real Estate Economics*, California Department of Real Estate, prepared by Dr. William Hippaka, pp. 142–143, 1974, Sacramento, CA.

and sellers are assumed to be fully knowledgeable and able to handle all transactions themselves. Because the real estate market is imperfect, the real estate professional's role is to help buyers, sellers, landlords, and tenants to overcome these imperfections.

Real estate professionals can provide the following services:

1. Increase buyer and seller knowledge by:

   a. Providing current market information regarding selling prices and rents.
   b. Advising clients and customers on investment opportunities.
   c. Providing information on alternative methods of financing.
   d. Helping the parties to close the real estate transaction.

2. Increase the number of market participants by persuading owners to offer their property for sale and by encouraging people to acquire real estate. These efforts can increase the number of buyers and sellers and help to reduce one of the major imperfections of a real estate marketÅtoo few participants.

Impact of the Internet

As more data becomes available on the Internet, the traditional role of the real estate agent as a fountain of information will be reduced. With a few clicks on a search engine, consumers can find most properties offered for sale, determine fair market prices, and find sites that tell you step by step how to buy, finance, or sell a home. As more and more consumers utilize the Internet, many of the information functions of the real estate professional outlined above will fade away. The primary role of the real estate agent will be that of a facilitator, time saver, and adviser. Buyers and sellers will be very knowledgeable, but may still use real estate professionals for advice, for negotiations, and to handle the time-consuming details needed to close a real estate transaction.

Once of the major economic impacts of the Internet has been to reduce the role of the so-called "middleman." Use of the Internet has greatly reduced the needed number of travel agents, stock brokers, insurance agents, mortgage brokers, and so on. Consumers log on and then buy direct, cutting out the middleperson. Only the future will determine what impact this will have on the needed number of real estate agents.

REVIEWING YOUR UNDERSTANDING

How the Real Estate Market Reacts to Changes in Demand

1. If the demand for apartments increases, what will happen to vacancy rates? The price of apartment buildings?

2. Will an increase in real estate demand raise mortgage interest rates in the short run? In the long run?

3. If contractors build too many homes, what will happen to sales prices? Why?

4. As a broker, you have been asked by a consumer group to justify the need for the services of a real estate agent. What are some things you should point out?

CHAPTER SUMMARY

Real estate markets have unique economic characteristics that separate them from other markets. For example, real estate buyers and sellers may not be fully informed about real estate values and market trends. The transfer of real property requires a legal and technical knowledge not possessed by the average person. Each real estate parcel is unique, isolated, and tied to a single, fixed location. Real estate is purchased infrequently and often represents the largest single investment an individual will ever make. Once a real estate use is established, it tends to have a long physical and economic life.

These characteristics create a need for an expert to advise the uninformed. The expert's role is filled by real estate professionals, who provide buyers and sellers with the market information needed to make rational real estate decisions. However, as more information becomes available on the Internet, the real estate agent's role will change from information provider to facilitator.

The analysis of any real estate market requires the understanding of some basic facts about the supply and demand of real estate. The supply of land per se is fixed—it cannot be expanded. The supply of land for various uses is fixed in the short run. Thus, changes in current real estate values usually are the result of shifts in demand, not in supply.

Changes in demand result from changes in population, income, credit, lifestyles, and governmental action. Long-run changes in the supply of real estate structures are influenced by the rate of new construction, conversion, and demolition. However, each segment of the real estate market, whether residential, commercial, industrial, or rural, reacts differently and therefore must be analyzed separately. Some foreign ownership of U.S. real estate has created debates regarding the "selling of America."

IMPORTANT TERMS AND CONCEPTS

Fixed land supply

Fixed short-run land uses

Real estate demand changes

Real estate market characteristics

Real estate professional's role

REVIEWING YOUR UNDERSTANDING

1. Which of the following is a characteristic of an imperfect real estate market?
   a. many and equal numbers of buyers and sellers
   b. highly knowledgeable buyers and sellers
   c. all products are alike
   d. fixed location

2. In a real estate "seller's market":
   a. supply exceeds demand
   b. prices are declining
   c. there are many qualified buyers but few properties for sale
   d. mortgage interest rates are very high

3. One of the key economic features of real estate is:
   a. relatively fixed supply
   b. fixed demand
   c. mobility
   d. low unit cost

4. An increase in demand will have what short-run impact on real estate prices and rents?
   a. prices and rents should decrease
   b. prices should decrease, but rents should increase
   c. prices and rents should increase
   d. prices should increase, but rents should decrease

5. The use of real estate brokers tends to make the real estate market:
   a. less than perfect
   b. more imperfect
   c. more nearly perfect
   d. does not influence the market one way or the other

6. Multiple listing services of a local real estate association tend to make the real estate market:
   a. less than perfect
   b. more imperfect
   c. more nearly perfect
   d. does not influence the market one way or the other

7. If the demand for commercial real estate increases, but "no growth" controls prevent new construction, rents per square foot in the short run should:
   a. increase
   b. decrease
   c. remain the same
   d. shift downward

8. All of the following can influence the demand for real estate *except:*
   a. population
   b. mortgage interest rates
   c. rates of construction
   d. lifestyles

9. "Six months free rent" as a concession is in reality a:
   a. reduction in rent
   b. sign of an increase in the need for construction
   c. sign of an increase in demand
   d. sign of a decrease in supply

10. Foreign ownership of U.S. real estate:
    a. provides needed capital for U.S. citizens
    b. in the short run increases government revenues
    c. helps maintain real estate prices
    d. does all of the above

11. Numerous and knowledgeable buyers and sellers, in which neither party has control, describes which of the following?
    a. perfect market
    b. imperfect market
    c. mixed economy
    d. command economy

12. In real estate, a "buyer's market" usually occurs when:
    a. demand exceeds supply
    b. numerous properties are for sale
    c. interest rates are low
    d. there are plenty of qualified buyers

13. The supply of land is fixed, but in time the intensity of land use can be increased.
    a. true
    b. false

14. Overbuilding tends to increase when:
    a. demand exceeds supply
    b. lenders tighten up on construction credit
    c. government imposes "no growth" controls
    d. supply exceeds demand, but new construction continues

15. All other things being equal, if population increases and mortgage interest rates decline:
    a. commercial rents should decline
    b. more renters should start to buy homes
    c. the economy should be heading for a recession
    d. resale of existing homes should go down

16. Which of the following is considered a real estate supply variable?
    a. consumer tastes
    b. population
    c. income
    d. rate of construction

17. A change or shift in the demand for real estate is caused by:
    a. changes in the availability of mortgage credit
    b. population changes
    c. income changes
    d. all of the above

18. According to the law of demand, as local home prices drop, the:
    a. demand for homes should decrease
    b. quantity of homes demanded should increase
    c. supply of homes will increase in the short run
    d. vacancy rate for homes should increase

19. Foreign ownership of real estate tends to increase when the:
    a. value of the dollar increases
    b. U.S. economy and the country of the potential foreign investor are in recession
    c. value of foreign currency increases compared to U.S. currency
    d. barriers to free trade are increased

20. Which of the following actions by real estate agents tend to make the real estate market more competitive?
    a. establishing uniform rates for sales commissions
    b. encouraging more owners to list their homes for sale
    c. member-only access to multiple listing information
    d. not explaining information about the various options for home financing

Questions 21–25 are based on Chapter 5 Case & Point, "Demand and Supply Graphics"

21. An increase in demand is illustrated by a:
    a. shift of the demand curve to the right
    b. shift of the demand curve to the left
    c. movement along the demand curve
    d. decrease in the quantity demanded

22. A decrease in supply is illustrated by a:
    a. shift of the supply curve to the right
    b. shift of the supply curve to the left
    c. movement along the supply curve
    d. increase in the quantity supplied

23. In Figure 5.10, as demand increases, while supply remains the same:
    a. prices increase
    b. supply decreases
    c. equilibrium remains the same
    d. quantity decreases

24. Once in equilibrium, an increase in demand and supply at the same time by the same amount will:
    a. decrease price
    b. increase price
    c. increase quantity
    d. shift the demand and supply curves to the left

25. According to Figure 5.16, a short-run decrease in demand for real estate will:
    a. decrease prices and rents
    b. increase prices and rents
    c. decrease supply
    d. decrease quantity

CASE & POINT

Demand and Supply Graphics
Perfect Markets—Basic Principles

According to economic theory, prices and output in perfect markets are established by the smooth interaction of demand and supply. To visualize this, economists use graphic lines. For theory purposes straight lines are used in this appendix. In the real world demand and supply lines have curves.

Demand   Demand is the total quantity that buyers are willing to buy at a given time at certain prices. Figure 5.1 illustrates the downward slope of the demand curve reflecting the law of demand, which states that the lower the price, the more consumers will buy; the higher the price, the less they will buy.

Looking at Figure 5.2, notice that as you move along the demand curve from point X to point Y, the price declines from Px to Py. The quantity increases from Qx to Qy. At lower prices the quantity that existing buyers are willing to purchase increases. If you move back from point Y

Figure 5.1   Demand Curve.

Figure 5.2 Movement Along the Demand Curve.

to *X*, prices will increase from *Py* to *Px*, and quantity will return from *Qy* to *Qx*.

Therefore, a change in price does not move the demand curve right or left; instead, a change in price results in movement up or down along the existing demand curve.

Supply Supply is the total quantity that sellers are willing to sell at a given time at certain prices. Figure 5.3 illustrates the upward slope of the supply curve reflecting the law of supply, which states that sellers or producers will offer more goods and services for sale as prices increase and fewer as prices decrease.

Looking at Figure 5.4, notice that as you move from point *A* to *B*, prices increase from *Pa* to *Pb*. Quantity increases from *Qa* to *Qb*. As prices increase, the existing suppliers, motivated by profits, will increase their output. If you move back from *Pb* to *Pa*, the decline in price will cause suppliers to cut back in quantity from *Qb* to *Qa*.

Equilibrium Figure 5.5 illustrates the point at which the demand and supply curves intersect and buyers and sellers establish prices in the marketplace. This intersecting point is called the *equilibrium*.

Figure 5.3   Supply Curve.

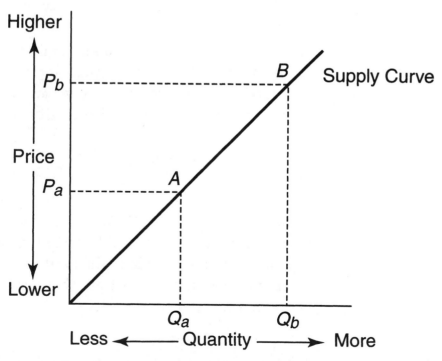

Figure 5.4   Movement Along the Supply Curve.

Figure 5.5   Demand and Supply in Equilibrium.

At any higher price, some buyers will refuse to purchase, thereby creating a surplus. Sellers will then mark down the price to the equilibrium point in order to sell the surplus. At any price lower than the equilibrium point, sellers will not supply enough goods and services because profit potential is too low. Only at the equilibrium price will demand and supply be balanced and the market cleared.

Increase or Decrease in Demand and Supply   Markets are dynamic, and equilibrium is constantly changing as buyers and sellers shift back and forth. The impact these changes have on market prices will depend on the direction and intensity of the change in demand or supply.

Changes in demand are caused by changes in population, income, personal tastes, credit, substitute products, and advertising. Changes in supply are caused by changes in the cost of production, new technology, and shifts in optimism or pessimism regarding the economic future. Figures 5.6 and 5.7 illustrate that any increase in demand or supply is shown by a shift to the right.

Figures 5.8 and 5.9 illustrate that any decrease in demand or supply results in a shift to the left.

Figure 5.6   Increase in Demand.

Figure 5.7   Increase in Supply.

Figure 5.8   Decrease in Demand.

Figure 5.9   Decrease in Supply.

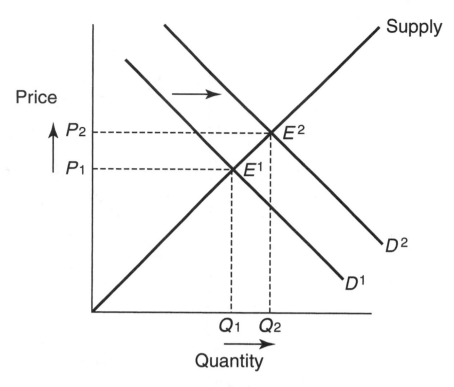

Figure 5.10   Increase in Demand, Supply Curve Remaining the Same.

Figures 5.10 and 5.11 illustrate the impact of an increase or decrease in demand with the supply curve remaining the same. If demand increases while the supply curve remains fixed, prices increase from *P1* to *P2*, quantity produced increases from *Q1* to *Q2*, and a new equilibrium is established at *E2* (Figure 5.10). If demand decreases while the supply curve remains fixed, prices decrease from *P1* to *P2*, quantity produced decreases from *Q1* to *Q2*, and a new equilibrium is established at *E2* (Figure 5.11).

Figures 5.12 and 5.13 illustrate the impact if supply increases or decreases while the demand curve remains the same. If supply increases while the demand curve remains fixed, prices drop from *P1* to *P2*, quantity produced increases from *Q1* to *Q2* because of the increased number of suppliers, and a new equilibrium is established at *E2* (Figure 5.12). If supply decreases while the demand curve remains fixed, prices rise from *P1* to *P2*, quantity produced decreases from *Q1* to *Q2* because of the decreased number of suppliers, and a new equilibrium is established at *E2* (Figure 5.13).

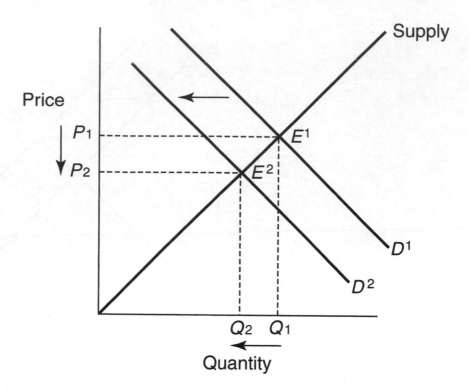

Figure 5.11   Decrease in Demand, Supply Curve Remaining the Same.

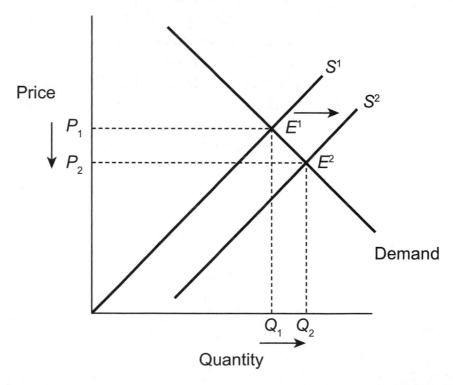

Figure 5.12   Increase in Supply, Demand Curve Remaining the Same.

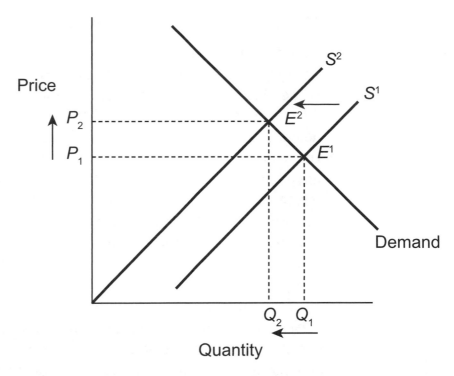

Figure 5.13 Decrease in Supply, Demand Curve Remaining the Same.

Test Yourself: Based on demand and supply, what will happen to price and quantity when:

1. Demand increases and supply decreases at the same time?

2. Demand decreases and supply increases at the same time?

3. Demand increases and supply increases at the same time and at the same amount?

4. Demand decreases and supply decreases at the same time and at the same amount?

Answers

1. You should get a large increase in price and a decline in quantity.

2. You should get a large decrease in price.

3. You should get no change in price, but an increase in quantity.

4. You should get no change in price, but a decrease in quantity.

Demand and Supply for Real Estate

Short-Run Impact

As mentioned earlier, a fundamental principle of real estate economics is the recognition that the total amount of land is fixed. The land surface cannot be increased or decreased according to the whims of demand. However, the *intensity of land use* can change, and in time this will increase or decrease the supply of real estate units. However, any change in the intensity of land use takes time. If the demand for residential or other real estate projects was suddenly to increase, developers would need considerable time to acquire land and obtain permits and financing. Figure 5.14 illustrates a down-sloping real estate demand curve with a short-run fixed supply curve, intersecting at equilibrium.

If the supply of real estate is fixed in the short run, any change in current market prices and rents will be determined by local changes in demand. When the demand goes up, prices and rents rise as buyers and renters attempt to outbid one another for a fixed supply. When the demand goes down, prices and rents decline because a decrease in demand creates some vacancies, and owners and landlords attempt to fill these vacancies by lowering prices and rents. Figure 5.15 illustrates how an increase in demand increases prices or rents, but this

Figure 5.14 Real Estate Demand Curve with a Short-Run Fixed Supply.

Figure 5.15   Increase in the Demand for Real Estate with a Short-Run Fixed Supply.

short-run increase cannot immediately increase the supply of real estate. Therefore, the price and/or rent levels of the existing real estate supply increase from *P1* to *P2*.

Figure 5.16 illustrates how a decrease in demand decreases prices or rents, but this short-run decrease cannot immediately decrease the supply of real estate. Therefore, the price and/or rent levels of the existing supply decrease from *P1* to *P2*.

Long-Run Impact

In the long run, once financing and building permits are obtained and construction is completed, the supply of real estate units offered for sale or rent can be increased. When this occurs, the supply curve for real estate will increase by shifting to the right. This will then create a new equilibrium for prices/rents and quantity. If the new increase in supply matches existing demand, prices and rents should remain stable. If the new construction exceeds demand, overbuilding will have occurred and prices and rents should decline as owners attempt to reduce the excess supply.

Figure 5.16 Decrease in the Demand for Real Estate with a Short-Run Fixed Supply.

PART TWO
UNDERSTANDING
REAL ESTATE MARKETS

CHAPTER 6
REGIONAL AND COMMUNITY ANALYSIS

PREVIEW

In a pure sense there is a technical difference between a *community*, a *city*, and a *town*. In an effort to simplify, however, the three terms will be used interchangeably to refer to a centralized location where people live and work. A *region* will refer to a group of communities in a surrounding area. This chapter examines the factors that contribute to the location and economic health of a community. Section 6.1 discusses the origins of communities and describes how these origins affect the development of the community. Section 6.2 explores the reasons that cause a city to either grow or decline. Section 6.3 outlines techniques used to forecast a region's economic growth. The Case & Point at the end of the chapter looks at Americans on the move. When you have completed this chapter, you will be able to:

1. Discuss how communities are formed.

2. List the economic factors that cause communities to change.

3. Describe the major tools used to forecast a region's economic growth.

4. Locate data sources that help you forecast your community's economic growth.

6.1 The Origins of Communities

E conomic activity has a major effect on both the location of a community and the value and use of real estate within the community.Once the roots of a community are understood and current local economic trends interpreted, a forecast can be made of what might happen to the value of real estate within the community.

The History of Communities

Early human beings lived as nomads. They migrated with the seasons and the availability of natural foods or wild game. In time, they selected caves or other shelters in areas they visited repeatedly. They began to build simple structures at various locations in their journey. This style of life was typical of the Native American Indian tribes before the Europeans arrived.

At some point, early people began to build small clusters of dwellings in fixed locations; these were the earliest towns. Knowledge of these early people is very limited. It is believed that the first towns arose around 7000 B.C. in the valleys of the Tigris and Euphrates rivers, known as Mesopotamia, now part of Iraq. From the long history of communities, two important themes emerge: the reason why the original town location was selected and the reasons for the economic survival of the town after its beginning.

What Determines Community Location?

Every community faces the initial decision of where to locate. The factors that influence the choice of a site depend on why the community is being formed. Among early nomads, important factors often included water, sources of food, and protection from enemies. Later, the factors sometimes involved social reasons, such as sites chosen for their religious significance or for governmental purposes like regional development. But the majority of community sites appears to have been chosen because of their commercial significance. Commercial influences result in the formation of the following three types of cities:

1. The central city

2. The transportation service city

3. The special-function city

Central Cities

A community that is a central city performs a variety of services for a surrounding area. The services provided usually include commercial, social, religious, and governmental. Such communities tend to be evenly spaced throughout the productive countryside, each surrounded by the hinterland, or "tributary area," that it serves. Thus, when forest land is converted to agriculture, the growing population provides an opportunity for the start of a series of such central market cities. The California Central Valley and the American Midwest are examples of areas with many central market cities.

Transportation Service Cities

In the second category are cities performing services along transportation routes. These cities form at locations called nodes. Among the many types of nodes are those at a "break-cargo" point, which is a place where a shift in the transportation system or route, or an obstacle, requires the unloading and reloading of the transport vehicles. At this point, the goods being carried can be repackaged ("break-bulk"), processed, wholesaled, or otherwise manipulated more easily than elsewhere. Possible break-cargo points include ports, major rail intersections, freeway intersections, river forks, and mountain passes. Points at which transportation systems require service function in a similar manner, as shown by the many old railroad watering stops in the western United States, such as Ogden, Utah, and San Bernardino, California.

Special-Function Cities

The third type of commercial city concentrates on one special function or service, such as mining, government, or retirement. Examples of special-function cities include resorts (e.g., Palm Springs, California), lumbering centers (e.g., Eureka, California), government centers (e.g., Washington, D.C.), and university (e.g., Davis, California).

Reasons for American City Locations

A study of American cities indicates a range of reasons for community origin. Some towns, such as Fort Bridger, Wyoming, were originally protection sites. Rossmoor (a senior-citizen development in Walnut Creek, California) is a more recent protection community. Salt Lake City was a religious community created at a site chosen to provide protection by distance and isolation. Break-cargo points include such ocean ports as San Francisco Bay, Baltimore, Seattle, San Pedro, and San Diego. River forks were factors at Pittsburgh, Pennsylvania,

Figure 6.1 First plat of Los Angeles. (*Source:* Richard M. Hurd, *Principles of City Land Values*. New York, The Record and Guide, 1903, p. 39.)

and Sacramento and Stockton, California. Denver, Colorado, and Truckee, California, owe their origins to mountain passes. The first plat of Los Angeles (Figure 6.1) suggests that the river and the ford over it were important to the early town's location.

How the City's Origin Fits In

There are several keys to explaining a city's origin. *Topography* (the shape of the earth's surface) often influences where cities are initially located. For example, protection-type communities tend to be located at sites that offer some security, such as islands or mountaintops.

Moreover, all communities must have some contact with the world around them. The transportation systems then in use, combined with local topography and the area's purpose, determined where the initial city was sited. It may have been at the ship landing, the railroad station, or the stage depot. This location is the point of contact with the outside world and becomes the focal point for the new city's growth.

The origin of a city, and the factors that influence its location, shape the placement of buildings and streets in early years. In turn, these original buildings and streets have a major impact on the shape and layout of the town many years later, as it matures into a city. Therefore, to understand the factors that form a community's size, shape, and layout, a person must know the reason for its origin. Once the reasons for its origin are known, a person can better understand its growth pattern. When a city's growth pattern is understood, a real estate investor is better able to predict future paths of growth. These growth patterns, plus a reading of the area's mandated general plan, provide the information needed to analyze the community growth aspects of real estate investment opportunities.

REVIEWING YOUR UNDERSTANDING

Origins of Communities

1. What determines a city's location?

2. What are the three types of commercial cities? Give some local examples of each.

3. How does transportation affect the location of communities?

6.2 Why The Community Grows

The continued survival of communities requires that the residents' needs for food, clothing, shelter, and other necessities are met. Few communities are completely self-sufficient. Therefore, each community must be able to pay for the imported goods that it needs. It must export goods, earn money, and use the money to buy needed imports.

The Community as an Economy

Economic success is so essential to the continued existence of a community that economists are frequently hired to study and forecast the community's economic health. They pay particular attention to how a community develops export goods and services to pay for its imported goods and services. This is very similar to the principles of international trade that exist between countries. All businesses and employees are separated into two broad categories. Companies that produce goods and services locally to be shipped outside the community or region are called *basic industries* or *basic employment*, and companies that produce goods and services locally for use by people within the community or region are called *local* or *secondary industries or employment*. Economists then analyze the trends within these two categories to forecast the economic strength and growth potential for the community and its surrounding region.

The Need for New Export Jobs

Economic success of a community can take several forms. The simplest would be continued survival of a fixed population at a fixed standard of living. More complex forms would involve either growth in population ("volume" changes), growth in the economic welfare of individuals ("per capita" changes), or both.

Community survival without population or income change is not common in American society because the rate of births and immigration has been historically higher than the rate of deaths. These increasing numbers of people must be housed and fed. Communities have expanded their economic capacities in order to provide these necessities.

Outside forces, moreover, tend to upset the stable economic existence of a community. For example, the advent of the automobile created new jobs in some areas but eliminated jobs (such as making buggy whips) in others. As a result of changes in technology, tastes, resources, or other factors, all goods and services have somewhat limited lifetimes. New goods and services must be developed to replace those that become obsolete and unwanted. Thus, even a currently stable city finds itself in a race to encourage new jobs. Projected increases in population require further job (and export) increases if the new workers are to be employed.

Where Do Export Goods and Services Come From?

In the early days of a town's existence, its export opportunities are restricted by the community's limited size and capabilities. Often, the only possible export is some simple local resource, such as cattle, grain, ores, timber, or fish. For other communities, the only available export may be labor skills, exported for the day or the week or the year. When the workers bring their earnings back, the money supports the community. This is evident today as Mexican nationals work in the United States and return and/or send money to their families in Mexico. On a small scale, the same process happens when people live in a suburban area with few jobs and commute to the city to work. The "export product" for the suburb is workers.

As the community grows, additional resources can be developed into export items. Often, some existing export resource requires processing that can be done locally, leading to the export of processed goods instead of raw materials. In time, the processing develops local skills, which become a new marketable resource.

If the shift in exports from resources to processed goods is successful, cities that were originally formed for resource exploitation can still survive when the resource is exhausted, by having the raw materials shipped to local processing plants to use their skilled work force.

A complex example is Detroit, which was originally a wheat-shipping port. Its workers learned how to repair broken steam engines of wheat ships, then how to make needed spare parts, and finally how to make entire engines. They became so expert at manufacturing steam engines and similar machinery that early automobile designers were drawn there for technical help with engine designs.

This analysis of community economic growth focuses on the products or services that are developed. Readers will find *The Economy of Cities*, by Jane Jacobs, a fascinating presentation of this type of analysis.[1] Jacobs suggests that two main community growth methods are important. The first method generates new export products. The second method develops local production of goods that were previously imported. When this happens, the product is no longer imported or the import quantities are reduced. In turn, this change frees export earnings that can be used to buy some other needed imports. In the Detroit example, workers learned to make spare parts that had previously been imported. This was a key step in the evolution of Detroit from a port to a manufacturing center.

Production Efficiency

The efficiency of production is a third path to economic growth. A fixed work force could export more goods if local businesses could increase productivity. This would mean increasing output without added labor, by using more sophisticated equipment. However, this path to economic growth may be resisted by workers because the increase in productivity acts to reduce the number of workers needed for a particular production level. This means firings, retraining, and change, which some firms and workers resist. From society's

[1] Jane Jacobs, *The Economy of Cities*. New York: Random House, 1969.

view, however, increased productivity is good because the freed worker can be used to produce other goods and services. Thus, the total amount of goods and services available to the community can grow without any increase in the numbers of workers or hours worked. Alternatively, the hours worked can be reduced without a reduction in the standard of living. Either way, welfare per capita is improved.

Modern Growth

Studies show that two major factors currently influence regional economic change. The first factor is the growth rate of an area's export business base. As mentioned earlier, growth in businesses that create export goods and services is the key. In recent times, the emphasis has been on "glamour" businesses. These are companies with rapid growth potential and low pollution emissions. For example, every community that wishes to grow has attempted to attract high-tech, digital, and biomedical companies.

The second major factor impacting regional economic change is the shift of businesses from one area to another. This shift can occur whether the company's national or worldwide business is growing or declining. The fact that a company moves to a new area will generate new jobs and income for the area—even if the company is in a stagnant industry. Of course, the area the company leaves then suffers the loss of jobs and income. The shift in businesses from the Midwest to the South, Southwest, and West is a modern-day example.

Changes in technology, population base, and availability of resources have been the main reasons for this shift. Then within these new growth areas competition is created as to which specific area wins the prize. A notable example here is the shift of businesses from the high-cost, high-tax, and occasionally not so business friendly California to low-cost, low-tax, business friendly Nevada. Table 6.1 lists several factors that businesses look for when seeking a new location.

A Summary of Regional and Community Growth Theory

In general, especially for smaller regions, community growth requires increases in basic employment, usually by the creation of new export goods and services. These new exports and their production are created either by the expansion of existing firms or by the addition of

Table 6.1 Business Location Factors

Raw Materials	cost _____ availability _____
Selling Markets	near _____ far _____
Transportation	cost _____ availability ___
Labor	cost _____ quality _____ quantity _____
Water	cost _____ quality _____ quantity _____
Energy	cost _____ quantity _____
Community Attitude	positive _____ negative _____
Taxes	high _____ low _____
Site Cost	high _____ moderate _____ low _____
Environmental Controls	restrictive _____ moderate _____
Employee Housing Cost	low _____ moderate _____ high _____

new businesses. The factors that influence business locations, discussed at length in Chapter 10, are summarized here.

When considering locations, businesses generally seek the least expensive access to needed inputs and outputs. This means to the inputs of land, labor, capital, and entrepreneurship, and to its output markets.

For each community, the availability of land, skilled labor, raw materials, business skills, and final markets is fairly fixed at any one time. Many communities will not have the resources or skills that particular industries need, but over a period of years, changes in technology, natural resources, population, and community attitude can alter the desirability of any community for business locations.

Setting Community Goals

Each community or region should review its economic future: *to decline, to hold stable*, or *to grow*. The decision is sometimes made politically, as when the area votes for or against community growth. At other times, the decision is an economic one as the demand for local products and skills either increases or decreases.

Growth in Population

One choice concerns the level of overall population growth. An increase in export production is the most common path toward population growth. However, issues of pollution and changes in lifestyles are often raised.

Clearly, every community must encourage new ideas, new products, and/or new fields of work to replace those that decline. In the process, it is hard to stop with *just enough* replacement jobs. Indeed, the small town with a rapidly growing new-employment category may find population growth all but impossible to stop. On the other hand, an area that has historically exported natural resources may find it difficult in maintain a healthy economy once the resource becomes depleted.

Growth in Welfare

The second type of economic change for a community is to improve its income per person—its per capita welfare. There are wide variations across communities and states in per capita income. Some of these are explained by differences in population composition, such as comparing the ages of people in the area, since per capita income could be lower in a city with many young children than in a city with mostly older couples. A population composed of workers with limited skills or limited education, for example, has a lower per capita income than one with advanced skills.

However, the type of employment in the area is the main determinant of differences between the *existing* per capita income of cities. The higher per capita incomes are found with high-salaried occupations. These are usually in businesses with a large amount of machinery, technology, and other capital investment in relation to the numbers of workers. On the other hand, businesses that are labor intensive usually seek out existing low-wage locations. This means that *past* differences in community income levels tend to get reinforced in the future. Low-income communities tend to be chosen as locations for companies that need low wages, whereas higher-income communities often have skills or facilities that attract high-wage companies.

However, the factors that influence all new community jobs are important. Many factors, such as technology or transportation changes, can produce major new higher-income opportunities in low-income areas. With recent cutbacks in high-tech digital and software companies, former high-cost-of-living communities have been losing jobs to lower-cost communities as these companies relocate. Examples include shifts of technical companies from California to Arizona, New Mexico, and Nevada. For the individual community, the important factor in both population growth and per capita growth is an awareness of its weaknesses and strength as a business location and a willingness to respond to opportunities.

Trying to Diversify

Finally, the community may have other economic goals besides those involving population growth or per capita growth. One example is of a single firm or industry being so successful that it dominates the entire area. If it ages and declines, it will drag the city down with it.

As cities develop skills drawn from their early resources, their businesses tend to specialize in these resources and skills. This is desirable because these skills become major exports. However, if these skills become obsolete because of new materials or processes, entire cities can be put out of work. Thus, most communities today prefer not to be one-industry towns. They prefer a *diversification* of companies, industries, and job types.

REVIEWING YOUR UNDERSTANDING

How the Community Grows

1. Why must each economic community usually have some export trade? Why must there be new products or services to export?

2. How does a community generate new exports?

3. Explain the difference between growing companies and shifting companies. How do they choose locations?

4. What are the two factors influencing changes in per capita income?

6.3 How to Study A Community

The economic study of a community or a region can be approached informally or formally. Most businesspeople and investors are continually watching community progress for signs of strength or weakness. Informally, they are watching the forces of supply and demand when they observe population, employment, and income changes. Although keen observation and instinct are invaluable investment tools, concrete economic studies can provide a factual basis for improved judgment decisions. This section reviews the traditional ways to analyze community growth, stressing the two major techniques now used for regional study: economic base analysis and input-output study. The section ends with a discussion of sources of information on regions and communities.

Traditional Community Analysis

A number of supply and demand factors have been traditionally used to study and analyze communities. Analysis of supply factors has emphasized the inventory of existing structures and their size, price, age, and condition. The cost of new construction, availability of suitable land, zoning, financing, and utilities have also been considered important.

The most important demand factor is population, both in total numbers and by age, education, or other categories (population demography). Population change is the focus of growth. Because people must have jobs, employment characteristics of the town are also studied, including wage rates, types of jobs, and unemployment rates.

Basic Employment

The most important long-term influence on a community's population and employment is its basic or export employment. Because basic employment differs from one town to another, towns can be classified according to the dominant type of basic employment. Some towns concentrate on industry, some on commerce, some on resorts, some on government, and some on resources. There are several classification systems; one, distinguishing towns as *central places, transportation service centers*, or *special-function towns*, was introduced in Section 6.1.

These classifications indicate the major activity in the town's economic base. This information can be combined with data on community origin to see how basic employment has changed since the community was founded. In turn, it is important to discover what factors have caused the changes in basic employment.

All this information is necessary in order to forecast the future of a region and its communities. Understanding past changes in the economic base will help predict future changes. Even knowing the current economic base may tell something about the area's future. This is particularly true of extractive resource regions, whose future depends

Special Interest Topic

The Multiplier Effect

As noted earlier, increasing the number of basic or export jobs is important to growth of any community. And for every new *basic* job, some additional *local* or secondary employment is created, in schools, shops, and the like. The ratio of new local jobs for every new basic job is called the *multiplier*. Economists who study basic employment have found that all areas do not have the same proportion of workers in basic or export jobs. This proportion varies with the size of the community, as shown in the listing below.

Community Size	Number of Local Jobs Added for Each New Basic Job
Very large cities	2.0
100,000 people	1.0
50,000 people	0.5

This ratio of local to basic jobs is significant. An addition of 100 new jobs in basic employment will actually have a greater effect on total employment. This is called the *multiplier effect*. It is easy to see why chambers of commerce want to obtain large, new manufacturing plants in their communities, because of the multiplied effect on total employment and the resulting increase in such areas as population and retail sales.

on the size of reserves of the timber, oil, fish, or other harvested resource.

Regional Economic Studies

The two main techniques used to conduct a regional economic study are: (1) economic base study and (2) input-output study.

The *economic base study* approach forecasts population growth by forecasting basic employment. The starting data are the numbers of current jobs in the area, broken down by export and non-export companies. The first step is to forecast how employment in each basic industry in the region will change, either by assigning some fraction of the nationwide growth in that industry or by projecting past local trends of employment. The forecasts of employment by industry are then totaled to make a forecast of basic employment for the region.

The next step is to convert the forecast of basic employment to a forecast of total employment, using the ratio or multiplier of export to local employment. Next, the forecast of total employment is converted to a population forecast for the total community by using the ratio of workers to people (*the labor participation rate*). In turn, population forecasts can be converted to land-use forecasts or other specialized studies.

These economic base studies require enormous amounts of data and analysis and are therefore quite expensive. They are not practical for small communities and would not be reliable in such cases, simply because a single new factory could move into a small town for reasons impossible to predict. For the large community or region, however, the studies have value.

Another, but less common, approach is the input-output method. In this type of study, researchers examine the resources that go into the economic activity of the community (inputs). They then calculate the goods and services (outputs) of the producing sectors of the community on the basis of where they are distributed or shipped. Outputs that are used locally as inputs for other producers must be identified separately.

Input-output analysis requires extensive amounts of data, which can be difficult to obtain. When the data are available (usually for very large regions), this method provides a full understanding of what happens in the economy of the region. For instance, the dollar amounts of all imports and exports can be determined. The production of various industries is totaled, as well as the breakdown of customers by product. In this way, one can see the flow of money through the community. This is one of the major features of input-output analysis.

Gatekeeping Syndrome

In rapidly growing areas there often is a tendency for old-timers to resent newcomers. The many changes, and the environmental impacts of growth, generate opposition. Once the newcomers get in, they try to keep out "new" newcomers on similar grounds. In another kind of gatekeeping, a large portion of Western land is owned by the federal government and environmental groups are attempting to minimize any development of a vast portion of this land to preserve the natural environment. These and numerous other factors are creating controversy over growth. There are hundreds of polarized groups fighting one another to press their own viewpoint.

Sources of Data

The major source of information about current and past regional and community conditions is the United States Census Bureau publications, including the most recent censuses of population, housing, and manufacturing. Many specialized analyses are generated from Census Bureau information by universities and public and private data centers. State and federal labor and employment offices are good sources of additional data, as are state and local chambers of commerce. Research publications from banks, universities, and regional Federal Reserve banks are also very helpful.

In general, only the larger areas have been studied and reported on. However, the scope of this coverage is improving. Some county and city planning departments and regional planning groups now have or are developing elaborate and detailed data centers.

Forecasts have most often been available from state and federal agencies, although some were produced as regional studies. Regional forecasts of specific types (especially transportation and population) are now available for many regions, and they are being updated and expanded. Various specialized forecasts (transportation, land use, pollution, water demand, and sewage) are being combined. The errors of some earlier forecasts are also being reviewed as planners seek to improve forecasting accuracy.

REVIEWING YOUR UNDERSTANDING

How to Study a Community

1. Why is the economic base important in studying a region?

2. What is an input-output study?

3. What is the multiplier effect?

CHAPTER SUMMARY

This chapter stressed that the purpose of regional and community analysis is to understand the economic activity in the area and its direct effects on real estate supply and demand.

The origin of communities results from the combination of site characteristics and commercial or social factors. Commercial factors play a more important role in cities founded recently, both in America and throughout the world. The origin of a city has tremendous influence on the layout of major buildings and street patterns in subsequent years.

Community growth depends on economic factors because communities are not self-sufficient; they need many imported goods. Volume growth of a city, practically speaking, is usually limited by the growth of jobs that produce goods or services for export. These export earnings, in turn, pay for the necessary imports. Exports at the time of a city's origin were usually related to the community's material resources, but in time the skills learned from handling these resources became more important.

Community studies examine such factors as basic employment, population, income, and other specific land-use factors. The two major types of such studies are economic base studies and input-output studies. There is a variety of source material available for persons wishing to engage in community analysis.

IMPORTANT TERMS AND CONCEPTS

Basic (export) employment	*Input-output analysis*
Break-cargo (break-bulk) point	*Secondary (local) employment*
Central city	*Special-function city*
Demography	*Transportation service city*
Economic base study	

REVIEWING YOUR UNDERSTANDING

1. A city formed at a "break-cargo" point is called a:
   a. central city
   b. transportation service city
   c. special-function city
   d. economic city

2. Growth of a region is most closely tied to what kind of jobs?
   a. local
   b. secondary
   c. basic
   d. internal

3. In terms of economic base analysis, a computer software company would be considered what kind of business?
   a. export
   b. import
   c. secondary
   d. local

4. In terms of economic base analysis, a residential real estate brokerage business is what kind of business?
   a. export
   b. basic
   c. manufacturing
   d. secondary

5. If a region's population expands rapidly, while jobs and government welfare decline, the per capita standard of living as measured by goods and services will probably:
   a. decrease
   b. increase
   c. remain the same
   d. escalate

6. If the multiplier effect for a local economy is that 1 export job creates 1.5 secondary jobs, an increase of 100 basic export jobs should create a total of how many new jobs in the area?
   a. 67
   b. 100
   c. 150
   d. 250

7. When selecting a new location for a factory, a company will usually check which of the following items?
   a. environmental requirements
   b. community attitudes
   c. transportation systems
   d. all of the above

8. The underlying principle of economic base analysis states that for a region to grow economically, it must:
   a. export more than it imports
   b. import more than it exports
   c. increase secondary business faster than basic business
   d. decrease basic industries

9. For some people, the disadvantages of economic growth include:
   a. more people
   b. traffic congestion
   c. additional pollution
   d. all of the above

10. The advantages of economic growth include more:
    a. goods and services
    b. jobs
    c. financial security
    d. all of the above

11. To stimulate economic growth, an increase in local jobs must occur before there can be an increase in export jobs.
    a. true
    b. false

12. A group of cities or communities in a surrounding area is usually called a:
    a. town
    b. region
    c. locality
    d. township

13. It is believed that the world's first towns and villages were located in:
    a. Europe
    b. Latin America
    c. the Middle East
    d. New Zealand

14. A "central city":
    a. is located midway between two large cities
    b. performs a variety of services for a surrounding area
    c. contains the central government offices for the region
    d. is usually located at a river fork, mountain pass, or ocean port

15. A city location selected to be convenient to a resource is described as a:
    a. special-function city
    b. resort city
    c. node
    d. break-cargo location

16. Original locations of cities tend to be influenced by:
    a. topography
    b. transportation
    c. both *a* and *b*
    d. neither *a* nor *b*

17. Two measures of community economic growth are:
    a. expansion and integration
    b. per capita and overall growth
    c. annexation and divestment
    d. local jobs and the multiplier

18. Greater productivity influences growth by:
    a. allowing the same number of workers to produce more export goods
    b. reducing the number of jobs
    c. creating more instability through changes
    d. interrupting government efforts to limit growth

19. When a community learns to make objects that previously had to be imported:
    a. the loss of imports hurts the local economy
    b. additional earnings are generated to pay for goods and services
    c. added jobs are tied up in local employment, hurting growth
    d. there is no net effect on the local economy

20. In an economic base study, a population forecast for a region is estimated by using a ratio of workers (or jobs) to people. This is called:
    a. job multiplier
    b. labor force participation rate
    c. demography
    d. topography

21. A city can grow in population, even if its export jobs are in industries that are not growing nationwide.
    a. true
    b. false

22. Moderately increasing productivity is considered socially desirable by many people, if the increase in productivity:
    a. lowers per capita living standards
    b. improves per-person welfare
    c. fulfills government objectives for slow growth
    d. eliminates private jobs

23. If a city's export jobs are mostly in one industry:
    a. such concentration is considered desirable
    b. diversification should be a key community goal
    c. real estate investment potential is enhanced
    d. the town's future is guaranteed

24. A shift of jobs in an industry from one city to another can cause some cities to grow even when the industry's overall growth is in decline.
    a. true
    b. false

25. Input-output analysis studies:
    a. whether production efficiency can be improved
    b. which jobs should be reclassified from basic to export
    c. what resources go into community economic activity, what goods and services are produced, and where they are distributed
    d. how long it takes on average to convert inputs to outputs

CASE & POINT

"Where Are We Moving To?"

The Sunbelt Boom

The Sunbelt states of the South and West have experienced major growth since the 1940s, because of their perceived pleasant climates and lifestyles, the desire of city dwellers to escape urban problems, excellent retirement communities, tourist attractions, and the shift in new employment opportunities. In the case of the South, the lack of unions, lower wages, and inexpensive real estate were initial factors. Today, the cost differentials are not as great as they once were, but still are an important factor. The Southwest states of Arizona, New Mexico, and Nevada are among the fastest-growing states in the union.

The losers in this shift were the Midwest Rust Belt (from Chicago east to Pittsburgh) and farm states such as the Dakotas, Iowa, etc. and some Northeastern states. In some cases these "loser" states have drawn together to provide a more united political front, in an attempt to stem the flow of business and government projects to the Sunbelt states. At other times these "loser" states fight over the shrinking job base.

The Rocky Mountain High

Mountain states such as Colorado, Utah, and Idaho initially gained growth in the 1970–1980 period, then suffered in the 1980s when the decline in resource extraction businesses (oil and shale) declined. During this period, overbuilding glutted the residential and commercial real estate markets, resulting in foreclosures and a massive drop in real estate prices. By the mid-1990s to the present mid-2000s, these problems are behind them and the mountain states are once again attracting businesses and experiencing large percentage gains in population.

Pacific Northwest's Green Acres Beckon

Northern California, Oregon, and Washington, bountiful in forests and rain, have been attracting people and some businesses. The Seattle-Tacoma metro area of Washington has experienced especially rapid growth. Microsoft and Boeing have been the major employers. Several rating agencies have selected this area as one of the more "ideal" in the United States. However, by the mid-2000s, Boeing moved its headquarters to Chicago and severe competition from European-based Airbus Company, plus a malaise in the airline industry, caused a drop in Boeing employment. The long-run economic impact of this is currently unknown. The issue of no state income taxes in Washington and no state sales taxes in Oregon could attract some retiring baby boomers later in the 2000s, as these retirees attempt to seek a more rural setting and stretch the money in their financial retirement plans.

U.S. Census Bureau Data

According to the U.S. Census Bureau, the fastest-growing metro areas for 1990–2000 by percentage growth were:

1. Las Vegas, NV
2. Naples, FL
3. Yuma, AZ
4. McAllan, TX
5. Austin, TX

From July 2003 to July 2004, the fastest-growing areas with a population of 100,000 or more were:

1. Port St. Lucie, FL
2. Elk Grove, CA
3. North Las Vegas, NV
4. Gilbert, AZ
5. Cape Coral, FL
6. Moreno Valley, CA
7. Chandler, AZ
8. Mirmar, FL
9. Rancho Cucamonga, CA
10. Roseville, CA

CHAPTER 7
COMMUNITY GROWTH PATTERNS

PREVIEW

This chapter describes how a community takes physical shape, how land use determines the community's layout, and where its population settles. Section 7.1 explains the factors that determine land-use patterns. Section 7.2 illustrates basic city growth patterns. Section 7.3 describes what happens to growth patterns as the community population increases. The Case & Point at the end of the chapter presents both U.S. and California Population Statistics. When you have completed this chapter, you will be able to:

1. List the major forces influencing the shape, layout, and density of a community.

2. Describe how each force affects the future shape of the community.

3. List the basic patterns of community growth.

4. Explain how land use in a community is a dynamic, evolving pattern that can be studied to forecast the path of growth for potential real estate investments.

7.1 Land-Use Patterns

The initial reason for establishing a community often determines its shape, the pattern of land use, and even how land is allocated among users. In the many cities laid out by the church in medieval Europe, church leaders made land-use decisions, primarily for religious reasons. Similarly, in cities whose original function was to protect the residents, military and police considerations dictated the location of shops, homes, and manufacturing sites.

However, as stressed in Chapter 6, to continue to develop, communities must become economically successful, whatever the reasons were for their initial location. Therefore, economic motives will eventually influence how land is allocated among competing land users.

How Economics Determines Land Use

In a market economy, there is competition among the various buyers of each product. In the absence of controls, goods and services go to the highest bidder. There is a similar competition among potential users of a site, and land goes to the user who is willing to pay the highest price. Appraisal books call this the "highest and best use."

According to the *principle of highest and best use*, the best use of land is the legal use that will produce the highest capitalized net income return to the land after allowing for the cost of the building. In most cases, this means that the value of a site is determined by how much rent it will bring, and possible tenants are considered according to how much rent each could pay at that site.

Why Patterns?

Even though land use is determined by the rent-paying ability of different legal users, why do communities form patterns of land use? The answer seems to be tied to an interesting set of rules. Thus, similar users cluster together at favorable locations, even with the absence of government zoning. Commercial users cluster with other commercial users, homeowners locate near other homeowners, and so on.

What Are the Rules?

A series of rules appears to control the economic process of developing land-use patterns.

Rule 1: Competition of Uses

When a number of potential users, each with a different idea, seeks the same site, competition raises the asking price of the land, until the highest bidder wins. It is assumed that the highest bidder's price was based on an expectation regarding the property's ability to produce rent and generate a profitable net income.

Rule 2: Economics of Succession

If a site is vacant and open to all legal uses, the type of development will usually be determined by the most profitable use. However, if there is a building on the site, a user who can occupy the existing improvements has an advantage over other users. The improvements will be demolished only when a new use is profitable enough to pay for the site, the old building, the demolition cost, and the cost of the new building.

Rule 3: Comparative Advantage

Each site has unique advantages and disadvantages for particular uses. Some locations may have favorable natural endowments (raw materials, climate, topography, or water, for example). Other locations may have access to many buyers or to by-product materials from other facilities. Still other locations might have good schools, suppliers, favorable government regulations, or other institutional advantages.

The advantages and disadvantages of a particular site will give a comparative advantage to whichever land use gets the greatest net benefit from that unique set of advantages and disadvantages.

Rule 4: The Rule of Imperfection

The ideal pattern of land use rarely exists because the information needed to make a perfect decision is often not available. Unwise property development or unusual social or political situations will also impede the highest and best use. Sometimes the community will interfere with the market (by zoning, for example) to avoid disruptions that market forces would otherwise cause. Thus, land-use patterns are never completely perfect or completely predictable.

Rule 5: Principle of Change

Nothing is static or fixed; therefore, the highest and best use is always changing. Technical, social, and economic changes continually alter the structure of the community and the pattern of ideal land use.

These five economic rules are important determinants of land-use patterns. Every community furnishes repeated examples of each rule. The student should particularly think about *comparative advantage*—why each use is located where it is. Examples: Industrial users cluster together because favorable utilities and transportation routes are nearby. To locate elsewhere could incur additional costs that can cut into profits or drive up prices with the danger of losing sales. Retail stores group to form "one-stop" shopping convenience. Homes are built near one another because water and other needed services are nearby and already in place.

The Noneconomic Factors in Land Use

In addition to economic forces, social and political forces influence land-use decisions. Political influences take the form of decisions carried out by state and local authorities executing the law, whereas social influences operate more subtly through group pressures. Political, social, and economic determinants of land use can operate independently of each other.

Political or legal effects on land-use decisions result from community attitudes on land use expressed through the police power and the power of eminent domain. Police power refers to the right of the community to regulate private behavior in order to protect the public's health, safety, and welfare. Eminent domain is the right of the community to buy for full value any site that the community needs to use. Zoning laws provide one of the most noticeable examples of police power. This topic is so important that most of Chapter 13 is devoted to political land-use controls.

Social controls on land use are less noticeable than political or economic ones. The past forms of social control involved unwritten understandings or common viewpoints that certain land-use decisions would or would not occur. Past examples of such unwritten rules included ethnic neighborhood limits, the importance of downtown stores over neighborhood stores, and the superiority of detached homes over multiple-unit structures. Such social controls could influence both political and economic decisions. They are separated to point out that they are based on social notions, opinions, and/or biases rather than on any kind of objective, established, factual bases. Social controls are becoming less influential as political controls replace them.

REVIEWING YOUR UNDERSTANDING

Why There Are Land-Use Patterns

1. The three major community forces that influence the land-use system are economic, _____, and _____.

2. How does competition influence land use?

3. List the five rules of economic land-use allocation. Explain each.

7.2 Looking at the Structure of Communities

This section examines typical patterns of land use in small communities. Four dominant factors are analyzed: accessibility, topography, transportation, and origins. A clear understanding of these four factors is necessary for the study of more complicated, larger communities discussed in Section 7.3.

Why Study Community Land-Use Patterns?

The study of a community's land-use pattern helps to show how this pattern has influenced the value of individual real estate parcels. As one real estate parcel changes value, it could have a domino effect on the use of surrounding parcels. This in turn will influence the investment potential of the area.

Investors look at the structure of land uses in a community to understand what changed in the past and what caused this change. From this, a person may be able to predict what future influences and changes might occur. As James Vance wrote, "The more we understand the original purpose of a city's physical components, the more meaningful is its present pattern and the more we learn about the processes at work in the city's structure."[1]

Viewing the Small Community

How can a community's structure be examined? The answer depends on the tools available. We can use maps that show types of

---

[1]James E. Vance, Jr., *Geography and Urban Evolution in the San Francisco Bay Area*. Institute of Government Studies, University of California, Berkeley, 1964, p. 3.

land use, values, number of people per square mile, automobile traffic, pollution counts, telephones per square mile, crime rate per block, or any other factor that seems important. In addition to maps, U.S. Census Tract data can be used to show population, the number of households, houses, ages of homes, conditions of structures, fire alarms per city block, and any other available data.

This information could relate to the city either at one moment or over a period of time. Capturing the city at one moment shows how the parts of the city differ at that instant. Tables and maps that show changes over time go one step further and allow researchers to see differences as they emerge.

Simple Circles—Accessibility

One of the earliest concepts of how communities are arranged was developed in Bavaria by Johan von Thünen in 1826. Von Thünen was the first to suggest that the shape of communities followed a predictable pattern. He wrote that if we simplify a city by choosing a flat, level site with farmland all around, the city would take the shape of a circle. In the center would be the land uses to which everyone needs access, such as community meeting places, churches, courtyards, and community food stores. Around these central uses would be a simple ring with the homes of the village people. Von Thünen's concept of accessibility is fundamental to the study of land-use patterns.

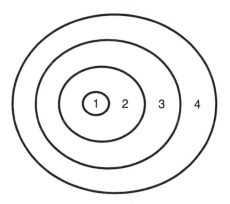

Figure 7.1 A simplified pattern of land use in cities. Von Thünen (1826): 1, central facilities; 2, homes; 3, crops; 4, grazing. Burgess (1920): 1, commercial and offices; 2, older homes, warehouses, and manufacturing; 3, low- and middle-cost housing; 4, higher-priced homes and shops. (*Sources:* Park, Burgess, and McKenzie, eds., *The City*. Chicago: University of Chicago Press, 1925; Von Thünen, *Der Isolierte Staat*, 1826.)

In addition, von Thünen wrote that land uses beyond the city would be distributed in similar circles or rings. Closest to the city would be farms growing perishable produce and those requiring intensive, frequent care by farmers. Farther out would be farms with crops requiring less care or transport. The farthest lands would be used for grazing by animals that could transport themselves and for growing timber.

Others have since applied von Thünen's ideas to American communities. Burgess presented the concept of concentric rings in 1920. In the inner ring would be shopping centers, department stores, and offices for lawyers, bankers, accountants, and government. In the second ring would be older homes undergoing a succession of uses as the first ring expanded. In addition, there would be warehouses, wholesaling activity, and on one side of the city, manufacturing. In the third ring from the center, Burgess suggested we would find low- and medium-cost housing, whereas higher-priced homes and shops would be located in the outer edges of the community. Figure 7.1 illustrates the concepts of von Thünen and Burgess.

The Importance of Topography

Von Thünen simplified everything by assuming that villages were located on flat plains and that they used the transportation systems of 1826: walking, pack animals, and slow carts. These two assumptions were important to his conclusion. His central concern was the importance of transportation cost or effort, and his pattern of uses provided people with the easiest access to those places they had to go to most often or most urgently.

However, when a city site is not level, the round pattern begins to change. For example, if a city had its origins as a protection site and is located on top of a ridge, with steep slopes on two sides, there will be little economic activity on these steep slopes. The city would be strung out along the ridge top in each direction, and its circular shape would become a ribbon. This is one example of the effect of topography on city shape. Topography—the shape and slope of the land— changes the shape of cities in several ways.

Topography may explain the city's location. Similarly, topographical features can attract added development or impede growth. Features that are attractions to growth include pleasant lake shores, level land, and—for their views—gentle hills. Features that are barriers to growth include steep hills, ravines, marshes, swamps, and riverbanks. Von Thünen's concept of a round city assumed a town on a level site. As we introduce topography, the shape changes. Figure 7.2 shows how topography modifies the round city shape.

Figure 7.2 The influence of topography on the circular city.

Transportation

Topography also has an obvious effect on transportation. It is easier, cheaper, and faster to travel on level land than up or down steep hills. The circular city developed in the first part of von Thünen's work was based on transportation by foot, pack animal, or cart. These are all transportation systems that we would describe as slow and dispersed or *random*. Random means that one can go from any place to any other place with equal ease. Later, von Thünen's study explores the effect of other systems of travel.

Twentieth-century communities had transportation systems that von Thünen did not foresee. The influence of each on city shape differs. The automobile driven on a city street is a random transportation system similar to a person on foot, but it is capable of moving far greater distances in the same time period. Automobile cities, therefore, tend to be circular, like von Thünen's, but extremely spread out, with lower population density. Streetcars and subways, on the other hand, cannot move randomly; they must move along rail lines. They are "linear" or "axial" transportation systems. Such rail systems, however, are strongly influenced by topography. Freeways are a combination of the two types of transport: The car itself tends to give a circular shape to the city, but freeways produce a series of linear extensions. Simple examples of these are illustrated in Figure 7.3. When we add modern transportation systems to von Thünen's simplified model of a community, we see that *the transportation system or systems in use will affect the density of the town as well as its shape.*

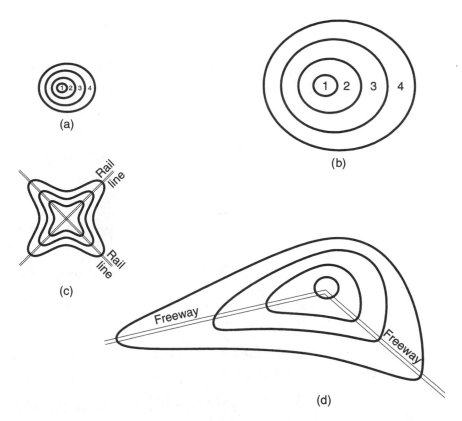

Figure 7.3 Effects of transportation on city shape for cities with 100,000 people. (a) Small size attributable to foot transportation; round shape by random access. (b) Large size attributable to auto transportation; round shape by random access. (c) Small size attributable to streetcar transportation; star shape from linear access. (d) Large size attributable to auto transporttion with two freeways; linear shape from linear access.

The Existing City: Origins

The fourth factor that influences community structure is history: How was the community first built? When the first building was erected, it influenced where the second building would be—probably close to the first, but not too close. When the first store was built, it is likely that it was located in the center of the existing housing cluster. Similarly, when the first government structure was built, it was usually located in the middle of the existing community. The city probably grew around its center—shops next to shops, homes next to homes, and offices next to offices.

This type of development occurred because there is a locational advantage for each type of land use at some particular location. Each new user wants the same locational advantages that existing competitive users have. This means that the community's origin continues to play a major part in the location of new buildings because the new buildings tend to develop near existing buildings. This, then, is the tremendous power of the existing investment in the community to draw additional investment toward it. In time, this original area will have built up a commanding number of economic and cultural attractions for many land uses. Only very high land prices or traffic congestion stops the constant pressure of new uses seeking to obtain these existing locational advantages.

REVIEWING YOUR UNDERSTANDING

Looking at the Structure of Communities

1. List the four dominant factors in community shape. Give an example of each.

2. How does each of these four factors influence the population density of a city?

3. List four examples of how topography influences a city.

7.3 Modern City Growth Patterns

This section combines the four factors of accessibility, transportation, topography, and origin with the additional elements that appear in the larger community. The result is a fairly realistic model of the pattern of land use in American communities.

Proximity Versus Accessibility

If the community grows, population exerts greater and greater pressures on the downtown central zone. These growing pressures involve larger numbers of people seeking to work, shop, and visit in this central area. Congestion increases (whatever the transportation system) until the advantages of the downtown area—its accessibility and central location—begin to disappear. For the person who lives on the edge of the city and needs to buy a few things, the shopping trip downtown becomes uneconomic. At some point, it becomes feasible for some types of land uses to leave the downtown area and move to the outskirts to gain better access to their outlying customers. This movement can be a gradual creep, one store moving a little farther out than the last, or a sudden leapfrog to the city's fringe.

This process illustrates the continual tug of war between the two main influences. The first, *proximity*, comes from the original location of the city, the high investment in existing buildings, the central location of the city center, and its proximity to the entire community. These factors represent the established, the fixed, and the past. The second is *accessibility* (the original reason for the central core) and the influence of transportation and transportation change on accessibility. These factors speak for change and the future.

Each land-use decision throughout the community involves a weighing, often consciously, of these two factors. Should we put the building in the safe location near where the last one was built? Or should we pioneer farther out along the transportation routes that have emerged in recent years? Quick investor response to the San Francisco Bay Area Rapid Transit System (BART) in the late 1960s is an excellent example of a new transportation system bringing shifts in the balance between proximity and accessibility and the system's impact on real estate values. When new transportation systems are initiated in other metro areas, the same investor response and favorable impact on real estate values takes place. Outlying suburban areas tend to benefit most when a new transportation system is created because of improved accessibility to the central core. All of the station locations along the route also benefit because of the increased traffic exposure and accessibility.

The Complex City

As the community gets larger, it requires more than one transportation system. Most communities now combine linear types of transportation with random types: subways and automobiles, for instance. Even in communities on level ground, with streets forming a grid, some streets will be one-way and some will be widened, arterial routes. These changes introduce linear features into an otherwise random street pattern.

Each use that moves away from the downtown along a linear route pulls the circular shape of the community with it. Sometimes a use will leapfrog, or jump still farther out, as most shopping centers have done. These outlying centers in turn become mini-downtown areas with their own forces of proximity (also called "gravity" or "centrality") flowing out in minicircles around them, as shown in Figure 7.4. Because these leapfrogging users of land are primarily seeking better accessibility to customers, they usually locate near an intersection of two or more transportation routes. This may be where two arterials meet, at a major freeway off-ramp, or (best of all) at a freeway-freeway intersection. Such locations can become complete new downtowns because of the drawing power that their growing mixtures of uses create.

Enter the Wedge

Our analysis so far has involved a city that has no better or worse side. Thus, we have assumed that you and I would live anywhere in the residential ring that lies on the outskirts of the city. This is not so in practice, and one example is our preference for locations that are easier to reach. Homer Hoyt's classic 1939 study, *The Structure and Growth of Residential Neighborhoods in American Cities,* concluded that higher-priced homes took the best acreage in the outskirts of the city. These houses tended to cluster into one segment of the outer circle. As the community grew, and as new houses were added in the suburbs, the higher-priced homes were added just beyond the existing high-priced areas. In this fashion, the higher-priced sector became a wedge. Medium-cost and low-cost homes sorted themselves out

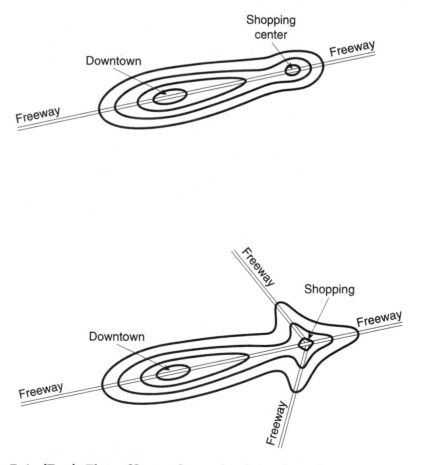

Figure 7.4 (Top) The effect of a suburban shopping center on community shape. (Bottom) The added effect of a second freeway.

similarly. The medium-cost homes typically sought to be near prestige locations, leaving the poorest area for development of lower-priced homes. In fact, one author called these poorer areas "sinks," because they were often areas with poor drainage. Hoyt mapped the shifts in location of better residential areas in a number of American cities; several of his maps are reproduced in Figure 7.5.

Hoyt then pointed out that the retail district in the city followed the higher-priced homes. As these homes concentrated to one side of the city and moved out toward the suburbs in a wedge, the better residential shops moved to that side of the downtown core. The wholesale and manufacturing uses generally oriented themselves out of the way of such high-priced commercial uses. This sorting process often left manufacturing located on the side of the downtown core closest to the area of low-priced homes.[2]

Hoyt further found that the wedge shape of the high-priced home area endured for a long time. Its direction of movement was toward the higher ground, but it also moved away from areas that were impossible to build on or that involved such dead-end developments as extending to the end of a peninsula or toward a riverbank. He found that changes in the direction of high-priced home movement occurred very slowly because of the long life of real estate improvements. He noted that industry and manufacturing tended to be close to such transportation sources as waterfronts, railroads, airports, and highways. Retail business, on the other hand, might be found at highway intersections and at any similar population cluster away from highways.

Political and Social Factors

As indicated earlier, we rarely find an ideal community growth pattern. Part of the reason is that factors like topography have subtle effects because they are based on people's *feelings* about topography. A good example is that hills and high ground can be an attraction to growth, especially of high-priced homes, and can also be a barrier to growth because of the high utility and transportation costs associated with getting there. The question of whether a particular hillside will be an attraction or a barrier to growth is difficult to predict. Moreover, the amount of attraction may change as transportation, utility systems, and people's tastes change.

---

[2]Contrary to Hoyt's theory, in some industrial cities old abandoned factories have been turned into shopping malls and condominiums. The success of these projects has varied.

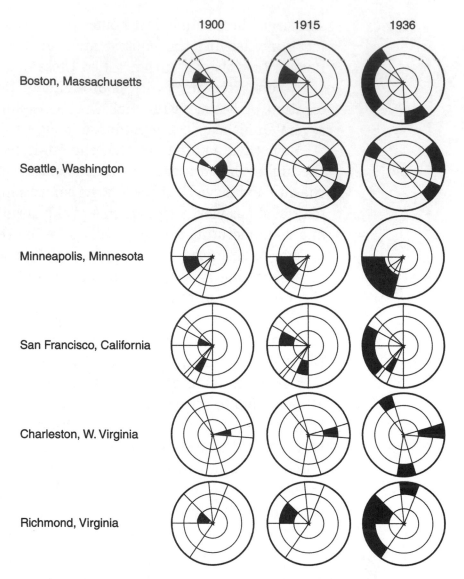

Figure 7.5 Shifts in location of fashionable residential areas in six American cities, 1900–1936. Fashionable residential areas indicated by solid black. (*Source:* Homer Hoyt, *The Structure and Growth of Residential Neighborhoods in American Cities*. Washington, DC, Federal Housing Administration, Government Printing Office, 1939, p. 115. This study is considered a classic by modern urban planners.)

The process is also complicated by factors other than the "big four"—accessibility, transportation, topography, and community origins. Political factors also influence community location and direction of growth. In some instances, political boundaries of cities are absolute barriers to growth, with no construction permitted outside the city limits. Sometimes these limitations are county boundaries, and growth of the city or community in that direction may be blocked. In other instances, city and county boundaries are not the problem. Instead, growth is hampered by boundaries of sewer or water districts.

Political factors are not limited just to the boundary problem. Communities establish general plans to express community feelings about land use, land-use patterns, and growth patterns. These planning decisions create land controls and restrict or direct growth patterns. For example, a community could pass an ordinance that reserves prime flat land for agriculture, so-called "green belts," despite its suitability for residential development. A community can also state what types of structure it desires or the density at which development can occur. Thus, there may be insufficient land to meet market wishes for one type of structure and excessive land for other types.

Community Attitudes

There are other social influences on the community's growth pattern and land-use pattern. One is the community's attitude toward transportation systems, alternatives, and change. The refusal of voters in a dense urban area to approve the financing of a rapid transit system probably means that the transportation system will be more random and less linear or axial than if the financing had passed. This will affect the overall density of the region and the clusters of secondary downtowns, or secondary concentric centers, that occur in a large region.

Even individual decisions can influence community growth patterns. An example is the farmer whose property is on the community's outskirts, in the path of development. Should this farmer hold and farm the land well past the time developers seek to use it, development pressures will be directed toward other available lands to the sides or beyond. The farmer could create a large island or barrier to growth. In other cases, however, the farm owner whose land is somewhat remote from development may become eager to sell, and by skillful merchandising, vigorous promotion, and use of politics, the farmer may encourage development far earlier than would otherwise be the case.

The Results

Thus, there are many factors that influence community growth patterns. Their effects, and the end result, are complicated and interwoven. It is possible, however, to describe how these forces interact, and the best description is the widely quoted statement by the pioneer urban economist Richard Hurd in his *Principles of City Land Values* (1903):

> Cities originate at their most convenient point of contact with the outer world and grow in the lines of least resistance or greatest attraction, or their resultants. The point of contact differs according to the methods of transportation, whether by water, by turnpike or by railroad. . . . The influence of topography, all-powerful when cities start, is constantly modified. . . . The most direct results of topography come from its control of transportation. . . .
>
> Growth in cities consists of movement away from the point of origin in all directions, except as topographically hindered, this movement being due both to aggregation at the edges and pressure from the center. Central growth takes place both from the heart of the city and from each subcentre of attraction, and axial growth pushes into the outlying territory by means of railroads, turnpikes and street railroads. All cities are built up from these two influences, which vary in quantity, intensity and quality, and resulting districts overlapping, interpenetrating, neutralizing and harmonizing as the pressure of the city's growth brings them in contact with each other. . . . Residences are early driven to the circumference, while business remains at the center, and as residences divide into various social grades, retail shops of corresponding grades follow them, and wholesale shops in turn follow the retailers, while institutions and various mixed utilities irregularly fill in the intermediate zone, and the banking and office section remains at the main business center. Complicating this broad outward movement of zones, axes of traffic projectshops through residence areas, create business subcentres, where they intersect, and change circular cities into star-shaped cites. Central growth, due to proximity, and axial growth, due to accessibility, are summed up in the static power of established sections and the dynamic power of their chief lines of intercommunication.[3]

Each sentence in this quotation has great significance. Reread the passage and take each sentence as a full, separate thought. Stop at the end of the sentence and ask yourself what it means in terms of the cities and communities that you have known. It is striking that Mr. Hurd was so successful in capturing the dynamic combination of factors in such clear language so long ago.

---

[3] Richard M. Hurd, *Principles of City Land Values*, New York, 1903, pp. 15–16.

Other Views

Comments by Burgess, Hoyt, and others do not seem to disprove or take a position opposing what Hurd said but rather emphasize one view or another of the complicated whole. For example, Harris and Ullman suggested in 1945 that the dominant concept in city shape was that of *multiple nuclei*. Their thought was that each land use responds in a different way to topography, transportation, and other influences. Similar uses tend to cluster together in nuclei, illustrated in Figure 7.6. The city thus created appears to be star-shaped. The multiple-nuclei concept explains how uses become located in different places in the community.

Others have stressed socioeconomic linkages and have pointed out that locational desires of families are the force in shaping cities. Families choose their residential location for social and economic needs. Businesses and public facilities follow them in order to be of service. This humanistic viewpoint of community shape, however, falls short of analyzing the factors that influence family residential choices. These turn out again to be amenities of location, topography, transportation, and political and social constraints on growth. Again we find a viewpoint that seems to restate Hurd.

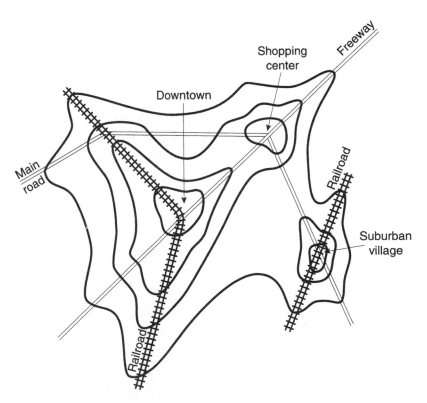

Figure 7.6 Multiple nuclei in city growth patterns.

Figure 7.7 The superblock grid system of city land use. Landuse codes: I, industrial; C, commercial; A, apartments; H, houses. (*Source:* After Barlowe, *Land Resource Economics*, 1972. Prentice Hall, Englewood Cliffs, N.J.)

Richard Nelson suggested in 1958 that there are four urban models. The largest is the metropolitan commercial center, which he calls Commerce City. Next in size is the medium-sized city, which he calls Center Town. Third is the rural trading area (Countyville), and fourth is the dormitory suburb for a larger city (Forest Lake). He suggests that land-use patterns in Countyville are predominantly the circular-zone concepts of von Thünen and Burgess. Sector (wedge) theory seems to become more relevant or visible in the larger Center Town. The largest community, Commerce City, shows the patterns described by the sector theory and also begins to demonstrate the multiple-nuclei concept. His fourth model, Forest Lake, is a satellite community, unlike the other three. It has a layout that will vary as determined by its relationship to its parent city.

In 1972, Barlowe suggested that suburban areas surrounding large cities increasingly show a land-use pattern of large grids. In these grids, the major avenues and cross streets are lined with commercial and industrial uses or sites, whereas the enclosed superblocks and the interior streets are reserved for residential uses. Figure 7.7 illustrates this pattern. Both Nelson and Barlowe sharpened our perception of how communities are structured. Nelson's four cities, in particular, seem to agree with the California experience. Both Nelson and Barlowe are consistent with the model that Hurd presents.

The Effects of Transportation Change

Nevertheless, there are ways in which Hurd's language cannot help us understand today's city. One major change since his time has been the effect of transportation on manufacturing and wholesale activities. Air freight, trucks, and freeways have freed wholesalers from the need to locate close to their retail customers. Indeed, many wholesalers now service an entire state, a region, or sometimes an entire country from one warehouse. These shifts in wholesale location do not violate Hurd's general concepts, but his language about the specific location of wholesalers is generally no longer valid.

Manufacturing, too, has thrown off its former ties to the railroad line and has gone beyond the need to locate in the center of the community, where the railroad yard and unloading spurs were located. Once freed from these constraints, manufacturing can follow other locational factors. One is a need for inexpensive land as industrial factories shift to single-story buildings. The addition of worker parking heightens this need.

The ties that once bound many types of land use to the inner zone are now weak. In the past, both wholesale and manufacturing had to be located in the central community to have reasonable accessibility to their shipments, customers, and needed technical assistance such as patent lawyers and banks. The transportation revolution of the twentieth century has liberated these land uses from the central zone.

Another significant force, and one that is critical for the future, is the explosion in communication capabilities. Although the telephone and the mail were present in 1903, the era in which many businesses required physical proximity to their customers (because interactions between people required a physical meeting) is at an end. Suburban movement of office buildings is one recent example of this change. Photocopying, FAX machines, computers, and the Internet are both a cause and a result of this major swing. In many downtown areas today, the remaining establishments consist primarily of specialty retail stores and those wholesale and office corporations that require face-to-face contact, such as jewelry or fashion clothes wholesaling, and lawyers, who often must negotiate directly.

Special Interest Topic

Largest Cities by Population in the U.S. and California

United States	Rank	California
New York	1	Los Angeles
Los Angeles	2	San Diego
Chicago	3	San Jose
Houston	4	San Francisco
Philadelphia	5	Long Beach
Phoenix	6	Fresno
San Diego	7	Sacramento
San Antonio	8	Oakland
Dallas	9	Santa Ana
San Jose	10	Anaheim

Source: U.S. Census Bureau 2004; California Department of Finance 2003.

These changes, which expand and extend the ideas Hurd presented, produced results that he did not foresee. The bursting concept first expressed by Babcock in the 1930s is another notion not anticipated by Hurd. Babcock notes that a new use need not locate adjacent to the most recently built similar use. Rather, it is possible for it to leapfrog over intervening uses to a new location, in advance of the gradual linear movement of the community toward that location. Shopping centers, big box retailing, and outlet malls are our premiere example of bursting out. Suburbanized office buildings, research parks, and manufacturing plants also illustrate the concept. This change has resulted from the tremendous increase in mobility that the automobile has given American society, although this is a change in the *scale* of mobility rather than a difference in the *type* of mobility. It allows us to go farther, faster, and in more directions than any other transportation system. The full impact pollution caused by automobiles will have on this trend is not yet apparent, but change certainly will occur.

REVIEWING YOUR UNDERSTANDING

Modern City Growth Patterns

1. What is meant by proximity and accessibility as forces in shaping cities? Give an example of the influence of each in your city.

2. Explain how the home location preferences of high-income people influence the layout of cities.

3. Give five examples of how political and social factors can influence city shape and layout.

4. What does the concept *multiple nuclei* mean? What effect do they have on the shape of cities?

5. Give five examples of the ways that the car and truck have changed the shape and layout of cities.

CHAPTER SUMMARY

This chapter has discussed how the community gets its shape, layout, and population density. The patterns of community development are important because they tell what factors have influenced land uses and changes.

The major forces influencing community growth patterns are (1) accessibility, (2) transportation, (3) topography, and (4) community origins. For any given parcel of land, one use has a comparative advantage over all other uses because of the effects of these forces. This comparative advantage is reflected by the amount of rent that the highest and best use is able to generate. Nearby sites, which have similar characteristics, attract similar uses to them. This leads to clusters or nuclei of similar uses.

In addition to economic forces, political and social pressures affect land-use decisions. Public land-use controls and eminent domain are the two most common types of political forces. Social pressures are varied but are a main influence on land use. All three forces spring from "we, the people," but in different ways, with different effects and mechanisms.

Small cities tend to have simple land-use patterns, generally a series of concentric rings of different land uses. Larger cities develop pie-shaped wedges that expand through several rings. This results from the gradual development of a higher-priced side or sector, in the residential and commercial rings. When we turn to large metropolitan areas or complexes, we see that a number of small concentric communities grow until they meet. The resulting pattern of land uses has a number of centers, both from suburban areas and from new clusters around major transportation intersections. Each center or nucleus has rings of uses around it, but each center may serve a specialized function.

In each case, the location of land uses seems to be the result of the competition between the drawing power of the existing buildings and the changing accessibility to people that is provided by growth of the community and its transportation system. The former is dominated by the origins and early transportation features of the town, and the latter owes much to topography, social and political influences, and the current transportation systems.

IMPORTANT TERMS AND CONCEPTS

Accessibility

Comparative advantage

Competition of uses

Concentric growth

Economic succession

Growth:

   Attraction

   Residence

Linear (axial) growth

Multiple nuclei

Topography

REVIEWING YOUR UNDERSTANDING

1. When land is allocated to the legal user who pays the highest price, economists call this the principle of:
   a. balance
   b. highest and best use
   c. economic succession
   d. change

2. The impact that zoning has on community growth patterns is what type of force?
   a. economic
   b. physical
   c. social
   d. political

3. The circular or concentric theory of growth has the city growing:
   a. around the downtown central core
   b. along transportation lines
   c. from several points such as suburban shopping centers
   d. from the highest to the lowest topographic points

4. The multiple nuclei theory of growth has the city growing:
   a. around the downtown central core
   b. along transportation lines
   c. from several points such as suburban shopping centers
   d. from the highest to the lowest topographic points

5. The growth of a community along transportation lines such as freeways or rapid transit routes is best described as:
   a. spatial
   b. axial or linear
   c. sporadic
   d. circular

6. In real estate land use, accessibility means:
   a. similar zoning
   b. ability to get in and out of a site
   c. social factors that determine use
   d. nearness to other businesses

7. According to the classic study by Homer Hoyt, *The Structure and Growth of Residential Neighborhoods in American Cities*, higher-priced homes tend to be built:
   a. on flat land
   b. near transportation systems
   c. near industrial parks
   d. on hillsides

8. The physical shape of a city can be changed by:
   a. new transportation systems
   b. topography
   c. new technology
   d. all of the above

9. No-growth policies by city governments are an example of what type of force?
   a. political
   b. economic
   c. physical
   d. social

10. The future growth patterns of large U.S. cities will be heavily influenced by:
    a. transportation systems
    b. environmental concerns
    c. telecommunications systems
    d. all of the above

11. Which transportation vehicle or system is considered random?
    a. trains
    b. automobiles
    c. subways
    d. trolleys

12. Comparative advantage means the:
    a. increased benefit that a particular building gives to a particular site
    b. locational benefit gained by a site being in the central area of a town
    c. increased benefit that a particular property gains from the advantages it may have over less desirable properties
    d. locational forces that shift town growth away from desirable areas

13. When an existing building is demolished and a new, more profitable building is constructed, this is an application of:
    a. the economics of succession
    b. the principle of change
    c. highest and best use
    d. all of the above

14. The pattern of land use in cities is based solely on the interplay of private market forces.
    a. true
    b. false

15. The four dominant factors in land-use patterns for small cities are:
    a. origins, social issues, politics, and change
    b. topography, transportation, economics, and politics
    c. topography, transportation, social issues, and change
    d. origins, accessibility, topography, and transportation

16. Land use tends to seek that location that has the best combination of benefits and minimal problems. This is called:
    a. zoning
    b. comparative advantage
    c. eminent domain
    d. concentric growth

17. Accessibility and topography have strong influences on land-use patterns.
    a. true
    b. false

18. In modern U.S. cities, land-use patterns are no longer influenced by major transportation systems.
    a. true
    b. false

19. After a town is formed, proximity and _____ are in a continual tug of war over the locations of new buildings.
    a. productivity
    b. import goods
    c. obsolescence
    d. accessibility

20. Leapfrogging is the label applied:
    a. when a new town is established
    b. when a new location is selected well away from existing central locations
    c. to the process of growth established by a new freeway
    d. when property is rezoned

21. The wedge describes the manner in which:
    a. a new transit system alters the pattern of land uses
    b. a shift of a major government building changes uses
    c. the principle of change influences government policies
    d. concentric rings of uses break into slices of different values

22. The ever-increasing use of electronic equipment such as FAX machines and interactive TV should lessen the need for additional office buildings in downtown areas of major U.S. cities.
    a. true
    b. false

23. Without zoning laws, similar land uses tend to cluster together: residential with residential, commercial with commercial, manufacturing with manufacturing, because of the principles of:
    a. change
    b. substitution
    c. decreasing returns
    d. comparative advantage

24. The location of manufacturing districts is most flexible when the main transportation system is:
    a. railroads
    b. trucking
    c. waterways
    d. airlines

25. The growth in use of communication systems changes land-use patterns by:
    a. increasing the power of existing locations
    b. making cities more linear in shape
    c. reducing the need for physical proximity to other uses
    d. reducing the leapfrogging tendency

CASE & POINT

United States and California Statistics: Population and Race

All data taken from the U.S. Department of Commerce, Bureau of Census and/or California Statistical Abstract

Table 7.1 Population

Year	United States	California	California as a Percentage of U.S. Total
1950	150,790,000	10,472,000	6.9%
1960	178,140,000	15,550,000	8.7%
1970	201,895,000	19,663,000	9.7%
1980	225,621,000	23,511,000	10.4%
1990	247,983,000	29,558,000	11.9%
2000	280,954,000	33,968,000	12.1%
2003	289,588,000	35,733,000	12.3%

Table 7.2 United States Breakdown by Race, 2000 Census

Subject	Number	Percent
RACE		
Total population	**281,421,906**	**100.0**
One race	274,595,678	97.6
White	211,460,626	75.1
Black or African American	34,658,190	12.3
American Indian and Alaska Native	2,475,956	0.9
American Indian	1,865,118	0.7
Alaska Native	97,876	0.0
Both American Indian and Alaska Native	1,002	0.0
American Indian or Alaska Native, not specified	511,960	0.2
Asian	10,242,998	3.6
Asian Indian	1,678,765	0.6
Chinese	2,432,585	0.9
Filipino	1,850,314	0.7
Japanese	796,700	0.3
Korean	1,076,872	0.4
Vietnamese	1,122,528	0.4
Other Asian category	1,061,646	0.4
Two or more Asian categories	223,588	0.1
Native Hawaiian and Other Pacific Islander	398,835	0.1
Native Hawaiian	140,652	0.0
Samoan	91,029	0.0
Guamanian or Chamorro	58,240	0.0
Other Pacific Islander category	99,996	0.0
Two or more Native Hawaiian or Other Pacific Islander categories	8,918	0.0
Some other race	15,359,073	5.5

Table 7.2   United States Breakdown by Race, 2000 Census *(Continued)*

Subject	Number	Percent
Two or more races	6,826,228	2.4
Two races including Some other race	3,001,558	1.1
Two races excluding Some other race, and three or more races	3,824,670	1.4
Two races excluding Some other race	3,366,517	1.2
Three or more races	458,153	0.2
HISPANIC OR LATINO		
Total population	**281,421,906**	**100.0**
Hispanic or Latino (of any race)	35,305,818	12.5
Mexican	20,640,711	7.3
Puerto Rican	3,406,178	1.2
Cuban	1,241,685	0.4
Other Hispanic or Latino	10,017,244	3.6
Not Hispanic or Latino	246,116,088	87.5
RACE AND HISPANIC OR LATINO		
Total population	**281,421,906**	**100.0**
One race	274,595,678	97.6
Hispanic or Latino	33,081,736	11.8
Not Hispanic or Latino	241,513,942	85.8
Two or more races	6,826,228	2.4
Hispanic or Latino	2,224,082	0.8
Not Hispanic or Latino	4,602,146	1.6

Table 7.3 California Breakdown by Race, 1990 and 2000 Census

	1990 Census		2000 Census		Change 1990–2000	
	Number	% of total	Number	% of total	Number	Percent
Excluding Hispanic or Latino:						
White	17,029,126	57.2	15,816,790	46.7	(1,212,336)	(7.1)
Black	2,092,446	7.0	2,181,926	6.4	89,480	4.3
Native American	185,065	0.6	178,984	0.5	(5,081)	(2.8)
Asian	} 2,710,353	9.1	3,648,860	10.8	} 1,042,243	38.5
Pacific Islander			103,736	0.3		
Other	56,093	0.2	71,681	0.2	15,588	27.8
Multirace	n.a.	–	903,115	2.7	–	–
Hispanic or Latino	7,687,938	25.8	10,966,556	32.4	3,278,618	42.6
Total	29,760,021	100.0	33,871,648	100.0	4,111,627	13.8

n.a. Not available

Department of Finance
Demographic Research Unit
(916) 322–4651
http://www.dof.ca.gov

Table 7.4 Total Population of California Cities, January 1, 2003 and 2004

County and city	2003	2004	Percent change	County and city	2003	2004	Percent change
CALIFORNIA	35,612,000	36,144,000	1.5%	Clayton	10,950	11,000	0.5%
				Concord	124,700	124,900	0.2%
ALAMEDA	1,487,700	1,498,000	0.7%	Danville	43,100	43,250	0.3%
Alameda	74,300	74,400	0.1%	El Cerrito	23,500	23,400	−0.4%
Albany	16,700	16,700	0.0%	Hercules	20,450	21,700	6.1%
Berkeley	104,000	104,300	0.3%	Lafayette	24,350	24,300	−0.2%
Dublin	36,150	38,350	6.1%	Martinez	36,800	36,800	0.0%
Emeryville	7,500	7,675	2.3%	Moraga	16,500	16,450	−0.3%
Fremont	206,800	209,100	0.1%	Oakley	26,950	27,550	2.2%
Hayward	143,900	144,600	0.5%	Orinda	17,800	17,750	−0.3%
Livermore	77,600	78,600	1.3%	Pinole	19,500	19,550	0.3%
Newark	43,700	43,750	0.1%	Pittsburg	60,900	61,500	1.0%
Oakland	408,500	411,600	0.8%	Pleasant Hill	33,600	33,600	0.0%
Piedmont	11,050	11,050	0.0%	Richmond	101,100	101,700	0.6%
Pleasanton	66,600	67,200	0.9%	San Pablo	30,750	31,050	1.0%
San Leandro	80,900	81,500	0.7%	San Ramon	46,950	48,600	3.5%
Union City	69,900	70,200	0.4%	Walnut Creek	65,800	66,000	0.3%
Balance of County	138,200	139,100	0.7%	Balance of County	156,900	157,400	0.3%
ALPINE	1,280	1,280	0.0%	DEL NORTE	28,000	28,250	0.9%
Balance of County	1,280	1,280	0.0%	Crescent City	7,350	7,550	2.7%
				Balance of County	20,650	20,700	0.2%
AMADOR	36,650	36,850	0.5%				
Amador	210	210	0.0%				
Ione	7,475	7,525	0.7%	EL DORADO	165,900	168,100	1.3%
Jackson	4,080	4,100	0.5%	Placerville	10,200	10,150	−0.5%
Plymouth	1,080	1,070	−0.9%	South Lake Tahoe	23,850	23,600	−1.0%
Sutter Creek	2,450	2,480	1.2%	Balance of County	131,800	134,400	2.0%
Balance of County	21,350	21,450	0.5%				
				FRESNO	845,600	862,600	2.0%
BUTTE	210,800	212,700	0.9%	Clovis	76,500	80,900	5.8%
Biggs	1,810	1,810	0.0%	Coalinga	16,050	16,700	4.0%
Chico	68,700	71,300	3.8%	Firebaugh	6,200	6,575	6.0%
Gridley	5,775	5,775	0.0%	Fowler	4,360	4,600	5.5%
Oroville	13,300	13,350	0.4%	Fresno	450,600	456,100	1.2%
Paradise	26,750	26,750	0.0%	Huron	6,925	6,975	0.7%
Balance of County	94,400	93,800	−0.6%	Kerman	10,050	10,650	6.0%
				Kingsburg	10,550	11,150	5.7%
CALAVERAS	42,750	43,350	1.4%	Mendota	8,200	8,650	5.5%
Angels City	3,370	3,440	2.1%	Orange Cove	8,775	9,250	5.4%
Balance of County	39,400	39,900	1.3%	Parlier	12,250	12,250	0.0%
				Reedley	21,450	21,750	1.4%
				Sanger	20,000	20,500	2.5%
COLUSA	19,750	20,100	1.8%	San Joaquin	3,510	3,570	1.7%
Colusa	5,600	5,625	0.4%	Selma	21,000	21,800	3.8%
Williams	4,040	4,230	4.7%	Balance of County	169,200	171,200	1.2%
Balance of County	10,150	10,250	1.0%				
				GLENN	27,400	27,750	1.3%
				Orland	6,450	6,525	1.2%
CONTRA COSTA	992,700	1,003,900	1.1%	Willows	6,350	6,375	0.4%
Antioch	99,100	100,600	1.5%	Balance of County	14,600	14,850	1.7%
Brentwood	33,000	37,050	12.3%				

Table 7.4 Total Population of California Cities, January 1, 2003 and 2004

County and city	2003	2004	Percent change	County and city	2003	2004	Percent change
HUMBOLDT	128,800	130,000	0.9%	LOS ANGELES	9,966,200	10,103,000	1.4%
Arcata	17,000	17,100	0.6%	Agoura Hills	21,900	22,150	1.1%
Blue Lake	1,170	1,170	0.0%	Alhambra	88,800	89,700	1.0%
Eureka	26,200	26,250	0.2%	Arcadia	55,500	55,900	0.7%
Femdale	1,410	1,390	−1.4%	Artesia	17,000	17,200	1.2%
Fortuna	10,900	11,100	1.8%	Avalon	3,470	3,500	0.9%
RioDell	3,190	3,210	0.6%	Azusa	47,100	48,150	2.2%
Trinidad	310	320	3.2%	Baldwin Park	79,500	80,300	1.0%
Balance of County	68,600	69,400	1.2%	Bell	38,200	38,650	1.2%
				Bellflower	76,300	77,000	0.9%
IMPERIAL	152,600	156,600	2.6%	Bell Gardens	45,700	45,950	0.5%
Brawley	22,850	23,800	4.2%	Beverly Hills	35,300	35,700	1.1%
Calexico	32,200	32,600	1.2%	Bradbury	920	940	2.2%
Calipatria	7,675	7,850	2.3%	Burbank	104,400	105,400	1.0%
BEL Centro	39,550	40,500	2.4%	Calabasas	22,550	22,900	1.6%
Holtville	5,750	5,825	1.3%	Carson	94,700	96,300	1.7%
Imperial	8,575	9,425	9.9%	Cerritos	54,200	54,700	0.9%
Westmorland	2,210	2,250	1.8%	Claremont	36,050	36,350	0.8%
Balance of County	33,800	34,300	1.5%	Commerce	13,150	13,350	1.5%
				Compton	96,900	97,900	1.0%
INYO	18,450	18,500	0.3%	Covina	48,650	49,100	0.9%
Bishop	3,640	3,630	−0.3%	Cudahy	25,400	25,650	1.0%
Balance of County	14,800	14,900	0.7%	Culver City	40,200	40,550	0.9%
				Diamond Bar	58,900	59,500	1.0%
KERN	708,400	724,900	2.3%	Downey	111,600	112,800	1.1%
Arvin	14,150	14,500	2.5%	Duarte	22,350	22,600	1.1%
Bakersfield	268,900	279,700	4.0%	El Monte	121,800	123,500	1.4%
California City	11,150	11,300	1.3%	El Segundo	16,700	16,850	0.9%
Delano	42,300	43,200	2.1%	Gardena	60,000	60,600	1.0%
Maricopa	1,140	1,140	0.0%	Glendale	202,500	205,300	1.4%
Mcfarland	10,700	11,150	4.2%	Glendora	51,400	52,000	1.2%
Ridgecrest	25,800	25,850	0.2%	Hawaiian Gardens	15,550	15,700	1.0%
Shafter	13,450	13,700	1.9%	Hawthorne	87,300	88,200	1.0%
Taft	9,025	8,950	−0.8%	Hermosa Beach	19,350	19,550	1.0%
Tehachapi	11,450	11,700	2.2%	Hidden Hills	2,000	2,020	1.0%
Wasco	22,400	22,850	2.0%	Huntington Park	63,900	64,500	0.9%
Balance of County	277,900	280,900	1.1%	Industry	800	800	0.0%
				Inglewood	116,800	117,600	0.7%
KINGS	137,400	141,400	2.9%	Irwindale	1,490	1,490	0.0%
Avenal	15,450	16,200	4.9%	La Canada Flintridge	21,200	21,400	0.9%
Corcoran	21,250	22,150	4.2%	La Habra Heights	6,050	6,150	1.7%
Hanford	44,850	46,300	3.2%	Lakewood	82,200	83,100	1.1%
Lemoore	21,250	21,900	3.1%	La Mirada	48,850	50,100	2.6%
Balance of County	34,700	34,850	0.4%	Lancaster	125,900	129,200	2.6%
				La Puente	42,600	43,050	1.1%
LAKE	62,300	63,200	1.4%	La Verne	32,900	33,250	1.1%
Clearlake	13,750	13,950	1.5%	Lawndale	32,800	33,200	1.2%
Lakeport	5,100	5,125	0.5%	Lornita	20,800	21,000	1.0%
Balance of County	43,450	44,150	1.6%	Long Beach	480,400	487,100	1.4%
				Los Angeles	3,859,400	3,912,200	1.4%
LASSEN	34,150	34,850	2.0%	Lynwood	72,500	73,000	0.7%
Susanville	17,650	18,100	2.5%	Malibu	13,300	13,550	1.9%
Balance of County	16,500	16,750	1.5%				

Table 7.4 Total Population of California Cities, January 1, 2003 and 2004

County and city	2003	2004	Percent change	County and city	2003	2004	Percent change
Manhattan Beach	36,250	36,600	1.0%	Ross	2,350	2,350	0.0%
Maywood	29,150	29,400	0.9%	San Anselmo	12,350	12,350	0.0%
Monrovia	38,400	38,800	1.0%	San Rafael	57,000	56,900	−0.2%
Montebello	64,600	65,200	0.9%	Sausalito	7,350	7,325	−0.3%
Monterey Park	63,300	63,900	0.9%	Tiburon	8,775	8,775	0.0%
Norwalk	108,600	109,500	0.8%	Balance of County	69,000	68,700	−0.4%
Palmdale	127,100	131,300	3.3%				
Palos Verdes Estates	13,900	14,100	1.4%	MARIPOSA	17,550	17,650	0.6%
Paramount	57,200	57,700	0.9%	Balance of County	17,550	17,650	0.6%
Pasadena	142,000	144,000	1.4%	MENDOCINO	88,400	89,200	0.9%
Pico Rivera	66,100	66,800	1.1%	Fort Bragg	6,900	6,900	0.0%
Pomona	156,300	158,400	1.3%	Point Arena	480	480	0.0%
Rancho Palos Verdes	42,750	43,200	1.1%	Ukiah	15,900	15,900	0.0%
Redondo Beach	66,500	66,900	0.6%	Willits	5,050	5,025	−0.5%
Rolling Hills	1,930	1,960	1.6%	Balance of County	60,100	60,900	1.3%
Rolling Hills Estates	8,050	8,125	0.9%	MERCED	227,000	232,100	2.2%
Rosemead	56,200	56,700	0.9%	Atwater	26,200	26,400	0.8%
San Dimas	36,400	36,750	1.0%	Dos Palos	4,620	4,790	3.7%
San Fernando	24,500	24,750	1.0%	Gustine	5,175	5,225	1.0%
San Gabriel	41,500	41,900	1.0%	Livingston	11,150	11,700	4.9%
San Marino	13,400	13,600	1.5%	Los Banos	29,400	30,650	4.3%
Santa Clarita	162,700	164,900	1.4%	Merced	68,200	69,800	2.3%
Santa Fe Springs	17,100	17,750	3.8%	Balance of County	82,300	83,600	1.6%
Santa Monica	89,200	90,300	1.2%	MODOC	9,550	9,650	1.0%
Sierra Madre	10,950	11,050	0.9%	Alturas	2,880	2,840	−1.4%
Signal Hill	10,250	10,650	3.9%	Balance of County	6,675	6,800	1.9%
South El Monte	21,950	22,100	0.7%				
South Gate	100,200	101,400	1.2%	MONO	13,400	13,500	0.7%
South Pasadena	25,250	25,500	1.0%	Mammoth Lakes	7,500	7,475	−0.3%
Temple City	34,650	35,300	1.9%	Balance of County	5,900	6,050	2.5%
Torrance	144,200	146,200	1.4%				
Vernon	95	95	0.0%	MONTEREY	415,600	421,400	1.4%
Walnut	31,400	31,700	1.0%	Carmel-By-The-Sea	4,080	4,100	0.5%
West Covina	110,400	111,400	0.9%	Del Rey Oaks	1,650	1,650	0.0%
West Hollywood	37,250	37,750	1.3%	Gonzales	8,300	8,425	1.5%
Westlake Village	8,750	8,825	0.9%	Greenfield	13,000	13,150	1.2%
Whittier	86,300	87,000	0.8%	King City	11,350	11,500	1.3%
Balance of County	1,044,200	1,064,700	2.0%	Marina	18,950	19,100	0.8%
				Monterey	30,300	30,250	−0.2%
MADERA	131,500	135,300	2.9%	Pacific Grove	15,500	15,600	0.6%
Chowchilla	14,400	15,450	7.3%	Salinas	149,700	152,200	1.7%
Madera	47,150	48,350	2.5%	Sand City	280	310	10.7%
Balance of County	70,000	71,500	2.1%	Seaside	33,400	33,300	−0.3%
				Soledad	24,550	26,200	6.7%
MARIN	249,800	250,200	0.2%	Balance of County	104,600	105,700	1.1%
Belvedere	2,130	2,130	0.0%				
Corte Madera	9,375	9,350	−0.3%	NAPA	130,100	131,600	1.2%
Fairfax	7,300	7,300	0.0%	American Canyon	12,350	13,150	6.5%
Larkspur	12,000	12,000	0.0%				
Mill Valley	13,600	13,600	0.0%				
Novato	48,550	49,400	1.8%				

Table 7.4 Total Population of California Cities, January 1, 2003 and 2004

County and city	2003	2004	Percent change	County and city	2003	2004	Percent change
Calistoga	5,250	5,200	−1.0%	Colfax	1,790	1,780	−0.6%
Napa	74,900	75,900	1.3%	Lincoln	19,900	23,050	15.8%
St Helena	6,050	6,000	−0.8%	Loomis	6,350	6,225	−2.0%
Yountville	3,290	3,260	−0.9%	Rocklin	46,000	48,900	6.3%
Balance of County	28,250	28,100	−0.5%	Roseville	93,300	96,900	3.9%
				Balance of County	103,500	102,600	−0.9%
NEVADA	95,100	96,100	1.1%				
Grass Valley	11,900	12,050	1.3%	PLUMAS	21,000	21,100	0.5%
Nevada City	3,010	3,000	−0.3%	Portola	2,180	2,190	0.5%
Truckee	14,750	15,000	1.7%	Balance of County	18,800	18,900	0.5%
Balance of County	65,500	66,000	0.8%				
				RIVERSIDE	1,719,000	1,776,700	3.4%
ORANGE	2,975,400	3,017,300	1.4%	Banning	25,600	27,200	6.3%
Aliso Viejo	43,900	44,850	2.2%	Beaumont	13,900	16,350	17.6%
Anaheim	337,200	343,000	1.7%	Blythe	21,300	21,950	3.1%
Brea	37,900	38,950	2.8%	Calimesa	7,400	7,350	−0.7%
Buena Park	80,200	80,600	0.5%	Canyon Lake	10,600	10,650	0.5%
Costa Mesa	111,500	113,000	1.3%	Cathedral City	47,700	48,600	1.9%
Cypress	47,900	48,450	1.1%	Coachella	27,000	27,650	2.4%
Dana Point	36,250	36,550	0.8%	Corona	138,200	141,800	2.6%
Fountain Valley	56,200	56,500	0.5%	Desert Hot Springs	17,300	17,700	2.3%
Fullerton	131,400	134,200	2.1%	Hemet	62,700	63,800	1.8%
Garden Grove	169,800	171,000	0.7%	Indian Wells	4,430	4,430	0.0%
Huntington Beach	196,900	198,800	1.0%	Indio	54,900	59,100	7.7%
Irvine	164,800	171,800	4.2%	Lake Elsinore	33,300	35,350	6.2%
Laguna Beach	24,550	24,750	0.8%	La Quinta	30,700	32,500	5.9%
Laguna Hills	32,800	33,000	0.6%	Moreno Valley	151,200	155,100	2.6%
Laguna Niguel	65,100	65,700	0.9%	Murrieta	68,200	77,700	13.9%
Laguna Woods	18,200	18,300	0.5%	Norco	25,400	25,500	0.4%
La Habra	61,200	61,500	0.5%	Palm Desert	44,300	44,800	1.1%
Lake Forest	77,300	77,700	0.5%	Palm Springs	44,350	44,250	−0.2%
La Palma	15,950	16,050	0.6%	Perris	38,500	41,300	7.3%
Los Alamitos	11,800	11,950	1.3%	Rancho Mirage	15,100	15,500	2.6%
Mission Viejo	97,300	97,800	0.5%	Riverside	276,300	277,000	0.3%
Newport Beach	79,900	80,800	1.1%	San Jacinto	26,250	26,700	1.7%
Orange	134,500	136,700	1.6%	Temecula	75,700	77,500	2.4%
Placentia	49,050	49,900	1.7%	Balance of County	458,600	477,000	4.0%
Rancho Santa Margrita	48,800	49,000	0.4%				
San Clemente	60,700	63,100	4.0%	SACRAMENTO	1,311,700	1,335,400	1.8%
San Juan Capistrano	35,200	35,850	1.8%	Citrus Heights	87,300	87,000	−0.3%
Santa Ana	347,000	349,100	0.6%	Elk Grove	85,900	109,100	27.0%
Seal Beach	24,900	24,950	0.2%	Folsom	63,900	65,600	2.7%
Stanton	38,400	38,600	0.5%	Galt	22,050	22,150	0.5%
Tustin	69,700	70,300	0.9%	Isleton	840	830	−1
Villa Park	6,150	6,200	0.8%	Sacramento	433,400	441,000	1.8%
Westminster	90,600	91,500	1.0%	Balance of County	618,200	609,700	−1.4%
Yorba Linda	62,600	64,000	2.2%				
Balance of County	109,800	112,800	2.7%	SAN BENITO	56,300	57,100	1.4%
				Hollister	36,600	37,000	1.1%
PLACER	283,500	292,100	3.0%	San Juan Bautista	1,610	1,720	6.8%
Auburn	12,600	12,650	0.4%				

Table 7.4 Total Population of California Cities, January 1, 2003 and 2004

County and city	2003	2004	Percent change	County and city	2003	2004	Percent change
Balance of County	18,100	18,400	1.7%	SAN JOAQUIN	616,500	630,600	2.3%
				Escalon	6,675	6,700	0.4%
				Lathrop	12,100	12,450	2.9%
SAN BERNARDINO	1,842,100	1,886,500	2.4%	Lodi	60,300	60,800	0.8%
Adelanto	19,500	21,250	9.0%	Manteca	57,500	59,700	3.8%
Apple Valley	59,200	61,300	3.5%	Ripon	11,650	12,300	5.6%
Barstow	23,150	23,200	0.2%	Stockton	262,600	269,100	2.5%
Big Bear Lake	5,900	6,025	2.1%	Tracy	70,000	74,100	5.9%
Chino	71,000	72,100	1.5%	Balance of County	135,700	135,500	−0.1%
Chino Hills	73,400	76,400	4.1%				
Cotton	50,500	50,800	0.6%	SAN LUIS OBISPO	255,400	258,200	1.1%
Fontana	146,500	154,800	5.7%	Arroyo Grande	16,450	16,600	0.9%
Grand Terrace	12,150	12,250	0.8%	Atascadero	27,300	27,700	1.5%
Hesperia	68,200	70,300	3.1%	El Paso De Robles	26,750	27,200	1.7%
Highland	47,700	49,250	3.2%				
Loma Linda	20,800	20,950	0.7%	Grover Beach	13,050	13,250	1.5%
Montclair	34,500	34,750	0.7%	Morro Bay	10,500	10,500	0.0%
Needles	5,250	5,375	2.4%	Pismo Beach	8,675	8,725	0.6%
Ontario	166,500	167,900	0.8%	San Luis Obispo	44,250	44,200	−0.1%
Rancho Cucamonga	147,400	154,800	5.0%	Balance of County	108,500	110,000	1.4%
Redlands	67,900	68,800	1.3%				
Rialto	97,100	98,100	1.0%	SAN MATEO	709,200	712,400	0.5%
San Bernardino	195,100	196,300	0.6%	Atherton	7,125	7,175	0.7%
Twentynine Palms	25,250	25,950	2.8%	Belmont	25,100	25,100	0.0%
				Brisbane	3,600	3,640	1.1%
Upland	72,200	72,700	0.7%	Burlingame	27,900	27,950	0.2%
Victorville	72,800	77,700	6.7%	Colma	1,180	1,280	8.5%
Yucaipa	45,650	47,450	3.9%	Daly City	103,000	103,300	0.3%
Yucca Valley	18,050	18,700	3.6%	East Palo Alto	31,350	31,500	0.5%
Balance of County	296,500	299,400	1.0%	Foster City	29,450	29,450	0.0%
				Half Moon Bay	12,150	12,250	0.8%
SAN DIEGO	2,976,100	3,017,200	1.4%	Hillsborough	10,850	10,850	0.0%
Carlsbad	90,800	93,000	2.4%	Menlo Park	30,450	30,400	−0.2%
Chula Vista	200,700	209,100	4.2%	Millbrae	20,450	20,450	0.0%
Coronado	26,450	26,450	0.0%	Pacifica	38,150	38,200	0.1%
Del Mar	4,530	4,560	0.7%	Portola Valley	4,440	4,480	0.9%
El Cajon	97,100	97,600	0.5%	Redwood City	75,100	75,100	0.0%
Encinitas	61,400	62,600	2.0%	San Bruno	40,450	41,250	2.0%
Escondido	138,800	140,500	1.2%	San Carlos	27,450	27,650	0.7%
Imperial Beach	27,750	27,800	0.2%	San Mateo	92,600	93,100	0.5%
La Mesa	56,000	56,000	0.0%	South San Francisco	60,100	60,400	0.5%
Lemon Grove	25,500	25,600	0.4%				
National City	60,000	57,000	−5.0%	Woodside	5,300	5,400	1.9%
Oceanside	170,700	173,300	1.5%	Balance of County	63,000	63,500	0.8%
Poway	50,100	50,600	1.0%				
San Diego	1,281,400	1,294,000	1.0%				
San Marcos	63,900	67,400	5.5%	SANTA BARBARA	410,300	414,800	1.1%
Santee	53,800	54,000	0.4%	Buellton	4,200	4,460	6.2%
Solana Beach	13,400	13,450	0.4%	Carpinteria	14,350	14,350	0.0%
Vista	93,200	94,000	0.9%	Goleta	30,800	30,850	0.2%
Balance of County	460,600	470,000	2.0%	Guadalupe	6,250	6,300	0.8%
				Lompoc	41,750	42,250	1.2%
				Santa Barbara	90,200	90,500	0.3%
SAN FRANCISCO	789,700	792,700	0.4%	Santa Maria	81,900	85,300	4.2%
San Francisco	789,700	792,700	0.4%	Solvang	5,425	5,425	0.0%

Table 7.4 Total Population of California Cities, January 1, 2003 and 2004

County and city	2003	2004	Percent change	County and city	2003	2004	Percent change
Balance of County	135,300	135,300	0.0%	Fairfield	102,600	103,600	1.0%
				Rio Vista	5,650	6,275	11.1%
				Suisun City	26,900	27,400	1.9%
SANTA CLARA	1,719,500	1,731,400	0.7%	Vacaville	94,000	95,100	1.2%
Campbell	38,050	38,200	0.4%	Vallejo	120,200	121,100	0.7%
Cupertino	51,900	52,600	1.3%	Balance of County	19,650	19,700	0.3%
Gilroy	44,700	46,200	3.4%				
Los Altos	27,550	27,500	−0.2%				
Los Altos Hills	8,300	8,350	0.6%	SONOMA	469,500	472,700	0.7%
Los Gatos	28,750	28,750	0.0%	Cloverdale	7,450	7,925	6.4%
Milpitas	64,700	64,600	−0.2%	Cotati	6,825	7,025	2.9%
Monte Sereno	3,480	3,500	0.6%	Healdsburg	11,600	11,600	0.0%
Morgan Hill	34,750	35,500	2.2%	Petaluma	55,600	55,900	0.5%
Mountain View	71,600	71,600	0.0%	Rohnert Park	42,300	42,150	−0.4%
Palo Alto	60,100	60,200	0.2%	Santa Rosa	153,400	154,400	0.7%
San Jose	919,600	926,200	0.7%	Sebastopol	7,750	7,750	0.0%
Santa Clara	105,200	107,200	1.9%	Sonoma	9,550	9,675	1.3%
Saratoga	30,300	30,300	0.0%	Windsor	24,350	24,800	1.8%
Sunnyvale	131,800	131,700	−0.1%	Balance of County	150,700	151,600	0.6%
Balance of County	98,900	98,900	0.0%				
				STANISLAUS	483,000	491,900	1.8%
SANTA CRUZ	258,900	260,200	0.5%	Ceres	36,450	37,350	2.5%
Capitola	10,100	10,050	−0.5%	Hughson	4,930	5,225	6.0%
Santa Cruz	55,400	56,300	1.6%	Modesto	203,500	206,200	1.3%
Scotts Valley	11,600	11,600	0.0%	Newman	7,775	8,300	6.8%
Watsonville	47,500	48,300	1.7%	Oakdale	16,750	17,100	2.1%
Balance of County	134,300	134,000	−0.2%	Patterson	13,700	14,150	3.3%
				Riverbank	17,300	18,200	5.2%
				Turlock	62,300	64,200	3.0%
SHASTA	173,200	175,700	1.4%	Waterford	7,675	7,850	2.3%
Anderson	9,625	10,050	4.4%	Balance of County	112,700	113,300	0.5%
Redding	86,300	87,300	1.2%				
Shasta Lake	9,875	10,050	1.8%				
Balance of County	67,500	68,300	1.2%	SUTTER	83,800	85,500	2.0%
				Live Oak	6,475	6,550	1.2%
SIERRA	3,560	3,520	−1.1%	Yuba City	48,700	50,800	4.3%
Loyalton	870	880	1.1%	Balance of County	28,600	28,150	−1.6%
Balance of County	2,700	2,650	−1.9%				
				TEHAMA	57,900	58,700	1.4%
SISKIYOU	44,600	44,850	0.6%	Corning	6,850	6,875	0.4%
Dorris	880	880	0.0%	Red Bluff	13,500	13,550	0.4%
Dunsmuir	1,890	1,880	−0.5%	Tehama	440	440	0.0%
Etna	770	770	0.0%	Balance of County	37,100	37,850	2.0%
Fort Jones	660	660	0.0%				
Montague	1,460	1,470	0.7%				
Mount Shasta	3,650	3,650	0.0%	TRINITY	13,300	13,450	1.1%
Tulelake	1,010	1,000	−1.0%	Balance of County	13,300	13,450	1.1%
Weed	3,000	2,960	−1.3%				
Yreka	7,325	7,325	0.0%				
Balance of County	24,000	24,250	1.0%	TULARE	388,600	396,800	2.1%
				Dinuba	18,400	18,600	1.1%
				Exeter	9,650	9,900	2.6%
SOLANO	412,200	416,500	1.0%	Farmersville	9,300	9,775	5.1%
				Lindsay	10,600	10,700	0.9%
Benicia	27,050	27,000	−0.2%	Porterville	42,200	43,150	2.3%
Dixon	16,200	16,350	0.9%	Tulare	46,550	47,700	2.5%

Table 7.4 Total Population of California Cities, January 1, 2003 and 2004

County and city	2003	2004	Percent change	County and city	2003	2004	Percent change
Visalia	99,500	102,700	3.2%	Simi Valley	117,700	118,800	0.9%
Woodlake	6,975	7,000	0.4%	Thousand Oaks	124,000	126,100	1.7%
Balance of County	145,500	147,300	1.2%	Balance of County	95,200	95,400	0.2%
TUOLUMNE	56,600	56,900	0.5%	YOLO	181,100	184,500	1.9%
Sonora	4,620	4,650	0.6%	Davis	63,800	64,500	1.1%
Balance of County	52,000	52,300	0.6%	West Sacramento	36,450	38,000	4.3%
				Winters	6,575	6,875	4.6%
VENTURA	791,600	802,400	1.4%	Woodland	51,600	52,500	1.7%
Camarillo	60,500	61,700	2.0%	Balance of County	22,800	22,600	−0.9%
Fillmore	14,700	15,150	3.1%				
Moorpark	34,550	34,900	1.0%				
Ojai	8,000	8,100	1.3%	YUBA	63,800	64,800	1.6%
Oxnard	181,800	186,100	2.4%	Marysville	12,750	12,800	0.4%
Port Hueneme	21,800	22,150	1.6%	Wheatland	2,730	3,180	16.5%
San Buenaventura	104,300	105,000	0.7%	Balance of County	48,350	48,850	1.0%
Santa Paula	28,950	29,100	0.5%				

Totals may not add due to independent rounding. Excludes estimated census undercount.

Department of Finance
Demographic Research Unit
(916) 322-4651
http://www.dof.ca.gov

Table 7.5 California Median Income and Poverty Status, 2000 Census

County	Median income in 1999 dollars		Income in 1999 below poverty level a/			
			Percent of population for whom poverty status is determined			
	Households	Families	All ages	Related children under 18 years	65 years and over	Percent of families
California	$47,493	$53,025	14.2	19.0	8.1	10.6
Alameda	55,946	65,857	11.0	13.5	8.1	7.7
Alpine	41,875	50,250	19.5	27.4	10.1	12.0
Amador	42,280	51,226	9.2	13.1	5.4	6.1
Butte	31,924	41,010	19.8	23.8	7.3	12.2
Calaveras	41,022	47,379	11.8	15.6	6.2	8.7
Colusa	35,062	40,138	16.1	19.5	8.2	13.0
Contra Costa	63,675	73,039	7.6	9.8	6.0	5.4
Del Norle	29,642	36,056	20.2	26.7	8.2	16.4
El Dorado	51,484	60,250	7.1	7.6	5.0	5.0

Table 7.5 California Median Income and Poverty Status, 2000 Census (*Continued*)

| County | Median income in 1999 dollars | | Income in 1999 below poverty level a/ Percent of population for whom poverty status is determined | | | Percent of families |
	Households	Families	All ages	Related children under 18 years	65 years and over	
Fresno	34,725	38,455	22.9	31.7	9.9	17.6
Glenn	32,107	37,023	18.1	26.3	7.6	12.5
Humboldt	31,226	39,370	19.5	22.5	7.2	12.9
Imperial	31,870	35,226	22.6	28.7	13.6	19.4
Inyo	35,006	44,970	12.6	16.0	8.3	9.3
Kern	35,446	39,403	20.8	27.8	10.5	16.8
Kings	35,749	38,111	19.5	25.9	8.8	15.8
Lake	29,627	35,818	17.6	22.8	7.3	12.9
Lassen	36,310	43,398	14.0	16.1	7.8	11.1
Los Angeles	42,189	46,452	17.9	24.2	10.5	14.4
Madera	36,286	39,226	21.4	28.6	9.0	15.9
Marin	71,306	88,934	6.6	6.9	4.5	3.7
Mariposa	34,626	42,655	14.8	16.5	9.0	10.5
Mendocino	35,996	42,168	15.9	21.5	7.7	10.9
Merced	35,532	38,009	21.7	28.4	10.7	16.9
Modoc	27,522	35,978	21.5	29.7	8.6	16.4
Mono	44,992	50,487	11.5	12.2	1.9	6.3
Monterey	48,305	51,169	13.5	17.4	6.8	9.7
Napa	51,738	61,410	8.3	10.6	5.6	5.6
Nevada	45,864	52,697	8.1	9.5	4.9	5.5
Orange	58,820	64,611	10.3	13.2	6.2	7.0
Placer	57,535	65,858	5.8	6.3	3.8	3.9
Plumas	36,351	46,119	13.1	16.7	6.4	9.0
Riverside	42,887	48,409	14.2	18.5	7.6	10.7
Sacramento	43,816	50,717	14.1	20.2	6.6	10.3
San Benito	57,469	60,665	10.0	11.4	8.5	6.7
San Bernardino	42,066	46,574	15.8	20.6	8.4	12.6

Table 7.5 California Median Income and Poverty Status, 2000 Census (*Continued*)

County	Median income in 1999 dollars		Income in 1999 below poverty level a/			
			Percent of population for whom poverty status is determined			Percent of families
	Households	Families	All ages	Related children under 18 years	65 years and over	
San Diego	47,067	53,438	12.4	16.5	6.8	8.9
San Francisco	55,221	63,545	11.3	13.5	10.5	7.8
San Joaquin	41,282	46,919	17.7	23.7	10.0	13.5
San Luis Obispo	42,428	52,447	12.8	11.4	5.9	6.8
San Mateo	70,819	80,737	5.8	6.0	5.1	3.5
Santa Barbara	46,677	54,042	14.3	16.3	6.2	8.5
Santa Clara	74,335	81,717	7.5	8.4	6.4	4.9
Santa Cruz	53,998	61,941	11.9	12.5	6.3	6.7
Shasta	34,335	40,491	15.4	21.0	7.3	11.3
Sierra	35,827	42,756	11.3	14.3	2.2	9.0
Siskiyou	29,530	36,890	18.6	26.6	7.3	14.0
Solano	54,099	60,597	8.3	10.3	6.3	6.1
Sonoma	53,076	61,921	8.1	8.4	5.7	4.7
Stanislaus	40,101	44,703	16.0	20.5	8.8	12.3
Sutler	38,375	44,330	15.5	21.3	7.7	12.1
Tehama	31,206	37,277	17.3	24.0	9.2	13.0
Trinity	27,711	34,343	18.7	26.2	7.2	14.1
Tulare	33,983	36,297	23.9	32.6	10.5	18.8
Tuolumne	38,725	44,327	11.4	16.2	4.0	8.1
Ventura	59,666	65,285	9.2	11.6	6.3	6.4
Yolo	40,769	51,623	18.4	16.0	7.4	9.5
Yuba	30,460	34,103	20.8	27.6	7.8	16.3

a/ Poverty status was determined for all persons except institutionalized persons, persons in military group quarters and in college dormitories, and unrelated individuals under 15 years old.

Household: A household includes the related family members and all the unrelated people who occupy a housing unit.

A person living alone in a housing unit, or a group of unrelated people sharing a housing unit is also counted as a household.

Family: A family is a group of two people or more(one of whom is the householder) related by birth, marriage, or adoption and residing together, all such people (including related subfamily members) are considered as members of one family.

Source: U.S. Department of Commerce, Bureau of the Census, SF3, http://www.census.gov/

CHAPTER 8
NEIGHBORHOODS: CLUSTERS OF LAND USE AND VALUE

PREVIEW

Chapter 8 describes the clusters of similar land uses and values called neighborhoods. Section 8.1 illustrates how to locate neighborhood boundaries. Section 8.2 describes how the study of neighborhoods can be used to identify changes that will influence individual property values. Section 8.3 analyzes neighborhood decay and the tools used to reverse the decline. The Case & Point at the end of the chapter explores the advantages and disadvantages of government versus private decision making regarding neighborhood preservation. When you have completed this chapter, you will be able to:

1. Define neighborhood and explain how to locate the boundary of neighborhoods.

2. Discuss how neighborhoods influence real property values.

3. List the four forces that affect neighborhood change.

4. Describe the process of neighborhood decay.

This information will help you to analyze the strengths and weaknesses of neighborhoods in your local community.

8.1 The Neighborhood as a Foundation of Value

C hapter 7 discussed how growth starts from the initial origins of the community and then discusses the forces that lead to a predictable pattern of expansion. This section shows how neighborhoods make a bridge between community land-use patterns and the values of individual parcels.

What Is a Neighborhood?

A neighborhood is a cluster of properties of relatively similar land use and value. Neighborhoods frequently have occupants with similar characteristics. In residential areas, occupants may have similar income levels, education, and status.

Neighborhoods exist because topography, transportation, and social and political influences have different effects on each type of land use. Thus, similar uses will be influenced in similar ways and will tend to cluster together. On the other hand, land uses can conflict, such as an airport locating in a residential neighborhood. This potential problem is usually addressed by zoning ordinances, which restrict land uses in a zone to a few narrow categories. Variances are granted only when applicants show that they are not injurious to the zoning categories. Similar controls can be achieved by the use of private deed restrictions.

Neighborhood Location and Property Values

There is an old saying that there are three factors that determine the value of a property—"location, location, and location!" This saying emphasizes that real estate has a fixed location, which means the value of an individual parcel is determined by, and cannot escape, the features or forces that surround it.

The value of a property is also a function of the physical property itself. That is, a large house on a large lot is worth more than a small house on a small lot, assuming that all other factors are the same. Other physical characteristics of the property, such as age, condition, quality, charm, renovation, mechanical features, and special equipment, are also part of what gives that property its value. However, the example of a brand-new automobile assembly plant in the middle of the Sahara Desert is used by many appraisal teachers to illustrate the relative importance of the physical property versus its surroundings.

In this case, despite the newness, excellent condition, functional layout, and quality materials of the assembly plant, the plant is not worth much because it lacks necessary features around it, such as utility and transportation systems and availability of skilled workers, raw materials, and markets for its products.

Another example is that of building identical homes on different sites. One site may be close to downtown, whereas another may be in an older suburb on the last available lot. A third site may be in a new suburb surrounded by similar newer homes. Finally, a fourth site might be in a rural area on a lot in a farmer's field. Although the houses are identical and were built by the same builder at the same time, each will have a different market value because of its individual location.

Defining Location

If property value is heavily influenced by location, the question is asked, What is location? *Location is the sum of all the topographical, transport, and other influences on land use that characterize a particular neighborhood or nucleus.* Location means almost the same thing as neighborhood. Location refers to the proximity to transportation, employment, shopping, and desired cultural facilities, and the influence of any nuisance that is found in the area. Location is also the sum of all the characteristics of the people who are present in the neighborhood. When people refer to the neighborhood, they are emphasizing the general characteristics of the area. Location refers to how these characteristics apply to a specific site.

Neighborhood Boundaries

Where does one neighborhood end and another begin? Neighborhood boundaries occur where the location starts to change. In some cases, a neighborhood boundary will be sharply defined, as by a lake, river, marsh, freeway, or similar distinct barrier to development. In other cases, neighborhoods lack such sharp boundaries; instead there is a gradual merging of neighborhoods. Sometimes two adjacent neighborhoods could be considered as one because they differ only slightly in their characteristics. On the other hand, one could subdivide any neighborhood by using minor differences among its several parts. You can see that *neighborhood* is not a precise term and that boundaries are usually not exact.

The type of boundary also varies for different types of neighborhoods. For example, the neighborhood for central financial district office buildings in larger cities may be set by the cluster of the existing financial office buildings.

Industrial developments tend to have defined boundaries set up by the zoning ordinance or at the point where the existing industrial park stops. However, if the industrial district contains a mixture of other uses, the boundary becomes uncertain. For example, many older areas have industrial buildings and residential buildings mixed together. This type of mixture has characteristics that could make it a neighborhood of its own, separate from adjoining areas that contain only industrial buildings. Also, a trend often called "new urbanism," where new construction has commercial use below and residential units above, blurs traditional neighborhood categories.

Thus, neighborhood boundaries are usually defined by geographic features, political boundaries of some kind, or by transitions in the existing pattern of land use. The boundaries are often vague and imprecise; however, many observers "on the ground" agree on what constitutes a local neighborhood.

REVIEWING YOUR UNDERSTANDING

Neighborhoods as Foundations of Value

1. What determines the boundary of a neighborhood?

2. How small can a neighborhood be? How large?

3. What do occupants of a neighborhood have in common?

8.2 Neighborhoods as Barometers of Change

Although a neighborhood is a collection of relatively similar occupants, structures, and uses of land, there are slight differences among properties in the neighborhood. These variations could be among the lots, structures, occupants, or locations. When the forces that determine land use in the community are changing, their effects will be noticed first in those places that are most vulnerable to change. When the small changes over the months are similar, it indicates that the neighborhood is responding to the new forces pushing on it. An example would be conversions of homes to small offices along a busy street.

Forces for Change

All forces for neighborhood change can be described as physical, economic, social, or political. Within these broad headings, there are several different possibilities.

Physical Factors

Physical factors for neighborhood change include the effects of time and the elements. They include weather—from routine fading and settling to the sudden tornado or flood—as well as earthquakes, slides, soil creep, and fault creep. Fires can be a physical factor for change, as can pollution.

Political Factors

Political factors that cause neighborhoods to change range from taxation to education. They include the effects of a radical city council on a conservative neighborhood and of a traditional city council on an unorthodox neighborhood. Examples of these effects include the willingness or failure to provide the level and type of police and fire support that the neighborhood seeks. Political factors can combine with physical issues; one example is governmental land-use controls in neighborhoods that use septic tanks. Some areas were subdivided many years ago, using, say, 50- by 100-foot lots. But sanitary standards today, depending on the soil, might require that five or more lots be purchased, to get a building permit if a septic tank is to be used. Or other homes, built with a septic tank, might be required to pay for a sewer line extension.

Social Factors

These can consist of national or local factors, or a variety of lifestyle and age factors. Examples include the type of conflict faced by a neighborhood with predominantly older residents when younger couples move in. The conflict can be over children playing, loud music, residence upkeep, or other issues that result from the differences in the characteristics of younger and older households.

Social conflicts can be among the most destructive to neighborhood stability. They are exceeded only by physical catastrophes such as fires and floods. At various times in the past, changes in the nationality, race, or religion of neighborhood occupants have panicked owners into hasty flight. Fortunately, as society becomes more comfortable with diversity, such an extreme reaction is expected to be rare in the future.

Economic Factors

The most obvious economic factor that causes neighborhoods to change is the *steady transition of a neighborhood* to lower-income use as its structures get older. Although this is not a hard-and-fast rule for all neighborhoods, it pertains to most neighborhoods. A second economic factor is that *locations will vary in their economic stability*. Thus, one neighborhood might be heavily occupied by workers from nearby electronics or auto factories. A swing in the business cycle within this neighborhood may cause more variation in the unemployment rate than another neighborhood occupied by people with a more varied mixture of jobs.

Transportation influences are a third economic factor. Because income differences affect the transportation capabilities of households, a bus strike, for example, will have different economic impacts on different neighborhoods. Closure of a bus company can have a permanent effect on one neighborhood's values but have no effect on another neighborhood that is also served by the bus line. The residents of the latter had the means to seek alternative transportation whereas the others did not. The effect of a transportation change on a neighborhood involves the social class of the occupants as well as their income levels. For instance, in a downtown high-income apartment, automobile ownership may be as low as in a low-income residential neighborhood, leaving both areas dependent on various forms of public transit.

Combinations

Physical, political, economic, or social factors can become involved with each other. Protection from floods is surely a political issue and social responsibility. Damaging civil riots may involve all four factors in a most complex and distressing pattern. Nevertheless, it is helpful to categorize these factors in order to understand the forces at work in a neighborhood. Table 8.1 provides an outline of the forces for neighborhood change.

Types of Neighborhood Change

As stated earlier, neighborhoods are a sensitive barometer of change in a city. The effects of change will be different in residential, commercial, or industrial neighborhoods. Nevertheless, the following broad categories suggest what to look for as signals of a changing neighborhood.

Condition

Age is an inescapable physical force, creating change in every neighborhood. Regardless of the category of land use, there is a

Table 8.1 A Summary of the Forces for Neighborhood Change

Physical	*Social*
Time	Conflicts
The elements	Age
Weathering	Lifestyles
Tornados	Demography
Floods	Ages
Earthquakes	Household sizes
Fires	*Economic*
Pollution	Job stability and diversity
Political	Aging of buildings
Facilities	Transportation cost and availability
Provided	
Omitted	
Taxes	
Amount	
Kind	
Philosophies	

constant struggle to maintain the condition of the real estate. Stable, unchanging neighborhoods almost always appear well maintained. Other neighborhoods show signs of trouble when conditions deteriorate and needed repairs accumulate. This is a warning that at some future time more rapid change must occur.

Turnover

Surprisingly, a stable neighborhood does not necessarily mean stable ownership. The reason is that, like buildings, owners and occupants age. If there is no turnover in owners, then their average age gets steadily older. This increasing age has implications for use, maintenance, and the demand for neighborhood properties. Will there be adequate future demand when owners' ages force the sale of an increasing number of properties? A reasonable level of turnover, then, is a sign of a stable neighborhood age balance. Too much turnover, however, represents a response to some unpleasant neighborhood force.

What is a normal turnover rate? The level will differ for owners of different property types. Downtown commercial properties usually have the slowest turnover rates, whereas residential districts vary widely, depending on the age, income, and employment characteristics of the occupants.

Use Change

Changes in property use cause neighborhoods to change. When a change in use starts to occur, the first changes are usually at the boundaries of the neighborhood. They may involve demolition of a house for construction of a new store, for example. Often, however, the early changes do not involve demolition, but rather conversion to another use. In the above example, instead of demolishing the house, it might be converted to an office or to a light commercial use like a hair salon or a preschool nursery. Not all changes occur, even when they are economically feasible. Many use changes are regulated by zoning ordinance, and a use permit, a variance, or rezoning would be needed. Some owners in neighborhoods try to resist change by blocking these new uses through application of political pressure against local government officials and agencies that have approval power—the "not in my backyard syndrome" (NIMBY).

Density of Occupancy

Sometimes when it is not feasible or legal to change the use, a more subtle change will occur—an increase in the density of use. A homeowner may rent out rooms; an industrial manager may sublease an unused portion of a plant; a store owner may sublease space for an affiliated venture; an office tenant may seek someone to share space. Increases in density are another way to get more income from an existing structure. The desire to increase income suggests that the existing income of the structure is inadequate to cover its costs, perhaps because the existing use is no longer as successful as it once was at this location. Density changes are usually temporary, until economic conditions improve enough to justify a full conversion to a new use or else a healthy economic return to the prior use. In either case, however, the meaning is clear: the neighborhood is changing its characteristics, for better or worse.

The Meaning of It All

What does all this change mean? How does it affect real estate markets and values? The most important concept to realize is not whether a change is for better or worse, but that a change is occurring. Once it is recognized that a neighborhood is changing, these changes can be studied to determine the forces causing the shift. Changes are considered signals for the future—predictors of the direction of real estate values. Common indicators of neighborhood change are turnovers, shifts in usage, increases in density, and increases or decreases in upkeep and maintenance. An understanding of the patterns of city growth, outlined in Chapter 7, should be combined with an understanding of the forces of neighborhood change. This combination will help to forecast the investment potential of individual properties within the city and neighborhood.

REVIEWING YOUR UNDERSTANDING

Neighborhoods as Barometers of Change

1. List four forces that produce neighborhood change. Give two examples of each.

2. List five visible effects of neighborhood change.

8.3 As Neighborhoods Age

 ging is a constant force for change. The changes that age imposes affect every neighborhood regardless of use.

Progressive Decay

Age exposes property to the weathering effects of the elements and to wear and tear from use. Without care and maintenance, buildings deteriorate and decay with age. The comment has been made that houses do not wear out but neighborhoods do. Do neighborhoods die? Like people, do neighborhoods have a life cycle of childhood, maturity, and decline?

It is obvious that some type of a "life" sequence does occur in all neighborhoods. In its childhood, a new neighborhood will have only a few new buildings. The remaining area will be vacant lots or older, pre-existing uses. As a neighborhood advances to adulthood, most of the land will have been developed, and the initially high rate of new construction will slow down. However, construction may continue for some years as the last remaining lots are slowly developed. During the maturing or middle-aged stage of a neighborhood, the condition of buildings generally remains good. Occupancy is typically stable, and the properties generate adequate income.

In time, however, the community changes. These changes begin to have their effect on the neighborhood, and decline sets in. Deteriorated buildings and other signs of decay are noticeable. This sequence can be observed in many neighborhoods, but the age of the neighborhood does not seem to follow the sequence in predetermined steps. Areas such as Georgetown in Washington, D.C., are several hundred years old and have never been more desirable than they are now. Other areas appear to reach maturity and turn downward in 25 years, as in some of the lower-priced residential subdivisions built in the early 1980s.

The End Result

It should be noted that neighborhood life cycles do not lead inevitably to the same death. In some cases, a declining neighborhood is redeveloped for a new use. This might involve the commercial expansion of the downtown area or expansion of nearby industrial areas. The conversion to a new use can be accomplished by private money, or it can be aided by governmental urban-renewal programs.

In other cases, a neighborhood simply continues to decline. The dying process drags on and produces a neighborhood that is truly a social horror. In some extreme cases, the neighborhood becomes so miserable that many city blocks of property are totally abandoned.

Wow! What Happened?

Most interesting, however, are older deteriorated neighborhoods that neither change uses nor slide into blight. At some point, some factor or group of factors emerges to produce a slow, gradual stabilization of certain neighborhoods and even reverse their decline. Remember that the properties are still aging; weather and constant use are still beating them down. Therefore, the process that stabilizes such a neighborhood *must* be positive and forceful to overcome the continuing pressures of time!

This process of stabilization is not well understood, but is very significant to the real estate community. Here is why. When a city's population is growing, there is ample economic pressure to convert a deteriorating older neighborhood to new land uses. But when the city's population is not growing or even is declining, there tends to be no demand for new land uses. So the demand to convert an old decaying neighborhood to a new use would be weak or not even present. Enduring the deteriorating slums, the other extreme, is an even worse answer. The process of neighborhood renewal, then, is critical if society is to have pleasant, stable older neighborhoods in cities with stable or declining population.

The Rehabilitation Cycle

Evidence suggests that in a number of older American residential neighborhoods, property has repeated the same life cycle a series of times. Neighborhood life cycles reviewed: Each cycle starts with neighborhood properties well maintained, modernized, and occupied by stable uses. The cycle then turns to a gradual decay of the neighborhood. This leads to a period when the neighborhood has deteriorated and prices of homes have fallen. In some instances, home prices will sink quite far before the recovery begins. The neighborhood has a high turnover rate, and occupants tend to have low incomes. Density is high, and maintenance is low. Illegal uses can be common, and abandoned homes are seen, often in the center or heart of the neighborhood.

The Recovery Period

The cycle then enters a recovery period, attracting new occupants who are different in income levels and density of occupancy from present occupants. These people are often called "urban homesteaders." This change usually appears first on one side of the neighborhood, toward the better-maintained or more attractive areas that are adjacent. These new occupants rehabilitate and remodel the structures that they buy and occupy (see Figure 8.1). They are pioneers who show the way to additional buyers, so that a gradual renaissance of the neighborhood occurs. Prices begin to rise at this stage, and enthusiasm grows, often to an evangelical pitch! This is the rehabilitation phase of the neighborhood cycle.

However, over the years the enthusiasm wears off. As the forces of aging continue, the neighborhood reaches a mature state again and starts to deteriorate once more. This cycle of decay and rebirth can be repeated indefinitely, unless it is interrupted by a major change in land use.

The American Experience

Many older American cities have experienced these repeated rehabilitation cycles. In some cases, the cycle has had a very wide swing, from decayed slum to prestige address. Certain examples are well known, such as Georgetown in Washington, D.C., and Back Bay in Boston. Others are not well known and could be only a few blocks in area. Some swings of the cycle may only be ripples: a small and unnoticed

Figure 8.1   Signs of neighborhood recovery. (*Source:* Boston Redevelopment Authority.)

deterioration of some houses for several years, and then a gradual recovery. Nearly every major article on housing rehabilitation now mentions another neighborhood where this cycle has been observed.

History shows that residential neighborhoods need not deteriorate into slums—that deterioration, once begun, can still be stopped. However, there is still the question of how to halt or reverse deterioration.

It is well to remember that American cities are far younger than those in some other areas of the world. Our understanding of neighborhood aging and feasible life of structures is less complete than those who have wrestled with the problem for over 2,000 years (as Rome has) or over 4,000 years (as Cairo has).

Learning to Fight Decay

How is neighborhood decay arrested and rehabilitation encouraged? What is this magical process that can fight off the forces of aging? Indeed, not every decaying neighborhood can be preserved. To try would be to try to freeze change or to deny that change exists! Neighborhood declines that should *not* be reversed might include areas on the fringe of a growing downtown commercial area, where land conversion is feasible, or a neighborhood so influenced by a new transportation system that it is best to encourage change.

Imagine an older residential section that has had a new rapid transit station placed in the middle of it. The traffic, noise, and congestion from the station can destroy the residential amenities that single-family residential owners require. The transportation shift also changes the characteristics of the neighborhood's location by changing its accessibility. This could change the neighborhood's ideal use from private homes to new apartments and apartment conversions. These uses are oriented to easy transportation access and are historically more tolerant of congestion and noise.

Destabilizing Forces

Forces other than age also contribute to neighborhood decline. In many communities, for example, the general plan and zoning ordinance show older residential neighborhoods as intended for some other use. This is a policy statement that the neighborhood is to be changed. It is a serious error if, in fact, the community seeks to stabilize and save the existing use of the neighborhood.

In addition, many people have commented that property taxes often work against neighborhood stabilization. They point out that a professional tax assessor is required to reevaluate a remodeled property because of its higher value. However, this leads to a higher tax, which penalizes the person who remodels and continues to occupy the building. Assessors have also usually placed low values on slum properties because the owner can demonstrate limited property income and major deterioration. Deteriorated property thus usually has much lower taxes than rehabilitated buildings in the same neighborhood.

In many communities, the process of change has included population shifts. In some cases, extreme antagonism occurred between the group departing the neighborhood and the group entering. Such hostile transitions often hasten neighborhood deterioration during times of change.

With some effort, the community could try to minimize the destructive effects of market pressures for new uses. If the land use in a neighborhood is going to change, for example, from residential to commercial, the changes should be encouraged first at the edges of the neighborhood, where the impact will be less noticeable. The heart of the neighborhood could be fully protected from the change for a while. Thus the new use can be gradually phased in without years of growing blight and neighborhood problems.

A Summary of Preservation

The foregoing discussion highlights how the forces of change put pressure on a neighborhood and what stabilizing actions are available. Fighting neighborhood decay involves locating the negative forces in time to correct the problem or to fight the negative influence. Just who should fight decay—government or private enterprise—is debatable (see this chapter appendix). However, those who take action should comprehend neighborhood forces and effects if they are to obtain the desired results. A thorough knowledge of urban land economics is the key to understanding.

REVIEWING YOUR UNDERSTANDING

As Neighborhoods Age

1. Why is age such an important factor in neighborhood change?

2. What are the phases of a neighborhood life cycle? What steps are involved in the rehabilitation phase?

3. Why is rehabilitation significant to the future of American cities?

4. Give examples in your community of deteriorating neighborhoods (not just residential uses) that have recovered, or of neighborhoods deteriorating because of negative factors that can be changed.

CHAPTER SUMMARY

This chapter has discussed the clusters of similar land uses called neighborhoods. As noted in Chapter 7, land uses tend to form clusters of similar uses, drawn together by their mutual need for the characteristics of a particular location or place in the pattern of the city.

Because real estate is not movable, its value is influenced by the location of the property as well as its characteristics. Location is the combination of all the influences on land use that are characteristic of a particular place in a community. A neighborhood is simply an area of similar uses and similar locational influences.

Neighborhood boundaries are sometimes set by physical objects (freeways) or political borders (city limits). In other cases, one group of uses will blend into another with no definable boundary. Neighborhood size varies with the use and location.

The study of neighborhoods is important because changes that eventually affect individual values are first visible at the neighborhood level. Investors and homeowners need to interpret neighborhood changes early enough to protect their investments.

Examples of forces that change neighborhoods include physical elements such as age and weather, political factors like school quality and taxation, social factors including group conflicts and group attitudes, and numerous economic influences. Often, the forces behind changes are complex or obscure. Thus, the early *effects* of these forces usually are the first indication of change.

The physical condition of properties is a sensitive indication of change because both age and weather cause deterioration. The rate of turnover of occupants and owners is also a measure of stability. Other barometers of neighborhood trends are changes in uses and density of occupancy.

Aging of property is an especially important force because of its constant negative pressure. Neighborhoods and properties start out new, become mature, and frequently decay in a predictable cycle. The length of time of the cycle varies and so does the end result. Some decayed neighborhoods are redeveloped to a new use, either by private or governmental effort. Others become stagnant slums.

Some areas, however, neither change their major use nor slide into blight. Rather, they extend the neighborhood cycle into a new phase of rehabilitation, which repairs and restores the old structures and brings the neighborhood back to its mature, stable stage again. Some American cities have older neighborhoods that have gone through a number of such rehabilitation and decay cycles.

Not every decaying neighborhood can be preserved. However, interest in neighborhood preservation is increasing. The process involves locating those forces that hurt the neighborhood and correcting them. Thus, aging is met by renovation efforts. Economic pressures for land changes can, rightly or wrongly, be blocked by zoning or redirected to limit the impact of change.

IMPORTANT TERMS AND CONCEPTS

Change in use	*Neighborhood cycle*
Deterioration or decay	*Neighborhood obsolescence*
Forces for change:	*Preservation*
Economic	*Rehabilitation cycle*
Physical	
Political	
Social	

REVIEWING YOUR UNDERSTANDING

1. A cluster of properties of relatively similar land use and value is a:
   a. neighborhood
   b. location
   c. city
   d. block

2. The value of a property at a particular location is created by which force?
   a. political
   b. economic
   c. physical
   d. all of the above

3. A political factor that causes a neighborhood to change is a(n):
   a. earthquake
   b. change in lifestyles
   c. rezoning
   d. new transportation route

4. An economic factor that causes a neighborhood to change is:
   a. an earthquake
   b. change in lifestyles
   c. rezoning
   d. a new transportation route

5. Which of the following can establish neighborhood boundaries?
   a. rivers
   b. zoning
   c. private deed restrictions
   d. all of the above

6. An ideal stable residential neighborhood would have:
   a. no turnovers
   b. high turnovers
   c. reasonable turnovers
   d. high percentage of commercial properties

7. All neighborhoods will:
   a. decline
   b. age
   c. stabilize
   d. appreciate

8. High turnover, falling prices, and deferred maintenance are signs of what phase in the life cycle of a neighborhood?
   a. beginning
   b. stabilization
   c. deterioration
   d. rehabilitation

9. When an attempt is made to save a residential neighborhood from decay, which of the following requires the most in new construction costs?
   a. preservation
   b. prevention
   c. rehabilitation
   d. reconciliation

10. A study of changes in city growth patterns, coupled with shifts in neighborhood uses, helps to predict:
    a. changes in values of properties located in the neighborhood
    b. future appreciation rates
    c. good investment opportunities
    d. all of the above

11. The reason people say that "location, location, and location" are the three factors that determine property value is:
    a. people cannot find property without knowing its location
    b. real estate has a fixed location
    c. demand for real estate cannot move from place to place
    d. buyers typically must choose the particular location, regardless of other property characteristics

12. Proximity to employment is irrelevant in studying neighborhoods.
    a. true
    b. false

13. Many residential neighborhoods have _____ defined boundaries.
    a. very clearly
    b. vaguely
    c. physically
    d. legally

14. Residential neighborhoods are typically considered to contain about 1,000 households:
    a. true
    b. false

15. Compared to the boundaries of residential neighborhoods, commercial neighborhood boundaries are:
    a. typically more precise
    b. typically much less precise
    c. more likely to be set by physical features
    d. much more influenced by social issues

16. The exact same home, built at three different locations in the same subdivision, will always have the same value.
    a. true
    b. false

17. A physical force that causes real estate values in a neighborhood to change is:
    a. population trends
    b. weather and the elements
    c. lifestyle changes
    d. business cycles

18. The greatest influence for neighborhood change comes primarily from:
    a. national trends
    b. regional factors
    c. local factors
    d. physical changes

19. Preservation refers to:
    a. maintaining a neighborhood
    b. rebuilding a neighborhood
    c. demolishing a neighborhood
    d. investing in a neighborhood

20. Neighborhood changes appear first at the:
    a. end of the neighborhood life cycle
    b. center of the neighborhood
    c. edge of the neighborhood
    d. recovery stage

21. The first phase of a neighborhood life cycle is:
    a. stability
    b. development
    c. decline
    d. rebirth

22. Assuming no redevelopment, the last phase of a neighborhood life cycle is:
    a. stability
    b. decline and/or slum
    c. steady maturity
    d. increasing values

23. Neighborhood change is usually:
    a. welcomed by all residents
    b. occurring in some manner at all times
    c. accomplished swiftly
    d. not reflected in property values

24. The value of a particular parcel of real estate is *most* influenced by:
    a. national trends
    b. state trends
    c. city trends
    d. neighborhood trends

25. The main reason real estate investors should take the time to study neighborhood trends is the impact these trends have on future cash flows and property values.
    a. true
    b. false

CASE & POINT

Neighborhood Preservation: Two Viewpoints

Viewpoint 1—Government Aid Approach

When a community decides that a neighborhood should be preserved, then the resources of the entire community should be put to work. One could just wait to see if the neighborhood recovers by itself, but many do not. Instead, an active effort is required. Aging and obsolescence can be countered by maintenance and remodeling. Property owners who are willing to do this should be encouraged and provided with the necessary funds by loans or outright grants and other public assistance. Owners or tenants who refuse to maintain their properties must be persuaded to do so by social pressure or legal force.

In addition, government resources must be focused to help stabilize the neighborhood. Examples include more frequent street sweeping, increased police patrol, more street lighting, diversion of through traffic, and added speed bumps or stop signs. Code enforcement may be increased to reduce illegal changes in use or increases in density, as well as encourage renovation and maintenance. Government's use of tax dollars can result in a good return for taxpayers.

Viewpoint 2—Free Market Approach

Keep government out of the neighborhood preservation business! The free market of supply and demand will be a better (more honest and more neutral) determinant of the highest and best use of land than will a government agency. Given a reasonable amount of time, the profit motive will stimulate maintenance of an existing use or a transition to a more economically feasible use. Government's track record of mandated neighborhood preservation is a tale of waste, mismanagement, corruption, blown up (razed) housing projects, and silly economics.

Indeed, because local government officials are more responsive to the opinions of local voters, they do not do what makes economic sense. Instead, they tend to be biased in favor of the existing land users, as opposed to a change to a higher and better use. This means government tends to resist change. But when a population is growing, or demographics are changing, or major transportation shifts are occurring, one cannot resist all change. Therefore, the government should leave neighborhoods alone and let the forces of supply and demand do the allocation.

CHAPTER 9
HOUSING MARKETS

PREVIEW

Chapter 9 explores factors that influence residential property values. Section 9.1 discusses the demand for housing and what causes changes in demand. Section 9.2 focuses on the supply of housing, including new construction and existing structures. Section 9.3 reviews the effects of governmental actions on the market for residential property. The Case & Point at the end of the chapter discusses the political controversy over gated housing developments. When you have completed this chapter, you will be able to:

1. List the major forces influencing supply and demand for residential real estate.

2. Discuss how to obtain forecasts of national and local housing market trends.

3. List the major effects of governmental activity in the housing market.

This information will help you to anticipate changes in residential markets in your area.

Housing Markets

Communities contain many different land uses, but the most common is residential housing. Housing land use includes homes, apartments, hotels, motels, and boarding homes. This chapter concentrates on homes and apartments. In previous chapters, it was noted how the allocation of land in a mixed capitalistic economy occurs mostly in the marketplace. There buyers and sellers interact, and eventually a price is determined and a real estate sale takes place. Government has a powerful influence on the final outcome of a real estate sale and the future use of the property. In this chapter attention is focused on two main topics: (1) How do the laws of supply and demand influence the residential housing market? and (2) What impact does government intervention have on the housing market?

9.1 The Demand for Housing

The demand for housing should be studied from two points of view. The first view looks at total demand, or the numbers of housing units needed in a given market. The second view looks at the composition of housing, such as unit size, age, location, condition, and whether the units are intended for owner occupancy or for rent. Housing analysis involves numbers and preferences.

The demand for housing is influenced by three major factors: (1) population and demographics, (2) effective income and related credit issues, and (3) tastes and lifestyles.

Population

The most important influence on housing demand is population. Put simply, housing is for people, and their presence or absence affects housing demand. Thus, major growth in community population must be followed by growth in the number of housing units.

Demography

Sheer numbers of people are not the only influence on the demand for housing. A second issue is *demography*, which is a breakdown of the composition of a population according to age, sex, occupation, income level, and other socioeconomic variables. Demography is important because people of different demographic characteristics have different housing needs. For example, young children live with their parents. By the time they are 18 or so, some have moved into their own apartments. By age 30, the great majority have moved into a housing unit of their own.

Therefore, two neighborhoods with the same total populations, but with different demography, will have different housing needs. One neighborhood might contain mostly older, retired people living in apartments. Some might be couples and some single persons. Only a few would have any children living at home. Another neighborhood might be made up of single-family homes occupied by middle-aged, middle-income families. This second neighborhood would have far more children and thus larger families. Although the population is the same in both neighborhoods, the number of housing units would be less in the second, as a result of the larger average family size. The neighborhoods would also differ in terms of the need for more or fewer schools, shops, and public transportation.

The Importance of Population Trends

Of all the factors that influence housing demand, population is the most important. Luckily, population information is readily available. Demographic change is especially easy to follow because of the time delay before babies become adults. Researchers can forecast the demography of the next 10 years by adding 10 years to the present age composition of a population and then adjusting for births, deaths, and in-and-out migration, both domestic and foreign. Migration varies greatly by region, so forecasts are more reliable in slowly changing areas than in rapidly changing areas.

Each region has its own demographic breakdown, and future changes in each will be different. In some areas, the children will grow up and want apartments. In others, the middle-aged couples will grow older, find big homes burdensome, and put their houses up for sale. In another area, the young apartment dwellers may be marrying, having children, and seeking larger dwelling units. For the nation as a whole, the 1980s had a strong housing demand as the baby boomers of the 1950s became the homebuyers of the 1980s.

However, many forecasted that the 1990s could be different as the fewer "pill babies" of the 1960s and 1970s come of homeowner age. The drop in the forecasted number of household formations in the 1990s led some economists to forecast that in some regions the housing market would become a buyer's market, in sharp contrast to the seller's market of the 1980s, and in some cases this did occur. But it must be remembered that local real estate trends can differ from national trends. In certain areas, such as California, Florida, and Texas, massive foreign immigration generated a sharp increase in housing needs. By the mid-2000s, housing demand was strong in most of the United States due to an expanding population, and fueled by low interest rates and liberal financing.

Divorce Rate

The high rate of divorce in the United States also influences housing demand. With no increase in population, an increase in the divorce rate will create need for additional housing units. If the divorced person remarries, the additional demand is temporary; if the person decides to remain unmarried, the demand increase is permanent. Uncoupling by unmarried people living together can have the same result as a divorce.

In high-divorce-rate states, such as California, the divorce rate is a major factor contributing to the demand for housing. The divorce and uncoupling rate is seen by some as offsetting the decline in demand attributable to fewer household formations as the median age of the population rises. Needless to say, this trend is not well received in some circles!

Sources of Information about Population and Demography Trends

Population and demographic breakdowns are frequently available from county or state planning offices. Their projections range from 10 to 50 years. The longer-range forecasts, however, are less reliable. Good information on population characteristics is compiled every 10 years when the national housing and population censuses are taken. The government tries to estimate and update the information each year. When attempting to gather this information, be sure to check with the U.S. Department of Housing and Urban Development, local universities, utility companies, planning departments, or private research firms to see that research has already been done.

Income

The second major item influencing housing demand is income. People who lack money cannot afford adequate housing, however great their housing needs. When people have a housing need, and if their income is sufficient to pay the costs of housing, they create an effective demand for housing. For some people, too many bills to pay or mouths to feed restrict the money available for housing. Thus, when analyzing income as a factor in housing demand, one focuses on that portion of people's total income available for housing use.

Income levels, like population, affect not only total housing demand but also the composition of that demand. Higher incomes often lead people to leave rental units and buy homes or condominiums. People of lower incomes sometimes find they must share housing accommodations with their parents or other people, which is called "doubling up." When their income increases, they frequently move out and seek a dwelling of their own, a process called "undoubling."

Income Changes

A rise in income can cause a change in the type of unit and amenities demanded. Examples include the addition of swimming pools, family rooms, extra bathrooms, and the like. A decline in income, however, leads to more modest housing and perhaps to doubling up. Income levels must also be compared to current housing costs. In the 1980s housing costs rose more rapidly than income. Although the demand for housing increased during this period, this affordability problem kept demand from rising further. But in the early to mid-1990s, housing prices leveled off or declined in some areas, while incomes held steady. This led to an increase in house affordability.

Then by the mid-2000s, housing prices soared much faster than incomes, and affordability became a major problem.

Availability of Credit

Buying a home is the largest single purchase most people make, and few people have the resources to pay cash for a home. The availability and cost of mortgage credit has an important influence on people's ability to buy, and, therefore, it has an impact on the demand for housing. Lower mortgage interest rates have the effect of increasing demand for housing at given levels of income.

A significant increase in housing demand in the past century has occurred because of liberal changes in mortgage credit. Real estate loans have gone from two- to five-year interest-only loans, renewed at the lender's discretion, to 30- to 40-year fully amortized loans. Special loan features, such as below-market adjustable "teaser" rates and interest-only loans, plus other innovations, have allowed many people to acquire a home they otherwise would not have been able to afford. The massive housing boom that followed World War II was aided by the Federal Housing Administration (FHA) and other government programs that liberalized financing standards.

It is clear that future changes in mortgage credit will also affect housing demand. Any U.S. capital shortages in the future will bring hard times to the real estate housing market. Economists closely watch the U.S. savings rate and the rate of foreign investment for signs of shift. If the savings rate rises and/or foreign investment in the U.S. capital market increases, that will spell good news for the housing market. If the opposite occurs, hard times could hit the housing market. The size of the U.S. budget deficit also has an impact on the availability and cost of mortgage money. If the U.S. government must finance a large deficit, it can crowd out the private sector, driving up interest rates. If plentiful affordable housing is a national goal, society will need to establish capital priorities and reorganize financial institutions so that mortgage credit can remain affordable. Starting in the late 1980s and carrying through today (2005), structural changes in the real estate industry via lower down, or no-down, payment requirements, longer amortization periods, more liberal qualifying ratios, and a fluid and active secondary market, have helped drive up the percentage of home ownership.

Changes in Taste

The third major factor influencing housing demand is taste or lifestyle. The most basic need for housing is little more than shelter from animals and the elements. As people seek a better standard of living, they respond to their own desire or their friends' expectations of what life ought to be. Thus, where people choose to live is not only a function of income and credit but also of personal preference. For example, some people choose to place most of their wealth in their home, whereas others might choose a modest principal residence, plus a getaway vacation home. Still others decide to spend the minimum on housing and use the extra money for investments, leisure, or hobbies.

Can Consumer Taste and Lifestyles Be Forecasted?

No one can say how long a particular fancy will last or how widespread it will become. The only certainty is change itself. However, real estate analysts should constantly monitor the market for change. Students of marketing suggest that taste changes appear first in people who are fashion conscious, then trickle down to the general population. Will housing styles be as volatile as clothing fashion? Will Santa Fe and Mediterranean housing motifs be like the miniskirt? Are huge houses on small lots in, and condos out? No one knows for sure, but because of tradition and the long life of homes, changes in housing taste tend to occur slowly. This usually allows builders to adjust their inventory so as not to be stuck with unsold, unappealing homes. For existing homes, updating and remodeling are ways to maintain appeal and value.

One additional note: a major reason for the increase in new home prices has been the buyer's desire to have an increase in square footage. If today's new homes were only 1,500 square feet like the homes built in the 1970s, the cost would be considerably less than the 2,500+ square foot homes of the 2000s.

Special Interest Topic

$$$ Affordability Index $$$

The National Association of REALTORS® and the California Association of REALTORS® have constructed a housing affordability index. The index comprises these three basic elements:

1. Determine the median home price for the area. Median means half of the sale prices were above and half of the sale prices were below.

2. Select the prevailing interest rates on standard home loans. Usually defined as a 20 percent down, 80 percent conventional home loan, most often using fixed rate loans.

3. Determine the household income level for the area.

Calculating the Affordability Index

1. Determine the median price home, say $400,000.

2. Calculated the loan payment for an 80% loan at the current interest rate, at say 6%. Then 400,000 × 80% = 320,000 loan @ 6% for 30 years = $1, 918.56 payment for principal and interest. Then add in monthly property taxes and insurance for a PITI monthly payment of say $2,500.

3. Calculate the monthly income needed to qualify for a monthly PITI payment of $2,500 using 30% qualifying ratio (payment should not exceed 30% of your monthly income). Then $2,500 ÷ .30 = $8,333 × 12 mos. = $100,000 (actual $99,999) annual income needed to qualify for a $320,000 loan, and a $400,000 home.

4. Then using census data, determine how many households have incomes of $100,000 or more, say 30,000 households. Next, determine the total number of households in the area, be it city, county, state or national; say the area has 100,000 households. Then the affordability index is calculated as follows:

$$\frac{30,000 \quad \text{qualifying households}}{100,000 \quad \text{total households}} = 30\% \text{ affordability index}$$

This means that only 30% of the households in the area can afford to buy the median priced home. A high percentage is good news for the local housing market, while a low percentage is not. Current national and local affordability index ratings are published in REALTOR® magazines and available on their websites.

REVIEWING YOUR UNDERSTANDING

The Demand for Housing

1. What are three major forces influencing housing demand?

2. How does demography affect housing demand?

3. How does mortgage credit affect housing demand?

4. What do people's tastes have to do with housing demand?

9.2 The Supply of Residential Housing

It is important to note that housing differs from many other economic commodities because a very large percentage of the demand is met by the supply of units already in existence. In boom years, new construction has added around 2 percent per year to our national housing stock. Most local areas experience a similar percentage increase. The existing stock is thus 98 percent of all the housing supply in any particular year. In summary, economists consider the supply of real estate housing fixed in the short run. Therefore, change in supply is viewed as a slow process occurring over a long period of time. The supply of housing must be studied from two viewpoints: (1) the total number of units and (2) the quality or suitability of the units.

Evaluation of Supply

The supply of housing at any future time will consist of units currently available, minus those units lost as a result of fires, demolition, and conversions to other uses, and then increased by buildings con-

Table 9.1 Changes in Housing Stock, Sometown

	21,214	Existing stock, end of previous year
Less	− 137	Demolitions during current year
	21,077	
Less	− 7	Housing units converted to other uses
	21,070	
Plus	+ 4	Other units converted to residences
	21,074	
Plus	+ 38	Added units to existing structures
	21,112	
Plus	+ 393	New construction
	21,505	Existing stock, end of current year

verted to housing and by new construction. The process is illustrated in Table 9.1.

Demolition and Destruction

In a changing community, all land use will eventually become the wrong use of the site at some future time. Changes in the community almost guarantee that this will happen. As a better use comes along, land values rise. The existing building decreases in value as it gets older and decreases more if the existing use is affected by new buildings with better uses. At a certain point, it becomes economically profitable to tear down the old building and build a new one to reflect the new highest and best use of the land. At this point the old structure has reached the end of its economic life. This economic life can end *long* before the building has reached the end of its physical life, depending on its location and the rate of change of the community.

Not all buildings are torn down because they have reached the end of their economic lives. Some are destroyed by fire, earthquakes, and other disasters. Some buildings are demolished in order to build public improvements such as highways and schools, or for urban renewal. In many American communities, demolition for urban renewal and highway purposes noticeably reduces the existing housing stock.

Thus, in forecasting future housing supply, analysts do not assume that the existing stock will be there forever. Some of the units reach the end of their physical lives. Other units will be torn down at the end of their economic lives for construction of nonresidential properties. The probable rate of demolition for various public purposes must also be taken into account. In some communities, the number of homes demolished to make way for new public improvements exceeds the number demolished because of a loss in economic life. Fortunately, public projects are planned far in advance, and their impact can be anticipated.

Conversion and Its Effects on Supply

In addition to demolition, the housing stock is changed by conversions. Conversions can increase the number of housing units by converting houses or other structures into apartments or flats. On the other hand, some conversions may change a residential unit into an office, medical center, or other nonresidential use, and this reduces the housing supply. One must combine the additions and subtractions to determine what net effect conversions have on the local housing market.

In general, conversion is not a major force in the change of housing supply. Data on past conversions are obtainable from the same building permit sources as demolition and construction data.

New Construction

New construction varies greatly from year to year and, especially, from area to area. It is also the largest element in the yearly change in housing supply. New construction occurs only when the required resources are available. These are the classic four elements of land, labor, capital, and entrepreneurial skills. Similarly, the costs of obtaining these resources must be in balance with each other and with the housing prices found in the marketplace. Changes in the availability of these resources will change their prices and affect the ability to build for a profit. Past experience demonstrates that shortages in these resources do occur. For example, land shortages can result from environmental restrictions or governmental attitudes toward the zoning of land. Labor shortages can result from attempts to increase housing construction beyond the limits of the available trained work force. Capital shortages, or a so-called "credit crunch," consisting of a shrinking money supply and high interest rates, have restricted new housing construction. Shortages of capital also show up as shortages of raw materials, because the raw materials require plants, mines, wells, and the like to produce them. Entrepreneurial shortages are less common in this country because the nature of house construction encourages people in the housing industry to learn development skills. Other countries with different social attitudes, however, have had difficulty in obtaining sufficient people with necessary development skills and knowledge.

Forecasts of new construction thus have to consider the availability of related resources. In fact, the major factors influencing recent variations in new construction (see Tables 9.2 and 9.3) have been changes in the cost and availability of capital and the current state of the local economy.

Future Supply Trends

Many observers say that increasing restrictions on new construction and lack of key resources will create a housing shortage in the future. Increasing shortages have driven up the cost of land, capital, labor, and many of the raw materials that are needed by the construction industry. With rising costs, a developer will build new housing only when home prices are expected to go up as fast or faster than costs. Some forecast that future housing costs and prices will continue to increase faster than buyer incomes, thereby causing a reduction in the demand for new housing construction. The renovation and remodeling of the existing housing stock may be a more significant factor for the future housing supply than has been true for the last several decades.

Some advocates say that the construction of second units (Granny units) is the best solution for a housing shortage. However, this idea has met with resistance by local governments and residents.

Is the Housing Suitable?

At any given time, the housing supply consists of existing dwelling units. You remember from Chapter 5 that two special features of real estate are its long life and fixed location. Thus, the suitability of existing housing becomes most important.

What About Housing Condition?

Because of the long life of housing structures, the condition of existing housing is an important issue. Few houses are built of materials that will last for a long period of time without maintenance. Thus, housing units are vulnerable to deterioration over their

Table 9.2 New Housing Units Authorized in California (in thousands)

Year	Total	Multiple	Single
1980	144,987	58,355	86,832
1990	164,394	60,219	104,175
2000	167,682	42,945	105,595
2003	195,682	56,920	138,762

Source: California Statistical Abstract, Department of Finance.

Table 9.3 Median Sales Price of Existing Single-Family Homes, by Region California, 1982-2003

Year	Statewide	Los Angeles	San Diego	San Francisco	Orange County	Central Valley	Palm Springs/ Lower Desert	San Luis Obispo
1982	$111,800	$119,259	$102,665	$128,090	$129,641	$72,200	$85,197	–
1983	114,370	118,543	103,077	133,730	131,456	73,210	94,909	–
1984	114,260	121,270	104,417	134,131	130,668	74,600	90,353	–
1985	119,860	124,787	111,517	145,129	132,758	75,600	84,751	–
1986	133,640	135,393	123,003	166,318	144,441	77,310	87,972	–
1987	142,060	146,630	134,073	176,796	163,218	82,410	95,714	–
1988	168,200	178,889	153,410	212,863	203,860	87,190	97,952	–
1989	196,120	214,831	181,922	260,722	241,708	97,370	112,629	$164,150
1990	193,770	212,130	183,210	259,000	242,358	116,330	118,410	201,730
1991	200,660	218,580	187,510	262,420	239,680	118,730	122,990	190,980
1992	197,030	210,790	183,110	259,250	230,860	119,430	125,140	181,210
1993	188,240	195,430	176,930	256,200	217,210	115,890	120,580	182,520
1994	185,010	189,170	176,010	255,580	214,540	113,370	120,600	169,390
1995	178,160	179,900	171,600	254,450	209,400	108,410	115,140	162,980
1996	177,270	172,886	174,450	266,660	213,370	107,480	110,630	166,090
1997	186,490	176,517	185,210	286,470	229,840	109,140	121,110	179,270
1998	200,100	191,700	207,100	321,070	261,700	114,980	132,840	180,880
1999	217,510	193,960	231,630	363,200	280,900	120,600	133,330	208,290
2000	241,350	215,300	269,410	454,560	316,240	133,380	149,300	248,310
2001	262,350	241,370	296,610	475,890	355,620	157,250	180,990	262,170
2002	316,130	290,300	364,240	517,060	412,650	189,210	223,420	326,710
2003	372,720	354,740	424,880	558,100	487,020	224,830	262,140	381,750

Year	Northern California	Northern Wine Country	Monterey	Ventura	Riverside/ San Bernardino	Santa Barbara	Sacramento	Santa Clara
1982	$87,610	$91,697	$113,890	$130,890	$78,770	$131,333	–	–
1983	85,650	94,723	112,585	128,664	80,424	131,743	–	–
1984	87,448	n.a	120,740	120,687	81,551	132,022	$76,138	–
1985	89,661	98,077	129,119	128,531	85,058	134,979	77,843	–
1986	92,098	111,323	146,057	142,155	92,117	153,289	82,308	–
1987	93,672	119,128	161,787	159,072	96,170	149,064	86,865	–
1988	102,426	132,470	185,658	204,311	106,729	204,984	94,640	–
1989	115,075	160,802	232,191	247,658	124,122	233,071	111,690	$275,270
1990	143,801	179,178	237,732	238,792	132,127	219,578	137,460	268,890
1991	135,020	185,740	233,660	234,930	135,400	215,760	135,500	256,640
1992	137,600	194,030	226,280	222,519	136,230	219,530	133,950	248,260
1993	138,800	190,640	222,750	211,600	134,480	209,340	127,500	246,510
1994	136,960	188,760	225,060	206,640	129,110	217,870	124,970	254,390
1995	136,830	189,250	226,510	199,900	120,950	208,210	119,480	255,260
1996	137,250	182,350	234,250	205,720	115,240	211,940	115,310	273,830

Table 9.3 Median Sales Price of Existing Single-Family Homes, by Region California, 1982-2003 (Continued)

Year	Northern California	Northern Wine Country	Monterey	Ventura	Riverside/ San Bernardino	Santa Barbara	Sacramento	Santa Clara
1997	141,840	191,340	259,000	219,300	114,340	242,220	116,100	316,250
1998	150,300	211,740	283,370	233,770	121,500	243,670	123,780	364,740
1999	161,830	245,600	333,810	254,950	128,670	272,740	131,500	399,380
2000	179,120	304,960	403,610	295,080	138,560	302,260	145,200	521,240
2001	196,510	344,800	426,270	322,560	156,690	335,540	173,150	524,320
2002	236,730	374,610	451,220	372,400	176,460	376,350	210,230	547,500
2003	283,990	425,490	491,600	462,520	220,940	402,740	247,630	556,470

Los Angeles: Arcadia, Beverly Hills, Citrus Valley, Culver City, Diamond Bar, Downey, Foothill, Glendale, Hacienda-Rowland, Los Angeles, LA Pacific West, Malibu, Montebello, Palos Verdes Peninsula, Rancho Southeast Pasadena/San Marino Board, San Fernando Valley, Santa Monica, South Bay, Southwest LA, Venice and West San Gabriel Valley.

San Francisco Bay Area: Berkeley, Contra Costa, Marin, Oakland, Palo Alto, San Francisco, San Jose, San Mateo-Burlingame, Santa Clara, Solano and Southern Alameda.

San Diego: Coronado, East San Diego, North San Diego (Carlsbad, Oceanside, San Dieguito). San Diego and South San Diego Bay Cities.

Orange County: Irvine, East Orange, Huntington Beach-Fountain Valley, Orange Coast, Orange Coast Pacific West AOR and South Orange.

Central Valley: Bakersfield, Fresno, Lodi, Merced, Modesto, Sacramento, Stockton and Visalia.

Palm Springs/Lower Desert: Palm Desert, Palm Springs and Desert Communities West.

Monterey: Monterey Peninsula and Santa Cruz.

Northern Wine Country: Mendocino, Napa and Sonoma (North Bay AOR).

Northern California: Chico, Clear Lake, Humboldt, Paradise, Placer, Siskiyou and Tahoe Sierra.

Riverside/San Bernardino: Corona-Norco, East Inland Empire, Inland Empire West, Inland Valleys and Rim of the World.

Ventura: Camarillo, Conejo Valley, Oxnard, Simi Valley and Ventura.

Santa Barbara: Lompoc, Santa Barbara and Santa Maria.

High Desert Area: Antelope Valley, Barstow, Palmdale and Victor Valley.

Pismo Coast, Atascadero, Paso Robles and San Luis Obispo Board of Realtors report home sales for the statewide sample but are not reported in a separate region.

n.a. Not available

Note: Movement in regional sales prices should not be interpreted as measuring changes in the cost of a standard home. Prices are influenced by changes in costs and variations in the characteristics and size of homes actually sold.

California Association of Realtors
Research and Economics
(213)739-8200
http://www.car.org/

lifetimes. The extent to which this has happened is of major interest to the real estate economist. Many older homes are not receiving adequate maintenance and are gradually deteriorating. When this happens to an entire neighborhood, a blight sets in. The decaying condition of the neighborhood seems to deter people from further maintenance, so that the blighted area gets worse and bigger. This has led to the complete abandonment of whole blocks of buildings in areas of cities like New York, Detroit, and Cleveland. Such abandoned houses effectively reduce the supply of housing units because people refuse to move into the area. This condition, which need not occur, is being carefully studied by urban policymakers and is a central issue for the future.

What About Housing Features?

Buyers and renters tend to seek amenities, which are the benefits of ownership or occupancy. These can include physical features such as space, age, condition, and appointments. Some features can be measured by objective scales or techniques. Other amenities, however, are not so objective. They depend on taste, status, and public opinion. These features are often faddish as well as hard to measure. Forecasting residential markets is thus complicated by the difficulty of forecasting the attitudes of buyers, sellers, renters, and landlords toward amenities. Buyers and sellers in the past have periodically changed their views on the importance of such amenities as newness, unconventional architecture, and suburban versus central living. Future changes must be considered in forecasting the housing market.

One example of this concept is the issue of the density of occupancy. The federal government has used one person per room as a housing goal. Some segments of the housing market are seeking lower density, and others are choosing higher densities to free income for other purposes. Over the last 20 years, the trend in new home construction has been to reduce average density, or increase the number of rooms relative to the number of occupants.

How will density be in the future? Will crushing home prices force extended families to stay together and share housing costs? Some new subdivisions in the Inland Empire of California are advertising "up to eleven bedrooms."

As buildings age, it becomes more likely that some aspect of the housing unit will not suit people's changing desires for amenity features. Major changes in the features, design, or equipment of houses occur surprisingly slowly. However, the lifetime of an average house is long enough that some elements of design become out of date, old-fashioned, unworkable, inefficient, or irreparable. As this happens, the housing unit becomes increasingly obsolete unless corrected by remodeling. Thus, a study of neighborhoods must consider the amount of obsolete features and remodeling rate.

What About Housing Location?

Another unique characteristic of real estate is its fixed location. Because of this, it is possible for changes in the community to make a certain use of the land no longer suitable, that is, locationally obsolete. Thus, a building that is nearly new, but at a changing location, could become so obsolete as to be torn down, causing a fair amount of economic waste. This waste can be reduced if the building has the flexibility to be converted to another profitable use.

The problem of fixed location is compounded by the long life of buildings as compared with the rate of change of the community in which the buildings are located. This has been especially true of rapidly growing communities in the western United States. This type of obsolescence, which shortens the economic life of the building, has a noticeable influence on the rate of demolition in the affected community. Thus, over the years, as a community's population mix or demography changes, the housing supply must meet these demand changes to maintain equilibrium.

Suitable for Whom?

In general, the long life of residential real estate means that the building must have sufficient flexibility to meet the changing needs of a long-term occupant or the needs of a series of users. This need for flexibility is a major reason for the slow and cautious rate of change in building design. Only the rich can afford to risk large sums to build a radical design that others may not be willing to buy.

Long life also means that the product can expect to be occupied by people of differing backgrounds and income. Because older units are generally in poorer condition, more obsolete, and less desirable than new ones, their values are generally less than new ones. Thus, housing units are typically occupied by lower-income users as the units get older. Most housing for lower-income occupants comes from this process, which is called *filtering*.

Filtering

Filtering is a central part of the residential market, given the long life of dwellings and the changing needs and tastes of people. Problems that develop during the filtering process have to do with the condition and obsolescence of the unit. Housing units are clearly capable of periodic renovation and renewal if social and economic circumstances so dictate. The American student of real estate should realize that housing units in many other countries are expected to last hundreds of years. In many European cities it is not unusual to live in a building that is more than 300 years old. These buildings are given repair and periodic remodeling and provide adequate housing at costs less expensive than new construction. The existence of slums in the United States is *primarily* a breakdown in the ongoing repair and renovation process that dwelling units must receive as they filter through a series of occupants and owners.

REVIEWING YOUR UNDERSTANDING

The Supply of Housing

1. What are the two central issues or viewpoints of housing supply?

2. How important is demolition to housing supply?

3. What is the impact of new construction on housing supply and what causes the rate of new construction to vary?

9.3 Governmental Housing Programs

Why is the government involved in housing programs? The reason frequently given for governmental intervention in the housing market is to change some unsatisfactory aspects of the usual working of supply and demand. Examples cited to justify government regulations include the need for a disclosure requirement because of the buyer's inadequate knowledge, the need to prevent discrimination by sellers or brokers, and the need to provide housing for low-income people. Government intervention in the housing market comes in the form of either housing regulations or outright financial support.

Regulating the Housing Market

One set of governmental actions restricts or regulates the housing market. These policies are intended to halt some action that the market would otherwise allow. Zoning and planning ordinances are common examples. In most communities zoning regulations forbid commercial uses in a residential zone. This regulation follows a belief that someone would put in a commercial use if it were not prohibited and that such a use would have detrimental effects on the residential area.

Others argue that profit motives would cluster similar land uses in the absence of zoning. Each owner, seeking to maximize property values, would only locate next to similar users. Therefore, a commercial building placed in a residential area would not be the highest and best use and would not normally occur. If by chance it did occur, market forces would soon render the building uneconomical and make it a candidate for demolition and another use.

Subdivision laws are another type of government restriction. Local, state, and federal subdivision laws require complicated and expensive approval procedures. These regulations are government's response to the belief, right or wrong, that some developers would put together an inadequate subdivision and that buyers would be unaware of the deceit and later would be unable to correct the problem by the market pressures of supply and demand. See Chapter 13, "Land-Use Controls," for more details.

Building and housing standards are also regulated by government codes. These codes specify *minimum* housing construction standards. This again assumes that some builders would provide inadequate or dangerous construction if not watched and that most buyers are not knowledgeable enough to do the watching. These regulations, in theory, are intended to protect uninformed buyers.

As discussed further in Chapter 13, "Land-Use Controls," regulatory governmental actions in the real estate market have sharply increased in recent years. No-growth and slow-growth policies by some local governments have restricted the supply of housing. This in turn has driven the price of the existing housing stock out of the reach of many would-be home buyers. The future will probably see even more government regulations. Most other industrialized countries have more restrictions on the housing market than the United States and offer some specific clues to future changes in the United States.

Encouraging Housing Production

The second group of governmental policies attempts to support or encourage housing production. These policies include programs to reduce shortages of land, labor, or capital. Examples are urban renewal for land assembly, organized apprenticeship programs for skilled labor training, and the huge program of federal home loan insurance.

Federal actions affecting financing have been an especially important (and changing) factor in the residential market. Government actions supporting housing production often seek to correct housing

Special Interest Topics

Rent Controls—Do They Make Economic Sense?

Rent control is a controversial topic with emotions and misconceptions running rampant on both sides of the issue. From a purely economic point of view, rent controls make little sense. The issue has been repeatedly studied by both liberal and conservative economists, and most agree that rent controls do not solve housing problems. Rents are high because demand for apartment housing is high and supply is inadequate. The solution is to either decrease demand for rental units or increase the supply.

Rent controls do neither. Rent controls artificially depress rent levels, which in turn increases the quantity demanded instead of reducing it. Rent controls reduce returns and yields on apartment investments, thereby discouraging the construction of new units or the conversion of large homes into apartments. In short, rent controls tend to perpetuate the ill they are supposed to cure!

Condo Conversions—Good or Bad?

One of the most interesting developments has been the conversion of existing apartment buildings to condominiums. The conversion rate is spurred by:

1. An increase in demand for owner-occupied housing.

2. An opportunity to gain greater profits for apartment owners whose rents have not kept pace with costs and inflation, especially in areas hit by rent controls.

3. An inability to build new housing because of environmental and other controls.

When apartments are converted to condominiums, the supply of housing for purchase increases, while the supply of housing for rent decreases.

Several local governments have enacted ordinances restricting the rate of conversions because of the concern that lower-income people will be priced out of the rental market. When condo conversions are restricted, government is essentially declaring that the demand for rental units shall take precedence over the demand for owner-occupied housing—that is, renters shall have priority over owners.

shortages in less profitable parts of the market. These have included housing for the elderly, the poor, college students, and nursing homes.

Many of these government programs have not produced the desired results and have been dropped. Some, like FHA loan insurance, have been so successful that they have encouraged the market to pick up the idea in the form of private loan insurance. When this happens, the need for governmental action is reduced, and the program, in some cases, may be discontinued. In general, despite changes in the various programs, the overall degree of governmental involvement in the housing market has been increasing. The most obvious examples have been the efforts to meet capital shortages and the subsidies for low-income and elderly housing. Both programs are expected to continue to grow. It is clear, however, that the exact form of governmental action will change from year to year.

It is important to stay abreast of changes in government programs in order to know which are likely to affect housing supply and demand. It is also important to remember that many government housing programs fail to achieve their goals and in some cases have been harmful to local real estate values. A real estate analyst should study all existing and proposed government housing programs to estimate what impact they will have on local housing prices.

REVIEWING YOUR UNDERSTANDING

Governmental Housing Programs

1. What are the two ways government intervenes in the housing market?

2. Give two examples of government actions that restrict the supply of housing and two ways government helps to increase the supply of housing.

3. In the future, will government increase or decrease its role in the housing market? Why?

CHAPTER SUMMARY

The residential market is made up predominantly of homes and apartments. The demand for housing is influenced by population and demography, income and credit terms, and consumer taste and lifestyles. However, housing demand really consists of groups of demand for units of differing ages, locations, sizes, features, and so forth. Housing supply is dominated by the existing stock of housing units. New construction, demolitions, and conversions will alter this supply. Repair and renovation of older units are important to maintain the supply of housing, in light of the long life and fixed location of real estate. The importance of house amenities was also stressed. Governmental programs were shown either to restrict or to help market behavior. An overriding concern is the lack of affordability in the housing market. The problem is especially acute in high-population, high-cost areas such as the urban and coastal sections of California.

IMPORTANT TERMS AND CONCEPTS

Affordability index	*Economic life*
Condo conversions	*Effective income*
Credit availability	*Filtering*
Demand composition	*Housing-unit mix*
Demography	*New construction*
Demolition	*Rent controls*
Doubling up	

REVIEWING YOUR UNDERSTANDING

1. Which of the following is considered a demand variable in the housing market?
   a. construction rates
   b. population change
   c. government growth controls
   d. demolition rate

2. If the supply of housing units is fixed, and demand decreases, the price of homes should:
   a. increase
   b. remain the same
   c. decrease
   d. not react

3. The number of real estate listings by brokers has increased and the number of qualified buyers has decreased. This is a(n):
   a. buyer's market
   b. seller's market
   c. unbalanced market
   d. underbuilt market

4. Which of the following is a supply factor that influences the housing market?
   a. cost of consumer credit
   b. taste and lifestyle
   c. population
   d. no-growth policies by local government

5. The median home price is $450,000, the monthly PITI for an 80% loan is $3,000, and the qualifying ratio is 30%. What household income is required to qualify for the median price home?
   a. $120,000
   b. $108,000
   c. $90,000
   d. none of these

6. When a homeowner trades up to a larger new home, this frees his or her smaller older home for a first-time home buyer. This process is called:
   a. trading down
   b. exchanging
   c. filtering
   d. leveling

7. The increased migration rate to the Sunbelt and West Coast states, coupled with a high divorce rate in these states, should increase the demand for:
   a. housing
   b. growth controls
   c. jobs
   d. all of the above

8. If housing costs rise beyond the income level of one household unit, two or more households may share a home. This process is called:
   a. cohabitating
   b. equity sharing
   c. time sharing
   d. doubling up

9. The study of a population by groupings such as sex, occupation, and income levels is called:
   a. diminution
   b. demography
   c. demonstrats
   d. demostatistics

10. The number of people of entry-level homeowner age can be estimated by adding a certain number of years to the age of the present population, then adjusting for death rates and in-and-out migration.
    a. true
    b. false

11. Which of the following is a direct influence on the demand for housing?
    a. labor supply
    b. construction cost
    c. divorce rate
    d. technological changes in home construction

12. If personal income increases faster than the increase in home prices, affordability will:
    a. increase
    b. decrease
    c. remain the same
    d. cause the demand curve for housing to shift to the left

13. Availability of mortgage credit has a significant impact on the demand for housing. Which of the following should decrease mortgage interest rates?
    a. increase in the U.S. budget deficit
    b. a tighter monetary policy by the Federal Reserve
    c. capital shortages
    d. increase in the U.S. savings rate

14. How people choose to spend their household dollars influences the demand for housing. This variable is called:
    a. taste
    b. demography
    c. crowding out
    d. amenity

15. Which of the following *will not* add to the housing supply?
    a. commercial to residential conversions
    b. new home construction
    c. demolition of housing units
    d. zoning changes that allow an increase in the number of homes per acre

16. The economic life of a building can end before its physical life.
    a. true
    b. false

17. Occasionally, a home's value may be below its outstanding mortgage balance. Which of the following can lead to this "upside-down" situation?
    a. the housing supply exceeds demand
    b. the owners took out a 125% loan
    c. the local economy declined
    d. all of the above

18. When homes in a neighborhood deteriorate, this is called:
    a. blight
    b. downsizing
    c. blockbusting
    d. filtering

19. Over the last 20 years the average density level (people per square foot) of new home construction has:
    a. increased
    b. decreased

20. Which government actions tend to restrict or regulate the housing market?
    a. zoning
    b. subdivision laws
    c. building codes
    d. all of the above

21. Which government actions tend to expand the housing market?
    a. public housing
    b. FHA insurance
    c. income tax deductions for home interest and property taxes
    d. all of the above

22. Rent controls tend to increase the:
    a. quantity of apartment units demanded
    b. supply of apartment units
    c. rate of return on apartments
    d. upgrading of apartments

23. A local law prohibiting the conversion of apartments to condominiums is another way of stating that owners shall have a priority over renters.
    a. true
    b. false

The housing market you are studying is comprised of the following elements: sewer and water moratoriums have been in place for three years, and a large corporation has recently decided to move its headquarters and 500 employees to the city. Construction loan funds are difficult to obtain because of a crisis in the financial markets. A new slowgrowth initiative has qualified for the ballot for the next local election. Citizens are complaining about local traffic congestion. Based on this information alone, answer Questions 24 and 25.

24. In the near future, the greatest increase in values should be in:
    a. unimproved land zoned residential
    b. unimproved land zoned commercial
    c. unimproved land zoned industrial
    d. new homes in a recently completed subdivision

25. In the short run, the value of existing homes should:
    a. increase
    b. decrease
    c. drop sharply
    d. stay the same

CASE & POINT

Gated Communities—American Apartheid?

In some areas, because of the fear of crime, there has been a trend to develop housing in gated developments. In some cities, owners in existing ungated subdivisions have petitioned local government to abandon streets in order to create gated communities. These developments are surrounded by high walls and usually contain higher-priced homes. Within such communities there can be found schools, parks, recreation facilities, and occasionally convenience stores. A common feature is their own security police force. In short, gated communities are a sort of reverse prison, designed to keep so-called undesirables out, instead of a traditional prison that keeps undesirable people locked up.

Gated communities generate many questions:

1. If this trend continues, will the United States end up with housing patterns similar to many Third World countries, where well-to-do and professional people live in guarded homes, surrounded by squalor, poverty, and squatters?

2. If government planners deny the right to create gated communities, will this be an infringement of a person's constitutional right to select the housing of his or her choice?

3. Where does the freedom of choice end and the need for an inclusive community begin?

4. If gated communities are denied in one city but allowed in a nearby city, will the former city end up with all poor people while the latter city ends up with all affluent people?

This politically incorrect topic may ultimately need to be addressed.

CHAPTER 10
COMMERCIAL AND INDUSTRIAL MARKETS

PREVIEW

This chapter discusses the major influences on the value and uses of commercial and industrial property. Section 10.1 and Section 10.2 examine the economic, social, and political forces that affect business real estate. Section 10.3 focuses on commercial properties, and industrial properties are the subject of Section 10.4. The Case & Point at the end of the chapter explores major changes in retailing and the impact on land use. When you have completed this chapter, you will be able to:

1. Explain how economic trends influence the value of business property.

2. List and define the four major forces that determine the selection of commercial sites.

3. Describe the elements that signal a change in commercial real estate markets.

10.1 Business Real Estate

*B*usiness real estate includes both commercial and industrial real property. The benefits of ownership of business real estate differ from the benefits of owner-occupied homes. For the homeowner, in addition to any appreciation potential, the price paid for the home is influenced by the personal benefits of ownership, including amenities such as status, security, pride of ownership, school district, and so on. These amenities are not directly related to the home's ability to produce rent. For business properties, these personal amenities are less important than the specific economic factors that influence the property's ability to generate rent and maintain value.

The business property road to value runs as follows: Economic trends influence current business profits. Business profits in turn determine the business owner's ability to pay rent. Rents then help to determine the property's net operating income. Finally, net operating income establishes a business property's market value. Thus, changes in current economic trends can have a greater near-term impact on business real estate values than on home values, that is, downturns or upturns in real estate value may occur first in the commercial, as opposed to residential, market. (See Figure 10.1.)

Figure 10.1 Road to value.

10.2 Major Economic Characteristics

Demand Is Tied to the Business Cycle

The demand for business real estate is tied to current economic activity. When the economy is booming, sales are up and the need for more commercial and industrial space increases. When business slows down, sales decline and most businesses put expansion plans on hold.

Supply Factors

Changes in the supply of business real estate depend on the rate of new construction, conversions, and demolitions. Because construction takes so long, supply cannot immediately match increases in demand. Business property development projects take years to package. The work needed to meet government requirements is especially time consuming. Also, no-growth and environment groups frequently challenge major development projects in court or by referendums at the polls. Then, once a project is finally started, a "pipeline effect" takes place. Even though a shift in the business cycle may reduce the demand for more business square footage, it is difficult to stop a project in mid-construction. As a result, the business real estate market has a history of building booms, followed by slow construction activity as the excess inventory is worked off.

Financing Is Critical

Because business real estate is often expensive, buyers usually borrow money to purchase property. Borrowing is also a standard investment tool when one seeks leverage and income tax advantages. The availability and cost of financing affect the profitability and value of real estate investments. During severe credit crunches, many proposed developments never get off the drawing board for lack of money.

Because the availability of mortgage money is so important, developers cater to the building preferences of lenders. For example, many lenders favor commercial property occupied by national businesses with good credit ratings. As a result, projects aimed for local, smaller tenants may never get built.

Lenders may dictate building design, layout, or the wording in leases. In many ways, lenders hold veto power over proposed business buildings. This veto power, and a healthy skepticism, can be a valuable check on the overenthusiasm of some developers. On the other hand, 25+ years ago, the savings and loan fiasco and the resulting crisis illustrate how some lenders financed many ill-conceived business real estate developments.

Government Controls

In addition to the restraints that may be imposed by lenders, the development and use of business real estate are subject to government controls. Governmental land-use controls were developed many years ago in response to problems in residential areas and later were broadened to restrict use in commercial and industrial districts. Real estate economists study government requirements because land-use patterns in many areas are dominated more by government controls than by economic forces. Community concern about business property development is more vocal than about any other land use, except for mines, heavy industry, landfills, and power plants.

Income Tax Impact

It is an accepted fact that tax law changes affect investor/owner behavior. Changes in income tax laws have been used to either stimulate or suppress the rate of business real estate development. The Economic Recovery Act of 1981 gave business property owners accelerated depreciation and tax credits to stimulate construction, to help the economy recover from a major recession. Then the Tax Reform Act of 1986 reversed the process by eliminating accelerated depreciation, lengthening straightline depreciation, and enacting passive loss rules, all designed to reduce the rate of business property construction. Any major tax changes in the mid to late 2000s must be watched, as they will also have an impact on the supply and demand for business property.

Buyers and Sellers Are Sophisticated

Contrary to many in the home market, buyers and sellers of business properties are often highly knowledgeable about the real estate market. Both buyers and sellers have access to attorneys, accountants, appraisers, and real estate specialists. Frequently, the buyer or seller is a financial institution, insurance company, or a real estate investment trust. Sophisticated foreign investors also are becoming a powerful force in the U.S. real estate market. These enlightened buyers and sellers frequently insist on using a well-trained, investment-oriented real estate agent. As mentioned in Chapter 5, investors in business properties create a more perfect market by being highly knowledgeable about the product—that is, real estate.

Using Leases

Many investor-owners rent out business properties on long-term leases because the owner wants protection against vacancies and rent losses. The length of the lease and the tenant's credit (or other guarantees against default) are very important to investors. A long-term lease is also important because it is a contract to pay money. Both lenders and investors study the lease carefully. The key elements in the lease are the length of the lease, the rent, the risks, and any special lease insurance or guarantees.

In relying on a long-term lease, one major risk is that the tenant might default. Thus, the stability and credit rating of the tenant are important factors. Buyers usually review the lease to be sure that it is binding, but many leases contain loopholes. In case the tenant defaults on the lease, the prudent investor must study what the value of the real estate would be *without* the lease and also estimate the strength of any lease guarantees.

Default is not the lessor's only risk. A major concern to a landlord is the risk that inflation will reduce the purchasing power of the rent money collected on the lease. Therefore, many business leases allow rent increases to match all or a portion of the rate of inflation. In addition, it is common to require the business tenant to pay the landlord's operating expenses, such as property taxes, building insurance, and maintenance. These are called "net leases," with an escalator clause tied to the rate of inflation. In other cases, the tenant agrees to pay any *increase* in expenses over the initial year.

In the past, problems caused by eminent domain takeovers of private property by government agencies have led many attorneys to insert eminent domain clauses in business leases. These clauses spell out the rights of the parties regarding trade fixtures, such as shelves and other items, attached by the tenant, loss of business and relocation cost provisions, and other related items. Thus, today's business leases are written with much more concern for the effects changing times will have on people and property values than was true just a decade or two ago.

REVIEWING YOUR UNDERSTANDING

Business Real Estate

1. How do changes in economic trends influence business property values?

2. What are three types of risk in leased real estate and how can they be reduced?

3. Explain why purchase money financing is important to business real estate.

10.3 Commercial Property

Commercial property, sometimes called income property, is a broad term that includes various subcategories such as retail, office, lodging, and multiuse buildings that combine both commercial and residential use. Although each subcategory has unique economic characteristics, for simplicity this section discusses general principles that apply to most commercial properties.

What Are the Major Forces?

There are four major forces that have an impact on commercial real estate markets: local community forces, comparative advantage forces, customer convenience forces, and the unique forces of a particular type of business.

Local Community Forces

Local community forces are important to the value of commercial properties because these properties are used to provide goods and services to the local community. Local community forces include trends in population, demography, taste, effective income, and purchasing power.

Increases in local population or income produce additional demand for commercial goods and services. This in turn creates demand for more retail stores, offices, and the like, in proportion to the increased change in purchasing power and population. Increases in other variables such as changes in consumer taste have similar impacts.

Comparative Advantage Forces

Commercial space users want a location where they will have a comparative advantage over their competitors. Comparative advantages are created by favorable items such as transportation, positive government controls, the proper combination of stores, and natural land features.

Transportation influences retail store locations because customers, other than through catalog or Internet sales, must visit a store to purchase goods. The easier to reach (or more accessible) a store, the better the customers like it, and the more likely they will continue their patronage. Locations where people already congregate (e.g., at transportation hubs or nodes) are among the most convenient. Offices and warehouses also need good transportation for access by their customers, employees, suppliers, and shippers.

Government controls also influence commercial locations. Some highly desirable locations may not be zoned for commercial use, which means that less desirable locations must be used because of their commercial zoning. Government controls can also affect the value of a particular location by placing restrictions on lot sizes, yard and parking allowances, building height, setback, and other density items.

A third category of comparative advantage is a favorable *combination of stores*. Simply put, some stores benefit from being near other stores in a proper mix. For example, several high-fashion stores can locate adjacent to one another and have a greater combined sales volume than if they were separated (for example, Rodeo Drive, Beverly Hills). Favorable combinations also exist for office buildings: Legal offices benefit from proximity to one another and to the courthouse; medical offices seek proximity to a hospital.

Finally, *natural features* can be a comparative advantage. Some sites are more level, drawing uses that need level sites. In addition, climate can play a role if there are noticeable local differences in wind, fog, rain, or snow.

Customer Convenience Forces

The differences in how customers shop for various goods and services influence the location needed. Stores that sell *convenience goods*, like razor blades, hosiery, and everyday groceries, must be located close to their customers. Some products (gasoline) should be convenient to the commuter, whereas others (cafeterias, florists) seek convenience to workers and shoppers. Most convenience stores, such as supermarkets that are oriented to homemakers, are located near residential areas.

Stores and offices that offer a specialized product or service have a different relationship to their customer. Specialty businesses find that customers will travel a much greater distance but frequently desire to have numerous alternative choices at one location. Thus, similar *shopping goods* stores often benefit from clustering in favorable combinations, such as car dealers on an "auto row."

The type of contact involved in customer relations has changed considerably. Improvements in communication systems and financial procedures have increased the customer transactions that can occur without face-to-face contact. This change is most noticeable with wholesaling. Improved truck transportation and standard product lines now allow wholesalers to be hundreds of miles away from the retailer, instead of a few city blocks. And increasing numbers of retailers market by Internet, catalogs, or TV ads, and take orders by credit card. Where is the "store" located? Who cares!

Effects of the Type of Business

The type of business activity influences the choice of location. For example, businesses handling inexpensive, bulky products such as sand and gravel need such a large amount of land that location becomes less important than land cost. Retailers of unique products with strong brand loyalty, such as Harley Davidson motorcycles, find that customers will travel long distances to reach them. Service offices such as accountants, appraisers, and consultants may find that they also have flexibility in where they locate. On the other hand, businesses such as real estate brokers must locate close to their customers to maintain visibility and loyalty. In general, the more common the business, the more its locations will be scattered through the community.

What Are the Patterns of Commercial Land Use?

Commercial land use is not uniformly spread throughout a city. Instead, as noted in Chapter 7, there are four general types of commercial neighborhoods or areas: the central business district, linear strips along main streets, local commercial clusters, and shopping and big box centers, and they tend to be concentrated in set areas. All commercial real estate users are concerned with linkage and accessibility. *Linkage* refers to the interrelationship between one business and others. *Accessibility* is the degree of ease by which a store or business can be reached by employees, customers, and suppliers.

The Central Business District

The central business district (CBD) lies at the center of the community's transportation system, nearly always close to the physical origins of the community. In the smallest town, the CBD may consist of stores at the main crossroads. In a very large metropolis, the CBD is many miles in area, divided into specific commercial neighborhoods.

Commercial uses typically cluster at the major intersection or the frontage of the main streets. In small towns, offices locate over retail stores. As the CBD becomes larger, office buildings cluster at locations a short distance from the main intersection.

Trends in the Central Business District

Even with advancements in telecommunications, the need to cluster near other businesses (linkage) is still an important issue to certain companies, which is why the downtown business area tends to maintain high land values. In the past several decades the following trends have occurred in central business districts in most major cities:

1. A huge office building boom in the 1980s changed the skyline of many cities. Since then, most CBD's office construction has slowed.

2. Major department stores have declined in both number and volume of sales. Many have closed and either gone out of business or moved to suburban shopping malls.

3. Movie theaters have closed and moved to the suburbs.

4. Attempts to create downtown malls by closing off streets have for the most part failed to produce good results.

5. Downtown hotels have suffered as more and more business meetings are conducted at airport hotels. In convention cities like San Francisco and Chicago, downtown hotels are still enjoying a brisk business, but many other cities have experienced a decline in the downtown hotel business.

6. Current attempts to revive the central business district include adding or improving rapid transit systems from the suburbs to the central city, the creation of sport complexes and convention centers, and a push to restore multiuse buildings to make it fashionable to live *and* work in the downtown area. One of the best examples is downtown San Diego.

Will central business districts return to the bustling round-the-clock activity of yesteryear? Or will they become strictly 8 A.M. to 5 P.M. cities that are abandoned at night? Only time and economics will tell.

Linear Strips

As people travel from the outlying districts to the downtown center, their movement concentrates on particular routes. This can result from the type of transportation system (buses and rapid transit) or from street widths and traffic controls. These avenues of heavy traffic attract commercial real estate uses. This exposure to the passing traffic can substitute for the more expensive downtown locations.

Many planners criticize commercial strips because they prefer cluster development. Most of the commercial uses occupying linear strips fall between the convenience-store and the shopping-store categories. These businesses do not need the neighborhood convenience of a grocery store, but neither are they big enough to pay downtown rents.

Some are commercial uses with marginal profits, others are easy access stores for those who travel on a particular road.

Local Commercial Clusters

The transportation pattern of the community often produces major crossroads away from the downtown area. These nodes become the focus of a local commercial cluster, similar to a small central business district. Usually these clusters are concentrated just off main streets. There has been a tremendous surge in retail store clusters. They are known as retail "power points" and are pulling sales from traditional shopping centers.

Shopping Centers

Detached suburban shopping centers date back to the 1920s. The modern central mall shopping center, with surrounding parking, was first built in the 1950s. Shopping centers are traditionally divided into three categories: neighborhood centers, community centers, and regional centers.

Neighborhood centers consist of a supermarket and a few other stores such as a drugstore, service station, and so on. These centers cater to the immediate neighborhood. People do not drive across town to shop at these centers.

Community centers have a department store, banks, variety stores, and some specialty stores, with restaurants clustered nearby. People will drive across town to shop at community centers.

Regional centers are large, planned projects containing several major "anchor" department stores. In addition, they include 50 or more national and regional specialty chain stores. Easy freeway access plus acres of free parking have made regional shopping malls a part of the American landscape. There is a trend toward clusters of large free-standing "big box" stores forming a regional center, as opposed to the traditional enclosed mall.

In the larger shopping centers, called super regional, traffic volumes are as great or greater than in central business districts. In addition, these centers have multiple stories and often contain dental, medical, legal, and accounting offices, and other businesses. Hotels and restaurants are often nearby, as are apartment complexes. To get better land use, newer regional centers are putting in multilevel parking areas.

These regional centers in turn attract office building developers. In some cases regional centers and the surrounding area became self-contained "cities." By the mid-2000s, the percentage of total retail sales by shopping centers was declining.

Interesting Changes

Of the many factors that influence commercial property location, three of the more fascinating are changes in transportation, services, and consumer tastes. These changes have had an interesting impact on commercial real estate.

The Automobile City

The late 1820s to the early 1900s were the railroad era for travel, both cross-country and intercity, and the 1920s to the present has been the age of the automobile. The growth of shopping centers and suburban office buildings and the decline of the downtown area reflect the swing from streetcars to automobiles. Will the automobile continue to be king? Or will a shift to rapid transit systems, spurred by air pollution and congestion caused by automobiles, once again change the desirable location sites for commercial real estate users? Will the Internet and telecommunications become the ultimate "transportation system," eliminating the need to physical travel for business purposes?

The Service Sector Explosion

As the U.S. economy continues its shift from producing goods to services, the need for service office space will continue to grow, while the need for manufacturing plants will decline. This process has been changing the face of American business centers. Office and service center building has expanded rapidly in the last two decades, especially office construction in downtown areas and along suburban freeways. In some areas by the mid-2000s supply of office buildings far exceeded the demand, leaving a tremendous amount of unused office space to be worked off. At the same time, the past growth in demand for office space has slowed way down. Will the office building market ever balance out to the point where supply and demand are equal? Witness the massive office space vacancy in the San Francisco Bay area after the dot.com collapse.

Shifts in Consumer Taste

Today's consumers are informed and knowledgeable. They seek better prices and a wider selection of goods and services. In the process, consumers have changed the methods used to deliver goods and services. This in turn has created a need for changes in commercial real estate use. Super regional shopping centers, with many stores, provided a wide array of merchandising and services, whereas clustered local power points provide convenience goods and services. But now many consumers are turning to warehouse clubs, or to "manufacturer

Special Interest Topic

Shopping Center Trivia

According to the International Council of Shopping Centers, the five states with the largest number of shopping centers are, in ranking order:

- California
- Florida
- Texas
- Illinois
- New York

The five largest shopping malls, as measured by leasable space, are, in ranking order:

- The Mall of America, Bloomington, Minnesota
- Del Amo Fashion Center, Torrance, California
- South Coast Plaza/Crystal Court Retail Center, Costa Mesa, California
- Lakewood Center Mall, Lakewood, California
- Woodfield Shopping Center, Schaumburg, Illinois

outlet" complexes, seeking better prices. Huge automobile dealerships line freeways, with groups of large freestanding building-supply and discount stores nearby.

Any gains in consumer disposable income will cause changes in consumer tastes. For example, additional income has increased the purchase of prepared foods and the number of restaurants, especially fast-food places. Also, increases in income increased automobile and airline travel and decreased rail and bus services. Income gains in the past have increased the construction of freeway and airport hotels and motels, and activity at downtown hotels, except for convention centers, has declined.

Is Your Local Commercial Area Changing?

Real estate is always changing. A reader should be able to determine whether a particular commercial neighborhood is stagnant, stable, or improving.

The Stagnant Commercial Neighborhood

At first glance, a stagnant commercial neighborhood seems all right. Stores and office buildings have been established for years. Building sales or changes of tenants are rare. However, this apparent stability or lack of change is deceptive. Buildings need upkeep and remodeling or else they become worn out and obsolete. A close look shows that the condition of properties in stagnant neighborhoods is usually deteriorating.

The lack of change in occupancy is also deceptive. Failure to make needed changes in sizes or types of retail stores creates problems. The lack of new faces and stores in the neighborhood is a sign of stagnation rather than stability.

The Stable Commercial Neighborhood

The stable neighborhood lacks these problems. Adequate maintenance and remodeling are occurring. New tenants move in, and new business owners buy out the old. The average age of the persons in business stays relatively constant. The types of businesses and offices in the area slowly change. Occasionally, new buildings appear, along with additions to and remodelings of existing buildings.

The Rapidly Changing Commercial Neighborhood

Recently built commercial neighborhoods change rapidly. Business-people are younger, and there may be many failures of new businesses as managers experiment and sort out the location factors and product mixes in the neighborhood. Sometimes, rapid changes strike an older commercial neighborhood, but most often, rapid change is stimulated by a major change in a freeway or transit system providing better access to the area. First signs often are an increase in property sales as speculators respond to the early clues of the transportation change. Upon completion of the new transportation system, increasing rent levels cause a rapid tenant turnover and an influx of new tenants or businesses.

Another rapid change occurs when the community's population sharply increases following the establishment of a major business. First come speculators, then construction, and then changes in rent levels, tenants, and types of establishments.

Finally, changes in smaller commercial neighborhoods can result from changes in surrounding residential neighborhoods. Changes in the surrounding residential neighborhood are followed by changes in the number and type of customers on the street, in how much stores sell, and in what they sell. In California and a few other states this is especially true in neighborhoods that have experienced a large influx of immigrants.

Making a Simple Market Survey

To make a simple commercial market survey one must look for change. Elements of change on the local level often have the greatest economic effect. However, occasionally a decision made on a state or national level will be crucial to the local economy. An example is the closing of a military base. Use the material presented in Table 10.1 as a framework for conducting a simple commercial market survey.

Community Economics

The economy of the community effects each commercial property in the area. Community economic changes can involve short-term local or national business cycles or long-term trends of permanent change. Therefore, it is necessary to view the national economic picture as well as what is happening to employment in the local community. Contact local planning agencies for recent forecasts of trends in a community's economic base.

Population Factors

Population changes in the community are related to community economic change. A growth in jobs usually means a growth in community population, although where there is a large nonworking

Table 10.1 Elements of a Commercial Market Study

A. The economy of the community

1. Predominant "export jobs"

2. Economic trends

B. Population factors

1. Composition

2. Preferences

C. Institutional factors

1. Transportation

2. Controls

3. Other

D. Supply characteristics

1. Physical (age, condition, etc.)

2. Occupancy, vacancy, and turnover

3. Economic activity

population such as retirees, population can increase without employment growth. Changes in demography are important to commercial property because demographic groups vary in income, spending habits, and so forth.

People's tastes also change. Changes in consumer preferences are among the most subtle influences on commercial property. Sometimes the analyst will find it advisable to "walk the street," asking businesspeople what changes they see in their customers.

Institutional Factors

Transportation change is one of the most dynamic institutional factors that affect real estate value. Is the present transportation system adequate? What are the problems and proposed changes in transportation? Are these changes likely? How will these transportation changes alter travel patterns? Other institutional factors influencing property values include government controls, with zoning as the starting point. Is the community general plan achieving what people want? Are government changes pending? If so, what impact will they have on real estate values? Are pollution problems apparent?

Supply Characteristics

What is the total number of existing buildings? What are the ages and conditions of the buildings? How much and what kind of new construction are there? Are there any trends in renovation or remodeling?

Similarly, information about the business occupants is important. What is the vacancy factor? Has there been much tenant turnover? What are business occupants' average age and length of stay? What is the satisfaction level of occupants with their general business situation, their customers, and location?

Economic data, if available, will sharpen your understanding. What is the number of commercial properties on the market? Are the numbers of sales increasing or decreasing? Are rent levels and values increasing? Are tenants renewing leases? What are the levels of retail sales in the area and how are they changing? If data are available, how are sales volumes changing for the various types of businesses? From this information, the direction of future change in a commercial neighborhood should become apparent. As discussed in Chapter 8, after noting changes, the real estate analyst should try to judge what forces are causing the changes, their strength, and at what pace the changes are occurring. Finally, the analyst tries to estimate what effect the changes will have on commercial real estate needs and investment opportunities.

REVIEWING YOUR UNDERSTANDING

Commercial Property

1. What is meant by linkage? Accessibility?

2. What are four types of commercial neighborhoods? Give an example of each from your city.

3. What are the characteristic differences among stagnant, stable, and rapidly changing commercial neighborhoods?

10.4 Industrial Property

As with commercial property, the demand for industrial property is tied to swings in the business cycle and the availability of mortgage funds. Linkage and accessibility, along with a good shipping system, are important for industrial site selection.

Theory of Industrial Location

A truism in industrial location is that a business seeks a location that reduces its costs and increases its profits. Obviously, no one location is ideal, so the choice involves compromises. Cost of land is a critical issue. However, land cost is only part of the picture. The availability of skilled labor may also be essential. Transportation costs to move raw materials to the plant and finished goods to market must be considered. Location of markets and raw materials sources thus become issues to consider.

Because of the importance of transportation costs, a plant that uses bulky raw material to make a lightweight, nonbulky finished product would seek to locate near the raw material, in order to reduce shipping costs. Processing of tons of ore to recover gold would be the extreme example of this type of location. One should consider what type of raw materials (or inputs) and what type of finished products (or outputs) are involved.

Melvin Greenhut found that new plant sites were selected for one of three main reasons involving the demand for the manufacturer's products, cost savings, or purely personal reasons. Greenhut calls plant sites chosen for easy access to customers *demand plants*. Plants

Table 10.2 Summary of Location Variables

Land cost	Energy, water, and sewage facilities
Transportation cost	Pollution and environmental requirements
Labor cost	Climate
Nearness to materials and markets	Housing cost
	Education facilities
Community attitudes	Personal, nonbusiness reasons
Tax levels	

located for their nearness to raw materials and a plentiful labor supply are called *cost plants*.[1]

In addition to demand and cost factors, business owners' personal preferences may dictate industry location. For example, the original Boeing family's preference to locate its aircraft factories in Seattle was a personal as well as an economic decision. Table 10.2 lists factors companies study when selecting an industrial site.

Others have classified industries as *market oriented, material oriented, labor oriented*, or *footloose*. The Los Angeles fashion garment industry, packed within a few blocks' radius, is the classic market-oriented industry. Industries oriented to their raw materials include steel mills, sawmills, and fish processing plants. Labor-oriented industries can locate either for low-cost labor, as do automobile plants in the southern United States, or for specialized skills, as do the computer software companies around the San Jose, California, area.

Footloose industries are considered capable of locating in any number of locations depending on personal factors. The number of footloose industries is increasing because of relative declines in the costs of transportation. Many times footloose industries locate midway between suppliers and customers.

The Changing Pattern of Industrial Locations

Early industrial communities were mostly in the eastern United States. Many had their origins in port towns such as Norfolk or Baltimore because of the inexpensive water transportation. Often, raw material access was important, especially for coal and timber. Most early manufacturing plants were located downtown for easy worker access and close to waterways or rail lines for raw materials transpor-

---

[1] Melvin Greenhut, *Plant Location in Theory and Practice*, University of North Carolina Press, 1956.

Table 10.3 Summary of Industrial Trends

1. Development of industrial parks with pleasant settings and employee parking lots.

2. Large, one-story buildings instead of multistory buildings.

3. Locations near airports, freeways, and major shipping ports.

tation. Some early plants were close to waterfalls, to use water power to run machinery. The New England textile mills, now all closed, were in this group.

Most of these past patterns are obsolete. Raw material transport is still important, but the orientation has shifted to a few expanded ports, like Oakland and San Pedro, California, and to airports and freeways. Because of its high product-handling cost, the multiple-story plant has been replaced by one-story plants. When combined with the need for automobile parking lots for workers, the one-story plant makes cheap land a necessity. These pressures have led to industrial parks, which are large clusters of industrial uses, often located well away from existing conventional districts. They feature inexpensive land and ample space for isolation from competitive or troublesome land uses. Table 10.3 is a summary of industrial trends.

For the most part, the industrial market has not suffered the dramatic boom and bust syndrome of the commercial office market. However, the accelerating rate of change in manufacturing and warehousing has sharply increased the rate of turnover in this market. Larger corporations often are cutting back, whereas spinoffs and startups are everywhere. With the high price of suburban housing, some industrial companies in certain California locations are having a difficult time attracting employees. Many potential transferees from other states have refused to relocate in California. Those that do often insist on housing subsidies from their employers.

The Industrial Market Study

For industrial market studies, the state of a city's major industries and its economic health are especially important. A city economically dependent upon a large single company or industry has a different industrial market situation from a city with a large diversified employment base.

Institutional factors are also important in making industrial market surveys. Are property tax rates reasonable? Are community attitudes receptive to industries of particular types? Is zoning appropriate? Are transportation systems adequate? What are the environmental constraints? Are educational facilities desirable and adequate for the needs of workers involved? Are needed support facilities, such as suppliers and financial, technical, and consulting people, readily available?

Supply characteristics are essential, too. An industrial market survey must examine the age, condition, and vacancy of existing buildings. The rate of new construction and absorption of that construction should be verified. What is the turnover? What is happening to the rate of property sales and prices? Are rents stable or increasing? Are investors happy with their investment experience? Is there land available for additional construction at appropriate locations? Are pollution and noise controls realistic and enforced in a nondiscriminatory manner?

In short, is the community going to be a successful location for a manufacturing operation, or are there factors (reasonable or unreasonable) that block the establishment or expansion of types of manufacturing processes? These factors then become important to the future of industrial land use in the community.

REVIEWING YOUR UNDERSTANDING

Industrial Property

1. List five things a company looks for when selecting a site.

2. What changes in industrial locations have occurred in your community in the past decade?

CHAPTER SUMMARY

Properties in commercial and industrial markets are diverse, but they share some common influences, especially the need for linkage and accessibility. Advancements in telecommunications has lessened, but not eliminated, this need. Many properties are leased, so that lease considerations are significant, especially in providing a landlord with security against risks such as default, vacancy, cost increases, inflation, and unforeseen economic changes.

The availability and costs of financing to purchase such properties are also important. The lender's requirements for design, lease language, tenant type, and the like also have significant effect.

Business properties are influenced by public requirements such as nuisance standards, environmental concerns, land-use controls, and others. The number and kinds of controls are increasing, and this crucial subject is discussed further in Chapter 13.

Some influences are especially important to commercial property. These are community economic forces, forces of comparative advantage, customer convenience forces, and the effects of the type of business. Because of these influences, commercial land uses occur in four different locations: the central business district (CBD), linear strips, local commercial clusters, and shopping and big box centers. Shopping centers are classified as neighborhood, community, regional, and super regional. Forces that generate changes in commercial locations include transportation changes, the paper and communications explosions, shifts in taste, and increased disposable income.

A particular commercial neighborhood can be either stagnant, stable, or improving. A market survey is a careful study of a commercial neighborhood and all of the forces that influence the neighborhood, in order to get the best possible description of the current state of affairs.

Special factors in industrial markets determine industrial location. Transportation, labor, materials, community attitudes, and markets are significant factors. There is a recent trend toward large suburban industrial parks. Industrial market surveys also seek to understand what forces are at work, what changes have occurred, and what current trends are forming. The goal is to develop an image of the community's future employment, population change, and industrial future. This is then used to determine the investment potential for business property.

IMPORTANT TERMS AND CONCEPTS

Accessibility	*Leasing for security*
Big box centers	*Linkage*
Central business district (CBD)	*Market-oriented industries*
Commercial strips	*Material-oriented industries*
Comparative advantage	*Shopping centers*
Convenience goods	*Community*
Footloose industries	*Neighborhood*
Industrial location theory	*Regional*
Labor-oriented industries	*Shopping goods*

REVIEWING YOUR UNDERSTANDING

1. Which of the following is *least important* for a business property investor?
   a. rent level
   b. noneconomic amenity
   c. credit rating of the tenant
   d. terms of the lease

2. Nearness to other compatible businesses is called:
   a. accessibility
   b. location
   c. linkage
   d. trading area

3. Which of the following regarding the commercial real estate market is generally false?
   a. Demand is tied to swings in the business cycle.
   b. Income tax law changes can influence the rate of construction.
   c. Lenders can have veto power over projects.
   d. Buyers and sellers are unsophisticated.

4. Once the building of a commercial or industrial project begins, it is difficult to stop even if it becomes apparent that the demand for the project has declined. This is known as the:
   a. gravity effect
   b. pipeline effect
   c. financial effect
   d. continuous effect

5. A thin line of commercial development along a city street is a:
   a. strip development
   b. power-point cluster
   c. neighborhood center
   d. community center

6. Small local clusters of trendy retail stores are called:
   a. power-point clusters
   b. regional centers
   c. megacenters
   d. super regional centers

7. Changes that have influenced the location of commercial properties include:
   a. the shift from emphasis on the production of goods to the providing of services
   b. increased use of the automobile
   c. changes in consumer tastes
   d. all of the above

8. Which of the following is a current trend in the industrial real estate market?
   a. large multiple-story buildings
   b. downtown locations
   c. industrial parks
   d. locating near upscale housing developments

9. A market-oriented industry tends to seek a location near its:
   a. raw materials
   b. customers
   c. lenders
   d. employees

10. Which of the following is considered a store selling "convenience" goods?
    a. minimarket
    b. jewelry store
    c. gun store
    d. high-fashion retail outlet

11. The ability of business to pay rent is influenced by economic conditions, leading to changes in property net income and value.
    a. true
    b. false

12. Development of business property tends to:
    a. lead changes in demand
    b. result when rents are dropping
    c. lag changes in demand
    d. not involve market changes

13. Project design, layout, numbers of tenants, and the like are often influenced by the lender.
    a. true
    b. false

14. Government income tax changes have tended to stimulate or suppress the rate of business real estate development.
    a. true
    b. false

15. Good leases add important value to business property. Regarding a net lease, a potential investor is *least* concerned with the:
    a. length of the lease
    b. risk of default by the tenant
    c. protection in the lease against inflation
    d. age of the building

16. Which type of shopping center tends to cater only to people within a single city?
    a. neighborhood
    b. community
    c. regional
    d. super regional

17. Changes in consumer tastes and lifestyles will not change commercial real estate patterns.
    a. true
    b. false

18. Which of the following is an example of a market-oriented commercial use?
    a. gravel pit
    b. lumber mill
    c. garment district
    d. clothing mill

19. The telecommunication explosion has altered the need for some businesses to seek a location near their customers.
    a. true
    b. false

20. The number of large department stores in the downtown area of most major cities in the United States is at an all-time high.
    a. true
    b. false

21. Linear commercial strips are:
    a. favored by city planners
    b. often of marginal economic quality
    c. usually weakest at major crossroads and strongest in midblock
    d. usually dominated by national or regional chain tenants

22. Outlet malls and warehouse clubs are new examples of changes in commercial real estate arising from:
    a. new zoning categories
    b. changes in building design
    c. changes in consumer taste
    d. changes in climate

23. A very low turnover rate over a long period of time in a commercial neighborhood is:
    a. a good sign
    b. irrelevant
    c. a bad sign
    d. a bad sign if store sales volumes are increasing

24. Which of the following is a trend in retail sales?
    a. increase in T.V. home shopping networks
    b. decrease in catalog sales
    c. decrease in credit card purchases
    d. increase in downtown department stores

25. Footloose industries tend to locate:
    a. to be close to their customers
    b. to be close to their workers
    c. because of personal noneconomic reasons
    d. to be close to raw materials

CASE & POINT

The Revolution in Retailing

BIG BOX STORES

It is clear that retailing has changed much in the past 50 years. The typical retail district of 50 or so years ago was located in the CBD and contained a few large department stores at key corners, plus small stores around it. The department stores were local or regional companies, and the small stores were nearly all locally owned and operated.

Over the years, retailing moved out to major regional crossroads intersections, creating the modern shopping center. The driving force was the increased accessibility created by automobiles, arterial roads, and expressways. Department stores merged into national or regional chains. The small stores grew larger, and many were regional or national chains or franchises.

The impacts of these retailing changes were profound. Most downtown department stores closed, along with many of the stores selling better-quality merchandise, as shopping trips shifted to the shopping centers. Downtowns of larger cities survived because of the tremendous growth of office land use during this time. However, downtowns of smaller towns were hurt, as office growth was more limited. The culture of the community changed, as well. People were less likely to meet downtown (except for those that worked there), and "hanging out at the mall" emerged as entertainment. The locational shifts in retailing also shifted the patterns of land values, as the values of rural lands fortunately close to arterial intersections exploded while downtown retail land lagged.

In recent decades, however, two new retailing influences have emerged. The first has been *the movement toward low-margin retailing*. Examples include the discounters, the warehouse clubs, such low-margin retailers as Wal-Mart, the super drug and grocery stores, and the outlet store craze. Generally, these stores have avoided the expensive enclosed malls of modern shopping centers and the premium retail locations. Many have located in relatively low-cost industrial locations with good freeway access. Most have featured self-service and minimal store finish. Selections often are limited and variable. These are known as "big box" stores.

The weaker department store chains have consolidated in a shakeout that is far from over, and the remaining central city retailers have fallen further behind. In a few cases, the decline in central city retail values has been pronounced enough to allow assemblage of numerous parcels, to create a retail project with parking and a cluster of different retailers that appeals to customers.

Such clusters arise in response to the second major new retail influence of the past 20 years: *the return of retailing as entertainment*. Its early manifestation was in "hanging out" at malls. As mall developers became more aware of this trend, they added more eating areas, often in a restaurant commons, and expanded central seating areas. These were followed by movie theaters, skating rinks, and other amusement areas. The culmination of this trend currently is the Mall of America in Minnesota, which has an amusement park and extensive recreation areas and is being promoted as a destination for excursion trips from hundreds of miles away! However, it is expensive to provide such an elaborate setting, and the result is likely to be higher rents to tenants and higher prices to customers.

Clearly, then, these two recent influences are somewhat in opposition. We should expect that the growth of low-margin retailing will involve convenience goods more than shopping goods. (The outlet store clusters manage to bridge both camps, as they offer somewhat lower prices for specialty shopping goods. The key, of course, is how low prices can be when more and more of the total sales are through outlet stores!) In addition, because of the economic strains of the 2000s, we can expect low-margin retailing to be the dominant influence.

What of the next 20 years, then? It seems clear that central city retailing is likely to continue to weaken. And smaller malls will be trapped between the pressure for low prices and an entertaining environment. But other issues are emerging. Specialty catalog sales are growing, even though old-time catalog sellers are closing down. Internet and cable shopping channels are growing even faster, but from a lower base. Will these grow to become a significant distribution channel, or will they remain a smaller specialty channel?

CHAPTER 11
RURAL AND RECREATIONAL
REAL ESTATE MARKETS

PREVIEW

This chapter, which concludes Part Two, "Understanding Real Estate Markets," emphasizes rural land uses. Section 11.1 explores agricultural property. Section 11.2 examines rural homes, from farmsteads and retirement homes to second homes and recreation rentals. Section 11.3 studies timberlands and similar resource properties. The Case & Point at the end of the chapter explores the issue of government subsidies for resource development. When you have completed this chapter, you will be able to:

1. List and understand the major factors influencing agricultural values and trends.

2. Discuss the important differences between rural homes and urban housing.

3. Understand the special problems and features of resource lands and trends in their uses and values.

11.1 Farmland Markets

Agriculture is a major land use in the United States, producing a tremendous amount of food and fiber (Table 11.1). The different farming uses such as orchards, irrigated croplands, dry croplands, and irrigated and dry pasture- and rangelands vary in value. However, there are common factors at work, determining how farmlands are used and what their value is. This section explores these key factors and discusses major trends.

Key Factors

Soil productivity
Rainfall
Growing season
Water supplies
Markets
Community facilities
Permits and quotas
Competition from other uses

Topography
Shape, size, and layout
Improvements
Access
Urban influences
Crop prices
Financing

Farmland use is determined by a combination of factors, the main concerns being which crops will grow, at what cost, and the estimated

Table 11.1 Leading Agricultural States and Counties

Top 10 States by Corp Value (2003)

1. California
2. lllinois
3. Iowa
4. Florida
5. Texas
6. Minnesota
7. Nebraska
8. Washington
9. Indiana
10. Kansas

Top 5 Agricultural Counties in California (2003)

1. Fresno
2. Tulare
3. Monterey
4. Kern
5. Merced

Source: U.S. Department of Agriculture and California Statistical Abstract, 2004.

yields of each. The more profitable crops are planted and the less profitable ones eliminated.

Soil Productivity

Formed from the interaction of the underlying rocks, the local climate, and the influences of topography, soils differ in many ways. Some soils (often on hillsides) are only a shallow layer on the rock, inches thick, whereas others (usually in valleys) are many tens of feet deep. Some are so sandy (many desert soils) that rainfall quickly drains out, whereas others are so silty that soils stay wet and rot plant roots.

Farm soils are generally placed in one of eight major classes, depending on their productivity or richness. Rural soil mapping is so complete that most established agricultural areas have detailed maps available from the Agricultural Extension Office, County Farm Advisor,

Figure 11.1 Soil class, slope, and erosion. A map of the soil and its capability. The symbols pertain to various aspects of soil and topography. For example: *10B1* refers to the kind of soil; the number *10* refers to the soil type; the letter *B* to steepness of slope; and number *1* to degree of erosion. The symbol *//e2* refers to the land capability unit; *//* designates the land capability class; *e* indicates the subclass; and *2* indicates the unit. Heavy lines on the map indicate boundaries of a capability unit. (*Source: Soil*, U.S. Department of Agriculture, Washington, DC, 1957.)

or comparable offices. Soil mapping often extends beyond the eight general classes to subcategories and to suitability for various specific crops. Figure 11.1 is an example, showing soil class, slope, and amount of erosion, and an overall productivity index.

Rainfall

The amount, timing, and nature of available moisture is every bit as important as the soil. In fact, it will have played a large part in developing the soil into its current form. Many marginal agricultural regions are well equipped with everything but natural rainwater, leaving low-value grazing as the only possible land use. Alternatives such as wells, irrigation projects, or cloud seeding can help change marginal soil into productive soil. However, most of the U.S. cropland relies on rainfall. As a result, much of the variation in farm production each year results from variations in when, where, and how much rain falls. Figure 11.2 shows this variation by location, but rainfall also varies with the seasons, as well as from year to year.

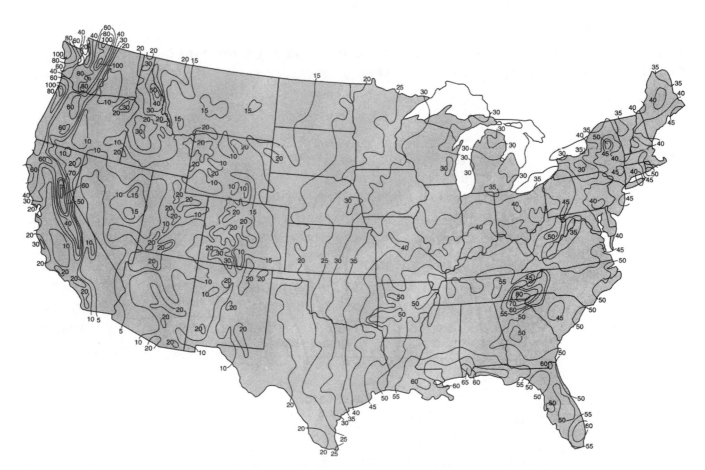

Figure 11.2 How rainfall varies. The average annual precipitation over the United States, in inches. (*Source: Soil*, U.S. Department of Agriculture, Washington, DC, 1957.)

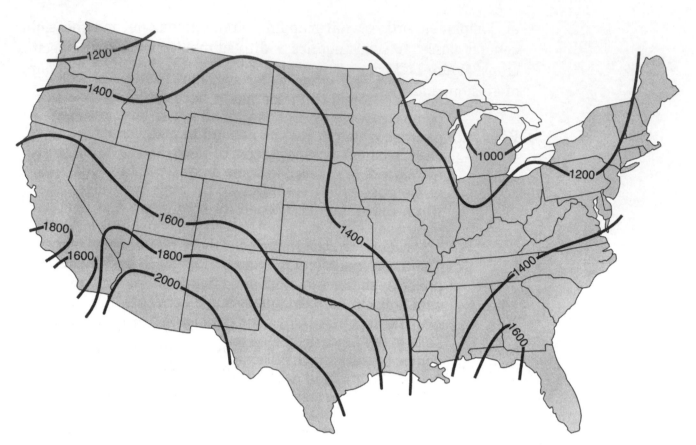

Figure 11.3 How sunshine varies. The distribution of solar energy over the United States, in BTU (British thermal units) per square foot on an average day. (*Source: Soil*, U.S. Department of Agriculture, Washington, DC, 1957.)

Growing Season

The amount of sunlight influences a farm's growing season. In some areas, like Alaska, only one crop can be grown in a year. In sunny areas, such as the Imperial Valley of California and the homestead region of Florida, year-round agriculture is practical. However, some crops are attuned to a particular climate and growing season. Oranges, for example, do not thrive in either a hot, tropical climate or a cool, temperate climate but grow best in a narrow subtropical belt that includes Florida, parts of Texas, and Southern California. Figure 11.3 maps the variation in the sun's energy across the United States.

Water Supplies

In addition to *rainfall*, other possible sources of water have become more important in recent years. Rainfall runoff in rivers has been used for irrigation in the past. Now, however, its use is subject to complicated water rights that tie up the available water during the drier parts of the year or divert it to storage reservoirs and urban water systems. The use of well water has been increasing for many decades. As more people pump, however, the underground water level recedes. The expense of larger pumps needed to pull water from deeper wells, plus the increasing cost of electricity, have reduced the numbers of new wells. In some areas small irrigation projects of the past have been followed by immense water projects, which have been developed for both urban and agricultural purposes.

However, irrigation projects must be properly managed. There are innumerable examples of failed ancient irrigation projects, such as in Mesopotamia and Jordan, and more recent projects, including parts of the Imperial Valley of California. The major problem is the gradual accumulation of various salts in the land, deposited from the water, until the land becomes so salty that it poisons most plants.

In many irrigated areas, the growth in nearby urban areas leads to growing conflict over the limited water. In time, urban dwellers tend to bid up the prices for available water. As irrigation water gets more expensive, saltwater and wastewater reclamation become more feasible as possible farm water sources. Good water is especially important to agricultural land use in certain areas, as some well and groundwater is so salty or full of chemicals (e.g., boron) that it kills plants.

Topography

The slope of the parcel, as well as gullies, rock outcrops, marshes, and the like, affect what the land can produce or how it can be farmed. Crops that are irrigated by flooding, such as rice, must be on level fields. Crops that are harvested by big machines, such as wheat, must be on fairly level land that is fairly dry at harvest time. The slope of a parcel is particularly important because steeper slopes usually have thinner layers of soil, are harder to work with machinery, and are also much harder to irrigate without causing soil erosion.

Shape, Size, and Layout

Shape, size, and layout all influence farm production, depending on the crops involved and the farming technology used. As a result of high prices, rice in Japan has been economically farmed with hand labor in steep plots of a few acres, whereas in California, mechanized rice farms on level terrain require hundreds of acres. Today, Japanese small plot rice production depends totally on government willingness to restrict rice imports and force domestic rice prices well above world market levels.

Improvements

This term covers a wide range of physical items found on farms and ranches. A milking parlor is an expensive but necessary building on a dairy farm. Underground drain tile, to keep fields dry enough, may be an equally necessary improvement for the asparagus farmer. Almost all farms and ranches have a variety of outbuildings for animals and equipment. The design and condition of these improvements must be appropriate if they are to have a positive effect on value. Changing crop demands can occasionally make existing improvements obsolete.

Access

Some good farms sell for less than others because of their remoteness. Remoteness can be the distance to markets to sell the farm's products or the distance to shops, stores, and services that farmers need. Isolated farms also have been less popular with farmers' families. In addition to the farmland price pressures caused by encroaching urban sprawl, the close-in farm will often be worth more than the remote one solely because of the time and cost of travel to and from the remote farm. However, there is a market for smaller, isolated farms for people seeking a more self-sufficient life away from cities.

Markets

Farmers and ranchers sell many crops through specialized marketing channels, such as stockyards and the grain elevator. Some specialty crops are very difficult to market *except* in the places where most of the production for that crop is centered. An obscure California valley might be an excellent small lettuce-production area, but the extra cost of shipping to Salinas, California, where its regional market for lettuce is centered, strips isolated producers of their profit margin. On the other hand, isolated locations with good access to major truck routes can sometimes economically justify agricultural produce.

Community Facilities

Rural areas, just like cities, can vary in the amount, variety, and quality of public and private services available, but most rural areas must settle for fewer of these services. Farmers are as interested as city dwellers in good schools, medical services, and adequate stores. Sad stories of inadequate rural health care and educational facilities have been highly publicized in the national media. Because of distance and low population, it is difficult to justify economically the cost of bringing topflight medical and educational facilities to rural areas. As farmer productivity has increased over the decades, rural population has declined. Rural community facilities have suffered.

Permits and Quotas

Governmental permission is sometimes needed to grow some crops, including tobacco, cotton, and sugar beets, and to produce fresh milk. Forest Service grazing permits allow a rancher to graze cattle on government land during the summer, sometimes doubling the number of cattle that a rancher can handle. These permits and quotas can be very important to the value of private land. The ability to hold and sell the permit to use government land can add to the value of a particular privately held ranch.

Government price supports and crop payments exert a similar influence for farmers. When a support program changes, farm incomes can change drastically, thereby influencing the choice of crop or value of farmland. Recent increases in the fees for grazing permits for ranchers in the western states are a case in point.

Competition from Other Uses

A particular rural parcel may have limited agricultural value but be of greater utility for other rural uses. Many of the rural recreational subdivisions created in the Sunbelt States in the 1960s were located in areas of poor farmland, where low prices made such subdivisions more profitable and thus economically more feasible for the developer. Similarly, some poorer farmlands, especially in the Northeast and Southeast regions of the United States, have potential value for tree farms that might equal their farmland values. Sand, gravel, and other resources may be mined, too, if the competing agricultural uses of the land are not profitable.

Urban Influences

Many states have farming areas close to urban areas, and land values in these locations have been driven up by speculators anticipating future city expansion. The nature and expectations of urban expansion, general planning, zoning, utilities, and transportation systems cause speculative premiums to be paid for rural land. However, such speculative premiums rise *and* fall.

Crop Prices

The prices of various farm crops rise and fall with changes in supply and demand. Farmland prices tend to swing with these changes in

Special Interest Topic

Agricultural Foreign Investment Disclosure Act

Although there is no federal law prohibiting foreigners from purchasing U.S. real estate, there has been a concern over foreign purchases of U.S. agricultural land. In 1978 Congress passed the Agricultural Foreign Investment Disclosure Act, which requires that a report be sent to the government within 90 days after the sale of farm or timberland to foreign investors. This law only covers parcels of one acre or more that produce $1,000 or more in output value per year. The purpose of the law is to monitor foreign purchases to see if further action is needed. The data developed as a result of this law suggest that such foreign purchases have not been very significant. On the other hand, anecdotal evidence suggests that many foreign investors simply chose to invest elsewhere after the law's passage.

crop prices. Soaring crop prices in the mid-1970s, coupled with wild inflation, generated record high farmland prices. Then the decline in crop prices in the 1980s, coupled with a drop in inflation, caused farmland prices to drop to levels below the balances on many existing farm mortgages and loans. The result was a wave of farm foreclosures. By the mid-1990s, crop prices stabilized and so did farmland prices and this trend continues today.

Financing

Farms are usually purchased and also operated with some borrowed capital. Today's fairly rapid changes in the availability and cost of all types of loans directly affect the profitability of farm operations. Higher loan interest rates increase the cost of operating a farm and thereby reduce farmland values. On the other hand, the expectation of inflation in the economy, although it produces higher loan interest rates, tends to stabilize farmland values as investors seek land investments to hedge against inflation. But investing in farmland as a hedge against inflation produces uses different from investing in farms for production of crops, distorting the entire economic process.

Special Interest Topic

The Farm Problem

The so-called "farm problem" is a classic example of supply exceeding demand, causing a drop in farm product prices and farm income. On the demand side, basic farm products, such as grains, have an *inelastic demand*, meaning that a large increase or decrease in price causes only a small change in the amount consumers are willing to buy. For example, if the price of wheat drops by 50 percent, people do not increase their consumption of wheat by 50 percent. You will not double the size of your meals if food prices drop by 100 percent! Meanwhile, on the supply side, technological advances in equipment, fertilizers, pesticides, water systems, land management skills, and so on, have greatly expanded the output of farm and ranch products. Each decade, fewer and fewer farmers are needed to feed us. In short, even with expanding exports to foreign countries, supply has exceeded demand, causing farm product prices to decline and farm incomes to fall.

The classical economic solution to the farm problem would be to allow farmers to fail, thereby reducing supply. This would cause production of farm products to fall to a point where supply and demand are in balance, at a price that would support the remaining farmers at a reasonable income. Why hasn't this happened? The reasons are many, such as: the need to "preserve an American way of life"; "farmers have fed a growing nation at great personal cost"; farmers sell in a nearly pure competitive market, but must buy goods and services in monopolistic competitive markets; and so on.

Government's Solution—Farm Aid

The past political solution to this economic problem has been to set up government programs to support farmers.

The major government farm aid programs are:

1. *Price supports*, in which the government guarantees the farmer a certain minimum price for crops. If consumers will not buy up all the output, the government buys the surplus at the support price. In theory, the government plans to resell the surplus in years when production is lower than demand, because of droughts and the like.

2. *Set-aside programs*, in which the government pays the farmer for not planting an allotted number of acres. Sometimes called "soil banking." Because the land is usually planted with crops that are plowed in, to increase soil fertility, these programs are considered to be good for the land.

3. *Increasing the demand for farm output:* by paying for research on new uses for farm products, by creating food stamps and other government programs designed to give food to U.S. citizens who cannot afford to pay, and by promoting food exports to foreign countries.

The Results to Date

Have government programs solved the "farm problem"? Most economists agree the answer is no. What went wrong? The farm aid programs to date have focused on keeping farm incomes up, instead of encouraging farmers to leave the farm and seek better-paying employment elsewhere. Why should a farmer leave if the government will guarantee loans or grant direct payment to stay! Another problem with government farm aid is that the greatest amount of aid has gone to the large corporate farmer, who needs increased personal income the least. The final critique of the past government farm policy is the tremendous cost these programs exact from U.S. consumers and taxpayers. There is no better demonstration of this than the large sums *still* spent to subsidize the growing of tobacco leaf.

Environmentalism

Although not a main factor until the 1970s, environmental protection and agricultural pollution controls are now an important factor affecting agricultural operations and thus farmland prices. Early environmental actions focused on broad-span, long-life pesticides such as DDT. Today, all pesticides are under government review. Agricultural burning, such as rice stubble and orchard cuttings, once common in rural areas, is now tightly controlled. Water pollution caused by chemical runoff from irrigation is a major concern. Environmental groups are lobbying heavily to restrict insecticides and other chemicals currently used in farming. If environmental and pollution constraints reduce the volume of crop production, the value of the farmland could be adversely affected. On the other hand, if environmental constraints reduce farm production, assuming demand increases or at least remains the same, the result could be higher unit market prices for the farmer. If this occurs, the price of farmland could rise or at least hold its present value. Only time will tell! In general, however, when there is a reduction in output of a given crop, prices rise *less* than the reduction in output, so that farmers' total receipts decline. This again illustrates *inelastic demand*.

Labor Relations

As farm operations have become larger and more specialized, they have needed more labor than any one farm family could supply. Seasonal labor crews have been necessary to handle key high-labor jobs. The scattered job locations and seasonal workload make it difficult for such crews to bargain effectively over wages and work conditions. In the 1970s, unionization, strikes, and jurisdictional fights affected some farm crops. Today, many farmers have successfully turned to mechanization and the use of smaller but more constant work crews. All of these changes have affected individual crop costs, profits, and land values.

Major Trends

Studies of agriculture over the past century document a huge increase in output per farmer. This increase has involved a sharp rise in average farm sizes, in mechanization, and in the invested capital per farm. However, there have also been big increases in output per acre, in specialization of farmers in one or two crops, and in the use of an increased petrochemical base of agricultural fertilizers and pesticides.

These trends have continued in recent years, but as mentioned before, concerns about the effects of agricultural fertilizers and pesticides may slow the rate of output per acre. There is increased experimentation with fertilizers and weed and pest controls with less long-term impact. Crop exports to other nations have grown dramatically in recent years and are expected to increase as world peace and trade treaties open up foreign markets not currently served by U.S. agricultural products. Improvements to world purchasing power and transportation have the potential to sharply increase demand for many products that once were luxuries.

The farm crisis era of the 1980s involved a large number of farm foreclosures, many of which were the result of rising farmland values in the 1970s and early 1980s. During these high-flying years, farmers and ranchers refinanced their land. These dollars were used to buy added equipment and land, or in some cases the money was used to purchase luxury goods or to acquire investments. Then when the price of agricultural products dropped or production dropped as a result of a drought, farmers and ranchers could not meet their loan payments. The result was a highly publicized wave of farm foreclosures in the 1980s. By the mid-1990s to the mid-2000s, stability had returned.

Another long-term trend is the growing split between a relatively limited number of efficient big producers and a large body of small, inefficient subsistence farmers, many of whom hold regular jobs and farm on the side. Intermediate-size farms appear to be dwindling.

REVIEWING YOUR UNDERSTANDING

Farmland Markets

1. List at least five factors that influence farmland values.

2. Explain several ways that climate affects these factors.

3. List three current trends in farming operations.

11.2 Rural Homes

An increasing number of people are turning to the rural land market for housing rather than farming. The reasons for the rural housing boom are many, but retirement and recreation are two of the more important factors. This section discusses new rural subdivisions and older homes separately, because of differences in marketing and in buyer motivations.

The New Subdivision

Most people have seen a newer rural subdivision or have received promotional information about one. Key features in the sales literature generally are the area's recreational facilities. The subdivision often includes some facilities within its boundaries, such as a lake, lodge, golf course, or tennis courts.

Rural subdivisions have primarily been marketed as second homesites or retirement areas for weary city dwellers. The subdivisions fall into several categories, generally based on the location of the site. Locations in the ski country have had strong demand, and most subdivisions in this category offer buildings with the land. Condominiums and cluster townhouses are common design features, but project facilities are sometimes limited in favor of maximum development of a nearby or affiliated ski slope. Some coastal beach subdivisions have had similar strong demand and regular building programs. Desert subdivisions have in some cases been successful, but others have been massive failures. The demand for these developments is tied to the ebb and flow of the general economy and the current demographics of the population. In boom times people tend to buy second homes; in recession times they tend to back off.

"Buy a Lot at Lost Acres"

Some rural subdivisions are in remote areas that had very limited demand for new homes prior to the subdivision. (This discussion, of course, ignores some subdivisions that are within the daily commuting range of a larger urban area and are essentially suburban.) Remote subdivisions have differed from ski condominiums in several ways, the limited preexisting demand being only one. Nearly all such tracts have concentrated on lot sales rather than sales of new buildings. Indeed, even several years after sale, usually less than 5 percent, and often less than 1 percent, of the lots have been built upon. Thus, the buyer is simply purchasing a site and the potential for future benefits. The seller often provides very generous financing, which makes the purchase easier.

The limited preexisting demand in the area means that such subdivisions must be sold by extensive marketing, often in other areas with more people. The low price for land only, coupled with a low down payment, have tended to attract buyers of limited economic means and experience, whose limited resources make second-home construction a rather distant possibility. As a result, sales discussions have often emphasized the benefits of land ownership and the profits to be made from the land investment. Unfortunately, this rosy future has not arrived for many buyers.

From your review of economic principles in Part One, as well as your experiences in the real world, you should be prepared to answer this question: Consider a subdivision in which 1,000 lots in a remote area are developed and sold, and only 10 lots are built on in the first four years. If the remaining 990 lots were bought for speculative profit, in hopes of selling for building in five years at higher prices, what will happen to lot resale prices? The laws of supply and demand are hard to evade. In other words, there never was any real, permanent demand for the lots; there was only a temporary, speculative fever created by an "overactive" sales pitch.

There are recreational subdivision lots that are worth less today than when they were sold 10 or 20 years ago, or 50 or 75 years ago! Moral: Not all land values go up—some go down!

Trends in Ski Country

The more successful ski and coastal subdivisions differ sharply from the examples above, because they have a strong enough demand to support immediate housing construction. The success of many of the initial subdivisions of this type led to a burst of favorable publicity, an increase in demand, and new imitators, who often had to pay higher prices for raw land. All of these factors produced rapid increases in values of the original subdivisions, which generated still more favorable publicity. It may take many years for the area prices to stabilize.

It is important to stress that the rate of second-home and recreational development is tied to movements in the economy and to cost of ownership. When the economy is booming, many people optimistically spend their discretionary income. When the economy is weak, some find they have to sell. The second-home and recreational property market is closely tied to swings in discretionary income.

Another issue influencing the market for second homes and recreational properties is price. Prices in many of these markets have risen rapidly. This results from high demand and increased building cost, because of escalating land prices, expensive building components, and added cost to meet environmental requirements.

As costs of projects rise, many families find that they use their second home too seldom to justify owning it. They then try to rent it out when they are not occupying it, for the weekend, the week, or the month. Experience with this growing supply of rentable buildings has led to sophisticated rural property-management firms and the concept of *time-sharing*, or ownership of a unit during a specified time block (e.g., the month of May). Unfortunately, some poorly conceived time-share projects, plus the growing volume of renters, the increasing vacancy ratios, and turnover of strangers, have tended to decimate the rural features that were original attractions of the projects. As owner usage declines, the space can be filled with renters, but only as long as renters are interested. In time, sale prices increasingly may reflect tenant rent levels and occupancy rates.

An Overview

The key factors of the newer rural subdivisions are their orientation to recreational attractions and their limited market. Even in the stronger markets, rising prices have reduced user demand and led to attempts to support ownership cost by part-time rental income. Investment motives have been a factor in a surprising number of rural purchases, often openly stated in vacant land subdivision transactions, but more subtly expressed in purchase of lots with houses and condominiums. The strength of *use* demand, as contrasted with *investment* demand, is the key issue, as it will have a major impact on future property values.

The Older Home

Older rural homes, as well as single rural lots or homesites, have entirely different market factors from the newer recreational subdivisions. Many recreational subdivision buyers are not aware of these differences and of the numerous buying choices they actually have.

The Local Marketplace

One of the major differences between new rural developments and older rural homes is that the older rural home is generally sold on a local market through the local newspaper, brokers, or word of mouth. This does not mean only local people are the buyers, for many newcomers look for housing using local information. However, this local market contrasts sharply with the mass-advertising urban market to which the new recreational subdivisions are sold. Historically, small-town prices have been much lower than prices for comparable locations in larger cities, because population pressure forces land and home prices up in larger cities. When recreational properties are sold on the urban market, their prices seem bargains in comparison to urban prices and tend to get bid up closer to urban levels. Rural markets, meanwhile, continue on their own way, at their own price levels.

Local influences in each local rural market determine the price level for homes and lots. Some towns and rural areas are declining in population as logging mills close or the number of farmers declines. Then home prices tend to be low or declining. Other rural areas gain new employment or an influx of retirees, and their population gains and home prices move higher. This increase is especially true for rural areas on the edge of urban growth or within a half-day's drive of major metropolitan areas.

On the Other Hand...

The older rural home, although often quite inexpensive by urban standards, is not always a bargain. Some factors taken for granted in the city can be major problems in the country. For example, city sewer mains and sewage treatment plants are not common in the country, but septic tanks are. Problems with sewers backing up, polluted wells, and saturated septic tank drain fields are all too common.

Water availability is also a problem. The polluted well is one aspect, the dry well another. Legal quarrels over water rights are occasionally a problem. Some residents have good water; others have water that is so salty or contaminated by agricultural chemicals that it is undrinkable or fatal to plants. Not all sites have water, but the only way to find out is to drill, which costs money.

Buyers of older rural properties may have trouble finding boundaries, obliging them to pay for a survey or risk later problems. They may also encounter problems with the condition of their dwellings. Older rural homes probably are more likely to have been built without building permits or code inspector supervision, or they may have had substantial owner alterations of varying quality. Even when new, heating, wiring, and plumbing systems often do not meet the standards expected of most urban homes. Deferred maintenance of roofs, chimneys, windows, and sills is common. Foundations may be far more casual, or even nonexistent, and damage from wood-destroying organisms (termites, fungus, and beetles) may be extensive.

Thus, the buyers of an older rural home must anticipate more problems, ask more questions, and look far more carefully than they would for an urban home purchase. The benefits of lower prices are there, but lower prices can be offset by high repair expense if the buyer is not wary. Even with today's higher standards of seller and broker disclosure requirements, urban buyers of older rural homes need to be very careful.

Who Buys What?

Buyers of such older rural homes are often quite different from buyers of recreational subdivision homes. Many are older, either retired or nearing it, and seek a less expensive or more peaceful retirement home than their former urban location. Others are young families with children, unable to afford the prices in recreational subdivisions, but eager to obtain a rural recreational second home. These contrast with the couples without children or well-to-do middle-aged families who buy many newer recreation subdivision homes. However, all these groups can occasionally be enticed into buying the recreation subdivision lot because of the lure of supposed profits on resale.

A final factor in the market for older rural homes is the relatively small job base in the area, particularly noticeable in areas dependent on one industry, such as logging, tourism, food processing, or a mine or other mineral operation. All too often, that industry will reach the end of its economic profitability and close or move its local operation.

When it does, the local area will go into a severe economic depression because of the loss of jobs. People will leave town looking for work, and real estate prices will fall. In time, people may return and prices may rise, but some towns never recover and become stagnant or even ghost towns, abandoned and worthless. The rural town with one major employer is thus a special risk, and the buyer should be wary.

REVIEWING YOUR UNDERSTANDING

Rural Homes

1. What are the two main categories of rural homes, and what is the principal difference between them?

2. How would you describe the past, present, and future demand for lots in a new recreational subdivision in a remote scenic area, where the main sales pitch is the investment and resale potential?

3. Explain four problems that the older rural home buyer may encounter that are generally little or no problem in urban homes.

11.3 Timber and Other Resource Lands

There are a number of different resources on rural lands and often on urban lands as well. These include timber, water power, oil, coal, gravel or rock, geothermal power, salt mines or ponds, and numerous ores, either strip-mined or underground, including iron, uranium, copper, salt, diatomaceous earth, and many others. Their location and marketing factors differ in many ways, making this subject far too complex for full coverage here. But this section will examine a series of related factors and trends that influence most resource lands. Each resource then brings its own market, processing, and locational characteristics to mix with these factors, to produce resource land prices and trends.

Key Factors

The most important fact about all resource lands is that *the demand for the resource*, and thus for the land, *is usually not connected to the local economy* or real estate market. Rather, the demand

Figure 11.4 Coal fields. (*Source:* Economic Research Service, *Our Land and Water Resources.* Washington, DC, Government Printing Office, 1974.)

and supply of the resource in nationwide or regional resource markets dominate. This is opposite, of course, to the usual land market. The map of coal fields in Figure 11.4 illustrates that the resource need not be located where the resource is used.

A second major factor is *transportation*. Most resource commodities are relatively bulky, low-valued materials, and their transportation cost *per dollar of value* is higher than most other transported goods. Most resource commodities also require some processing at a timber sawmill or smelter, reduction plant or crushing mill, which usually reduces the bulk considerably and increases the commodity's value per pound. The location of these processing plants, their transportation access, and their cost heavily influence the market for resource lands.

A third major factor is the *characteristic of the resource parcel* itself. The size of the ore body or timber stand is important, because a larger collection of the resource in one holding allows more potential revenue to cover the original costs for exploration, roads, permits, and the possible huge development expense before the first sale occurs. The land parcel size may also be important in other ways, either to provide a buffer from other property owners who might be injured by the operation if it were close to them, or as space for various support, maintenance, and resource-processing facilities. Parcel topography and shape may also have value, as well as the exact nature of the resource. Issues such as the chemical composition of ores, the species composition of timber stands, the thickness of ore bodies, the amount of dirt on top of the ore ("overburden"), the density and age of timber stands, and the amount of underbrush, all combine to determine what it will cost to prepare the resource, extract it, and ship it to the nearest market. The lower the cost, the more valuable is the land.

Related to this, but a distinctly different fourth factor, is the limiting effect of *environmental* and *pollution controls*, which will vary for different resources and in different political jurisdictions. Their effect is primarily to increase the cost of producing the resource or to require the product to assume directly the full costs of resource development, rather than imposing a portion of costs on people, animals, or lands downstream or downwind from the resource lands.

Finally, the fifth key factor found in markets for these resource lands is the presence of *special income and property tax laws* and *title laws and procedures*. That is, resource lands are generally treated as a special category by many government agencies, often in a favorable or preferential way. Income tax treatment includes depletion allowances for underground resources and capital gains treatment for timber sales. Special property tax treatment in California, for example, is primarily for timberlands, which have both potential for agricultural preserve taxation by contract and also constitutional restrictions on taxation of immature timber. Many states give preferential property tax treatment for agricultural land, in exchange for the landowner's promise to keep the land in farming and ranching.

Major Trends

As with the other land uses surveyed, there are clear trends in resource land markets. The extent and importance of these trends will vary from location to location.

One of the longest established trends is the slow-paced, gradual depletion of the richer resource concentrations and eventual development of what originally would have been inferior quality resources. Some firms today, in fact, are successfully reworking waste dumps of older mines and old oil wells. In part this is a result of higher resource prices, but sometimes new processing techniques allow low-cost utilization of minerals that once were too expensive to process, or even impossible to extract.

A second long-term trend is the general increase in resource market prices. Although some, like oil prices, have had ups and downs over the last 20 years, most have gone up. In the long run, nearly all resource goods have increased in price, as a result of supply cost increases, growing scarcity of quality resource concentrations, and worldwide rising demand. The increase in market price for processed resources often circles back to produce an increase in resource land prices, as, for example, for western timberlands.

More recently, the search to locate these lower quality resources has emphasized research in exploration techniques. The concepts and tools now in use are increasingly complex and expensive to own and operate, so that the small prospector on a burro is not a major source of today's resource discoveries. Instead, the source may be equipment on an airplane, a helicopter, or a space satellite, owned or controlled by larger corporations able to fund this type of study. With the end of the cold war, many former eastern European countries are opening up as a source of raw materials, a trend that could serve to increase worldwide supply.

Finally, the rapid increase in the environmental and pollution control costs directly paid by the resource developer is a major recent trend. Many new resource programs are more influenced by this than by any other factor. For some resource users, adequate pollution control instruments cost too much relative to current resource market prices. New technology, lower costs, higher prices, or some combination of these three will be necessary for continued resource production at lower pollution levels. Because of national differences in handling these issues, another result is international shifts in production of various resources.

All of these major trends are interrelated to the key factors initially covered. As mentioned before, different resources are being influenced by these trends at different rates, as are different areas of the country. The interplay of factors will determine what happens to resource land values in each region and category.

REVIEWING YOUR UNDERSTANDING

Timber and Other Resource Lands

1. List five key factors influencing resource land use.

2. Give two examples of each and explain their effect on resource land use or value.

3. List four recent trends in resource land use.

CHAPTER SUMMARY

This chapter has emphasized the important influences on markets for rural land uses, stressing agricultural property, rural homes, and resource properties.

Key factors in determining the use and value of farmland include soil productivity, rainfall, length of growing season, water supplies, topography, parcel size, shape and layout, and farm improvements. Other factors include access, markets, community facilities, permits and quotas, competition from other rural uses, urban influences, crop prices, financing, environmentalism, and labor relations.

Major trends include increases in output per farmer, in average farm size, in specialization, and in export orientation. More recently, trends include a decrease in farm foreclosures, use of natural as opposed to chemical fertilizers and insecticides, and increasing environmental requirements.

The rural home market is really two markets—new recreational subdivisions and older rural homes. Each market attracts a different type of purchaser, and each has its own advantages and liabilities. Investors in new rural subdivisions must beware of buying into areas for which there is likely to be little or no resale demand. Buyers of old homes must carefully inspect their prospective properties for problems and investigate the economic strength of the area they are considering.

Investors in rural lands for resource purposes should examine a series of key factors that relate to the cost of processing the resource. Recent trends in technology and the continued depletion of resource stocks have made the exploration and further exploitation of old resource areas attractive.

IMPORTANT TERMS AND CONCEPTS

Crop markets	*Resource processing plants*
Environmentalism	*Soil banking*
Local market	*Soil productivity*
Permits and quotas	*Time-sharing*
Pollution controls	*Topography*
Price supports	*Transportation*
Recreational subdivision	*Water*

REVIEWING YOUR UNDERSTANDING

1. The U.S. "farm problem" is caused by:
   a. demand exceeding supply
   b. supply often exceeding demand
   c. technological change occurring more slowly in agriculture than in other industries
   d. worldwide hunger

2. A technique used by the government to reduce the supply of farm products is:
   a. favorable tax breaks for farmers
   b. price supports
   c. soil banking
   d. guaranteed farm loans

3. Which of the following would *not* have an impact on the price of farmland?
   a. soil productivity
   b. direction of urban growth patterns
   c. access
   d. all have impact

4. Which of the following is a demand, as opposed to a supply, factor that influences the value of farmland?
   a. increased output per acre
   b. better pesticides
   c. government quotas on crop output
   d. low interest rate farm loans

5. A rural residential homesite subdivision is considered misplaced if after several years:
   a. no building occurs
   b. the resale market for lots is active
   c. extensive building occurs
   d. commercial stores are constructed

6. The demand for recreational real estate is increased by all of the following, *except* an:
   a. upswing in the business cycle
   b. increase in the cost of building
   c. improved transportation access
   d. increase in discretionary income

7. Purchase of the use of real estate for a particular two-week period is called:
   a. condominium
   b. equity-sharing
   c. time-sharing
   d. periodic tenancy

8. Which of the following is typical of older rural homes?
   a. easier to finance than urban homes
   b. rarely suffer from deferred maintenance
   c. private water and sewer systems
   d. prices always rise in future years

9. The value of timber and other resource land is tied to the demand for the resource itself. The market price of the resource is determined primarily by:
   a. supply and demand forces in the national and international market
   b. supply and demand forces in the local market
   c. government decree
   d. the health of the local economy

10. All of the following are trends in resource real estate markets, *except*:
    a. gradual depletion of resources
    b. less concern for environmental issues
    c. resource land prices shift with the market price of the resource
    d. improvements in resource extraction technology

11. Rainfall is very important to agricultural land value, especially if it occurs:
    a. in sufficient quantity
    b. at the right time, place, and amount
    c. during the growing season
    d. without too much erosion

12. The length of the growing season:
    a. does not influence the types of crops grown
    b. is determined by consumer preferences
    c. determines how many crops per year can be harvested
    d. has negligible effects on farmer incomes

13. Irrigation:
    a. is the only solution to food shortages
    b. does not have an impact on land value
    c. allows inexpensive farming of former mountain areas
    d. requires very careful land management

14. Topography refers to the:
    a. surface features of land
    b. placement of improvements on the land
    c. mineral content beneath the land
    d. support one piece of land gives to an adjoining parcel

15. A location near crop-processing facilities:
    a. is a necessity for only a few specialty crops
    b. is more for farmer convenience than profitability
    c. is highly desirable for many crops
    d. is not influenced by transportation systems

16. Past long-term trends in U.S. agriculture include:
    a. a sharp rise in average farm size, mechanization, and invested capital per farm
    b. big increases in output per acre and in use of fertilizers and pesticides
    c. greater specialization by farmers in one or two crops
    d. all of the above

17. The government farm aid program that pays farmers for not planting an allocated number of acres of a specific crop is called set-asides or:
    a. price supports
    b. soil banking
    c. tariff guarantees
    d. inelastic supply

18. In terms of less successful rural homesite subdivisions or so-called "premature subdivisions," many original buyers were too motivated by investment potential and less motivated by the intent to use.
    a. true
    b. false

19. Vacation or second homes are often:
    a. available to rent
    b. very similar in size, design, features, and appearance to urban homes of similar size and age
    c. of significantly better quality than urban homes of similar size and age
    d. located in dense urban areas

20. The least common type of new vacation home is the:
    a. condominium
    b. time-share
    c. retirement home
    d. mansion

21. Units in new vacation home developments are almost always sold by longtime established local real estate brokers.
    a. true
    b. false

22. Rural home prices:
    a. are influenced by local employment as well as demand from outsiders
    b. tend to be higher than comparable urban homes
    c. are easier to appraise than urban homes
    d. are not influenced by the ease of accessibility

23. Which of the following is normally *not* a concern when buying a rural vacation home?
    a. square footage of the home or unit
    b. condition of sewage facilities
    c. quantity and quality of the water supply
    d. boundaries of the local school district

24. When buying an older rural home, a smart buyer should assume that maintenance problems exist, and the buyer should carefully investigate before purchasing.
    a. true
    b. false

25. The price of resource land is influenced by:
    a. access to processing facilities
    b. environmental requirements
    c. cost to develop the resource
    d. all of the above

CASE & POINT

Should the Government Subsidize Resource Development?

Historically, many governments, including the United States, have subsidized resource development. For example, people are encouraged to prospect for valuable ore on land owned by the U.S. government (excluding parks and military bases) and to file a mining claim if they find something of value. The law then allowed people to buy the land for a low fixed price if they spend the required sum of money developing a proper mine.

Other government subsidies include preferential income and property tax incentives for resource extraction. Federal or state funds are sometimes spent to improve access to the area, to provide job training, or to provide flood control protection, if it will help with resource development. And sometimes the subsidy is more subtle, as when government agencies issue needed permits without requiring the resource developer to eliminate all material pollution or other impacts on the adjoining properties. Finally, sometimes a government agency will step in and acquire property needed for the resource project, using its power of eminent domain. This can allow a private project to go ahead, despite the refusal of local property owners to sell land necessary to the project.

What economic reasons are given for these subsidies or assistance? Today, the foremost reasons are increased private jobs and the need to increase government revenue. Most government jurisdictions are very aware that they can help or hurt job growth and business survival. The economic recession of the early 2000s has made the creation of new jobs a major priority of government. In addition, resource developments are usually large enough to generate substantial amounts of new property taxes. In addition, spending by the resource company and its new employees increase sales tax revenues.

A particular benefit of most resource developments is that the new revenue generated is much greater than the required government services. Police, fire, and school costs are low, and local jurisdictions may consider resource projects to be profitable and to be encouraged.

But are resource extraction projects really profitable? The answer, of course, lies with how we measure profitability. Every resource project, no matter how well designed, will have impacts or "spillover" effects on a surrounding area. Resource projects often have the potential for substantial air or water pollution; the degree of abatement or mitigation required by a firm is critical to the financial feasibility of the project and is heavily debated at public hearings. Clearly, then, resource projects are probably not as profitable to the government as they appear at first glance.

Resources are always competing with other resources for an economic use. We can build homes with lumber cut from trees, or we can now build homes with steel studs. We can use trees to make paper, or we can use other fibers like cotton (and papyrus) to make paper. Often, too, we can recycle or reuse existing resources.

The bottom line questions are: Should the government be subsidizing the development of resources or should resource extraction costs be left to the private market? What if the material the government subsidizes generates waste that is hard to get rid of? Should the government only subsidize recycling as opposed to new development? Clearly, the United States is entering an era in which we must look more closely at all of the subsidies for resource development and modify those that no longer make economic sense.

PART THREE
MAJOR INFLUENCES
ON REAL ESTATE
DEVELOPMENT

CHAPTER 12
THE ECONOMICS OF REAL PROPERTY TAXATION

PREVIEW

In an effort to raise needed revenue, governments levy various taxes on real estate. This chapter examines the impact that real property taxes have on private real estate activity. Section 12.1 reviews the principles of taxation with emphasis on what influences the selection of a particular type of tax. Section 12.2 outlines the effect of real property taxes on real estate values. Section 12.3 deals with the problems of real property tax reform. The Case & Point at the end of the chapter discusses tax terminology used by government officials, as opposed to economists. When you have completed this chapter, you will be able to:

1. List two basic taxing philosophies in the United States.

2. Describe why the property tax is used by local government.

3. Discuss why many economists feel that the real property tax is regressive and a burden on lower-income people.

4. Give three examples of how real property taxes can influence land usage.

5. Discuss current and proposed real property tax reforms.

12.1 The Principles of Taxation

W hy must the government collect taxes? What is the philosophy behind taxation? Why doesn't the government just print more money? Who bears the burden of taxes? This section answers these questions, thereby laying the foundation for understanding what impact property taxes have on real estate activity.

Taxes Can Be Used to Redistribute Wealth

The government levies taxes to generate revenue. The tax revenue is used to buy resources, which the government then redistributes in the form of governmental goods and services.

The taxing process can be viewed as follows: A tax on consumers or businesses reduces their spendable income. With less spendable income, consumers and businesses buy less, causing a drop in demand. This drop in consumer and business demand releases resources—unsold resources are left on the seller's shelf. The government then uses tax money to acquire these released resources. In short, a tax diverts some resources from the private sector (consumers and businesses) to the government sector. Once acquired, these resources are redistributed by the government according to the guidelines established by elected officials.

In addition to taxing, the government can obtain revenue by borrowing, charging fees and issuing fines, and by printing money. Fees, fines, and borrowing operate somewhat like taxes, in that spending in the private sector is reduced, thereby releasing resources for governmental use. However, printing money is an entirely different matter. Printing money does not reduce spending; it stimulates spending. During periods of prosperity and full employment, printing money can cause excessive spending and bring on massive inflation. Thus the government is reluctant to print money as its only source of revenue. Given all the alternatives—taxes, fines and fees, or printing money—taxation has become the major method for generating government revenue.

Pay Now or Pay Later?

It should be noted that in recent years, the U.S. government has borrowed heavily to raise money to fund current government spending. This avoids the politically troublesome need to raise current taxes. However, down the road when the borrowed funds are paid back, taxes will need to be increased. This technique, of borrow now and pay later, shifts the tax problem to future generations. The bottom line is that, as economists are fond of saying, there is no free lunch. Every government program must be funded. The funding choices are to pay for it now by increasing taxes or borrow the funds, which will cause an increase in taxes at some future time. Another choice is to cut future government spending to pay for current spending. This latter choice has not had a good track record!

The Theory of Taxation

In *The Wealth of Nations*, Adam Smith stated that a tax should be:

1. Equitable, *meaning that the tax burden should be spread equally among all citizens.*

2. Certain, *meaning that every taxpayer should know how much tax is owed, when it is due, and for what it is being used.*

3. Economical, *meaning that the cost of collecting the tax should be small in relation to the amount of taxes collected.* In other words, it is uneconomical to institute a tax that costs $1,000 to administer but only brings in $2,000 in tax revenue.

Two Philosophical Principles

There are two major alternative philosophies regarding taxation. The first is that taxes should be based on a person's ability to pay. In other words, the rich should pay a higher percentage of their income for taxes than do the poor. The federal income tax is an example of a tax based on the ability-to-pay philosophy.

The second major philosophy is that taxes should be paid according to the benefits received from the government. A bridge toll is an example of a benefits-received tax. If a person uses the bridge, he or she pays the toll. If the bridge is not used, the toll is not paid. This is a so-called "user" tax.

Both of these philosophies have their problems: Does taxing based on ability to pay stifle incentive? Does it encourage people to seek tax loopholes? Or worse yet, does it provide an excuse for illegal tax evasion? On the other hand, if taxation is based on the benefits-received or "user" philosophy, will only the middle- and upper-income citizens receive government services? Will the poor, who may need the government's help the most, be denied this help because they cannot afford to pay? Would this increase conflicts between the rich and the poor?

Major Taxes and Expenditures

Each level of government—federal, state, and local—uses several different types of taxation in an effort to generate revenue. Table 12.1 shows the major tax and the largest single expenditure for each level of government in the United States.

The major source of revenue for the federal government is the personal income tax. The largest federal expenditure is for income security, and the second largest expense is for national defense. Income security refers to various federal programs to assist the unemployed, disabled, people on welfare programs, the homeless, and so on. In times of war, defense expenditures can be larger than income security expenditures.

For most state governments, the major source of tax revenue is the sales tax, and the largest expenditures are for education and welfare. Those states without a sales tax, such as Oregon, usually use a strong state income tax as a substitute. Some states, such as California, use a combination of a sales tax and a state income tax. In California, the state sales tax and state income tax produce almost the same revenue.

When it comes to local government the property tax is by far the largest single source of tax revenue. Even with an increasing amount of local income and sales taxes, the property tax is still the main source of tax revenue for most local governments. The major expenditure by local government is for education, followed by public safety.

Is the Tax Progressive, Proportional, or Regressive?

One way of evaluating a tax is to determine how the cost of taxes relates to the taxpayer's ability to pay. To help analyze the burden of a tax, economists describe taxes as progressive, proportional, or regressive.

Table 12.1 Major Tax and Expenditure by Each Level of Government

Government Level	Major Tax	Largest Expenditure
Federal government	Personal income tax	Income security
State governments	Sales tax	Education and welfare
Local governments	Property tax	Education

A *progressive tax* increases in rate as the value of a taxable item increases. Thus, if taxable value increases from $1,000 to $2,000, the tax rate will also increase from perhaps 5 percent to 15 percent. A *proportional tax* retains the same rate as the value of the item being taxed increases. If the value of the taxable item increases from $1,000 to $2,000, the tax rate remains the same (5 percent at $1,000, and still 5 percent at $2,000). A *regressive tax* declines in rate as the value of the item being taxed increases. If the value of the taxable item increases from $1,000 to $2,000, the tax decreases, perhaps from 5 percent to 2 percent.

When evaluating a tax based on a taxpayer's ability to pay, economists frequently modify the definition of progressive, proportional, and regressive by substituting the word *income* for the phrase *value of the item being taxed*. Thus, a *progressive tax* in this sense means that when income increases, the percentage of the tax also increases. A *proportional tax* means that when a taxpayer's income increases, the percentage of tax remains the same. A *regressive tax* means that when the income of the taxpayer increases, the percentage paid in taxes decreases.

Evaluating Major Taxes—Who Bears the Burden?

The personal income tax is somewhat progressive in that the tax rate rises as taxable income increases, reflecting the ability-to-pay philosophy. However, it should be noted that higher-income individuals tend to make use of tax experts and tax loopholes to reduce their tax bite. So in the real world, the progressiveness of the income tax is not as steep as the tax charts indicate.

The sales tax appears to be proportional in that the tax rate remains the same as the value of taxable items increases. But if one plots the amount of taxes paid against the income level of persons paying the sales tax, the *impact* of the sales tax turns out to be regressive. The poor end up paying a higher percentage of their income for sales taxes than do the wealthy. Lower-income individuals spend a greater percentage of their income on items that are subject to the sales tax than do wealthier individuals. Poor people must spend all their income to live. Wealthy people do not spend all their income on taxable living expenses. They save a certain portion (savings are not subject to the sales tax) and spend some on nontaxable services. Assuming a sales tax rate of 7 percent, Table 12.2 illustrates a hypothetical example of the regressiveness of a sales tax compared with income.

Special Interest Topic

Are State Lotteries a Form of Regressive Taxation?

During the 1980s, state governments were looking for additional sources of revenue, and many turned to state-operated lotteries. Groups opposed to lotteries warned that the source of this revenue would be from those citizens least able to pay, because people who buy lottery tickets tend to come from low-income backgrounds. The money spent on lottery tickets would be better spent on food, health, clothing, and other essentials of life.

Groups in favor of a lottery argued that lotteries would raise money for education and other programs that benefit everyone, including low-income people. The alternative would be to cut education and other programs because people would refuse to vote for the required tax increases to maintain these programs. However, people would vote for a lottery, and some of the lottery revenue would be targeted for education and other needed programs.

What have been the results? When presented to the people for a vote, in almost every case the state lottery law passed. Did the prediction come true that the lottery would be used primarily by low-income people? According to a study by the National Bureau of Economic Research in Cambridge, Massachusetts, approximately 50 percent of all money spent on lottery tickets comes from 5 percent of the lottery players. This group's profile is predominately middle-aged and/or minority, with a blue-collar background.

Win $20 Million (and Get a Lot Less!)

If you beat the odds and win a $20 million lottery, how much do you really get? Most state lotteries are exempt from state, but not federal, income tax. Further, the proceeds are not paid up front, but rather in 20 equal annual installments.

Example: Twenty million dollars less approximately 35 percent for federal income taxes, leaves a balance of approximately $13,000,000, which, divided by 20 years, equals $650,000 per year. This $650,000 per year, discounted for the time value of money, say, 6 percent, for the next 20 years, equals a present value of $7,455,450, and this is the current value of your prize. Not shabby, but not $20 million!

Table 12.2 Example of the Regressive Impact of a Sales Tax

Income	Amount Spent Subject to Tax	Tax Rate	Sales Tax	Percent of Income
$10,000	$10,000	7%	$700	7%
$100,000	$30,000	7%	$2,100	2.1%

In an attempt to make the impact less regressive, many states have exempted food, rent, and utilities from the sales tax. Poor people tend to spend a major portion of their income in these areas, and by providing exemptions, low-income people gain some relief from the regressive nature of the sales tax.

Who Really Pays the Tax?

Ultimately, all taxes are paid by people. But the person legally responsible for the tax payment may be able to shift the tax cost to someone else. Example: Retail store owners may be required to pay sales taxes to state and local governments—the actual check for the tax is paid by the store owner. But the store owner collects the tax from the consumer at the point of sale. Therefore, although charged for the sales tax, the store owner does not bear the incidence of the tax. When studying what impact existing or proposed new taxes will have on society, economists also trace who will actually end up with the tax burden.

REVIEWING YOUR UNDERSTANDING

The Principles of Taxation

1. In addition to taxes, name three other sources of government revenue.

2. How does taxing according to ability to pay differ from taxing based on benefits received?

3. Describe the differences between progressive, proportional, and regressive taxes. What are some problems associated with a progressive tax? With a regressive tax?

12.2 Evaluating the Property Tax

Use of the property tax in the United States dates from the founding colonists, who brought to this country Britain's concept of taxing land. After the U.S. Constitution was written, the new federal government used excise, sales, and other forms of taxation, leaving the property tax for state and local governments. By 1900, state governments for the most part had also abandoned the property tax in favor of other forms of taxation. This left local government as the sole collector of the property tax. This tradition has continued; property taxes are still the major source of revenue for city and county governments. This section examines what impact real property taxes have on real estate values.

Local Government and the Property Tax

Why have local governments held on so firmly to the property tax? With so many people complaining about high real estate taxes, why do local governments continue to use this tax?

First, if the property tax is discontinued, a new tax would be needed to take its place. The levying of any new tax runs into massive political and administrative problems. So, for better or worse, there is a tendency to stick with the existing tax system. Second, a tax on real estate has certain advantages that other taxes do not have. Real estate is visible and immobile—real estate cannot be hidden from the tax collector. Also, unlike the income tax or the sales tax, property tax revenue does not fluctuate widely with short-term swings in the business cycle. People tend to pay their property taxes because the penalty for not paying is loss of the property, and for most people, this is too high a price to pay.

Local governments like the property tax because it provides a stable source of revenue. This in turn makes establishing annual local and county budgets an easier task.

Who Really Pays the Property Tax: Owners, Tenants, or Consumers?

Who actually pays the tax? The property taxes paid on owner-occupied homes are usually nonshiftable—the owner pays. There are no tenants or customers to whom the tax can be passed. However, the situation for rental and business-owned property is entirely different. In the long run, property taxes are one of the costs of doing business and

Special Interest Topic

The Dilemma of the City: Taxpayers Are Decreasing While Tax Users Are Increasing

TAX PAYERS

TAX USERS

When city congestion drove upper- and middle-income people to the suburbs, their places were often taken by poor people seeking jobs. When the jobs failed to materialize, the poor went on welfare and drew upon other government services. Many major cities now have a dilemma: Taxpayers are decreasing while tax users are increasing.

How can this problem be solved? Should the city raise taxes to generate the needed revenue? Or would a tax increase just drive out additional taxpayers? Should the federal government increase its subsidies to the cities? Will suburban and rural people resent paying taxes to support cities where they do not reside?

are shifted to customers—be they apartment tenants or business clients.

What about tax increases? Are they immediately shifted to consumers? If market conditions allow, landlords usually shift property tax increases to tenants in the form of higher rents. It must be recognized that this shift will occur only if there is a "landlord's market"—a a strong tenant demand and a limited rental supply. When this exists, property tax increases are easily shifted to tenants. On the other hand, in a "soft" rental market with many vacancies, property tax increases tend to be absorbed by the landlord for fear that higher rents would cause a loss of tenants.

What if the tenants are businesses? If landlords can shift property tax increases to business tenants, do these businesses then shift the taxes to their customers in the form of higher prices? Do businesses that own their property shift the tax to their customers? The answer depends on the condition of the market in which the tenant-business operates. If the market is highly competitive, business can shift the tax to customers only to the extent that other business competitors pay the same taxes. If Business A pays a tax of $10 and competitor Business B pays $5, then in order to remain competitive, Business A must absorb the difference. If both Business A and Business B pay the same tax, they both can shift the full tax on to customers.

When discussing who pays increases in property taxes, it must be realized that some properties are rented on long-term leases, which may control whether the tenant or the landlord absorbs the tax increase. Also, in some areas, governmental rent controls determine who shall pay the increase in taxes.

Property Taxes and Capitalized Real Estate Values

It was stated earlier that an increase in real property taxes that cannot be shifted to others (e.g., tax increases on owner-occupied homes) can reduce the value of real estate. How much value will the property lose? Will the loss be equal to or greater than the tax increase? The answers to these questions depend on how the tax monies are spent. If the government uses the increased revenue from property taxes for expenditures that benefit the taxpayer's home, such as street improvements, outdoor lighting, or neighborhood cleanup, the taxpayer's property values may remain stable or even increase. However, if the tax increases are spent in such a way that the taxpayer receives no benefits, the taxpayer's property will lose sales value. The amount of the maximum loss would be the capitalized value of the tax increase. Table 12.3 illustrates this concept.

When there is a property tax increase, the loss in real estate value is not the amount of the annual tax increase, but rather the loss is the tax increase capitalized over a number of years. Of course, this applies only if (1) the tax increase does not benefit the taxpayer's property, and (2) the tax increase is not shifted onto others in the form of higher rents or prices.

Table 12.3 Capitalized Loss Caused by Property Tax Increase

	Before	After	Change
Taxes	$1,000/yr.	$1,100/yr.	$100 tax increase
Net Income *divided by the*	$10,000	$9,900	$100 reduction
Capitalization Rate *equals the*	10%	10%	none
Value Estimate	$100,000	$99,000	$1,000 loss

$$\frac{\text{Net Income}}{\text{Capitalization Rate}} = \text{Value Estimate}$$

Is the Real Property Tax Regressive?

Do poor people spend a higher percentage of their income on real property taxes than do wealthy persons? If so, the property tax is regressive. If real estate taxes tend to take the same percentage of income regardless of how much is earned, the property tax is proportional, not regressive.

Real property taxes are levied at a tax rate multiplied times a value. Thus, higher-valued properties are charged the same tax rate as lower-valued properties. But studies reveal that when one plots the dollar amount of real estate taxes paid against the income levels of the taxpayer, the real property tax is regressive. Lower-income persons spend a higher percentage of their income on property taxes than do wealthy persons.[1]

Reasons for Regressiveness

Economists usually note two reasons for the regressiveness of the property tax. One deals with the tax assessment procedure; the other looks at the percentage of consumer income spent on housing. First, assessors may assess high-priced properties more conservatively than low-priced properties because (1) there are more low-priced properties, (2) they tend to be alike, and (3) they are bought and sold frequently. This gives the tax assessor plenty of current market information for assessment purposes. On the other hand, high-priced

---

[1]D. Netzer, *Economics of the Property Tax,* Washington DC, Brookings Institute, 1966, pp. 46–56.

Special Interest Topic

How the Budget Process Works

Local government expense budgets are established, then sources of revenue are estimated and subtracted from the budget. Any remaining unfunded expenses must be cut or paid for by increased taxes. Participants in the local tax procedure are:

- The *Board of Supervisors* or *City Council* members, who set the budget.
- The *auditor*, who maintains the tax rolls.
- The *assessor*, who appraises the property.
- The *tax collector*, who is responsible for actually collecting the tax.

properties are not as common, they are exchanged less frequently, and, therefore, the tax assessor has less information to work with. In addition, wealthy property owners are usually able to hire experts to challenge the assessor's value estimates. Not wanting to face the dilemma of a show-cause proceeding, the assessor may tend to assess the expensive property at a lower value. In essence, the assessment process may be regressive, and this in turn makes the tax regressive. However, property tax revolts, such as California's Proposition 13, have tended to even out the tax assessment process and defuse a portion of this argument.

The other main reason given for the regressiveness of the real property tax is that lower-income people must spend a higher percentage of their income on housing than do wealthy individuals. Although people do trade up to better housing as income levels increase, it appears that spending on housing does not increase as fast as gains in personal income.[2] If their income doubles, people usually will not double the amount they spend for a home. Therefore, as income rises, housing costs (and property taxes paid) become a smaller percentage of income. This is a classic example of regressiveness.

---

[2] Ibid., p. 57.

Real Property Taxes and Land Usage

Although the primary purpose of the property tax is to generate revenue for local government, it is also possible for government to influence land use by manipulating the property tax. Some examples of how real property taxes can influence land use are given below.

1. By exempting religious, educational, and charitable institutions from taxation, the government is, in effect, using taxes as an incentive to create more of these institutions.

2. Assessing rural land based on its suburban residential potential can force up property taxes to the point that rural owners must sell to developers. On the other hand, a low preferential tax treatment of rural property may create an incentive to keep the land rural, thereby maintaining open green space.

3. Taxing resources such as timber and minerals at full value may force quick exploitation tactics, whereas special tax concessions during growing periods may encourage resource development and conservation.

4. Some communities have used artificially low property tax rates to attract industries and other new businesses to occupy city-owned industrial parks. Other cities may pursue a "no-growth" philosophy by raising taxes in an effort to discourage commercial development.

5. High property taxes during economic depressions can cause private ownership to be converted to government ownership as property owners default on their tax payments. Many cities and counties acquired large land holdings during the major depression of the 1930s.

6. Higher property taxes can cause more intensified land use as property owners rent spare rooms and garages, plow more acres, use more fertilizer, and so on, in an effort to offset tax increases with higher incomes.

7. Cities may be tempted to encourage retail land use, which generates more local revenue by way of sales taxes, and discourage residential uses, which may generate a need for additional services that cost more than the property tax revenue brings in.

These are but a few of the many ways in which government can direct land use via changes in property taxation. It should be stressed that any special concession to one type of property shifts the tax burden to the nonexempt property. In your community, who pays for church exemptions? Veteran's exemptions? Rural property exemptions? New business exemptions? Homeowner's exemptions?

REVIEWING YOUR UNDERSTANDING

Evaluating the Property Tax

1. What are some reasons local officials give for continued use of the real property tax? How much of your local government's revenue comes from property taxes? What is your largest local government expenditure?

2. What is meant by "shifting" the property tax? When is it difficult to shift the tax?

3. How does an increase in real property taxes affect real estate values? How does it affect land use?

4. When people state, "Real property taxes are regressive," what do they mean by regressive?

12.3 Real Property Tax Reform

Real property taxes are despised by property owners and tenants, labeled as regressive by economists, attacked by politicians up for election, and lobbied against by real estate trade organizations. Why does such an unloved tax still exist? If everybody hates it, why hasn't it been eliminated? This section examines real property tax reform.

Political Realities

In spite of all its faults, the property tax, as mentioned earlier, does have a strong feature—it produces a constant, predictable source of revenue that does not fluctuate widely with short-term movements in the business cycle. Some local governments have experimented with other forms of taxation, namely sales and income tax, but have run into numerous political problems. Citizens resent new taxes. They approve the removal of existing taxes but fight the introduction of a new, substitute tax. So it appears that until an acceptable substitute tax is devised, the property tax will remain.

Current Reforms

If people are stuck with the real property tax, can it be modified to remove some of its inequities? Most criticism of the property tax concentrates on its regressiveness. Thus, many reform proposals are aimed at aligning property taxes more closely with one's ability to pay. Several reforms are currently under way that can help to reduce the regressive features of the real property tax.

Exemptions for Low-Income People

Some communities have provided property exemptions for low-income people, especially the older, retired property owner. This exemption reduces the tax bite for people with low or fixed incomes, thereby shifting the property tax burden to those with higher incomes.

Exemptions for Homeowners

Some states have enacted laws exempting from taxation a flat dollar amount of the value of owner-occupied residential property. For example, California homeowners are allowed a $7,000 exemption, which works as follows:

Appraised Value	$200,000
Less: homeowner's exemption	− 7,000
Assessed value for property tax purposes	$193,00

This gives some small degree of relief to homeowners, who are usually unable to shift the property tax onto others.

Upgrading the Professional Skills of the Assessor's Office

Many states have established uniform assessment procedures to correct possible inequities in local assessors' offices. Statewide assessment rates, mandatory review procedures, and professional appraisal training are a few of the reforms. In most areas, the assessor is an elected official, and some reformers advocate changing this to a civil service appointment to try to remove the possibility of political favoritism from the assessment procedure.

Placing a Limit on Property Taxes

A so-called "taxpayers revolt" began on June 6, 1978, when the voters of California passed Proposition 13, the Jarvis—Gann Initiative. Proposition 13 limits real property taxes to 1 percent of the "full cash

**THEORIES AND
THEORETICIANS**

HENRY GEORGE AND THE SINGLE TAX

Library of Congress

Henry George (1839—1897) was a reformist concerned about economic inequities. As a newspaperman in the San Francisco area, he wrote emotional articles about the problems of rising land values and profiteering. George outlined his philosophy in a book entitled *Progress and Poverty*, published in 1880.

George believed that land was a free commodity, like air and sunlight, and thus belonged to all the people. However, he did believe in other forms of private property ownership. Therefore, he proposed that all rents for land were an unearned surplus and should be taxed away and given to the government to help eliminate poverty. He envisioned that if landowners were charged 100 percent taxes on land value, they would still develop the land because profits made from improvements on the land would not be taxed. George concluded that if all land were taxed as surplus value, enough revenue would be generated so that no other form of taxation would be required.

His book was an instant success, and George became famous. He moved to New York where, in 1886, he came close to being elected mayor of New York. He died in 1897 while campaigning once again for the mayor's office.

Although the single tax has never been completely adopted in the United States, Henry George had a tremendous impact on the whole idea of equity and taxing according to the ability to pay. Some current reform proposals regarding higher taxation on land and less on improvements have their roots in George's philosophy.

value" of the real property, plus an additional amount for local assessment bonds.

Beginning with a retroactive cutoff date of March 1975, property taxes can only be increased by 2 percent per year. The real estate can only be reassessed to full cash market value upon sale or other specified transfer of title. The effect is to limit property tax increases to 2 percent per year, measured from the time a property owner acquires title. Thus, two homeowners, side by side with identically valued homes, could have vastly different property tax bills depending on how long each has owned the property. Several states have followed California's lead and enacted their own versions of Proposition 13.

Groups opposed to this property tax limitation concept have challenged the constitutionality of these laws on grounds of unequal taxation. Some groups attack the concept based on the observation that owners of commercial and industrial properties get a better break than do homeowners. This argument points out that homes are bought and sold more often than commercial and industrial properties. Therefore, homes are reassessed and taxed at the new market price more often than business properties, and this shifts more property tax burden from business property owners to homeowners. In 1992, the U.S. Supreme Court declared Proposition 13 to be constitutional.

Possible Future Reforms

Other reform possibilities include increasing the tax burden assigned to land and reducing the tax rate on improvements. If land is taxed at a higher rate than improvements, there would be an incentive to bring vacant land into use. Also, an incentive would exist for property owners to improve their properties without the fear of a large increase in assessed value. However, there may be some practical problems in implementing this proposal, such as opposition from groups who wish to keep land as open space.

Another reform proposal states that inefficient, overlapping community services should be combined into larger regional units to gain economies of scale. For example, instead of having individual city schools, water, sewer, road construction, and utility departments, there would be a combined regional system, thereby reducing overhead. However, others object that combinations such as this would isolate government from the control of local citizens.

Still another reform proposal would limit the amount of property tax revenue that can be spent on education and welfare, the two major expenditures of local government. Those in favor of this proposal believe that property owners pay a disproportionate share of the cost for educational and welfare programs. This proposal would, in effect, shift the tax burden for education and welfare from local to state government.

California's Proposition 13 has in effect done exactly that. By limiting local property tax revenue, the state of California has needed to increase its share of the cost for local education and welfare. This has started a controversy of local versus state control over schools and welfare programs. Critics of Proposition 13 point out that "he or she who pays, in this case the state, gets to call the local shots." These same critics also point out that property tax limitation proposals merely substitute one regressive tax (property tax) with another regressive tax (state sales tax or lottery).

Other Taxes Affecting Real Estate

People tend to forget that in addition to the property tax, there are many other taxes that affect real estate. Major examples include:

Special assessments	Transfer taxes
Inheritance taxes	Severance taxes on
Gift taxes	natural resources
Income taxes	

All of these taxes are controversial in their own right. Currently, the issue of the level of the real estate transfer tax is being hotly debated in many areas of the United States. In an effort to raise additional revenue, local governments are looking at the possibility of sharply increasing the tax on the sale of real estate.

REVIEWING YOUR UNDERSTANDING

Real Property Tax Reform

1. List four types of real property tax reforms.

2. List two types of real property tax exemptions. Who pays for these exemptions?

3. What was Henry George's idea?

CHAPTER SUMMARY

When government levies a tax, resources are diverted from the private sector to government for redistribution according to the decisions of elected officials. Taxes are based on either the ability to pay or on the benefits received. Any tax can be analyzed to determine who bears the greatest burden relative to their ability to pay. A progressive tax, like the federal income tax, places a heavier burden on the wealthy. A regressive tax, like the sales tax and property tax, places a greater burden on the poor.

The property tax is used primarily by local governments and in most cases constitutes the single largest source of total revenue received by cities and counties. The greatest criticism of the property tax is its regressivenessthe heaviest burden is placed on lower-income individuals. In spite of all its shortcomings, the property tax persists because it does have one saving grace: It generates a constant, steady, and predictable source of revenue that does not fluctuate widely with short-term movements in the business cycle. Unlike federal and state governments, which depend on fluctuating income and sales taxes, local government can accurately predict how much property tax revenue it will receive and can budget accordingly.

Property taxes can reduce real estate income flows. If the taxes are not spent in a manner that enhances real estate, property values decline. The loss in value is the capitalized amount of the property tax. Real property taxes can be used by local government to influence land usage. Preferential tax treatment will encourage certain kinds of development, whereas abnormally high taxes can discourage other development.

A number of property tax reforms are under consideration, including low-income exemptions, homeowner's exemptions, and upgrading the skills of tax assessment officials. However, reform does not mean replacement. In the immediate future, it appears that the property tax will remain as the primary source of revenue for local governments.

IMPORTANT TERMS AND CONCEPTS

Ability to pay	*Proportional tax*
Benefits received	*Real property tax*
Homeowner's exemptions	*Regressive tax*
Personal income tax	*Sales tax*
Progressive tax	*Single tax theory*
Property tax and land usage	

REVIEWING YOUR UNDERSTANDING

1. All of the following sources of government revenue reduce private demand, *except*:
   a. taxes
   b. borrowing
   c. user fees
   d. printing money

2. Two major taxing philosophies are (1) ability to pay, and (2):
   a. redistribution
   b. regressive
   c. benefits received
   d. better distribution

3. As the taxpayer's income increases, the tax rate increases faster. This is an example of a:
   a. progressive tax
   b. proportional tax
   c. regressive tax
   d. reverse tax

4. Which of the following property owners is least able to shift a property tax increase to others?
   a. homeowner
   b. apartment landlord
   c. retail store owner
   d. office building owner

5. When measured against the income of the taxpayer, all of the following are considered by most economists to be regressive, *except*:
   a. property tax
   b. income tax
   c. sales tax
   d. lottery tickets

6. If the prevailing capitalization rate for real property is 10 percent, an increase in real estate taxes of $500 that cannot be shifted and is not beneficial to the subject property will cause a loss in value of approximately:
   a. $500
   b. $5,000
   c. $50,000
   d. $500,000

7. Taxes are used by governments to:
   a. raise revenue
   b. redistribute income
   c. encourage or discourage a private activity
   d. do all of the above

8. A charge levied by government to a developer for the cost of upgrading a city road to accommodate the increased traffic caused by the proposed development is a(n):
   a. ability-to-pay charge
   b. benefits-received charge
   c. progressive charge
   d. proportional charge

9. The main advantage of a property tax for local government is that it:
   a. is popular with voters
   b. swings quickly with changes in the local business cycle
   c. places a greater burden on the wealthy, as opposed to the modest landowner
   d. is easier to predict property tax revenue compared to other taxes

10. Regarding property tax limitations such as California's Proposition 13, which of the following is true?
    a. the tax is evenly spread across all homeowners
    b. homeowners seem to get a better break than business property owners
    c. tax expenditure decisions have shifted from local to state government
    d. all economists agree that the limitations are beneficial

11. Ultimately, all taxes are paid by:
    a. people
    b. government
    c. businesses
    d. corporations

12. When government borrows on a long-term basis to pay for current expenditures, this shifts the tax burden to future generations.
    a. true
    b. false

13. During peace time, the largest expenditure for the federal government is:
    a. defense
    b. education
    c. income security and other entitlements
    d. employment costs

14. The largest expenditure for local government is:
    a. defense
    b. education
    c. income security and other entitlements
    d. employment costs

15. The major tax for the federal government is:
    a. sales tax
    b. excise tax
    c. income tax
    d. property tax

16. The major tax for local government is:
    a. sales tax
    b. inheritance tax
    c. income tax
    d. property tax

17. Which is considered a progressive tax?
    a. sales tax
    b. excise tax
    c. income tax
    d. property tax

18. The person legally obligated for a tax is always the same person who actually bears the burden for the tax.
    a. true
    b. false

19. Which item subject to taxation is the least apt to be hidden from the tax collector?
    a. income
    b. goods
    c. real estate
    d. profits

20. In a high demand market, if all businesses pay the same tax, there is a tendency to shift this tax to:
    a. stockholders
    b. customers
    c. other businesses
    d. employees

21. Lower-income people tend to spend a lower percentage of their income on housing costs.
    a. true
    b. false

22. Property tax exemptions for churches, veterans, and homeowners constitute a tax shift to owners of nonexempt properties.
    a. true
    b. false

23. The famous advocate of a 100 percent tax on land value as a substitute for all other taxes:
    a. Adam Smith
    b. Karl Marx
    c. John Maynard Keynes
    d. Henry George

24. Which of the following proposals would substitute one regressive tax for another?
    a. decrease property taxes and increase sales taxes
    b. decrease property taxes and increase income taxes
    c. decrease use of lottery revenue and increase income taxes
    d. decrease income taxes and increase sales taxes

25. Which of the following taxes can have an impact on real estate ownership?
    a. transfer tax
    b. inheritance tax
    c. gift tax
    d. all of the above

CASE & POINT

Tax Talk . . . Say What You Mean!

The so-called *T* word is so dreadful for elected government officials that the language of taxation in political circles has changed from the standard economic definitions. Here are some key tax concepts as used by economists and elected government officials.

Economists Say:	Elected Official Say:
"Tax"	"Revenue Enhancement" if they voted for the tax. If they voted against the tax they call it a "tax."
"Tax Burden"	"Fair Share" if they voted for the tax. If they voted against the tax they call it a "Tax Burden."
"Government Spending"	"Government Investment" unless they voted against the spending; then it is called "Pork."
"Tax Incentives"	"Tax Incentives" unless they voted against; then they call the incentives "Tax Loopholes."
"Tax Increase"	"Tax Reform" unless they voted against the increase; then they call it a "Tax Increase."
"Removing a Tax Deduction in Order to Raise Revenue"	"No New Taxes."
"A Need to Raise Taxes"	"Need for more government leadership" or "Need for public responsibility" or "The American people wish to increase their contribution."

The political reality is that many voters believe that "taxes are OK as long as I don't pay." This presents a major problem for elected officials, who need to raise government revenue to enact programs that voters demand. If the politicians openly raise taxes to provide government programs, there is a good chance they may have problems at the polls at reelection time. Likewise, if they fail to deliver the government programs, they may not get reelected. To solve this dilemma some elected government officials have resorted to the new language illustrated above.

CHAPTER 13
LAND-USE CONTROLS

PREVIEW

Land-use controls are controversial: Some people feel that land is a commodity to be bought and sold like any other product. They consider any type of land-use control an infringement on free enterprise. At the other extreme are those who believe land is a resource that belongs to all the people, the use of which should be completely controlled by public agencies. Somewhere in the middle is the view that land is both a commodity and a resource, which should be privately owned but used constructively to benefit society.

Section 13.1 outlines the major forms of private and public land-use controls. Section 13.2 summarizes the principles of urban land-use planning. Section 13.3 examines recent land-use trends, noting nationwide emphasis on the environment, coastal zoning, and pollution regulations. The Case & Point at the end of the chapter presents two viewpoints regarding property rights. When you have completed this chapter, you will be able to:

1. List two reasons for the current controversy over land-use controls.

2. List two forms of private land-use controls and two forms of public land-use controls.

3. Describe the three major steps in creating a comprehensive plan for a community.

4. Describe recent trends in land-use controls.

13.1 Types of Land-Use Controls

The current debate over public land-use controls has its roots in two economic concepts: (1) The supply of land at the right location is now scarce, and (2) many people view land as a resource, not just as a commodity.

In the frontier days, land was plentiful and inexpensive, and there was little concern over its use. Wastefulness was tolerated because of the seemingly inexhaustible supply. Land was treated as a commodity to be bought, sold, and speculated on, much like agricultural products.

With the settling of the West and the massive increase in urban population, land-use controls were deemed necessary to protect neighbors from each other and to protect and preserve the land. However, controls meant surrendering a degree of individual freedom and conflicted with the deep-rooted traditions of free enterprise and private property rights.

Today the land-use controversy centers on this question: To what extent can private land be controlled without destroying the principles of private property rights? There is no "right" answer to this question. Each person must make a decision based on his or her own interpretation of the issues. This section outlines private and public land-use controls.

Private Land-Use Controls

Private land-use controls refer to nongovernment regulation of land. Two major private controls are (1) economic highest and best use, and (2) private deed restrictions.

Economic Highest and Best Use

In a pure capitalistic economy, the basic control over land use is market allocation: The interaction of supply and demand will eventually determine the highest and best use of land. *Highest and best use is defined as that legal use that will produce the greatest net income attributable to the land at a specific location.* In theory, if the market is left alone, competitive bidding would eventually determine what is the most profitable use of the land. Once this use has been established, it will continue until a more profitable use comes along. The private market controls land use through the maximization of private profit.

In a pure capitalistic system, land control using the concept of economic highest and best use can work. But our capitalistic system is mixed, not pure, and the goal of private profit may not correspond with social goals. Under mixed capitalism, if private interests differ from social interests, private interests must frequently be modified to support social goals. In today's real estate market, the economic concept of highest and best use exerts a powerful influence on land use, but it is not the only one. Other private and public tools are used to modify land use in spite of profit considerations.

Private Deed Restrictions

Private land use can be controlled by the placing of restrictions in deeds. Private deed restrictions are commonly referred to as "covenants, conditions, and restrictions," or CC&Rs for short. The law of real property allows owners to limit the use of land by contract as long as the contract restrictions are not contrary to public policy. Although there are technical differences between a covenant, a condition, and a restriction, the basic concept is the same—they attempt to maintain property values by preventing land from being used in a manner that would be adverse to nearby properties. The importance of compatible nearby uses was stressed in Chapter 8.

Private deed restrictions are usually created in one of three ways: (1) Existing property owners get together and agree to create restrictions mutually beneficial to all parties; (2) an owner of a large parcel of land sells off a portion or portions and inserts restrictions in the deed to protect his or her remaining parcels from adverse uses by the new neighbor(s); or (3) a land developer creates blanket tract restrictions for a new subdivision.

Recent inroads made by public controls have somewhat diminished the use of private deed restrictions. However, many questions not usually controlled by zoning or by codes can be handled by private restrictions. Examples include architectural uniformity, landscaping standards, light and air easements, maintenance agreements, and homeowner association controls.

Public Land-Use Controls

Industrialization and urban crowding have created a need for public controls to maintain order and promote social harmony. One way to maintain order is to control the use of the land. Government can use one or all of the following powers to control land use: (1) police power, (2) the power of eminent domain, (3) government spending power, and (4) the power of taxation. As taxation was discussed in Chapter 12, this section discusses only police power, eminent domain, and government spending.

Police Power

Police power refers to the constitutional right of government to regulate private activity to promote the general health, welfare, and safety of society. Police power has often been used in the United

States to direct land use. Some major examples of police power include zoning ordinances, building and health codes, setback requirements, pollution abatement, and rent controls. Of the many police power enactments, zoning and subdivision regulations emerge as the most influential methods of controlling land use.

Zoning

Zoning refers to the division of land into designated use districts. In zoning's simplest form, these districts are divided into residential use, commercial use, industrial use, and rural use. Each use in turn can have several subclasses. For example, residential can be broken down into single-family, multifamily, and mobile home zones. Commercial zones are often divided into zones for retail, office, and wholesale space. Industrial zones can be divided into light industry and heavy industry, and rural zones into agricultural, resource, or recreational uses.

Zoning as a land control tool was not common in the United States until the 1920s. Prior to that time there was some doubt about the constitutionality of zoning, although early zoning laws can be traced to Colonial times. But in the 1926 landmark case *Euclid v. Amber Realty Company*, the Supreme Court held that zoning was a reasonable exercise of government police power. Since this decision, every state has passed legislation allowing individual cities and counties to enact zoning ordinances.

Early zoning ordinances were aimed at safety and nuisance control. The idea was to use zoning to protect individual property values by prohibiting offensive use of surrounding land. The use of zoning has gradually been expanded, and now it is used to promote the general welfare of the entire community.

Subdivision Regulations

Another important use of police power is subdivision regulation. Poorly conceived subdivisions, with inadequate streets and facilities, can become a burden to taxpayers in later years, when expensive redevelopment is needed to correct earlier oversights. Proponents of subdivision controls believe that the origin of slums and urban blight can be traced to inadequate regulations. Opponents disagree, noting that today's slums are the result of government ordinances that prevent land from rising to its economic highest and best use.

Today, subdivision regulations are used in most areas of the United States. Real estate developers are frequently required to provide water, sewer, storm drainage, paved streets, sidewalks, street lights, and school and park sites as a condition of being allowed to subdivide. The idea is to plan for the future at the inception and to require the purchaser of the subdivided lot, not the community as a whole, to pay the expense of

Special Interest Topic

Conflicts Between Police Power and Eminent Domain

Police power allows government to regulate private land without the payment of compensation, whereas eminent domain converts private property to public ownership and requires the payment of compensation. The question might be asked, How far can the government limit or interfere with the private use of land without taking the land for public use, which involves eminent domain and the payment of compensation? There is no clear answer. The line of distinction between the police power and eminent domain is fuzzy. Various courts have moved back and forth depending on the circumstances in each case.

added community facilities. Like all public controls, subdivision regulations are controversial in that they require the surrender of some individual rights in an attempt to promote the general welfare.

Eminent Domain

Police power allows government to regulate private land without the payment of compensation. The power of eminent domain is different in that it allows the government to acquire title to private land in exchange for the payment of just compensation. Eminent domain is used for a variety of government land-use projects such as highways, public housing, and urban renewal.

Most levels of government may exercise power of eminent domain regardless of how unwilling the property owner may be. The main issue in most eminent domain cases is the amount of compensation. The courts have ruled that the property's fair market value is the usual basis for determining compensation. In addition, most federal and some state agencies must also pay for moving and other miscellaneous expenses incurred by any occupant being displaced, whether owner or tenant.

Government Spending as an Influence on Land Use

Through its enormous spending power, the government can influence the use of land. The courts have held that the government can spend money for almost any purpose as long as it is for the benefit of the public. Government funds have been used to finance many types of real estate-oriented developments such as roads, dams, canals, and power facilities. In addition, governmental subsidies such as aid to farmers and FHA and VA (Veterans Administration) mortgage guarantees can influence land use. The spending power of the government is so great that it can direct some land use without the necessity of eminent domain, police power, or taxation.

REVIEWING YOUR UNDERSTANDING

Types of Land-Use Controls

1. List two economic concepts that are at the root of the current land-use controversy.

2. List two private land-use controls and give one example of each.

3. List two public tools for controlling land use. Give two examples of each.

4. How does the power of eminent domain differ from the police power?

13.2 Principles of Urban Planning

Since the early 1900s, the United States has shifted from a rural to an urban nation. In 1900, approximately 40 percent of the United States population lived in urban areas. By the mid-2000s, this percentage had increased to over 70 percent. Some states have even greater concentrations of population; well over 90 percent of Californians live in urban areas.

Most cities and suburbs were unprepared to handle this massive increase in urban growth. In some cases, the result has been over-crowding, slums, property tax problems, traffic congestion, and many other urban ills. Out of this confusion has risen the cry for better urban planning. This section describes the principles of urban planning.

Definition of Urban Planning

The dictionary defines *planning* as "thinking out acts and purposes beforehand." When applied to urban areas, planning can be defined as anticipating and achieving community goals in light of social, eco-nomic, and physical needs. Urban planning requires that a community analyze its assets and liabilities, establish its goals, and then attempt to achieve these goals using land-use control as a primary tool.

The word *planning* causes apprehension among some people, because they fear planning will mean loss of economic and political freedom. Those who support the concept of urban planning believe that directing a community's growth presents no threat to personal freedom.

Creation and Implementation of Urban Planning

The establishment of a community plan requires three major steps: (1) resource analysis, (2) formulation of community goals, and (3) implementation of the plan.

Resource Analysis

The first step in urban planning is to recognize the individual char-acter of the community. What are its strong points? What are its weak-nesses? To accomplish this, several substudies will be required, including an economic base study, a population trend study, a housing element study, a survey of existing land use, a city facilities study, and an analysis of the community's financial resources. Once a resource inventory has been taken, the next step is to formulate com-munity goals in light of its resources.

Formulation of Community Goals

The formulation of community goals is the most difficult phase of urban planning because of the conflict among various special-interest groups, each trying to secure its own definitions of the community goal. However, citizen input should be encouraged, because a community plan must be based on the desires of community residents as a whole, not on the desires of staff planners alone.

Once the goals are established, a comprehensive plan to achieve these objectives must be formulated. The plan is frequently referred to as the *general plan*, and it should encompass all social, economic, and physical aspects of the desired growth. The plan should be long range but provide for short-range flexibility as the need for modification arises. Under no circumstances must the general plan be viewed as an inflexible, permanent fixture that will never require modification. A community's attitudes and resources can change, and the general plan must be modified to recognize these changes.

Implementation of the General Plan

The final step in urban planning is to implement the general plan. The implementation phase requires local government to use police power, eminent domain, taxation, and control over government spending to enact the plan. These powers have been discussed earlier, but it should again be stressed that the two most powerful tools for implementing a community plan are zoning and subdivision regulations.

Zoning can be used to separate incompatible land uses, promote health and safety standards, preserve property values, and minimize the cost of public improvements, whereas subdivision regulations can

---

Special Interest Topic

Summary of Planning Terms

Planning commission—An appointed body of citizens charged with the responsibility of advising the elected board of supervisors or city council members in matters of land use.

Planning department—City or county staff employees who lend professional and technical assistance to elected officials.

Zone—An area defined on a map by a boundary line within which the land-use regulations are the same.

Rezoning—The process of changing the land-use regulations on specified property from one zone to another.

Variance—A deviation from the zoning regulations for a particular parcel.

Condition—A requirement imposed by the government in connection with the approval of a permit or a division of property.

Development plans—Plans showing the details of the proposed development. Normally includes a plot plan, architectural renderings, and statistical information relative to acreage, building area, units, and parking.

Subdivision—A division of property into five or more parcels.

Lot split—A division of property into two, three, or four parcels.

Architectural review—Certain zoning areas in which a special citizen group approves or rejects the proposal based on its architectural compatibility with the surrounding area.

Appeal—The right to request review of a negative planning commission decision. The appellate process goes from the planning commission to the board of supervisors or city council to the courts.

LuLu—Stands for Local Undesirable Land Use, a slang phrase.

NIMBY—Stands for Not In My Back Yard, a slang phrase.

Host Community Benefits (Impact Fees)—Payments by a developer to local government in exchange for the right to proceed with the building project.

be used to chart the quality and quantity of future land division. When these two tools are used in conjunction with other public controls, the general plan has the best chance of being implemented.

If the general plan has been well conceived, and if it represents a consensus of the community, the implementation should proceed with a minimum of friction. On the other hand, if the community plan fails to represent citizen input, or if public agencies misuse the tools of implementation, the plan will meet with failure.

The Need for Regional Planning

Historically, planning has been a local matter. Each community developed its own plans within the confines of its own territorial limits. In the process, each community attempted to optimize its own social and economic well-being, frequently at the expense of surrounding areas. For example, the placing of a smelly industrial plant on the border of one city has a spillover effect on the neighboring community downwind.

The growth of multicity metropolitan areas has underscored the need for more efficient planning on a regional basis for such projects as water and sewage systems, rapid transit, highway traffic patterns, airports, and pollution controls. Any attempt by individual cities to

THEORIES AND THEORETICIANS

Early American Planners

WILLIAM PENN (1644–1718)

Library of Congress

Systematic land planning in the United States began with William Penn in 1682. Penn, an English Quaker and founder of the Commonwealth of Pennsylvania, began in 1682 to plan and design the city of Philadelphia. Using a checkerboard grid, he mapped out the city and a surrounding system of agricultural villages to help feed the city inhabitants. As a land promoter, Penn traveled throughout Europe selling land in an attempt to populate his colony. Penn died in 1718, deeply in debt.

attack these problems can result in inefficient small-scale operations and needless duplication.

From an economic point of view, what might be needed is a regional government, with the power to tax and administer regional programs. However, from a political point of view, there is a widespread resistance to the creation of another layer of government. Moreover, local government officials are reluctant to surrender some of their power. What usually occurs is a compromise—a regional commission or district created to solve a single problem. Metropolitan

**THEORIES AND
THEORETICIANS**

**Early American
Planners**

PIERRE CHARLES L'ENFANT (1754–1825)

National Archives

L'Enfant was a French-born engineer and architect who fought for the colonies during the Revolutionary War. In 1791, L'Enfant was commissioned by George Washington to design a new federal city in the District of Columbia. Avoiding the grid street plan, L'Enfant designed a city of radiating streets with wide avenues and numerous parks. Two years later, a dispute with Congress led to L'Enfant's dismissal. Numerous disputes over compensation followed, and L'Enfant died in poverty in 1825, never seeing his dream city completed. However, many of his key ideas can be seen in the city today.

rapid transit districts, regional park commissions, and regional water quality control boards are some examples.

Regional planning is easiest to implement when the regional organization is given the power to tax and receive direct federal and state aid. If the regional commission depends wholly on annual grants from the treasury of individual cities within the geographic area, political infighting between cities tends to dilute the implementation of regional planning.

There seems to be a movement toward more planning on a regional basis. The impact of this planning will depend on the willingness to forgo some local control in favor of a regional commission. In some cases, local communities have little choice because national and state legislation may require regional controls. But, required or not, regional planning will work best if it can be proven to local citizens that the result will be better coordination and perhaps a savings of tax dollars. If the evidence is to the contrary, regional planning will meet tremendous resistance.

REVIEWING YOUR UNDERSTANDING

Principles of Urban Planning

1. What is the purpose of urban planning?

2. List three major steps needed to establish a community plan.

3. What are the two most powerful tools for implementing a community plan?

4. Why is regional planning being used?

13.3 Recent Trends in Land-Use Controls

As stated earlier, land-use controls are controversial. At the core of the controversy is the recognition that usable land is a scarce resource that needs some public controls. But how much control is needed? There are those who feel that recent land-use controls are too stringent, whereas others feel that more controls are needed.

Some recent and controversial land-use controls include: (1) control over premature subdividing, (2) pollution and environmental regulations, (3) slow-growth or no-growth policies, (4) the creation of new towns, (5) state and federal intervention in land-use controls, and (6) inclusionary zoning. Many of these are interrelated and are a by-product of the environmental movement.

Preventing Premature Subdividing

Public control over the subdividing of land has existed for decades, but there has recently been a concerted effort to control what is known as a premature subdivision. A subdivision is "premature" when home construction fails to take place after the subdivision lots are sold. Frequently, the developer has already dedicated the streets, sewers, and other off-site facilities to the local government. Local government then finds itself in the position of having to maintain the unused facilities. The lack of home construction fails to generate the needed property tax revenue, and the local government is put in a financial bind. For small, rural governments, this situation can be especially painful.

To prevent premature subdivision, some planning agencies require would-be developers to show the likelihood of home construction as one of the conditions for obtaining a subdivision permit. This requirement, along with the difficulty in meeting environmental regulations, has caused subdivision activity to decline in many rural areas.

Pollution and Environmental Regulations

Beginning in the 1960s and continuing today, there has been a tremendous amount of federal legislation dealing with pollution and environmental issues, including water and air quality, waste disposal, resource recovery, endangered species, coastal preservation, and environmental impact report requirements, just to name a few. State efforts at pollution and environmental protection have produced similar laws.

Much of this legislation seeks to regulate land use to minimize environmental damage. Before a construction project is approved, the developer must show what impact the proposed project will have on the environment. The permit-issuing agency then decides, after first consulting with experts and holding public hearings, whether to issue the permit.

Like other controls, pollution and environmental regulations increase the cost of land development in terms of both time and money. The contents of an environmental impact report will be discussed in more detail in Chapter 15, "Required Government Reports."

Slow-Growth and No-Growth Policies

For many years, communities and local business groups spent large sums of money advertising the amenities of their area in an attempt to attract industry and people. Their goal was more growth. However, increased congestion and pollution have led some communities to reverse their positions, adopting slow-growth or no-growth policies.

Communities can discourage growth by making it difficult to build a home or by preventing the establishment of businesses that will create jobs. Land-use controls can be an effective tool in discouraging unwanted growth. For example, a community can keep additional people out by converting vacant land to public parks. Or it can allow only the affluent to move into a community by creating zones for expensive homes. Another common slow-growth tool is to only allow a limited number of building permits each year. Builders competing for permits are required to submit proposals that are rated on how "beneficial" each is to the community. A community can prevent business expansion by creating tough pollution standards, levying excessive taxes, or by preventing the construction of new transportation facilities.

A case can be made *for* slow- or no-growth policies by stressing the need to preserve open space, to avoid pollution, to maintain the community's way of life, and to keep from straining community fiscal budgets. However, equally good cases can be made *against* no-growth policies by pointing out that they can discriminate against lower-income persons who are attempting to improve their status. A no-growth policy can freeze low-income people at their present level by reducing economic opportunities, which in turn can prevent upward social mobility.

On a national basis, the only effective no-growth policy is a decrease in the rate of population growth. However, on a state or local basis, no-growth can be achieved by shifting the burden of population growth to another state or community. This naturally leads to infighting and dissension among states and communities. Several court cases are currently attempting to resolve the no-growth question by delineating the right of the government to control growth and the rights of individuals to live and work where they please. Once this question is resolved, the answer will have a significant impact on local real estate activity.

The Creation of New Towns

Among planners a debate exists about whether urban density can best be relieved by (1) creating new towns in rural areas, (2) shifting people to existing smaller cities, or (3) leaving the countryside as it is and redeveloping the major cities to accommodate more people.

Planners who favor the creation of new towns believe that, in the long run, it is more economical to build entire new cities to handle population increases than to attempt to redevelop existing major cities. The new cities would be self-contained, so that people could live, work, and shop with a minimum of commuting. Columbia, Maryland, and Reston, Virginia, although several decades old, are two examples of such "new" cities.

Others feel that instead of building entire new cities, the government should encourage the growth of existing small towns. Greatest emphasis would be placed on enlarging towns in economically depressed areas, where such action would help fight chronic unemployment. A key proposal is to use government contracts or subsidies to entice businesses to relocate to the depressed regions.

Some planners are critical both of the new town concept and the idea of encouraging growth in existing smaller towns. They believe that the problems of urban America will not evaporate with the development of new cities. They also believe that it is improper to destroy the culture of existing rural areas by importing population from major cities. Instead, this group believes that the best solution is to redesign existing metropolitan areas to allow for living with a higher density. The planners note that by European standards our major cities are underpopulated and that through good design we can increase the number of people per acre without an increase in their feeling of being crowded. This can be accomplished by converting our existing horizontal parking space, residential areas, and shopping centers to high-rise buildings, thus instantly generating more space without expanding the city limits. However, planners who favor new towns or the expansion of existing smaller cities rebut by stating that given the opportunity, people prefer low- as opposed to high-density living.

Although planners disagree on the best solution for urban congestion, most do agree that any solution is going to require massive government assistance in at least two forms: land assemblage, using the government's power of eminent domain; and financial assistance to build initial off-site improvements such as streets, sewers, water plants, and other basic facilities. However, the building of new towns or reconstruction of existing cities need not be totally a government project. After the initial planning, land acquisition, and off-site development financing have taken place, the project can be turned over to private enterprise for completion. The combination of urban dwellers seeking better surroundings and profit-motivated businesses willing to provide these surroundings could produce the economic setting needed to help defeat urban congestion.

State and Federal Intervention in Land-Use Controls

In the past, land-use controls were essentially a local matter. Cities and counties enacted land controls to achieve their own goals. However, recent urban pressures have increased the amount of land regulation at the state and federal level. There is a feeling that some problems are too large for a single city to handle, or that self-interest causes some communities to seek a solution that has a detrimental effect on a neighboring community.

Metropolitan problems have led to the creation of regional commissions charged with overseeing the activities of all regions within the state. An example of a regional-state relationship is the California Coastal Zone Conservation Act of 1972. This act recognizes that the coast of California "belongs to all the people and that it has a delicately balanced ecosystem that should be permanently protected." The act requires local regions and communities to incorporate coastal planning into their general plan. Each local entity is charged with controlling coastal development within its area, but the state commission established guidelines that local planners must follow.

On a still higher level, there is considerable discussion whether the federal government should enact a comprehensive national land-use policy. The proposal would require each state to adopt a statewide environmental, recreational, and industrial land-use plan. The federal plan would require the establishment of industrial, conservation, and recreational sanctuaries. Federal grant-in-aid funds would be available to assist states in creating and maintaining the plan. To assure adoption, the federal government would use its power to withdraw federal aid and expenditures from any state that failed to comply with the regulations. This threatened loss of federal funds would assure state compliance.

People in favor of more state and federal land-use controls believe that an overall general plan for land use is needed. They note that many communities have general plans for development within local boundaries and that state and national governments should likewise have a general plan for land within their boundaries.

Opposition to state and national land-use controls comes from individuals who argue that the power of land regulation should be limited to local government. They fear that planning on a state or federal level would not be sensitive to local needs. Who is correct? Like most land-use controls, the correct answer depends on one's value judgment.

Inclusionary Zoning

Inclusionary zoning is a type of regulation that requires a developer of new residential housing to set aside a designated number of units for low- and moderate-income people. If the project is an apartment complex, the developer must rent a percentage of the units to low-income people at specified below-market rent. If the project offers houses for sale, a certain percentage must be sold at below-market prices. To assure that the units will remain available to low-income families after the initial sale, restrictions are inserted in the deed.

If a developer does not provide units per the inclusionary ordinance, either the building permit is denied, or in some cases an in-lieu fee is paid to the government entity. To entice builders to cooperate, many inclusionary zoning ordinances provide for density bonuses, by which the builder is allowed to construct more units per acre.

Again, "There is no such thing as a free lunch." Inclusionary zoning does incur a cost. The price of other units in the development usually must be increased to offset the losses the builder incurs on the below-market priced units. In essence, the buyers of regular units subsidize the buyers of the below-market priced units. Thus, the burden for providing affordable housing units is shifted from the government sector to the private sector. Inclusionary zoning laws are highly controversial, and the issue is constantly under legal challenge.

Land-Use Controls and the Real Estate Industry

The trend seems to be set—more and more public control over private land use. Instead of being just a vehicle for the production of profit, land will more than likely also be viewed as a resource to be used to achieve social as well as economic well-being. As this attitude toward land use expands, the real estate industry must participate in the decision-making process to present its views. Both property owners and the real estate industry must see that land-use regulations consider the views of all the citizens, not just those of a select few. The key is to eliminate the undesirable aspects of poor land management while maintaining the good qualities of private real estate ownership. This is a difficult task that will require cooperation and compromise from preservationists, conservationists, environmentalists, private real estate interests, government, and all other groups who are interested in real estate use.

REVIEWING YOUR UNDERSTANDING

Recent Trends in Land-Use Controls

1. List two examples of recent pollution and environmental regulations that have influenced land use in your area. Are they local, regional, state, or federal land-use controls?

2. Some economists state that no-growth policies are discriminatory against lower-income people. What reasons do they give to justify their statement?

3. Why have some recent land-use regulations come from state, as opposed to local, government?

CHAPTER SUMMARY

The current debate over public land-use controls has its roots in two economic concepts: (1) the supply of land at the right location is scarce, and (2) the public is viewing land as a resource, not just a commodity. Land-use controls can be divided into two broad categories: private controls and public controls. Private land-use controls include economic highest and best use decisions and private deed restrictions. Public land-use controls include the use of government police power, eminent domain, government spending patterns, and taxation. Increased urban density has created a need for land planning. Planning can be defined as "anticipating and achieving community goals in light of the community's social, economic, and physical needs."

The establishment of a community plan requires three major steps: (1) resources analysis, (2) formulation of community goals, and (3) implementation of the plan. Zoning and subdivision regulations are the two most powerful tools for implementing a community's general plan. With the growth of multicity metropolitan areas, some planning has shifted from the local community to regional commissions.

Recent trends in land-use controls include the prevention of premature subdivisions, pollution and environmental regulations, slow-growth or no-growth policies, the debate over the creation of new towns, and state and federal intervention. The trend seems to be toward more public control over private land uses. This has caused a polarization of the issue. There are those who feel present land controls are too stringent and are a threat to our economic system. Others believe that more controls are needed. Proper land-use control is a difficult issue that will require cooperation and compromise among all interested groups.

IMPORTANT TERMS AND CONCEPTS

Economic highest and best use   *Property rights*

Eminent domain   *Regional planning*

Environmental controls   *Resource versus commodity*

General plan   *Slow-growth policy*

Inclusionary zoning   *Subdivision regulations*

No-growth policy   *Urban planning*

Police power   *Zoning*

Private deed restrictions

REVIEWING YOUR UNDERSTANDING

1. The land-use controversy is a debate over whether land should be viewed as a resource or:
   a. a commodity
   b. an asset
   c. an investment
   d. a possession

2. Critics of government use of land-use controls feel that it infringes on:
   a. zoning
   b. property rights
   c. eminent domain
   d. equal protection

3. A real estate example of government use of police power is:
   a. zoning
   b. property rights
   c. eminent domain
   d. equal protection

4. A real estate example of private land-use control is:
   a. zoning
   b. eminent domain
   c. deed restrictions
   d. inclusionary exceptions

5. Private deed restrictions are created in all of the following ways, *except*:
   a. mutual agreement among property owners
   b. deed reservations
   c. blanket tract restrictions
   d. government action

6. Government can control private land use by:
   a. tax incentives
   b. police power
   c. government spending patterns
   d. all of the above

7. Which of the following best describes the current philosophy behind government zoning ordinances? The purpose of zoning is to promote:
   a. property rights
   b. general welfare
   c. city development
   d. traffic flow

8. A community's general plan exerts more government control over private land use than does a community's zoning laws.
   a. true
   b. false

9. The creation of a community general plan requires resource analysis, formation of goals, and:
   a. federal guidelines
   b. urban analysis
   c. health codes
   d. implementation

10. A wrench is to a mechanic as _____ is to a planner.
    a. money
    b. escheat
    c. zoning
    d. a public hearing

11. Which of the following is true?
    a. land-use controls reduce the cost of building homes
    b. environmental regulations reduce the cost of building homes
    c. it is usually easy and fast to obtain government permits for a new housing development
    d. government controls have probably increased the quality of homes

12. The legal use of land at a specific location that will produce the greatest net income is called:
    a. the right to use
    b. highest and best use
    c. intensified use
    d. economic use

13. Government taking of private land in exchange for just compensation is called:
    a. escheat
    b. police power
    c. forfeiture
    d. eminent domain

14. Government's design for the future of a community is called the:
    a. general plan
    b. economic base plan
    c. housing element plan
    d. demographic plan

15. The two most powerful tools for implementing a community's general plan are zoning and health codes.
    a. true
    b. false

16. When an individual parcel of land is given approval to deviate from a zoning regulation, it is called:
    a. rezoning
    b. CC&Rs
    c. variance
    d. restrictive use

17. A subdivision of vacant residential land is considered premature when:
    a. roads are paved prior to construction
    b. sewer and water improvements are put in before homes
    c. school sites are set aside for the future
    d. home construction fails to occur

18. Slow-growth policies that limit the number of annual home-building permits:
    a. are examples of supply and demand in balance
    b. tend to decrease local home prices
    c. tend to increase local home prices
    d. do not distort real estate market forces

19. A pro-growth government policy can bring more:
    a. jobs
    b. pollution and congestion
    c. housing construction
    d. all of the above

20. A no- or slow-growth government policy can bring reduced:
    a. jobs
    b. pollution and congestion
    c. housing construction
    d. all of the above

21. On a national basis, the only effective no-growth policy is a decrease in the rate of population growth. But on a state or local basis, no-growth can occur by shifting the population burden to another state or community.
    a. true
    b. false

22. A type of land-use control that requires a builder to set aside a certain number of units for low- to moderate income people as a condition for obtaining a building permit is:
    a. inclusionary zoning
    b. fair housing law
    c. affordable domain
    d. equal housing rights

23. Debates regarding the solutions to urban density include:
    a. creating new towns in rural areas
    b. shifting urban dwellers to existing smaller cities
    c. redeveloping urban areas to accommodate more people
    d. all of the above

24. Which of the following is a trend in land-use controls?
    a. more state and regional control as opposed to local control
    b. more environmental regulations
    c. more shifting of costs from government to subdivision buyers
    d. all of the above are trends

25. The trend seems set: Land in the future will be viewed by government as a resource, not just a vehicle for the production of profit.
    a. true
    b. false

CASE & POINT
Property Rights: Two Viewpoints

Historically, the word *property* did not only refer to the thing owned but also includes the right or interest that the owner had in the item possessed. Today, the word refers to both meanings.

Basic property rights are:

The right to possess
The right to use
The right to encumber
The right to dispose
The right to exclude others

The current controversy over land-use controls centers around the extent to which these private property rights should be amended to promote the public welfare. Here are two viewpoints.

Viewpoint 1

Government has gone too far. The U.S. Constitution bans the taking of private property without the payment of just compensation. All levels of government, whether federal, state, or local, in their desire to control private activity have come up with a sinister way of "taking" private land without paying for it. Government does this by placing excessive restrictive regulations on private landowners. Through zoning, building codes, health codes, and environmental laws, government has been able to box private landowners into a corner. The landowner cannot use the land, and government does not have to pay for it, because it is merely "regulating," not taking the land. Shame on the government for trampling on the rights of property owners! The reason government is taking this approach is simple: Citizens would not allow government to increase taxes to outright pay for the land, so government has come up with a sneaky way to circumvent basic property rights and the U.S. Constitution.

But at last, there appears to be some form of hope. In 1994, by a 5 to 4 decision, in the case of *Dolan v. City of Tigard*, the U.S. Supreme Court ruled that the City of Tigard, Oregon, could not require Florence Dolan to turn over 10 percent of her land for a storm drain and bicycle path in exchange for a building permit to enlarge her existing hardware and plumbing store. Perhaps this is the signal that will stop government from forcing private property owners to pay for public improvements.

Viewpoint 2

Get real! People do not "own" land; they are only the current caretakers. All of the land in the United States is owned by the government. If you don't believe it, don't pay your property taxes and see who gets the land! Government regulations over private land use are just another extension of laws needed to maintain an orderly society,—no different from the need for traffic lights.

When you purchase real estate you are granted the right to occupy it until you sell, give it away, or die. You purchase this right with the full knowledge that your use is subject to an existing permissive use called zoning. The price you paid for this right was based on this knowledge. Along with most investments, land ownership carries risks. Although your land was zoned a certain way at acquisition, there is no guarantee things will stay the same. Change is a fact of life. If the land is currently zoned agricultural and you wish to enhance its value by attempting to rezone it commercial or residential, you have the right to apply for a rezoning. But you do not have any God-given right to the change. You knew what the zoning was going in, and you took your chances.

Society is dynamic, not static. "Things happen." Therefore, if you wish to purchase the right to use real estate, you must recognize that as society changes, the allowed use of your land could also be changed by duly elected officials representing the wishes of a democratic society. Therefore, if your land is "down-zoned," you lose; if it is "up-zoned," you win. Welcome to the world of risk taking. If you don't like it, stay a renter!

CHAPTER 14
REAL ESTATE DEVELOPMENT

PREVIEW

This chapter outlines the principles of real estate development. Section 14.1 focuses on real estate construction activity, with special emphasis on the economic characteristics of the homebuilding industry. Section 14.2 deals with the development and building process and features flow charts that illustrate the steps in real estate development. The Case & Point at the end of the chapter explores the economic effects of the great wave of overbuilding in the 1980s. When you have completed this chapter, you will be able to:

1. List three categories of real estate construction.

2. List five economic characteristics of the homebuilding industry.

3. Differentiate between land development and construction.

4. Describe the six major phases of land development and construction.

14.1 Real Estate Construction

R eal estate construction is a major contributor to the economic expansion of the United States. Each year, new construction generates billions of dollars in income and directly or indirectly employs several million workers. This section outlines the various categories of real estate construction and then concentrates on the economic characteristics of the homebuilding industry.

Construction Activity

Real estate construction activity can be divided into three main categories: residential, nonresidential, and public works.

Residential construction includes single-family dwellings, condominiums, and multifamily apartments. The volume of residential construction is closely tied to movements in the mortgage money market, employment, and personal income. When people are working and mortgage credit is available at reasonable interest rates, residential construction tends to accelerate. During periods of high unemployment or tight mortgage credit, residential construction and existing home prices decline. (See Tables 14.1 and and 14.2.)

Nonresidential construction consists of retail and office buildings, industrial plants, and institutional buildings such as schools and libraries. Nonresidential construction activity usually parallels changes in the business cycle. When real GDP is growing and the economy is experiencing prosperity, nonresidential construction increases. When there is a downturn in economic activity, nonresidential construction tapers off.

Public works construction refers to the building of streets, sewer systems, highways, bridges, and public projects other than buildings. Many public works projects are financed by federal grants supplemented by local matching funds. During periods of economic

Table 14.1 Value of New California Construction

Type of Construction (millions of dollars)	1990	1995	2002
Residential	$20,686	$13,879	$33,305
Nonresidential	$12,735	$ 8,155	$14,529

Source: Statistical Abstract of California 2004.

prosperity, tax revenues for local and state governments increase, thereby stimulating public works construction. In economic downturns local tax revenues decline, but at the same time government attempts to fight a recession by increasing its spending. Although there are occasional exceptions, the changes in public works construction normally do not fluctuate as widely as do changes in residential and nonresidential construction.

Table 14.3 shows the value of California new construction by categories as a percentage of total construction for select years. These figures show that residential construction tends to be 60–70%, and nonresidential 30–40% of nongovernment new construction.

Table 14.2 Existing Home Prices—California, 1982–2003

Year	Statewide	Los Angeles	San Diego	San Francisco	Orange County	Central Valley	Palm Springs/ Lower Desert	San Luis Obispo
1982	$111,800	$119,259	$102,665	$128,090	$129,641	$72,200	$85,197	—
1983	114,370	118,543	103,077	133,730	131,456	73,210	94,909	—
1984	114,260	121,270	104,417	134,131	130,668	74,600	90,353	—
1985	119,860	124,787	111,517	145,129	132,758	75,600	84,751	—
1986	133,640	135,393	123,003	166,318	144,441	77,310	87,972	—
1987	142,060	146,630	134,073	176,796	163,218	82,410	95,714	—
1988	168,200	178,889	153,410	212,863	203,860	87,190	97,952	—
1989	196,120	214,831	181,922	260,722	241,708	97,370	112,629	164,150
1990	193,770	212,130	183,210	259,000	242,358	116,330	118,410	201,730
1991	200,660	218,580	187,510	262,420	239,680	118,730	122,990	190,980
1992	197,030	210,790	183,110	259,250	230,860	119,430	125,140	181,210
1993	188,240	195,430	176,930	256,200	217,210	115,890	120,580	182,520
1994	185,010	189,170	176,010	255,580	214,540	113,370	120,600	169,900
1995	178,160	179,900	171,600	254,450	209,400	108,410	115,140	162,980
1996	177,270	172,886	174,450	266,660	213,370	107,480	110,630	166,090
1997	186,490	176,517	185,210	286,470	229,840	109,140	121,110	179,270
1998	200,100	191,700	207,100	321,070	261,700	114,980	132,840	180,880
1999	217,510	198,900	231,630	363,200	280,900	120,600	133,330	208,290
2000	241,350	215,900	269,410	454,560	316,240	133,380	149,300	248,310
2001	262,350	241,370	298,510	475,890	355,620	157,250	180,990	282,170
2002	316,130	290,030	364,240	517,060	412,650	189,210	223,420	326,710
2003	372,720	354,740	424,880	558,100	487,020	224,830	262,140	381,750

Table 14.2 Existing Home Prices—California, 1982–2003 (Continued)

Year	Northern California	Northern Wine Country	Monterey	Ventura	Riverside/ San Bernadino	Santa Barbara	Sacramento	Santa Clara
1982	$87,610	$91,697	$113,890	$130,890	$78,770	$131,333	—	—
1983	85,650	94,723	112,585	128,664	80,424	131,743	—	—
1984	87,448	n.a	120,740	120,687	81,551	132,022	$76,138	—
1985	89,661	98,077	129,119	128,531	85,058	134,979	77,843	—
1986	92,098	111,023	146,057	142,155	92,117	153,289	82,308	—
1987	93,672	119,128	161,787	159,072	96,170	149,084	86,865	—
1988	102,426	132,470	185,658	204,318	106,729	204,984	94,640	—
1989	115,075	160,802	232,191	247,658	124,122	233,071	111,690	$275,270
1990	143,801	179,178	237,732	238,792	132,127	219,578	137,460	268,890
1991	135,020	185,740	233,660	234,930	135,400	215,760	135,500	256,640
1992	137,600	194,030	226,280	222,510	136,230	219,530	133,950	248,260
1993	138,800	190,640	222,750	211,600	134,480	209,340	127,500	246,510
1994	136,960	188,760	225,060	206,640	129,110	217,870	124,970	254,390
1995	136,830	189,250	226,510	199,900	120,950	208,210	119,480	255,260
1996	137,250	182,350	234,250	205,720	115,240	211,940	115,310	273,830
1997	141,840	191,340	259,000	219,300	114,340	242,220	116,100	316,250
1998	150,300	211,740	283,370	233,770	121,500	243,670	123,780	364,740
1999	161,830	245,600	333,810	254,950	128,670	272,740	131,500	399,380
2000	179,120	304,960	403,610	295,080	138,560	302,260	145,200	521,240
2001	196,510	344,800	426,270	322,560	156,690	335,540	173,150	524,320
2002	236,730	374,610	451,220	372,400	176,460	376,350	210,230	547,500
2003	283,990	425,490	491,600	462,520	220,940	402,740	247,630	556,470

Los Angeles: Arcadia, Beverly Hills, Citrus Valley, Culver City, Diamond Bar, Diamond Bar, Foothill, Glendale, Hacienda-Rowland, Los Angeles, LA Pacific West, Malibu, Montebello, Palos Verdes Peninsula, Rancho Southeast, Pasadena/San Marino Board, San Fernando Valley, Santa Monica, South Bay, Southwest LA, Venice and West San Gabriel Valley.
San Francisco Bay Area: Berkeley, Contra Costa, Marin, Oakland, Palo Alto, San Francisco, San Jose, San Mateo-Burlingame, Santa Clara, Solano and Southern Alameda.
San Diego: Coronado, East San Diego, North San Diego (Carlsbad, Oceanside, San Dieguito),San Diego and South San Diego Bay Cities.
Orange County: Irvine, East Orange, Huntington Beach-Fountain Valley, Orange Coast, Orange Coast Pacific West AOR and South Orange.
Central Valley: Bakersfield, Fresno, Lodi, Merced, Modesto, Sacramento, Stockton and Visalia.
Palm Springs/Lower Desert: Palm Desert, Palm Springs and Desert Communities West.
Monterey: Monterey Peninsula and Santa Cruz.
Northern Wine Country: Mendocino, Napa and Sonoma (North Bay AOR).
Northern California: Chico, Clear Lake, Humboldt, Paradise, Placer, Siskiyou and Tahoe Sierra.
Riverside/San Bernardino: Corona-Norco, East Inland Empire, Inland Empire West, Inland Valleys and Rim of the World.
Ventura: Camarillo, Conejo Valley, Oxnard, Simi Valley and Ventura.
Santa Barbara: Lompoc, Santa Barbara and Santa Maria.
High Desert Area: Antelope Valley, Barstow, Palmdale and Victor Valley.
Pismo Coast, Atascadero, Paso Robles and San Luis Obispo Board of Realtors report home sales for the statewide sample but are not reported in a separate region.
n.a Not available

Note: Movement in regional sales prices should not be interpreted as measuring changes in the cost of a standard home. Prices are influenced by changes in costs and variations in the characteristics and size of homes actually sold.

California Association of Realtors, Research and Economics, (213)739-8200, http://www.car.org/

Table 14.3 Value of New California Nongovernment Construction as a Percentage of New Total

	1990	1995	2002
Residential construction	61.9	62.9	70.0
Nonresidential construction	31.8	37.1	30.0

Source: California Statistical Abstract 2004.

Characteristics of the Homebuilding Industry

The homebuilding industry is noted for its booms and busts. Periods of high rates of construction are followed by hefty declines in buying and construction. Why does new residential construction fluctuate? Why isn't the rate of new home construction steady and predictable? The answer lies with the economic characteristics of the homebuilding industry, presented in the following list.

1. The industry is comprised of many small, independent builders and a few hundred large, corporate companies. This means that in some less-populated areas homebuilding is a local operation that cannot generate enough production to gain savings from large-scale building.

2. It is relatively easy to enter the homebuilding industry—a skilled construction worker can usually start a small company with a limited amount of capital. This ease of entry, coupled with inadequate capital backing, can generate a high failure rate in the smaller-scale segment of the homebuilding industry.

3. As a result of a long physical and economic life, residential homes last for many years. In any given year, the supply of new homes rarely adds more than 2 percent to the total supply of homes in the United States. In short, a home does not wear out rapidly, and thus the replacement demand is low. A homebuilder, unlike an automobile manufacturer, cannot count on the replacement market to bolster activity.

4. Home construction is heavily influenced by the actions of government. The government can stimulate housing construction with special financing programs such as the FHA, or it can retard housing construction through environmental controls or burdensome real property taxation, or, most important, increased interest rates.

Special Interest Topic

Manufactured and Mobile Homes

Skyrocketing land values and construction costs have priced many people out of the conventional housing market. Older people living on fixed incomes and others who own large homes may wish to reduce expenses by selling their existing homes and moving into less expensive quarters. For these people and many others, the answer has been manufactured and mobile home living.

Manufactured and mobile homes comprise 20—30% of all new single-family home sales in the United States. Mobile home dealers could probably increase their sales even more if a sufficient number of manufactured and mobile home sites could be located. In some areas, manufactured and mobile homes are allowed to occupy inferior locations only. This discrimination can be traced to the transient trailer-type camps of the 1930s. However, today's mobile homes are not trailers, nor are they very mobile. Studies have shown that four out of five manufactured and mobile homes are set on land sites and never moved again. In fact, it is becoming more difficult to distinguish the better manufactured and mobile homes from conventional homes. Some units come with wood shingle siding, step-down living rooms, two baths, and three bedrooms. Some have second stories. They can be purchased using FHA, VA, or conventional financing.

Special Interest Topic

The Price of New Homes Sets a Ceiling on the Price of Existing Homes

Whenever the demand for homes is strong, prices for existing properties tend to rise. What stops them from rising dramatically, however, is that they get too close to the cost of building a comparable new home. Buyers generally refuse to pay a high amount for an older home when the same money can purchase a new home. Thus, the cost of new homes sets a ceiling on existing home prices. The long-term price trend for older homes will follow along just under the cost trends for comparable new construction (including the impact of lot price trends).

5. The homebuilding industry depends on liberal mortgage credit terms, so that prospective homebuyers can finance the purchase of new homes.

From the preceding list, it is apparent that homebuilding can be a fragmented industry, comprised of many small-scale local builders who depend on the whims of others for their survival, counterbalanced by a few large-scale construction companies who can build thousands of homes in a single year. But in spite of handicaps, the homebuilding industry as a whole is making some innovative progress in construction technology, building design, and cost controls. The standardization of parts, the creation of better tools, and the prefabrication of building components have helped to streamline the construction process. To continue this rate of innovation will require a positive attitude from lenders, government, construction workers, and homebuyers alike.

REVIEWING YOUR UNDERSTANDING

Real Estate Construction

1. List two other categories of construction besides residential.

2. List five economic characteristics of the homebuilding industry.

3. Explain why lending institutions and governmental agencies are important to homebuilders.

14.2 The Development and Building Process

The creation of a new real estate project needs managerial talent to plan, coordinate, and control the factors of production (land, labor, and capital). This managerial skill is provided by developer-investors, contractors, and architects, all of whom are instrumental in the creation of a successful real estate development. This section outlines the development and construction process.

Land Development and Construction

The production of urban real estate can be broken down into two major categories: *land development* and *construction*. Land development refers to subdividing and preparing the land for building, and construction refers to the actual erection of buildings and improvements. However, before private land development and building construction begin, at least four factors should be thoroughly investigated: market analysis, government approvals, adequate financing, and a reasonable profit margin.

Market Analysis

Prior to undertaking a real estate project, a developer should conduct an in-depth market analysis to estimate whether adequate buyer demand exists for the proposed project. Market analysis techniques vary according to whether the study is for residential, commercial, industrial, or rural purposes. But regardless of the nature of the proposed project, certain questions need to be answered: What is the present and future demand for this type of real estate, in numbers and price levels? Is the proposed site a good location? Are buyers ready to purchase? At what price? With what features? If not now, when? What is the current and future supply? Are there other sellers? What does the competition plan to do in the future? Is now the right time for this project? These questions form the heart of a market analysis and should be answered before any firm commitments are made. The time to be concerned with sales potential is *before* the project begins, not after!

Government Approvals

A real estate project is not possible unless proper government permits can be obtained. Meeting government regulations, such as zoning, building codes, density maximums, environmental reports, and utility requirements, is an essential step in any real estate development. A developer must be familiar with the relevant government requirements for this project and must assess the likelihood of obtaining government approval. *The key factor is the time needed to obtain approval.* Long delays because of government "red tape" can cause a project to fail, the victim of missed sales and increased cost for land, labor, materials, and capital. A careful review of the time needed and the penalties for delays is essential. Government reports and their time delays will be discussed in greater detail in the next chapter. In addition, it is critical to identify all costs that governments will require the project to pay. These could include road and utility line extensions, annexation fees for various districts, and impact fees to provide such facilities as a new school or park needed for the project's occupants.

Adequate Financing

Real estate developers and investors rarely pay cash for their projects; they are usually strong believers in the principle of leverage (using a minimum amount of equity funds and a maximum amount of borrowed funds to control a large investment). The funds needed for land acquisition can come from several sources. The seller can carry back a purchase money deed of trust, the developer can form a syndicate and raise the needed capital by selling ownership shares, or the funds may be borrowed from a financial institution or a private party.

After land acquisition, the funds for construction usually come from traditional lenders—banks, thrift institutions, insurance companies, and mortgage companies. In addition to traditional sources, construction funds are occasionally available from pension funds, real estate investment trusts, and endowment funds. The importance of financing cannot be overemphasized. Without adequate funding, a real estate project, as developers put it, cannot "fly."

Figure 14.1 Feasibility study steps.

Adequate financing depends on two main variables: (1) the market potential of the project, and (2) the condition of the money market. If a developer can demonstrate to lenders that a strong market exists for the proposed project, and if lenders have funds available at reasonable interest rates, chances are the project will be funded. On the other hand, if the money market is tight and the supply of funds limited, a developer may find it impossible to borrow the needed capital, regardless of the market potential for the project. The project will have to be shelved because of the lack of mortgage credit.

Developers of larger projects increasingly consider the possible use of government-issued bonds, to pay for various needed road or utility work. These bonds can be a specific amount assessed against the parcel, usually described as a *special assessment*, or they can be a general bond, to be paid off by a group of properties, a whole area, or the entire city. Because these bonds are normally tax free to the investor who buys them, the interest rates are often cheaper than bank loans, despite the high costs of issuing them.

Profit Potential

After analyzing the market, estimating the cost and likelihood of government approval, and projecting the cost of financing, private developers can estimate the profit potential. If the profit return is too low relative to the costs and risks, the proposal is rejected as unfeasible. On the other hand, if the profit potential appears reasonable, the project commences.

Figure 14.1 summarizes the four studies that should be conducted before real estate development and construction take place.

When This Process Is Ignored, Overbuilding Can Occur

The four steps listed above are what *should* be done before ground is broken for a new project. However, during the 1980s, a tremendous amount of overbuilding occurred in the commercial real estate market in most cities across the United States. This created an excess supply of commercial office buildings and retail floor space. The reasons frequently given for this overbuilding include economic slowdown, income tax incentives, easy money from underregulated banks and savings and loans, tax base-hungry local governments, and massive foreign investment. Most of this overbuilding, and the resultant foreclosures, could have been prevented if realistic market studies had been conducted before the projects were developed. Instead, what occurred was analysis based on gut feelings, hopes, prayers, and a false reliance on perpetual increases in real estate values! From this perspective, then, the overbuilding was caused by (1) the collapse of old-time conservative banking, followed by (2) the failure of regulators to adopt and enforce meaningful restrictions to backstop the lenders, and then, (3) the failure of legislators to recognize the folly of such a splurge and to require and fund adequate regulatory action.

By the mid-2000s sanity had returned to the commercial real estate market.

Steps in Construction

Land development and construction take place in steps or phases. Figure 14.2 summarizes the major steps in land development and construction.

The *planning phase* encompasses market analysis, government approval procedures, arranging financing, and profit analysis.

Land procurement refers to the purchase of the property. In some cases, the purchase is just the acquisition of a single parcel. In other cases, however, land procurement may require the painstaking assemblage of several smaller parcels under different ownerships in order to create one larger parcel. Usually, the land is optioned, or contracted for, prior to the planning phase. Escrow then closes when government and lender approvals are obtained.

The *land preparation phase* is concerned with the clearing of land and the installation of off-site improvements such as utilities, streets, and gutters to make way for on-site construction. *Off-site* means off of the individual building site, but *not* necessarily off of the larger parcel.

The *construction phase* begins as soon as land preparation permits access. In construction, timing is a critical factor. Building is usually done in phases, frequently by different subcontractors. Blending each phase to eliminate delays is one of the most difficult aspects of managing construction. Delays between construction phases can occur

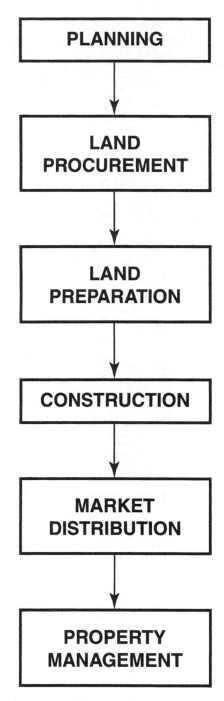

Figure 14.2 Major steps in land development and construction.

because of adverse weather, labor strikes, material shortages, and improperly estimated time requirements for various construction activities. Delays cost money, as interest accrues on construction loans and labor is paid for standby time.

The *market distribution phase* is concerned with the selling and transfer of property. Frequently, the sale takes place before construction

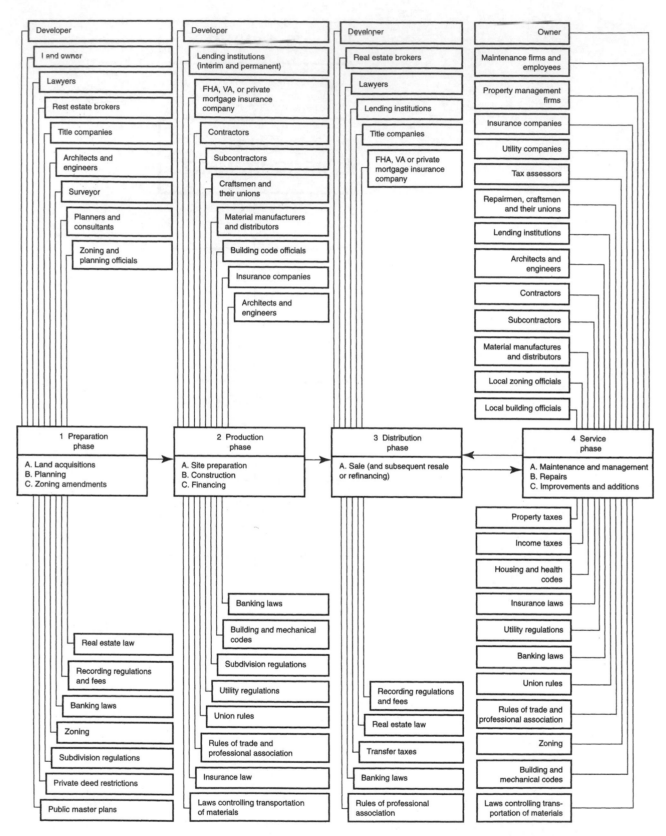

Figure 14.3 The housing process—major participants and influences. (*Source:* The President's Committee on Urban Housing, *A Decent Home*. Washington, DC, Government Printing Office, December 1968, p.115.)

begins. These are called "build to suit" projects. If the project is not pre-sold but is built on speculation, ideally the property is sold before construction is completed. In other cases the property is not sold until after completion. In any case, the actual legal transfer of title usually does not occur until the property is completed and ready for occupancy.

The *property management phase* refers to the maintenance and servicing of the development after construction. If the property is owner-occupied, the service and upkeep rests with the owner. If the project is tenant-occupied, frequently a professional property manager is hired to supervise the servicing of the property. Property management involves two major activities—physical upkeep and record keeping. Physical upkeep refers to maintenance and repairs; record keeping involves rent collection, ledger accounts, and the preparation of income and expense sheets for tax purposes.

Figure 14.3 is an expanded version of the construction process, outlining the individuals and institutions that are involved in each phase of construction.

The Cost of Construction Delays and Impact Fees

The old saying, "Time is money," is especially true in real estate development. Many real estate developers work on relatively thin profit margins, and any unforeseen delay can quickly erode profits. Construction delays can be caused by required government reports, mismanagement by developers, labor strikes, shortages of materials, adverse weather, changes in the mortgage money market, and so on.

Studies and reports by various universities and building trade associations state that somewhere between 20 and 40 percent of the price of a new home, depending on the location, can be directly attributed to government regulations. These high regulation costs are especially prevalent in states like California, where local governments have been sharply increasing fees (called *impact fees*) charged to developers for the right to obtain a building permit, in an attempt to make up for the property tax revenue lost through the passage of property tax reduction legislation.

Not only are developers asked to pay for direct costs, such as new streets, water, and sewer hookups for the project, they have been required to pay for schools, parks, and other community facilities that are not directly related to the project. Developers must recoup their impact fees by raising the prices they charge to the new property buyers. This can be viewed as a way for local government to raise money indirectly from property owners, to make up for the tax revenue lost by not being able to increase property taxes sufficiently to pay for these facilities directly.

REVIEWING YOUR UNDERSTANDING

The Development and Building Process

1. What is the difference between land development and construction?

2. List four things that should be considered before beginning a real estate project.

3. List six major steps in land development and construction.

CHAPTER SUMMARY

Real estate construction activity can be classified as residential, non-residential, and public works. The real estate development process flows in a series of phases or steps: planning, land procurement, land preparation, construction, market distribution, and property management.

The homebuilding industry is highly fragmented, consisting of numerous small builders, plus a few large corporate builders. Erratic homebuilding activity can be traced to the unpredictable nature of lenders, buyers, builders, labor unions, and government. Government impact fees have increased the cost of property ownership, as developers pass these costs on in the form of higher prices.

IMPORTANT TERMS AND CONCEPTS

Building construction

Construction process steps

Economic characteristics

Homebuilding industry

Impact fees

Land development

Nonresidential construction

Public works construction

Residential construction

Special assessment bonds

REVIEWING YOUR UNDERSTANDING

1. The three main categories of real estate construction are residential, nonresidential, and:
   a. mobile homes
   b. office buildings
   c. public works
   d. farms

2. The largest percentage of construction takes place in which sector?
   a. residential
   b. nonresidential
   c. public works
   d. farms

3. Fluctuation in the rate of new home construction is caused by:
   a. government actions
   b. availability of mortgage credit
   c. phases of the business cycle
   d. all of the above

4. Manufactured and mobile homes comprise approximately what percentage of new single-family home sales in the United States?
   a. 0—5
   b. 10—15
   c. 20—30
   d. 40—50

5. Regarding the prices of existing homes:
   a. prices are usually higher than comparable new homes
   b. prices are usually lower than comparable new homes
   c. prices are usually the same as comparable new homes
   d. prices are set by government actions

6. In terms of the factors of production—land, labor, capital, and entrepreneurship—the developer is the entrepreneur and therefore should earn:
   a. rent
   b. wages
   c. interest
   d. profit

7. Subdividing is considered:
   a. construction
   b. land development
   c. building
   d. assemblage

8. The first step in the real estate development process is to:
   a. do a market analysis
   b. obtain government approval
   c. line up the financing
   d. compute the return on investment

9. Impact fees are paid by developers to governments as a condition for issuing a building permit. In the final analysis the cost for these fees is ultimately paid by:
   a. developers
   b. lenders
   c. taxpayers
   d. buyers

10. Real estate development takes place in a series of phases. The first phase is:
    a. planning
    b. procurement
    c. construction
    d. property management

11. Financing for land development does *not* involve:
    a. banks
    b. tax-exempt bonds
    c. FHA
    d. pension funds

12. To obtain government approvals, developers will need to do all of the following, *except*:
    a. study environmental impacts
    b. show compliance with the community general plan
    c. agree to provide needed utilities and roads
    d. provide a net worth statement

13. As the business cycle changes, public works construction is usually less affected than residential construction.
    a. true
    b. false

14. The rate of nonresidential construction is projected to decline throughout the 2000s, primarily because of:
    a. environmental conflicts
    b. overbuilding during boom times and the dot.com collapse in the early 2000s
    c. shortages of materials
    d. shortages of labor

15. Manufactured and mobile homes today are:
    a. often moved
    b. more similar in appearance to regular homes
    c. found in all neighborhoods
    d. difficult to finance

16. The homebuilding industry:
    a. consists of many small, independent builders and several hundred large, corporate developers
    b. each year increases home construction output at a steady, even level
    c. is very difficult for newcomers to get into
    d. depends on tight mortgage credit terms to succeed

17. High impact fees and time delays caused by government "red tape" can increase construction costs 20 percent or more.
    a. true
    b. false

18. Innovation in homebuilding requires a positive attitude from lenders, government, construction workers, and homebuyers.
    a. true
    b. false

19. Which of the following people at a homebuilding project *would not* be providing entrepreneurial (management)skills?
    a. carpenter
    b. architect
    c. developer
    d. construction superintendent

20. Land development and construction take place in a series of phases. Which of the following is the correct order?
    a. planning, land procurement, construction, land preparation
    b. land preparation, land procurement, planning, construction
    c. land procurement, planning, land preparation, construction
    d. planning, land procurement, land preparation, construction

21. Market analysis in real estate seeks to answer which basic question?
    a. Is there adequate demand for the project?
    b. Are there sufficient utilities?
    c. Will existing transportation systems provide access?
    d. Can financing be obtained?

22. In planning a real estate development, "government approvals" means reviewing:
    a. income tax requirements
    b. Federal Reserve standards
    c. the need for legislative approvals
    d. the government-imposed costs, as well as the needed approvals

23. Funding for construction of small projects is primarily by:
    a. traditional lenders
    b. government-issued bonds
    c. pension funds
    d. endowment funds

24. The construction of freeways and bridges comes under the category of:
    a. residential construction
    b. nonresidential construction
    c. public works construction
    d. on-site construction

25. In recent years, there has been a trend of using government bonds to finance off-site improvements and then levying special assessments against each lot in the development.
    a. true
    b. false

CASE & POINT

Real Estate Economic History: California in the 1980s: "The Build-and-They-Shall-Come Syndrome," Followed by a Decline in the 1990s—2000s

The 1980s represent an interesting decade for those who study real estate economics. From this period real estate analysts gained a better understanding than ever before of how important the availability of money is to real estate development. In the 1980s, as money became available for almost any project, whether it made economic sense or not, more and more new projects lined up for funding.

A second lesson from the 1980s was the establishment of alternative ways for developers to profit from development. In the past, the developer's profit was gained only upon sale of the completed successful project. In the 1980s, however, most developers got income primarily by taking periodic payments from the loan funds toward "overhead costs." If the project failed, the developer started another project in another market, with a different lender, and repeated the cycle.

A third lesson from the 1980s was how much society had been relying on the concept of "lender's caution." Lender's caution disappeared when the inflation of the late 1970s led to high interest rates, which caused consumers to transfer funds from savings accounts to bonds and preferred stocks (disintermediation). Lenders, facing the very real danger that their institutions might go bankrupt, tossed caution out in the hope of earning enough profit from loan fees to save their jobs. But lender's caution had been the only lock on the door, because the politicians had eliminated the regulators, in the name of deregulation.

A fourth lesson from the 1980s is very sobering. Respected real estate commentators pointed out the folly of building such an excess of space as early as 1985. Yet the splurge continued on through 1986,

1987, 1990, and even, in some markets, 1992. Clearly, lenders, developers, and the country lost the ability to see something inappropriate happening and act to correct it.

As significant as these lessons from the 1980s are, they are minor compared to the lessons of the 1990s and early 2000s. Foremost is the new encounter with supply and demand. Previously, when there was a temporary oversupply of some type of space, real estate economists and appraisers would look at the amount of available space, divide that number by the annual (or monthly) amount leased, and conclude that in six months or so the market would be back in equilibrium. Because the vacancy was fairly minor and the absorption period short, rents did not appear to decline. But in the 1990s and early 2000s, the amount of vacant space has been very large. To make matters worse, in many markets new buildings have added to the supply, and tenants have downsized. As a result, the absorption period has stretched to two years, and then three years or more, and rents have started to soften: A tenant now, at a lower rent, is clearly preferable to a vacancy in the current market.

Along with the new focus on supply and demand, the market has discovered "negative absorption." As tenants have downsized, centralized, rationalized, gone broke, merged, or left town, the demand for office space has declined. Along with the available space in new buildings, the market has had to cope with growing amounts of available sublease space.

The drop in rents and demand has led inevitably to loan defaults and foreclosures, and then to the third major development of the 1990s and 2000s, the creation of systems to sell large amounts of real estate efficiently. The motive, of course, is to sell off all of the failed real estate projects and other real estate accumulated by lenders. In the process, the real estate auction has emerged as a major vehicle for unloading unwanted real estate. In addition, sophisticated investors have combined to buy large groups of properties using purchasing pools. Moreover, at the start of the 1990s the primary form of real estate security sold on Wall Street was the bond backed by residential mortgages, available for some decades through FHA, then FNMA, GNMA, and FHLMC. But by the mid-1990s, bonds backed by commercial mortgages began expanding rapidly. Finally, the 2000s has marked the rebirth of the Real Estate Investment Trust, a concept almost abandoned in past years but now returning with great force.

Other lessons from the 1980s and 1990s are numerous. One is that excessive supply created in one period does have short-term favorable impacts, such as added jobs in banking, construction, materials manufacturing, and brokerage in the 1980s. The added jobs increased incomes and state and federal income tax revenues. Governments collected rezoning and building permit fees and property taxes on the new buildings.

But the negative economic impact of excess supply comes back to haunt the economy in later years. Because of the earlier oversupply, no new buildings are built, so the previous extra jobs are lost as well as some core jobs. Businesses that depend on new construction, from architects to contractors to equipment rental firms, are badly hurt. Some go out of business. The lost jobs reduce incomes and income tax receipts, and increase unemployment. Meanwhile, the oversupply has led to reduced market rents in all buildings, new and old. The declining rents lower owners' abilities to make loan payments, leading to foreclosures of fully occupied buildings.

The last lesson of the 1980s and 1990s is the consequences of overbuilding for property owners. Because of the high vacancies and declining rents of office buildings and some retail and industrial areas, many loans have been foreclosed, or net cash flow has all but disappeared. Contrary to popular belief, all commercial property owners are not rich insurance companies; some building owners were older, middle-class people, and the money lost was partly their retirement savings. As a result, surveys show a significant number of people have found it necessary to adjust to less income or reduced savings for the future. This has curtailed their spending, a silent secondary economic effect of overbuilding.

CHAPTER 15
REQUIRED GOVERNMENT REPORTS

PREVIEW

This chapter briefly describes the reports that real estate developers must prepare to obtain government building permits. Section 15.1 discusses the types of reports required by federal, state, and local government agencies. Section 15.2 examines both the costs and the benefits of government reports. The Case & Point at the end of the chapter explores the wetlands controversy, an area of increasing regulation. When you have completed this chapter, you will be able to:

1. Explain the reasons given for requiring government reports before private real estate may be developed.

2. List the types of reports often required by federal, state, and local government agencies.

3. Describe both the costs and the benefits to real estate developers, property owners, and society of requiring government reports.

15.1 Types of Required Government Reports

Government agencies need reports to see that proposed real estate projects conform to land-use laws. Reports and investigations provide the basis for government agencies to approve, deny, or modify proposed real estate development. This section summarizes major legislation with which real estate developers must comply in order to obtain governmental approval for their projects.

Federal Legislation

Although there are many federal laws and agencies that regulate the use of real estate, the two most important agencies are the United States Department of Housing and Urban Development (HUD) and the Environmental Protection Agency (EPA).

The United States Department of Housing and Urban Development (HUD)

HUD is an umbrella department that oversees the activities of several federal agencies that influence real estate development. Some of the more important agencies are listed below.

1. The Federal Housing Administration *insures real estate loans made by approved lenders*. It is widely known as FHA.

2. The Public Housing Administration *helps to fund and supervise administration of low-rent housing projects*.

3. The Community Facilities Administration *provides funds to cities, counties, and colleges to construct public buildings and public works projects*.

4. The Urban Renewal Administration *provides financial assistance to local governments for slum clearance and rehabilitation*.

5. The Office of Interstate Land Sales Registration *regulates the interstate sales of subdivided land*.

This is only a partial list of HUD's activities, but it is obvious that many real estate projects fall under the jurisdiction of one or more of these agencies. When this occurs, HUD requires extensive reports to see that its regulations are being followed. Some typical report topics include relocation plans for persons being displaced by the proposed project, a statement of fair employment practices, equal housing opportunities questionnaires, environmental impact statements, a complete economic base analysis, and a detailed market analysis.

Environmental Protection Agency (EPA)

The EPA was created in 1970 and, along with the Council on Environmental Quality, is responsible for seeing that federal pollution standards are enforced. Some of the federal environmental legislation acts of special interest to real estate users are given below.

1. National Environmental Policy Act (NEPA) *requires the preparation of environmental impact statements on all federally assisted real estate projects.*

2. Federal Water Pollution Acts *regulate real estate development along waterways and underground water channels.* These acts have been used to halt real estate construction until adequate antipollution protection devices are developed. They require the preparation of an extensive report outlining the water pollution impact before a developer is allowed to grade the land or erect a building.

3. Clean Air Acts *control real estate development that could add to air pollution.* These acts have been used to deny building permits for industrial and commercial real estate projects on the grounds that additional development will aggravate air pollution. They require a complete report regarding air pollution standards before construction is allowed to proceed.

Other federal acts that influence real estate development include the Noise Control Act; the National Coastal Zone Management Act; the Flood Disaster Protection Act, which affects any real estate development in mapped flood plains; and the very controversial Federal Wetlands Act. (See appendix.) All of these acts require the submission of reports before real estate development is allowed.

State Legislation

In addition to federal reports, real estate developers must also comply with state laws that may require reports. State regulations of special interest to real estate include: state housing and construction codes, state sanitation and health codes, subdivision requirements, statewide zoning controls, and state environmental regulations.

State Housing and Construction Codes

Most states have passed minimum construction codes that require all new construction to meet state standards. As a condition for receiving a building permit, a developer must submit a plot map and building plans with detailed specifications. After a complete examination of the plans, making revisions where necessary, the state agency usually approves them. In many states, the code is adopted and enforced at the county or city level for most buildings. However, mobile homes and manufactured housing (modular homes) increasingly are regulated by state codes rather than local codes.

State Health and Sanitation Codes

State health departments regulate statewide health measures. County or city health departments usually play a major role in enforcement, as discussed later. Drainage, plumbing, sewage disposal, hazardous waste materials, and water supply all come under the jurisdiction of health and sanitation codes. Each health officer has the authority to halt any proposed development that fails to meet the legal standards. As a condition for obtaining a building permit, a developer must submit a report showing that the proposed project meets all health requirements, or must get health department approval for the project plans.

Subdivision Regulations

Subdivision regulation is one of the main tools used by state and local governments for controlling real estate development. Although subdivision laws are not new, amendments and changes are constantly being added by legislators. Usually, the primary law addresses the required approval process and content of any map that shows a division of an existing land parcel. In addition, some states like California impose a public report disclosure requirement prior to the first sale of any subdivided parcel.

State or local agencies usually require comprehensive subdivision reports, to ensure that a developer is complying with all subdivision laws before residential lots can be sold. A typical subdivision report must outline who holds title, flood and drainage conditions, water and sewage handling, land filling, roads and access, the nature of all utility hookups, complete plans for all off-site and on-site improvements, any major environmental impact, any seller financing, proposed marketing techniques, and many other technical items.

Statewide Zoning Controls

Historically, zoning has been a local matter. Cities and counties enacted zoning ordinances to achieve their own individual goals, applicable only to property within their boundaries. However, as urban growth pressures create problems that overlap city and county boundaries, state governments have been enacting new forms of state-wide zoning. Much of the recent legislation has been environmentally oriented, and states have assumed control over areas considered to have regional importance, such as coastlines, lake and river frontage, agricultural land, and desert areas. Statewide zoning also occurs in high hazard areas such as flood plains, earthquake faults, and land-slide areas. Here again, real estate developers often must submit reports showing that their proposed project conforms to these state zoning laws.

State Environmental Regulation

Since the late 1960s, state legislatures have been enacting environmental laws similar in nature to the federal legislation. Individual states have created special environmental agencies to ensure that the environmental impact of a real estate project is studied before a building permit is granted.

The typical procedure for the developer is to present the proposed real estate project to an environmental review board. In some cases, this will be the local planning commission. The review board then decides if the proposed project will have a significant impact on the environment. If the answer is negative, a *negative declaration* is issued, and the developer then proceeds with the project. If the review board concludes that the project will have a significant impact, the developer must then prepare and submit a comprehensive environmental impact report.

For report purposes, the *environment* is defined as all social, economic, biological, and physical surroundings. Thus, a typical environmental impact report contains a detailed analysis of how the proposed real estate project will affect each of these four areas. The report also requires that the developer outline the steps to be taken to counteract any environmental damage that might result from the real estate project. Usually, such reports must consider the proposed project and several alternatives, from no project at all, through a project version with many fewer impacts, perhaps to a project version with *greater* impacts. In addition, alternate ways to mitigate the impacts must be presented.

Once the environmental impact report is completed, it is submitted to the environmental review board as a draft. The general public is usually invited to make comments on the draft report. The draft report is then amended and submitted for a final decision by the review board. All environmental review board decisions, either for or against the proposed project, can be challenged in the courts.

Local Legislation

In addition to meeting federal and state requirements, developers must conform with local real estate codes. City and county governments nearly always have local planning, public works, building, and sanitation agencies that require the submission of reports or review and approve the project plans before a local building permit is issued. Typically, local reports or review are needed in the following areas: grading, construction details, lot design, street and other off-site facilities, zoning and architectural conformity, environmental impact, and impact on traffic, schools, police and fire service, and property tax.

Who pays the cost of these government reviews and reports? What is the trade-off between costs and benefits? Is it worth the red tape? These topics will be covered in the next section, but before you proceed, check your understanding by answering the following questions.

REVIEWING YOUR UNDERSTANDING

Types of Required Government Reports

1. What is the reason for having government regulatory agencies?

2. Why does the EPA wish to regulate real estate development?

3. In addition to housing codes, list four other state codes or regulations that require the preparation of a report.

15.2 Costs Versus Benefits

As mentioned in earlier chapters, "There is no such thing as a free lunch." Any use of resources, whether land, labor, or capital, incurs a cost that someone must pay. This section studies required government reports by comparing their costs with the benefits received.

Defining Costs and Benefits

To simplify their analysis, economists break costs and benefits into the following categories: private costs, social costs, private benefits, and social benefits.

Private costs are those expenses paid by a particular individual or business firm. They are the actual out-of-pocket money expenditures of that individual or business.

Social costs are the expenses paid by society as a whole rather than by an individual or business. For example, if a business pays for and constructs a $150 million factory, this is a private cost. But if the factory then pollutes the air, the pollution becomes a social cost paid by all, not just the factory owner or its customers.

Private benefits are rewards enjoyed by a particular individual or business and not by society as a whole. Private benefits are frequently stated in terms of money profits.

Social benefits are rewards that accrue to all of society, not just to an individual or business. For example, if a real estate developer builds a successful shopping center, the developer may reap private profit. In addition, if the project stimulates local business and increases employment and income, this could create a social benefit—a reward shared by all of society, not just the real estate developer.

Analyzing the Costs

The cost of required government reports can be broken down into private and social costs. *Private costs include preparation costs, review fees, holding costs, inflation costs, and overhead costs.* The cost of preparing government reports varies with the size and scope of the proposed project. But the consulting fees charged by attorneys, engineers, appraisers, economists, and environmental researchers can run hundreds or thousands of dollars per day, and when all the required reports are completed, the cost can be quite high.

Most government agencies charge a fee to review the report or to review the plans for compliance. These fees are growing faster than general inflation. Many governments are seeking to support planning or building department costs entirely from fees, rather than from general revenues.

The costs for holding unused land include expenses for property taxes, interest on land loans, minimum maintenance, and opportunity costs. *Opportunity costs* refer to the unrealized, potential earnings that the money tied up in unimproved land might have earned if invested elsewhere.

Inflation costs refer to the increase in material prices and wages that occurs during construction delays. The longer construction is delayed, the greater the likelihood that inflation will drive up the cost of construction.

Overhead costs are the costs that continue whether a developer is working or not. Overhead costs include such items as rent on the developer's office, bank payments on equipment, equipment maintenance, and fixed salaries for office workers.

Preparation, review, holding, inflation, and overhead costs are all private costs that are either absorbed by the developer or, in most cases, passed on to the developer's customers in the form of higher real estate prices.

What are the social costs of required government reviews and reports? Does society also pay a price as a result of required reports or reviews? Yes, society as a whole may bear some costs, such as a loss or delay of jobs and income. Another social cost might be an increase in consumer prices because of the cost-push inflation sparked by the increase in construction prices. At the higher selling prices, some consumers will not qualify, lowering the number of buyers.

Analyzing the Benefits

The benefits gained by requiring government reviews or reports on real estate projects can be broken down into social benefits and private benefits. *Social benefits include less environmental damage, better land planning, consumer protection, and the fostering of social integration.* Many of the recent land-use regulations have been aimed at protecting the environment. By requiring environmental reports, society benefits by knowing that potential environmental damage will be studied, along with project alternatives and impact mitigations, before a real estate project is approved.

Another social benefit frequently cited is better land-use planning. By requiring reports, the government can see that private land is not used in a manner likely to harm surrounding landowners or the community. Thus, noisy industrial uses are usually separated from residential uses.

Consumer protection is one very common benefit of government review or reporting requirements. The consumer thus benefits from an expert review of health and safety issues that may be extremely complex and all but impossible for the consumer to evaluate.

Still another benefit from government regulation is that it can be used to promote social integration. By requiring real estate developers to submit reports on social goals, such as minority employment in construction trades, equal housing opportunities, and relocation assistance to persons being displaced by the real estate project, disadvantaged persons are given a better chance to become a part of the social mainstream.

Are there any private benefits that real estate developers or their customers gain from requiring detailed reports? Yes, in the long run, the private costs paid by requiring government reports may be offset by private benefits such as higher real estate values. For example, it is possible that by requiring a careful study of the environment, a completed real estate project may be so harmonious in its surroundings that its value rises rapidly. This enhances the image of the real estate developer and generates profitable resale potential for the initial buyer of the real estate projects.

The Trend

As you can see, there are certain costs associated with government laws and reports and there are certain benefits. Do the costs outweigh the benefits? Or do the benefits outweigh the costs? Obviously, there are no easy answers. Each case must be analyzed independently, but the trend appears to be set—more and more government reports will be required before a real estate project will be approved.

If this is the case, can the costs be reduced without sacrificing the benefits? The answer is a resounding *YES*. One area that real estate economists, environmentalists, conservationists, and developers agree on is that the duplication of work required by the various levels of government must be eliminated. In many cases, a real estate developer must prepare the same information in four or five different forms to conform to separate, overlapping guidelines of different government agencies. What is needed is a simpler review system, where approval or denial is relayed more rapidly, thus saving both private and social costs.

REVIEWING YOUR UNDERSTANDING

Costs Versus Benefits

1. What is the difference between a social cost and a private cost and between a social benefit and a private benefit?

2. Define the following: preparation cost, review fees, holding cost, inflation cost, and overhead cost.

3. List three social benefits that result from government regulation of private real estate.

CHAPTER SUMMARY

Legislators pass land-use laws and then create government agencies to enforce these laws. As an enforcement tool, government agencies require real estate developers to submit reports verifying that public regulations are being met.

The cost of requiring government reports includes private costs such as preparation cost, holding cost, inflation cost, and overhead cost. Society also bears some costs, such as higher prices and loss of employment and income. The social benefits derived from requiring government reports in private real estate activities include less environmental damage, better land-use planning, consumer protection, and the fostering of social goals. Private benefits may include an increase in real estate values.

The trend seems to indicate that more government reports will be required in the future. The key is to streamline the reporting system so that both private and social costs can be reduced without sacrificing the benefits.

IMPORTANT TERMS AND CONCEPTS

Environment	*Private benefits*
Environmental impact	*Private costs*
Impact mitigation	*Social benefits*
Negative declaration	*Social costs*

REVIEWING YOUR UNDERSTANDING

1. The stated purpose of requiring government reviews or reports before a developer is issued a building permit is to:
   a. see that the project conforms to land-use laws
   b. allow environmentalists to delay or stop the development
   c. satisfy the lender's requirements for loan approval
   d. issue opinions as to the profitability of the project

2. Which law requires an environmental impact report on all major federal public works projects?
   a. Clean Air Act
   b. Hazardous Waste Materials Act
   c. National Environmental Policy Act
   d. Federal Projects Act

3. The environment includes:
   a. economic and social impact
   b. economic and biological impact
   c. economic, social, and biological impact
   d. economic, social, biological, and physical impact

4. Instead of a full environmental impact report, a small project with little if any impact on the environment can be approved using a:
   a. negative declaration
   b. payment of a waiver fee
   c. federal district attorney
   d. small claims court order

5. The final approval for the actual design and layout of a housing subdivision usually rests with the:
   a. federal government
   b. state government
   c. local government
   d. developer

6. The pollution of the air by an unregulated factory is what type of cost?
   a. private
   b. social
   c. customer
   d. environmental

7. The profit generated by owning a real estate building is what type of benefit?
   a. private
   b. social
   c. community
   d. environmental

8. The private costs incurred because of the delays of required government reviews and reports are called:
   a. holding costs
   b. environmental costs
   c. oversight costs
   d. impact fees

9. The benefits of requiring government approval before a real estate project can be built may include:
   a. higher property values
   b. reduced social costs
   c. less environmental damage
   d. all of the above

10. Economists, real estate developers, and environmentalists tend to agree that:
    a. the duplication of work required by various government agencies is wasteful
    b. real estate is a commodity to be bought and sold like corn
    c. environmental concerns will decrease as time goes on
    d. in the future, government will have a smaller voice in real estate development projects

11. The Federal Housing Administration:
    a. loans money for housing construction or purchase
    b. insures real estate loans made by approved lenders
    c. coordinates all federal efforts to increase housing production
    d. is responsible for environmental review of all housing developments

12. The Urban Renewal Administration:
    a. provides financial assistance to local governments for slum clearance and rehabilitation
    b. is responsible for assembling land parcels for new housing construction in rural areas
    c. is responsible for environmental review of all housing developments
    d. is a division of the Environmental Protection Agency

13. When federal funds are being used to buy property for a city or county project:
    a. the local agency is exempt from any need to prepare an environmental impact report
    b. the project ownership cannot be transferred to a private party
    c. no state regulations need be followed
    d. a relocation plan will be required, to assist people being displaced

14. EPA is a federal agency charged with:
    a. providing funds to local agencies to construct public buildings
    b. insuring real estate loans made by approved lenders
    c. enforcing federal pollution standards
    d. monitoring subdivision lot sales

15. The National Environmental Policy Act:
    a. requires preparation of environmental impact statements
    b. is the primary law affecting water pollution
    c. focuses primarily on wildlife protection
    d. has little or no effect on any local real estate activity

16. The Flood Disaster Protection Act:
    a. applies only to federal flood control projects
    b. affects development of property in mapped flood plains
    c. is the basis for water pollution control
    d. established the requirement for environmental impact reports

17. State health codes:
    a. often are enforced by county or city health workers
    b. regulate traffic patterns
    c. apply only to residential, not commercial, real estate projects
    d. cannot exceed federal health codes

18. The subdivision laws generally:
    a. apply when a single large building is to be occupied by more than one tenant
    b. set standards for approving and mapping any division of a parcel of land
    c. are enforced by federal, not state government
    d. define the required education and experience for residential developers

19. The potential earnings that money tied up in unimproved land could have earned if invested elsewhere are called:
    a. holding cost
    b. social cost
    c. opportunity cost
    d. preparation cost

20. A negative declaration is a:
    a. finding that a proposed project does not have a significant environmental impact
    b. finding that a proposed project is not located in an earthquake zone
    c. statement that a proposed project is exempt from federal air pollution regulations
    d. statement that a proposed project meets all regulatory requirements

21. The trend is toward more and more government reports in order to undertake a large development project.
    a. true
    b. false

22. Mitigation means:
    a. ways to reduce the environmental impacts of a project
    b. the alternative projects that the typical environmental impact report must study
    c. steps necessary to obtain permission to build in a flood plain
    d. the process of review that a proposed subdivision must go through

23. Environmental impact reports (EIRs) require a developer to list *not doing* the project as one alternative to reducing environmental damage.
    a. true
    b. false

24. Social costs of required government reviews and reports include:
    a. preparation costs and review fees
    b. overhead and holding costs
    c. better land-use planning
    d. higher prices to consumers

25. Social benefits of required government reviews and reports include:
    a. reduced demand
    b. greater profits for developers
    c. lower price appreciation
    d. better land-use planning

CASE & POINT

How Wet Is Wet?

In terms of required government permits, one of the most controversial is the U.S. Army Corps of Engineers 404 permit, which allows real estate development on designated wetlands. The Federal Wetlands Act was enacted in 1972 as part of the Federal Waters Pollution Control Act. This act requires the issuance of a permit by the Corps prior to allowing any land work or building in designated wetland areas, unless specifically exempt. Exempt activities are "discharges" for normal farming, forestry, and ranching operations. Another exemption from a permit is Exemption 26, which allows a landowner or developer to fill certain wetlands without a permit if no more than one acre of wetland is lost. Only one Exemption 26 is allowed for an entire project.

The original Federal Wetlands Act did not define wetlands, and each federal agency is allowed, by regulations, to define what is meant by wetlands. Thus, the definition of wetlands can differ among the Army Corps of Engineers, the Environmental Protection Agency, the Fish and Wild Life Service, and the Soil Conservation Service.

Now the problem begins: Any application for a 404 permit to develop on wetlands as defined by the Corps must be submitted for review to other federal agencies, which may have a different definition of wetlands. These other federal agencies have the power to deny the permit or impose mitigation requirements, which can be expensive. This in turn could make the proposed real estate project unfeasible.

Just what is meant by the term *wetlands?* The definition as used by the Corps and EPA is "areas that are inundated or saturated by surface or groundwater at a frequency and duration sufficient to support, and that under normal circumstances do support, a prevalence of vegetation typically adapted for life in saturated soil conditions." The definition then describes the character of wetlands as including: hydrology (presence of water), the presence of aquatic vegetation, or the presence of saturated soil. Corps and EPA guidelines then state that if land is saturated seven or more days per year, and aquatic vegetation is present, the area is considered wetlands. By these guidelines it appears that the definition of wetlands can change each year depending on seasonal rainfall.

How far can the definition of wetlands be stretched? In one case the U.S. Army Corps of Engineers argued that an isolated mudhole that could be used by migratory birds as a rest stop should be declared a wetland and come under the Corps' jurisdiction.

The actual 404 permit process consists of the following steps:

1. Preapplication consultation with the Corps.
2. Formal application submission for a permit.
3. Posting of public hearing notice by the Corps.
4. Public hearing for the public and interested parties.
5. A public interest review by the Corps.
6. A review by other related federal and state agencies.
7. A decision by the Corps.

In the process the landowner or developer will probably be required to prepare an environmental impact report and a cultural resource survey to determine what impact the project may have on the environment and if any culturally sensitive lands are involved. If approval is granted, it may require the developer to mitigate the damage by creating new wetlands significantly larger than the wetlands affected.

The message is clear: Prior to purchasing any land for real estate development a prudent investor should hire a competent wetlands consultant and a qualified attorney to inspect the land and conduct an inquiry with the appropriate federal and state agencies regarding the status of the land. Failure to do so could become very expensive in the long run.

PART FOUR

REAL ESTATE
INVESTMENT

*The Economics
of the Parcel*

CHAPTER 16
SUMMARY OF REAL ESTATE INVESTMENT PRINCIPLES

PREVIEW

This chapter looks at the economics of individual properties. Section 16.1 discusses basic investment principles. Section 16.2 demonstrates real estate cash flow analysis. Section 16.3 shows how cash flows are used to estimate offering prices and compute rates of return. The Case & Point at the end of the chapter contains a case study. When you have completed this chapter, you will be able to:

1. Define investment and list the five essential elements to consider when selecting an investment.

2. Complete a first-year real estate cash flow analysis.

3. Explain how real estate offering prices are determined.

4. Discuss how real estate returns are calculated.

16.1 Basic Investment Principles

*I*nvesting is defined in a variety of ways, such as placing money for profitable purposes, or extending capital in exchange for perceived profits. Another definition for investing, favored by many economists, is this: *Investing is defined as giving up present consumption in exchange for future benefits*. This definition focuses on the idea that investing is the opposite of consumption.

In one way or another, most people generate money. After-tax money can only be used in two ways: (1) spent or (2) invested. Every dollar spent is a dollar that cannot be invested; every dollar invested is a dollar that cannot be spent. Therefore, one must decide how much money to use for present consumption and how much to invest. Any money not used for consumption is automatically invested. Whether the investment is in the form of savings, stocks, gold, real estate, or idle cash, for better or worse, these are all forms of investments!

Obviously, some people invest very little. This may be because they need every dollar to subsist, or, if more affluent, they simply choose to consume now and not worry about the future. On the other hand, some people are active investors, giving up some current consumption to build a nest egg for the future. This section concentrates on real estate as an investment.

The Key Investment Factors

The five major economic characteristics of an investment are return, management, taxability, liquidity, and risk.

Return

Most investments involve an initial capital outlay, which if successful is followed by the recovery of benefits over a period of time. This recovery of benefits is the *return*, or economic reason for making the investment. A return can be in the form of money, such as rents from a building, or less tangible benefits (amenities), such as occupancy of a home. The returns can also vary in their timing; returns can arrive now or later and can come as one payment, a series of even payments, or as irregular payments. Common patterns include:

1. A series of payments over a period of time

2. A series of payments plus a large single end payment

3. A large single payment only

The higher the return the greater the value of the investment. However, a return two years from now or at some other distant time is worth less than a return today. Thus, in comparing investments, the amount of returns and the timing of their payment are all-important.

Management

Different investments require different types and amounts of *management*. Management is defined as the supervision needed to oversee an investment. A savings account needs almost no management, whereas an apartment building calls for a considerable amount. Various investments should be compared on the basis of the amount and skill of management time each requires. As "time is money," an investment that requires more management should produce a higher return to pay for the time and effort.

Taxability

Investments differ in how their earnings are *taxed*. Some investments, like certain municipal bonds, are free of income taxes. Others, like corporate dividends, are subject to corporate income tax and then to personal income tax. Investors are interested in the return received *after* taxes, so the taxability of the investment is important in evaluating investment alternatives. Taxability of real estate investments is so important (and complex) that all of Chapter 17 is devoted to the topic.

Liquidity

Liquidity refers to the ease and speed of converting the investment into cash. Investments differ in their liquidity. Blue-chip stocks on the New York Stock Exchange are highly liquid—you can sell them on any business day and receive your money in a day or so. Savings can be withdrawn in cash on the spot from a bank and therefore are very liquid. However, other investments, such as a loan to a new business, are illiquid—you might need to wait years to recoup your money.

Real estate is considered an illiquid investment. It is difficult to convert real estate equity to cash quickly. To convert real estate equity to cash there are two choices: (1) sell the property or (2) borrow against the property. Both of these take time and also cost money, in the form of seller closing costs or borrower loan costs. Therefore, it is frequently stated that one should only invest in real estate after seeing that liquidity needs have been met with other forms of investment.

Risk

Investments vary in the amount of risk. *Risk* is defined as the danger of loss in the value of the investment. Types of risk include financial, interest rate, purchasing power, social change, and legal change risk.

For many investments, *financial risk*—the loss of investment or earnings through failure to receive payments when due—is the greatest hazard. The financial risk of each investment varies, depending on the stability of the investment, the reliability (or uncertainty) of the investor's estimate of stability, and the margin or allowance that the investment has before little problems become big ones! Financial risk is particularly important to real estate investments because of the large up-front investment, slow returns, and the frequent use of borrowed funds.

Interest rate risk refers to the possible loss in value of an investment as a result of increases in market interest rates. This risk is usually associated with the market for corporate or government bonds. The basic rule is as follows: A decrease in market interest rates will increase the resale prices of existing bonds; or the opposite: An increase in market interest rates will decrease the resale prices of existing bonds.

For example, assume that in 2005 an investor bought a new bond, paying 10 percent interest only for 10 years, and the purchase price and the face amount is $10,000. Thus, the annual income is scheduled to be $10,000 × 10% = $1,000 per year for 10 years, then a full payoff of $10,000. Suppose the investor needs money and attempts to sell the bond in 2010 and finds that market interest rates have risen to 20 percent on this type of bond. This means that a buyer of this bond will only pay the investor $5,000 for the $10,000 bond! Why? If the existing bond pays interest at $1,000 per year ($10,000 × 10%), in order to earn 20 percent, the new buyer will invest $5,000 × 20% to generate the $1,000 interest paid on the existing bond. Thus, the market value of the bond has dropped from $10,000 to $5,000 because of changes in market interest rates.

Are there interest rate risks for real estate investments? Yes, the wide swings of market interest rates have produced real estate risks. For example, assume that an investor purchased a leased warehouse for cash in 2005 on the basis of an 8 percent return. The investor attempts to sell the warehouse in 2010 and discovers that buyers now demand a 10 percent return because of changes in market interest rates. This situation will reduce the selling price of the warehouse 20 percent below the investor's purchase price. This is an example of how a change in market interest rates can reduce the value of an otherwise secure investment.

Purchasing power risk refers to the possibility of loss attributable to inflation. The investor can receive the same dollars from the investment, but with inflation the dollars purchase less. Investments that pay a fixed dollar return, such as certain bonds, are vulnerable to purchasing power risk. Investments such as common stocks or real estate can provide protection from inflation and purchasing power risk *if* the net earnings increase with inflation. Since inflation eats away at investment dollars, many investors insist upon a higher rate of return to make up the difference. Thus, the fear of continued inflation leads to a demand for higher rates of return.

Risk of social change arises because every investment is vulnerable to social changes that can influence supply or demand and in turn can affect the earnings of an investment. Real estate investments are especially vulnerable because real estate is tied to a fixed location. For example, as urban dwellers leave a congested city for the suburbs, real estate values at the urban locations could decline in value.

Risk of legal change means that new laws may have an impact on an investment's ability to produce income. Changes in laws regarding taxes, pollution, zoning, and landlord-tenant relations have had a significant impact on real estate returns and values.

Other Risk Variables: Visibility and Specialization

Visibility means that the investment or the building or the co-owners are visible, or likely to be noticed, which affects the risk of social or legal change. A building occupied by a controversial tenant is more visible than one occupied by low-key tenants. The lease of an office building to the state government is more visible than a lease to an insurance company. An investment with a city council member as a partner is more visible than one with someone less well known. Visibility can also help an investment, as when a central corner location gets a prestigious tenant or when having a big-name tenant gets the landlord better loan terms or attracts buyers.

Specialization refers to the degree of uniqueness of a building. Often this means the cost of converting the building to other uses. A highly specialized building, such as a medical office building or a fast-food franchise restaurant, is more expensive to convert to other uses than a standard building and is therefore riskier.

The Investment Decision

Each investor approaches an investment decision in his or her own manner. Some are careful and analytic, whereas others just plunge in. The economic approach to decision making consists of balancing the characteristics and risks of investments against the requirements or needs of the investor. In this fashion an investor can analyze an investment in terms of returns, risks, liquidity, and so on, to see if it meets his or her needs.

The next section describes how to calculate the owner's cash flow on an income-producing property. Before you proceed, answer the review questions to test your understanding of the material in this section.

REVIEWING YOUR UNDERSTANDING

1. Define investing.

2. List and describe the five economic characteristics that affect an investment.

3. How would you rank real estate, high or low, in terms of these five economic characteristics?

16.2 Real Estate Cash Flow Analysis

It should be stressed that real estate is an investment that normally produces a slow recovery of profit and initial investment over a period of many years. The process of forecasting the amount of money received each year, including the year of resale, is called *cash flow analysis*.

The cash flow analysis for each year can be viewed as a series of steps. These steps are outlined in cash flow forms. Cash flow forms vary in steps and terminology, but a typical example is shown in Figure 16.1.

The Steps in Annual Cash Flow Analysis

To illustrate the steps in an annual cash flow analysis, look at the following case study:

Case Study

An older 20-unit apartment, with an asking price of $1,700,000, requires $500,000 cash down, plus a new loan of $1,200,000. Each unit rents for $800 per month; other income is $300 per month; and the vacancy/credit loss factor is 5 percent. Annual verified expenses are $43,100, and the annual fixed debt service for the $1,200,000 loan is $126,370.

Annual Cash Flow Analysis

1. Gross Scheduled Income ($800 × 20 units × 12 mos.)	$192,000
2. Plus: Other Income ($300 × 12 mos.)	+ 3,600
3. Equals: Total Gross Income	$195,600
4. Less: Vacancy/Credit Loss (5%)	− 9,780
5. Equals: Gross Operating Income	$185,820
6. Less: Annual Operating Expenses	− 43,100
7. Equals: Net Operating Income	$142,720
8. Less: Annual Debt Service	−126,370
9. Equals: Before-Tax Cash Flow	$16,350

Tax Benefit Analysis

10. Net Operating Income (Line 7)	$142,720
11. Less: Interest (Loan 1)	−119,700
12. Less: Interest (Loan 2)	0
13. Less: Cost Recovery (Depreciation)	− 38,760
14. Equals: Real Estate Taxable Income or	$ 0
15. Equals: Estimated Allowable Loss (If Loss)	$<15,740>
16. Times: Tax Bracket (times Line 14 or 15)	× .38
17. Equals: Taxes Saved or Paid	$ 5,981

Net Spendable Income

18. Before-Tax Cash Flow (Line 9)	$ 16,350
19. Plus/Less Taxes Saved or Paid (Line 17)	+ 5,981
20. Equals: Net Spendable Income (After-Tax Cash Flow)	$ 22,331

Figure 16.1 A cash flow analysis.

The first year's interest deduction on the loan totals $119,700, and the annual estimated depreciation for income tax purposes is $38,760. The potential investor is in a combined federal and state income tax bracket at the marginal rate of 38 percent. According to the investor's accountant, all passive losses can be used each year. No passive losses will be carried forward to reduce gain in the year of resale. (Passive losses are explained in detail in Chapter 17.)

Based on this information, a cash flow analysis is developed and presented in Figure 16.1.

Before-Tax Cash Flow

The first series of steps in cash flow analysis computes what is commonly called Before-Tax Cash Flow. It is also known as the Economic Cash Flow. (See Figure 16.1.)

Total Gross Income

The first figure is *Gross Scheduled Income*, and it is defined as the maximum amount of rents if 100 percent occupied at either current rents or market rents. *Current rents* refer to lease or contracted rents, and *market rents* refer to what the space or units would rent for if new tenants were sought. Whether current or market rents are being used should be noted by the analyst on the form. In the case study, the current rents are also the market rents; therefore, $800 × 20 units × 12 months = $192,000 Gross Scheduled Income.

Next, Other Income, if any, is added. *Other Income* refers to items other than rent, such as vending machine income, storage or parking space income, and so on. In the case study, the Other Income is $300 per month. Thus, $300 × 12 months = $3,600 Other Income. The combination of Gross Scheduled Income ($192,000) and Other Income ($3,600) equals *Total Gross Income* of $195,600 (Figure 16.1, Line 3).

Vacancy/Credit Loss

Then a dollar amount for Vacancy and Credit Loss (uncollected rents), estimated as a percentage based on experiences in the market, is subtracted from the Total Gross Income to arrive at *Gross Operating Income*. In the case study a 5% Vacancy/Credit loss factor results in $195,600 × 5% = $9,780, which is subtracted from $195,600 to equal $185,820 Gross Operating Income (Figure 16.1, Line 5).

Annual Operating Expenses

The next item deals with the property's annual operating expense estimate. In some properties, like leased commercial and industrial buildings, it is common for the tenants to pay operating expenses under what is known as a *net lease*. In other properties, such as residential rentals, the owner pays these operating expenses. The expense analysis usually starts with an examination of the property's past expenses as shown by property management records or the owner's income tax statements. It is important to note that operating expenses do not include loan payments or depreciation write-off. Annual operating expenses are the actual cost incurred to run the property, such as property tax and insurance, maintenance, repairs, management fees, utilities, and supplies. Loan payments are a financial cost to an owner who chooses to borrow rather than pay cash. Loan payments are not a charge to operate a property. Depreciation is a noncash income tax deduction that is not related to the property's physical operation. Depreciation is a paper write-off for tax purposes and therefore is not an actual out-of-pocket expense. Loan payments and depreciation are dealt with in cash flow analysis, but not as operating expenses.

Once past operating expenses have been verified, the expenses must be adjusted to reflect current information and the management policies of the new investor. When the adjustments have been made, they can be compared to expense data for other comparable properties to determine reasonableness. In some cases, funds will be set aside as reserves for replacement of major repairable items, such as new roof or carpets. This will be reflected in the annual operating expense deduction.

Net Operating Income

In the case study, annual operating expenses were given as $43,100 and are subtracted from the Gross Operating Income of $185,820 to give a *Net Operating Income* of $142,720 (Figure 16.1, Line 7). Net Operating Income is a key figure in cash flow analysis. First, it is the amount of money the property is estimated to produce to help cover the Annual Debt Service (loan payments for the year). Second, as shown later, the Net Operating Income is used by investors and appraisers to estimate the price or value of the property.

Annual Debt Service

The *Annual Debt Service* is simply the monthly loan payments (principal and interest), if any, times 12 months. Obviously, the size of the annual debt service is a function of the amount of cash down payment and the size and terms of the mortgage(s). In the case study, the $1,200,000 loan, based on a certain interest rate and term, was estimated to produce a monthly loan payment of $10,530.83, which when multiplied by 12 months yielded an annual debt service of $126,370 (Figure 16.1, Line 8).

Before-Tax Cash Flows

In the case study, Net Operating Income of $142,720 less the Annual Debt Service of $126,370 = $16,350 positive Before-Tax Cash Flow (Figure 16.1, Line 9). If the Annual Debt Service is ever larger than the Net Operating Income, the property will produce a negative Before-Tax Cash Flow.

Before-Tax Cash Flow is what the investor is estimated to keep after covering all costs, including loan payments, but before the payment of income taxes, if any, on the collected rents. In some circles this is known as the "Economic" Cash Flow. It is also described as "cash on cash," the investor's annual pretax cash return on cash invested.

Tax Benefit Analysis

In addition to Economic Cash Flow, there are income tax aspects to owning and operating rental real estate. The income tax aspects could be positive and add to Before-Tax Cash Flow, or they could be negative and reduce the Before-Tax Cash Flow. A tax benefit analysis computes the positive or negative impact income taxes have on cash flow.

Taxable Income or Loss for the year

To compute the taxable income or loss for the rental year, the Net Operating Income is listed, then the allowable interest deductions on the mortgage(s) are subtracted. It should be noted that only the interest portion of the loan payments, not the principal, is deductible for tax purposes.

The interest portion is computed using a financial calculator or amortization tables. In our case study the deductible interest is given as $119,700. There is no second loan, so the next step is to deduct the depreciation write-off, which is called Cost Recovery. (The depreciation rules will be explained in the next chapter on income taxes.) The figure of $38,760 given as depreciation in the case study is subtracted as indicated. Thus, Net Operating Income $142,720, less $119,700 interest, less $38,760 depreciation = ‹$15,740› tax loss for the year (Figure 16.1, Line 15).

Note that after deducting interest and depreciation from the Net Operating Income you could have income left over, which would be taxable income. However, in the case study, the interest and depreciation deductions exceeded the Net Operating Income, thereby generating a tax loss for the year. The loss of ‹$15,740› is a paper loss, not a real out-of-pocket cash loss! How is this so? The depreciation deduction of $38,760 was a noncash deduction for income tax purposes, and this deduction created the ‹$15,740› loss at no current out-of-pocket expense to the potential investor.

Taxes Saved or Paid for the Year

If an investor has a taxable income or taxable loss for the year, a set of rules called the passive income and loss rules apply. The passive rules will be discussed in the next chapter on income tax. Assuming that the ability to use the income or loss applies for the current year, a real estate investor then calculates the taxes saved or paid by multiplying the taxable income or loss by the marginal tax bracket for the year.

In the case study, the investor's marginal tax bracket is 38 percent. Therefore, the ‹$15,740› usable tax loss × 38% = a positive $5,981 tax savings (Figure 16.1, Line 17). How can a loss turn into a positive tax savings? First, remember the loss is paper, not real! Then, this paper tax loss of ‹$15,740› is used dollar for dollar to offset other income the investor has outside of the property. When $15,740 of other outside income is offset by the paper loss generated from the property, an investor would save $5,981 in taxes he or she otherwise would need to pay on that outside income. This $5,981, in the form of tax savings, increases the investor's current spending power.

Net Spendable Income

Net Spendable Income, also known as After-Tax Cash Flow, is the Before-Tax Cash Flow plus or minus the taxes saved or paid. This is the so-called "net bottom line." In the case study, the Before-Tax Cash Flow is $16,350, and the taxes saved are $5,981. Therefore, $16,350 + $5,981 = $22,331 Net Spendable Income (Figure 16.1, Line 20).

Multiyear Analysis

The cash flow steps given in Figure 16.1 reflect the first year's estimate. Although many small investment properties are purchased just using a one-year analysis, investors in larger properties usually insist upon a multiyear analysis, in which the cash flow is projected for each year of the investor's estimated holding period. Typical multiyear analysis periods are for 5, 10, 15, or 20 years.

Given a set of assumptions regarding future rent, vacancy, expense, loan payment, and tax aspect changes, the real estate analyst estimates a cash flow forecast for each subsequent year of the investor's projected holding period. The result is a Net Spendable Income estimate for each future year. Net spendable income is also known as after-tax cash flow. In some situations multiyear analysis is completed using before-tax instead of after-tax cash flow numbers.

Net Sale Proceeds

When the Net Spendable Income has been estimated for each year of the investor's projected holding period, the cash flow analysis is still not complete. One step remains: calculation of the Net Sale Proceeds.

Net Sale Proceeds, often called the *reversion* by appraisers, is the amount of money the investor is estimated to net, after close of escrow and payment of income taxes, when the property is sold at the end of the holding period. In some situations, sales proceeds are calculated omitting the income tax aspects. If this is the case, the result is called net from escrow or net from sale, excluding income tax aspects.

To calculate the Net Sale Proceeds the analyst estimates what the property can be sold for at the end of the investor's holding period 5, 10, 15, or 20 years later. This is done using an annual compound appreciation rate or a capitalization of net income approach based on the last holding year's Net Operating Income. (Capitalization of Net Operating Income will be discussed in the next section of this chapter.) Once the resale price is estimated, seller closing costs, old loan balances, and capital gain taxes are subtracted to produce the Net Sale Proceeds.

Referring to the previous case study, if the original price of the 20-unit apartment property is $1,700,000 and the annual appreciation rate is estimated to be 6 percent, the projected resale price in five years would be approximately $2,275,000 ($1,700,000 × 1.06, repeated five times). Then the seller's closing cost for the sale of a $2,275,000 property is estimated, say at 8 percent. The result would be a seller closing cost of $182,000 ($2,275,000 × 8%).

Next, the outstanding balance, after five years, on the original loan of $1,200,000 would be estimated using a financial calculator or remaining loan balance table. In our case study assume the remaining loan balance on the original loan amount of $1,200,000 after five years is down to $1,158,000. The next step would be to estimate what the capital gain tax would be on the profit when the property is resold for $2,275,000. This involves a series of substeps illustrated in the next chapter on income taxes. Let us assume that the capital gain tax came to an estimated $250,000. Then the net sale proceeds would be computed as follows:

$2,275,000 estimated resale price

— 182,000 seller closing cost (8%)

—1,158,000 outstanding balance on loan

— 250,000 capital gain tax on resale profit

$ 685,000 Net Sale Proceeds (net to seller upon resale)

Garbage In, Garbage Out

When doing a multiyear projection, a real estate analyst is required to estimate future changes in the subject property's rents, operating expenses, and value. Obviously, there are no guarantees as to what will happen to a property in the future. For example, who in the mid-1980s would have predicted the collapse of the Soviet Union and the subsequent impact it would have on real estate values in regions dependent on the defense industry, such as Southern California! Or the dot.com bust in the early 2000s and its negative impact on the commercial real estate market in the San Francisco Bay area!

When estimating future changes in rents, expenses, and values, bitter lessons have taught real estate analysts to use very conservative figures and require potential investors to sign a statement that these figures are only estimates and not guaranteed.

Summing Up Cash Flow Analysis

Cash flow analysis consists of three major steps:

1. Estimate the first year's Net Spendable Income (After-Tax Cash Flow).

2. Using a set of conservative assumptions, estimate each subsequent year's Net Spendable Income, for the length of the investor's holding period.

3. Estimate the net sale proceeds when the investor sells the property at the end of the holding period.

When these three steps are completed, the analyst has all the cash flow numbers—the amount of investment it takes to get into the property and the property's net bottom line estimates for each year of ownership, plus the Net Sales Proceeds in the year of resale. The next section discusses the various methods used to arrive at an offering price and several techniques used to compute rates of return once cash flow numbers are generated. Before moving on, review your understanding of cash flow analysis.

REVIEWING YOUR UNDERSTANDING

1. Recite the steps to arrive at Before-Tax Cash Flow.

2. Under the concept of tax benefit analysis, starting with Net Operating Income, list the steps to arrive at taxes saved or paid for the year.

3. If Before-Tax Cash Flow is a negative <$1,000>, and taxes saved is a positive $3,000, what is Net Spendable Income?

16.3 Estimating Price and Rates of Return

Once an investor decides to seriously consider making an offer on a particular property, the three key economic issues are: (1) the offering price, (2) the amount of the cash investment, and (3) the rate of return on the cash investment.

The Offering Price

Many investors make an offer to buy contingent upon a favorable appraisal made by a qualified appraiser. The issue here is not how appraisers arrive at value; that is the subject of a course in real estate appraisal. The issue is: What rules of thumb do investors use to arrive at an initial offering price? Investors' rules of thumb are as many and varied as are investors, but three common techniques are: Gross Rent Multiplier, Capitalization Rate, and price per square foot.

Gross Rent Multiplier

The formula for gross rent multiplier is:

$$\frac{\text{Asking Price}}{\text{Gross Scheduled Income}} = \text{Gross Rent Multiplier}$$

The investment property's Asking Price is divided by its Gross Scheduled Income to arrive at the property's Gross Rent Multiplier. In other words, "How many times does the potential rent go into the asking price?" Referring to our case study, the asking price for the 20-unit apartment property is $1,700,000, and the Gross Scheduled Income from Figure 16.1 is $192,000. Therefore the Gross Rent Multiplier is:

$$\frac{\text{Asking Price } \$1,700,000}{\text{Gross Scheduled Income } \$\ 192,000} = 8.85 \text{ Gross Rent Multiplier}$$

The 8.85 Gross Rent Multiplier itself is meaningless, until it can be compared to the market Gross Rent Multiplier for comparable properties. Investors and their real estate agents are usually aware of prevailing Gross Rent Multipliers and apply the following rule of thumb:

> The lower the property's multiplier below the market multiplier, the better the asking price. The higher the property's multiplier above the market multiplier, the worse (more overpriced) the asking price.

If the prevailing market multiplier for comparable 20-unit apartments is 10, the 8.85 Gross Rent Multiplier from the case study indicates a good buy. If the prevailing market multiplier is 7, then the case study's asking price of $1,700,000 seems too high. If in fact the market multiplier is 7, an investor would compute the maximum offering price as follows:

Gross Scheduled Income $\times$ Market Multiplier = Maximum Offering Price
Thus, $192,000$\times$7=$1,344,000 Offering Price.

The Gross Rent Multiplier approach, because it uses gross income instead of net income, ignores the impact that vacancies and expenses have on price. It is possible that two properties could have the same gross income, but because of various factors could have very different net operating incomes. Because of this shortcoming, the Gross Rent Multiplier is most often used for apartments and other residential properties. It is rarely used for commercial and industrial properties. Investors in commercial and industrial real estate generally prefer the Net Operating Income approach, called the Capitalization Rate.

Capitalization Rate

To arrive at an offering price using the Capitalization Rate approach, the following formula is used:

$$\frac{\text{Net Operating Income}}{\text{Asking Price}} = \text{Capitalization Rate (Cap Rate)}$$

Notice in the formula that the property's net operating income, not its gross income, is used, and it is divided by the asking price. The answer is expressed as a percentage. In essence the question is, "What percentage of the asking price is the net operating income?" Assuming an investor were to pay all cash and therefore have no loan payments, the Cap Rate would be the first-year before-tax rate of return if the investor paid the full asking price. In essence the investor is asking, "If I paid cash for the property, does the net income produce an adequate rate of return for my money?"

Using the 20-unit apartment case study in Figure 16.1, the Net Operating Income is $142,720, and the asking price is $1,700,000. Therefore the Capitalization Rate is:

$$\frac{\text{Net Operating Income } \$142,720}{\text{Asking Price } \$1,700,000} = 8.4\% \text{ Capitalization Rate}$$

The 8.4% Capitalization Rate is meaningless until the prevailing market Capitalization Rate for comparable properties is known. Most investors and their agents and consultants know the range of prevailing Cap Rates in the market for comparable properties. Once the market Cap Rate is estimated the following rule of thumb is usually applied:

The higher the property's Cap Rate above the market Cap Rate, the better the asking price. The lower the property's Cap Rate below the market Cap Rate the worse (more overpriced) the asking price.

If the prevailing market Capitalization Rate is 7.5 percent, while the property's Capitalization Rate at the asking price is 8.4 percent, this would indicate that the asking price is below market and on the surface appears to be a good buy. If, on the other hand, the prevailing market Capitalization Rate is 9.5 percent, the case study's rate of 8.4 percent is too low, meaning the asking price of $1,700,000 appears to be too high. If in fact the market Cap Rate is 9.5 percent, the investor figures the maximum offering price for the property as follows:

$$\frac{\text{Net Operating Income } \$142,720}{\text{Market Capitalization Rate } 9.5\%} = \$1,502,316 \text{ Maximum Price}$$

This Capitalization Rate technique is preferred by many investors because it closely parallels a more sophisticated capitalization approach used by appraisers to arrive at the market value of an income property.

Price per Square Foot

As a backup to the Gross Rent Multiplier and Capitalization Rate approach to estimate an offering price, many investors use the price per square foot technique. Here the offering price is divided by the square footage of the building to calculate the price per square foot. Then the price per square foot is compared to the price per square foot of other, similar properties to see if the price per square foot is in the market range.

Cash Flow Revisited

Once an investor establishes a price he or she is willing to offer (frequently below the asking price), another cash flow analysis is conducted. This new cash flow analysis looks at what the numbers will be if the lower offered price is accepted. A lower price usually means less money borrowed and a lower annual debt service. This results in less deductible interest and, because of a lower price, less annual depreciation write-off. All of this will have an impact on net spendable income and net sale proceeds upon resale. This will then have an impact on the investor's rate of return.

Amount of the Cash Investment

One of the major economic issues is the amount of cash needed to acquire the real estate investment. Obviously, the amount of cash required varies with the terms and conditions of the sale, as well as the current requirements of real estate lenders. Some investors prefer to pay all cash, whereas some investors attempt to buy without putting any personal money down. There are numerous seminars, some questionable, on how to buy real estate with no money down, but for the most part, these seminars only apply to small residential rental properties.

In most cases, investors are required to put 20 to 30 percent cash down, with lenders willing to finance the difference if the borrower and property meet the lenders' standards. The terms of the financing will depend on four major items: (1) the current state of the real estate market, (2) the current state of the financial markets, (3) the current state of the occupancy and cash flow of the property, and (4) the credit rating and financial strength of the investor. Once these issues are settled, the amount of cash invested for the purpose of computing rates of return is considered to be the cash down payment, plus all buyer's closing costs.

Computing Rates of Return

Formulas for computing rates of return on cash invested can be broken down into two general categories: (1) rates of return for the first year, and (2) rates of return for the entire holding period.

Rates of Return for the First Year

The two common calculations to arrive at the first-year rate of return are the before-tax cash on cash rate and the after-tax cash on cash rate. The first-year before-tax cash on cash rate formula is:

$$\frac{\text{First-Year Before-Tax Cash Flow}}{\text{Cash Invested}} = \begin{array}{c}\text{First-Year Before-Tax}\\ \text{Cash on Cash Rate}\end{array}$$

Referring to the 20-unit apartment case study shown as Figure 16.1, the Before-Tax Cash Flow is $16,350, and the cash invested is $500,000; thus:

$$\frac{\$16,350 \text{ Before-Tax Cash Flow}}{\$500,000 \text{ Cash Invested}} = \begin{array}{c}3.27\% \text{ Before-Tax}\\ \text{Cash on Cash Rate}\end{array}$$

The before-tax cash on cash rate ignores any impact that income taxes may have on the rate of return. The before-tax cash rate is also called the "economic" cash on cash rate.

Another common first-year calculation is the after-tax cash on cash rate. This formula is as follows:

$$\frac{\text{First-Year Net Spendable Income}}{\text{Cash Invested}} = \frac{\text{First-Year After-Tax}}{\text{Cash on Cash Rate}}$$

Referring to the 20-unit apartment case study, the Net Spendable Income is $22,331, and the cash invested is still $500,000; therefore, the after-tax cash on cash rate is:

$$\frac{\text{Net Spendable Income } \$22,331}{\text{Cash Invested } \$500,000} = \frac{4.47\% \text{ After-Tax}}{\text{Cash on Cash Rate}}$$

In both of these examples, at the asking price of $1,700,000, the first-year rates are low, indicating that the asking price is probably too high. If the investor offers a lower price that results in better cash flow numbers, the rates of return, both before and after taxes, should increase to an acceptable rate.

Occasionally, some people factor in the first year's principal payments on the loan and the first year's estimated appreciation to compute a first-year rate of return. This is the so-called "equity yield rate for the year." More sophisticated real estate analysts reject this concept, pointing out that a rate of return should be on a cash-equivalent basis. They note that principal payments and appreciation are only on paper until the property is refinanced or sold. They are not received as cash each year. They also point out that when a property is refinanced or sold, closing costs greatly reduce the actual cash received. Therefore, any equity yield computed prior to liquidating the investment will be overstated and can be a form of misrepresentation.

Multiyear Rates of Return

There are basically two types of calculations of multiyear rates of return used by real estate investors. They are the (1) Internal Rate of Return (IRR), and (2) Financial Management Rate of Return (FMRR). Both of these rates recognize the time value of money and use a discount system that reduces the future cash flows to a present value.

Multiyear rates are preferred over first-year rates because they reflect performance over a period of years, as opposed to a single year, and they recognize the time value of money. Simply put, the time value of money states that a dollar today is worth more than a dollar tomorrow. The idea is that the faster you get your money, the quicker you can put it to work to earn even more money. Conversely, the longer you wait to receive your dollar the less the dollar is worth, because of the opportunities missed by your money not being reinvested to earn even more money.

Real estate investments are influenced by the time value of money. Investors place cash up front as the down payment (present-valued dollars) and, over time, receive back annual cash flows, plus net sale proceeds upon resale (future-valued dollars). Therefore, the concept of discounted cash flow analysis to adjust for the time value of money is appropriate when computing rates of return for real estate investments.

Internal Rate of Return (IRR)

The Internal Rate of Return (IRR) is defined as that discount rate that reduces the future cash flows to just equal the amount of money invested. The calculation is done on certain financial calculators or a computer. The steps are as follows:

1. Once the IRR program is ready to run, the analyst enters the initial cash invested and the after-tax cash flows for each year in the order received, including the Net Sale Proceeds in the year of resale.

2. Then the calculator/computer discounts each year's cash flow to solve for a rate that will discount all the future cash flows to a present value that equals the amount of the cash invested. Once the discount rate is located, this is the Internal Rate of Return—the amount each dollar is earning while in the investment. The IRR evolved from the field of corporate finance and is a generally accepted standard measurement of performance among more sophisticated real estate investors and brokers.

Financial Management Rate of Return (FMMR)

There are several shortcomings in the calculation process of finding the Internal Rate of Return. A major problem is the IRR reinvestment assumption. The IRR assumes that as an investor receives each cash flow each year from the investment, these cash flows are immediately reinvested and they continue to earn a yield equal to the IRR until the investment terminates. This can be unrealistic if the annual cash flows are modest and the IRRs higher than normal market rates. Under these circumstances, the IRR is an overstated rate.

The *Financial Management Rate of Return (FMRR)* attempts to overcome this problem by readjusting each year's cash flows in light of a "safe" rate and a reinvestment rate that is a reflection of the real world. Once the adjustments are made, a new discount rate is computed, and this is known as the Financial Management Rate of Return. In today's investment world, the FMRR is generally considered a better reflection of actual performance than the IRR. However, many analysts consider the IRR better for comparing one investment against another investment.

The concepts of the Internal Rate of Return and the Financial Management Rate of Return presented here have been simplified. Readers who wish a more in-depth explanation of discounted cash flow analysis are encouraged to seek additional information by reading textbooks on corporate finance or by contacting the National Association of REALTORS® or the Appraisal Institute for their trade publications on discounted cash flow analysis.

REVIEWING YOUR UNDERSTANDING

1. Write down the formulas for the first-year before-tax cash on cash rate and the first-year after-tax cash on cash rate.

2. What is the definition of the Internal Rate of Return (IRR), and how does it differ from the Financial Management Rate of Return (FMRR)?

CHAPTER SUMMARY

Investing is defined as giving up present consumption in exchange for future benefits. Some people invest using hunches; others use an investment analysis procedure. When selecting an investment, the five economic characteristics to check are return, management, taxability, liquidity, and risk.

Real estate cash flow analysis is the process of estimating the amount of money an investor might receive each year of ownership, including the year of resale. When the cash flow process is completed, the Before-Tax Cash Flow, taxes saved or paid, and the Net Spendable Income for each year of ownership are forecast. Then the resale price of the property at the end of the investor's holding period is estimated and from this the Net Sale Proceed are forecast. Offering prices and rate of return estimates can be computed based on these cash flow numbers.

Offering prices are frequently based on the Gross Rent Multiplier approach and the Capitalization Rate approach and are double-checked by the price per square foot approach. Rates of return can be computed for the first year only, or can be based on a multiyear analysis of the investor's entire holding period.

The most common first-year rates are the before-tax cash on cash rate and the after-tax cash on cash rate. Multiyear rates of return should take into consideration the time value of money and use a discounted cash flow approach. The two most common multiyear rates are the Internal Rate of Return (IRR) and the Financial Management Rate of Return (FMRR). The Financial Management Rate of Return attempts to overcome the reinvestment assumption shortcoming of the Internal Rate of Return.

IMPORTANT TERMS AND CONCEPTS

After-Tax Cash Flow	*Liquidity*
Before-Tax Cash Flow	*Multi- vs. single-year analysis*
Capitalization Rate	*Net Sale proceeds*
Cash flow analysis	*Net Spendable Income*
FMRR	*Time value of money*
Gross Rent Multiplier	*Types of rates of return*
IRR	*Types of risks*
Investing	

REVIEWING YOUR UNDERSTANDING

1. The ability to convert an asset to cash quickly is called:
   a. management
   b. risk
   c. yield
   d. liquidity

2. The risk of loss because of an increase in inflation is:
   a. financial risk
   b. interest rate risk
   c. purchasing power risk
   d. social change risk

3. The decline in real estate values caused by a population shift from urban centers to the suburbs is an example of which risk?
   a. purchase power risk
   b. legal change risk
   c. social change risk
   d. financial risk

4. The maximum amount of rent assuming 100 percent occupancy is:
   a. gross scheduled income
   b. gross operating income
   c. gross rent multiplier
   d. gross domestic income

5. A contract in which the tenant agrees to pay all the operating expenses is a:
   a. gross lease
   b. net lease
   c. percentage lease
   d. residual lease

6. Which of the following *is not* considered a real estate operating expense?
   a. maintenance
   b. utilities
   c. management
   d. loan payments

7. In cash flow analysis, depreciation is:
   a. called cost recovery
   b. a noncash deduction
   c. an income tax concept
   d. all of the above

8. Before-tax cash flow is computed when:
   a. operating expenses are subtracted from gross operating income
   b. annual debt service is subtracted from net operating income
   c. taxes saved or paid is subtracted from net operating income
   d. vacancies are subtracted from gross scheduled income

9. According to the cash flow formula, a useable tax loss times a marginal tax bracket equals taxes saved.
   a. true
   b. false

10. Taxes saved or paid, plus before-tax cash flow, equals:
    a. net spendable income
    b. net rate of return
    c. net sale proceeds
    d. net operating income

11. Before-tax cash flow is $10,000, useable tax loss is ‹$5,000›, and marginal tax bracket is 30 percent; therefore, the after-tax cash flow is:
    a. $ 1,500
    b. $ 4,500
    c. $11,500
    d. $15,000

12. Resale price, less outstanding loan balances, less seller closing costs, less capital gain taxes, equals:
    a. net spendable income
    b. net rate of return
    c. net sale proceeds
    d. net operating income

13. $\dfrac{\text{Asking Price}}{\text{Net Operating Income}} = \text{Gross Rent Multiplier}$
    a. true
    b. false

14. All things being equal, the higher the subject property's gross rent multiplier above the market multiplier, the better the buy.
    a. true
    b. false

15. Comparable Property 1 sold for $500,000, with a gross scheduled income of $62,500. Comparable Property 2 sold for $450,000, with a gross scheduled income of $56,250. The subject property's gross scheduled income is $57,100. Based only on this information, the estimated market price of the subject property is:
    a. $456,800
    b. $420,500
    c. $357,200
    d. $318,750

16. The gross rent multiplier approach is most often used to esti-mate the probable resale price of:
    a. single-family homes
    b. apartment properties
    c. commercial properties
    d. industrial properties

17. $\dfrac{\text{Net Operating Income}}{\text{Price}} = \text{Capitalization Rate}$
    a. true
    b. false

18. All things being equal, the higher the subject property's capi-talization rate over the prevailing market capitalization rate, the worse the buy.
    a. true
    b. false

19. The discount rate that reduces the future cash flows to a present value just equal to the amount of money invested is called the:
    a. cash on cash rate of return
    b. equity yield rate of return
    c. internal rate of return
    d. accounting rate of return

Answer questions 20–25 based on the following case study:

Small rental in a semi-rural college area requires 30% down The small two bedroom home is listed for $300,000, and requires $90,000 down (30%), and a new loan of $210,000 (70%) @ 7% fixed, 30 years, payable $1,397 per month. The rent paid by four students totals $1,900 per month, vacancy factor 5%, there is no other income. Annual operating expenses $5,800. Interest deduction is $14,632 for the year, annual depreciation on improvements $7,636. Per the accountant, all passive losses can be used in the current year. Potential investor has a combined federal and state tax bracket of 36%. **Based on the listed price, answer the following questions.**

First-Year Cash Flow

20. What is the net operating income?

    $_____

21. What is the before-tax cash flow?

    $_____

22. What is the net spendable income?

    $_____

23. What is the annual gross rent multiplier?

    $_____

24. What is the capitalization rate?

    $_____

25. What is the after-tax cash on cash rate?

    $_____

CASE & POINT

Case Study—Older 10-Unit Apartment Building

The following is a practice case study and the answers can be found in the **Answers to Reviewing Your Understanding Questions** section toward the end of the book.

The asking price for a 10-unit apartment property is $1,200,000.

Income and Expense Data

Each unit rents for $1,000 per month, and vending machines and other income net $700 per month. The vacancy factor is 5%. Annual operating expenses (property taxes, insurance, repairs, and management) are estimated to run 30% of the gross scheduled income (Line 1).

Financing Data

Lenders will only grant a 75% loan, thus $1.2 million asking price × 75% = $900,000 loan at 8% fixed interest for 30 years = approximately $6,600 monthly loan payment. The down payment would be $300,000 (asking price $1.2 million × 25%).

Income Tax Information

Based on the loan above, the first year interest deduction is approximately $71,700 and the first year depreciation estimate is $28,400. The potential investor's combined federal and state tax bracket is 36%. Per the investor's accountant, all passive losses are useable in the current year. **Complete the problem below. Round all figures to the nearest dollar. Take all percentages two places past the decimal.**

First-Year Cash Flow Analysis

1. Gross Scheduled Income $
2. Plus: Other Income   +

3. Equals: Total Gross Income $
4. Less: Vacancy/Credit Loss   −

5. Equals: Gross Operating Income $
6. Less: Annual Operating Expenses   −

7. Equals: Net Operating Income $
8. Less: Annual Debt Service   −

9. Equals: Before-Tax Cash Flow $

Tax Benefit Analysis

10. Net Operating Income $

11. Less: Interest (Loan 1)   —

12. Less: Interest (Loan 2)   —

13. Less: Cost Recovery (Depreciation)   —

14. Equals: Real Estate Taxable Income or $

15. Equals: Estimated Allowable Loss (if loss) $

16. Times Tax Bracket (times Line 14 or 15)

17. Equals: Taxes Saved or Paid $

Net Spendable Income

18. Before-Tax Cash Flow (Line 9) $

19. Plus/Less: Taxes Saved or Paid (Line 17)

20. Equals: Net Spendable Income (After-Tax Cash Flow) $

As the investor's adviser, you are asked to answer the following questions:

1. What is the Before-Tax Cash Flow? $

2. What are the taxes saved/paid? $

3. What is Net Spendable Income? $

4. What is the Gross Rent Multiplier?

5. What is the Capitalization Rate?   %

6. What is the before-tax cash on cash rate?   %

7. What is the after-tax cash on cash rate?   %

8. If the prevailing cap rate in the market is 8 percent, what is the maximum that should be paid for this 10-unit apartment? $_____

Assume the investor purchases the property for the price computed in Question 8, and the new loan amount is for $806,063 at 8% for 30 years, payable $5,915 per month. Due to the lower price, assume that Annual Operating Expenses will now be reduced to $34,000 per year, the annual interest deduction will be $64,242, and the depreciation write-off will drop to $27,000 per year. All other figures remain as before.

9. What will be the new net spendable income?

10. With an investment of $268,687, what will be the new after-tax cash on cash rate of return?

CHAPTER 17
INCOME TAX ASPECTS OF INVESTMENT REAL ESTATE

PREVIEW

This chapter discusses the impact of the basic principles of federal income taxes on income-producing real estate. Some income tax aspects for homeowners are summarized as a special interest topic and are not stressed in this chapter. Section 17.1 of this chapter outlines the major income tax advantages of owning investment real estate. Section 17.2 discusses basis and depreciation rules. Section 17.3 briefly describes the passive loss rules. Section 17.4 illustrates how gain upon disposition is calculated and how gain and taxes can be deferred by installment sales and real estate exchanges. The Case & Point at the end of the chapter presents two views regarding the income tax deductibility of mortgage interest for homeowners.

The material in this chapter is basic and limited to federal, not state, income tax rules. This chapter is intended to illustrate how income taxes affect real estate investment decisions. Readers must recognize that income tax rules are subject to changes after the printing of this textbook. This textbook is not intended to be an aid for tax planning, for which all readers are encouraged to seek tax counsel. When you have completed this chapter, you should be able to:

1. List the major income tax advantages of owning investment real estate.

2. Describe how basis is established and why basis is important to real estate investors.

3. **Outline how operating expenses, interest, depreciation, and the passive loss rules affect a property's cash flow.**

4. **Discuss how gain or loss is measured upon resale and how installment sale reporting and Internal Revenue Code Section 1031 exchanges can spread or defer gain and taxes into future years.**

17.1 Major Income Tax Advantages

There are six major income tax advantages for owning income-producing real estate:

1. Interest on loans used to purchase or improve rental real estate is fully deductible against the rental income produced by the property. In some cases any leftover interest, according to the passive loss rules, might also be deductible against an investor's other income. However, interest paid on other types of loans, such as consumer loans, certain raw land loans, and even some aspects of home loans, may not be fully deductible for income tax purposes.

2. For income property owners, repairs, maintenance, management, property taxes, insurance, and other operating expenses are deductible. In contrast, homeowners can currently deduct only property taxes.

3. Income property owners can take depreciation (cost recovery) deductions to shelter rental income. Depreciation is a noncash deduction that has the same deduction impact as interest and operating expenses, which do require a cash outlay. Homeowners are not allowed to take depreciation.

4. Upon resale, if a property was held by an investor for the statutory time, it may qualify for favorable capital gain treatment, if allowed at that time.

5. A real estate investor is allowed installment sale reporting when the property is sold and the seller carries financing (paper). This may save the seller income taxes by pushing a part of the taxable gain into a lower tax bracket in future years.

6. If the investor follows the rules of Internal Revenue Code Section 1031, a real estate exchange can be used to defer all gain and taxes into another like-kind property.

Investor Versus Dealer

An investor is a person who holds property for a personal investment portfolio. A dealer is a person who acquires real estate as inventory to be resold to customers in the course of business. Why the distinction? The federal tax code treats investors and dealers differently. For example, real estate investors get all of the six major tax advantages listed in the preceding paragraph. On the other hand, real estate dealers are not allowed depreciation, capital gains, installment sales, and Internal Revenue Code Section 1031 exchanges.

Obviously, when analyzing a particular property it will make a significant difference, in terms of cash flow analysis, yield, and disposition strategy, whether the buyer is a dealer or an investor. There are no absolute, clear guidelines as to what behavior makes one a dealer or an investor. There are many gray areas that require the advice of tax experts based on individual circumstances. Factors to consider include the number of sales, length of holding period, sales after subdividing, and the like. For the remainder of this chapter it will be assumed that an investor position applies.

REVIEWING YOUR UNDERSTANDING

1. List six major income tax advantages of owning income real estate.

2. In terms of cash outlay, how do depreciation deductions differ from operating expenses and mortgage interest?

3. Compare the income tax differences between a real estate investor and a real estate dealer.

17.2 Basis and Depreciation

In addition to deductions for out-of-pocket operating expenses and interest paid on mortgages, an income tax deduction is allowed for depreciation, formally known as cost recovery. Depreciation is an annual bookkeeping deduction allowed by the tax code as a cost recovery for the theoretical loss in value of the property over time. In reality, the property could be appreciating in real value, but an investor is still allowed to take a depreciation loss deduction for income tax purposes. This has the impact of sheltering rental income without experiencing a cash expense or actual loss in value.

The depreciation deduction is allowed only on the improvements, not on the land. Please remember that this usage of the word *depreciation* is different from the use in appraisals.

How Much Is Deductible?

The dollar amount of depreciation allowed each year is a function of the taxpayer's basis in the real estate, the allocation between improvements and land, and the straight-line write-off period. *Basis* refers to the property owner's cost for income tax purposes. The allocation between improvements and land is determined by an appraisal or a set of guidelines. The straight-line write-off period is established by Congress.

How Does It Work?

First, the property owner's basis must be determined. Basis is important for two reasons: (1) Basis is the starting point for computing depreciation while the property is owned, and (2) basis helps to determine the gain or loss for income tax purposes when the property is disposed of.

The owner's initial basis in a property is determined by the method of acquisition, not by the value of the property. A $2 million property can be acquired one way and have a basis of $2 million. But the same property could be acquired another way and have a basis that is considerably lower. An investor must depreciate using basis, not value! The most common method to acquire title is to purchase the real estate. Basis upon purchase is usually the purchase price, plus a certain portion of the buyer's closing cost, called capitalized cost. During the investor's ownership, the basis will be increased by the cost of any capital improvements added and will decrease by the amount of allowed depreciation deductions.

Once the purchase price and capitalized closing cost have been determined, the next step is to allocate the basis between the nondepreciable land and the depreciable improvements. This allocation is done by use of an appraisal, comparable sales data, or sometimes the ratio established by the county tax assessor on the property tax bill. This allocation process is tricky and is subject to IRS challenge if the allocation does not reflect current market reality. Once the basis has been allocated between land and improvements, there is frequently further subdivision between real property and personal property, such as carpets, draperies, appliances, and so on, because of the different write-off rules for each.

The time periods for depreciating investments are set by law and have been subject to frequent changes. As of 2005, the depreciation

Special Interest Topic

Initial Basis of Real Estate

The following are various methods of acquiring title to real estate and how basis is initially determined:

1. If real property is acquired by purchase, the initial basis is the purchase price plus capitalized buyer's closing cost.

2. If real property is acquired by gift, the initial basis is the donor's adjusted cost basis, or market value at the date of gift, whichever is less.

3. If real property is acquired by inheritance, the initial basis is market value at the date of death of the decedent.

4. If real property is acquired by exchange, the initial basis is the market value of the new property, less the deferred gain from the old property.

5. The basis of a principal residence converted to a rental is the adjusted basis of the home or the home's market value on date of conversion, whichever is less.

periods for real estate were 27½ years for residential rental property and 39 years for nonresidential rental property. Real estate must use straight-line depreciation. However, the first and last year straight-line system must be modified by what is called the mid-month convention. Accelerated systems that allowed more than straight-line depreciation were abolished for all real estate acquired after December 31, 1986. Personal property depreciation has various time periods, with five to seven years being the most common. Personal property is allowed accelerated write-off using the 200 percent declining balance system. This 200 percent system must be modified using the mid-year convention. Both mid-month and mid-year conventions require slight modifications to the straight-line and 200 percent declining balance systems when calculating the precise dollar amount of depreciation. The details are beyond the scope of this text. For specific information readers are encouraged to consult a tax professional.

Example

An investor purchased an apartment property for $1 million, plus $5,000 in capitalized buyer closing costs. According to an appraisal, the allocation is 20 percent to land and 80 percent to building, with no personal property items. The first 12 months' depreciation could be estimated as follows:

$1,000,000   Purchase price

+   5,000   Plus: capitalized buyer closing costs

$1,005,000   Equals: Initial basis

×   .80   Times: Percent building ratio

$ 804,000   Equals: Depreciable building

then

$$\frac{\$804,000 \text{ depreciable building}}{27\frac{1}{2} \text{ years residential rental}} = \$29,236 \text{ estimated depreciated}$$

(actual amount will be slightly less because of mid-month convention— i.e., first year only 11½ months)

REVIEWING YOUR UNDERSTANDING

1. Discuss how initial basis is determined for real estate owners.

2. How is basis allocated between land and improvements? What is the length of depreciation allowed for residential and nonresidential rental real estate?

3. Purchase price for a small commercial property is $500,000, plus $3,000 capitalized buyer's closing cost. Land is 20 percent, building 80 percent, with no personal property. What is the approximate depreciation for the first 12 months?

17.3 Passive Loss Rules

*T*he Tax Reform Act of 1986 was a major overhaul of the federal income tax system. One of the act's many features was an attack on real estate tax shelters. The main purpose of a real estate tax shelter is to produce a paper tax loss (as opposed to an out-of-pocket cash loss) that can be applied against the investor's personal income. In short, paper tax losses offset other real income, resulting in a decrease in taxes owed and an increase in after-tax spendable dollars. In the meantime, the investment may appreciate, resulting in a capital gain upon resale. The purpose of the passive loss section of the Tax Reform Act of 1986 was to reduce the practice of using paper real estate losses to reduce otherwise taxable personal income.

Prior to the Tax Reform Act of 1986 any annual loss (rents, lower operating expenses, mortgage interest, and depreciation) could be used in the current year to offset any other current income of the investor. However, the general passive loss rules now state that real estate losses can only offset what is known as passive income. To understand the passive loss rules and their impact on real estate cash flow analysis requires an explanation of income classifications.

According to the Tax Reform Act of 1986, income is broken into the following three classifications:

1. *Active Income.* Income generated when the taxpayer materially participates in an activity that produces income. Examples include wages, commissions, profits from owner-managed business, and other similar activities.

2. *Portfolio Income.* Income from paper types of investments, such as interest on savings, dividends on stocks, and coupons on bonds.

3. *Passive Income.* Income generated when the taxpayer does not materially participate in an activity that produces income. Examples include limited partnership income, business ventures in which the taxpayer has no active role, and rents from rental real estate. The Tax Reform Act of 1986 states that rental real estate is considered a passive activity, even if the property owner actively manages the rental real estate. This provision was a deliberate attempt to keep rental real estate in the passive income category.

Passive Income/Loss Offset Rules

The general rule is that a passive loss can offset only passive income. Passive losses cannot normally be used to offset active or portfolio income. If passive real estate losses cannot be used in the current year because of a lack of passive income, then the passive loss must be carried forward to offset passive income that might arise in a future tax year. If future tax years do not produce suitable passive income, the carry-forward passive loss can be used to offset gain when the subject property is sold.

This change was a dramatic shift from the earlier position that a real estate tax loss could be used to offset any current income. By restricting the offset of annual real estate losses to passive income, if a real estate investor does not have passive income, the normal tax savings will not be realized in the current year. This reduces the investor's current cash flow, which in turn reduces the investor's current rate of return and lowers the interest in and willingness to invest in rental real estate.

$25,000 Exception to the Passive Loss Rules

The passive loss rules provide an exception to the general rule that passive losses can offset only passive income. This exception, known as the $25,000 real estate exception to the passive loss rules, allows a qualified rental property owner to use up to $25,000 of passive real estate rental losses to offset active or portfolio income each year, after first offsetting passive income. To qualify for this $25,000 exception, a taxpayer must meet the following tests:

1. The taxpayer must own 10 percent or more direct interest in rental real estate and not hold title as either a corporation or a tax-reporting limited partnership, which must file Internal Revenue Service Form 1065.

2. The owner must be active in the management of the rental real estate. "Active in management" means that the owner must deal directly with the tenants and make all management decisions or hire a property manager to deal with the tenants. If the owner hires a property manager, the two should confer periodically, and the management contract should specify that the owner is the decision maker regarding the operations of the property. If a property owner leaves all management decisions to a property manager and merely receives a check and accounting statements, the property owner will probably fail the active-in-management test and lose the use of the $25,000 rule.

3. For the tax year in question, the rental real estate owner's modified adjusted gross income must be $100,000 or less. If the owner's modified adjusted gross income for the year is more than $100,000, then the otherwise usable $25,000 is reduced $1 for every $2 the modified adjusted gross income exceeds $100,000. Thus, the $25,000 rule will be phased out entirely when a rental real estate owner's modified adjusted gross income reaches $150,000. Keeping with the spirit of the Tax Reform Act of 1986, this effectively reserves the $25,000 rule for moderate-income real estate investors.

For the real estate investors who meet this series of tests, up to $25,000 of passive losses can be used in the current tax year to offset active and portfolio income, reducing taxes owed. This in turn will increase the after-tax spendable income for the year and raise the current year's rate of return.

Professional Real Estate Exception

Qualified real estate professionals who spend at least 750 hours and more than one-half of all business time per year in real estate activities can use real estate losses to offset any business or personal income. In short, unlike other real estate investors, a qualified real estate professional does not need to follow the passive loss rules.

A qualified real estate professional can acquire income real estate and use any paper losses created by depreciation to offset any, not just passive, income. This gives a qualified real estate professional a decided investment advantage over a regular investor.

To determine who is a qualified real estate professional, one must turn to ever changing IRS interpretations. Examples of qualified real estate professionals include appraisers, property managers, loan brokers, and real estate agents who meet the hours and percentage of business rules and have been cleared by IRS interpretations.

Several other rules from the Tax Reform Act of 1986 have an impact on real estate investments but are beyond the scope of this chapter. Once again, readers are encouraged to seek competent tax counsel before entering into a real estate transaction.

REVIEWING YOUR UNDERSTANDING

1. What is a tax shelter?

2. What is the general passive loss rule?

3. What are the three tests to determine if the $25,000 exception to the general passive loss rule can be used?

4. What is the qualified real estate professional exception to the passive loss rules?

17.4 Calculating and Deferring Gain

Once owners decide to market their properties, a series of choices arise as to how to handle the gain upon sale. A real estate investor has three basic choices: (1) sell for cash and pay the tax on the gain, (2) sell and carry some equity in a note and deed of trust and report some gain as an installment sale, or (3) do not sell and instead do a like-kind Internal Revenue Code Section 1031 exchange and defer the gain and tax into the new property. This section outlines the basic principles of each choice.

Calculating Gain and Taxes Owed on Income Property

Step 1: Calculate Adjusted Cost Basis

Initial (original) basis

Plus: buyer's capitalized closing cost

Plus: capital improvements, if any

Minus: depreciation for term of ownership

Equals: adjusted cost basis on date of resale

Step 2: Calculate Gain

Resale price

Less: Seller closing cost

Less: Adjusted cost basis from Step 1

Less: carry-forward passive losses, if any

Equals: gain on sale

Step 3: Apply current capital gain treatment to the gain on sale to calculate the tax owed.

Use of an Installment Sale to Spread Out Taxable Gain

Section 453 of the Internal Revenue Code provides a way to spread over a number of years the gain and tax on the profit from a sale of an asset. This avoids paying the entire tax on the entire gain in the year of sale.

To qualify a sale as an installment sale, the seller must "carry back" financing on behalf of the buyer. The financing can be in the form of a note and deed of trust, a mortgage, a contract of sale, or other similar instruments. The seller "carry loan" must call for a due date in some year other than the same year as the sale. The seller carry loan can be either a senior or junior loan. Whenever the seller carries back paper, the installment method for reporting gain is automatic, unless the seller formally elects to take the entire tax in the year of sale. Installment sale reporting is allowed for real estate investors and homeowners. Real estate dealers are normally denied the use of installment sales.

Some advantages and disadvantages of an installment sale follow.

Advantages

1. It is a way to sell a property in a tight real estate market.

2. An installment sale can lower the tax owed on the sale by throwing all or part of the gain into a more favorable, low tax bracket year in the future.

3. Interest can be earned from the buyer on gain not yet reported.

4. The tax can be paid in the future with inflated (cheaper) dollars.

Disadvantages

1. Seller does not receive all of his or her equity in up-front cash, thereby incurring opportunity costs on reinvestment possibilities.

2. Seller may be in a higher tax bracket when money is collected from the buyer in a future year and thus may actually pay more in taxes than would have been the case in the year of sale.

3. Buyer could pay off the loan early and thereby force the seller to take gain in an unplanned, unfavorable tax year.

4. Buyer could default on the loan, and the seller could be forced to proceed with a foreclosure.

There are many other aspects to installment sales not covered in this brief summary. The installment sale technique for spreading out gain may or may not be a good tax move for a real estate seller. A real estate licensee should not give tax advice; however, a licensee should recognize that an installment sale is one of several choices a seller should discuss with a tax adviser.

Use of a Like-Kind 1031 Exchange to Defer Gain

Section 1031 of the Internal Revenue Code provides a way to move ownership from one income or investment property to another and not recognize taxable gain. Although the rules are complicated, the basic concept states that real estate held for income or investment can be exchanged, tax deferred, for any other real estate to be held

Special Interest Topic

Application of 1997 & 1998 Tax Law Changes to the Sale of a Principal Residence

1. The law now states that there will be no tax on a gain up to $250,000 for single home sellers and $500,000 for married home sellers who file a joint return. To qualify, the home must have been your principal residence for at least two out of the last five years. Only one spouse needs to have been the owner, but both spouses must have lived there for a two year period, and filed joint returns, to get the $500,000 maximum exemption. All age limits and requirements to buy another home have been eliminated.

2. This full exclusion can only be used once every 2 years. If a home is sold for a gain before the two year holding period, the gain will be fully taxable, UNLESS the sale is due to a job change, major illness, or unforeseen circumstances. Then a pro rata formula will be used to separate tax exempt from taxable gain.

Example: Assume the owner lived in the home for only 18 months, then due to a job change, the home was sold for a gain. The formula will work as follows:

$$\frac{18 \text{ months}}{24 \text{ months}} = 75\%$$

If homeowner is single, he or she would get $250,000 × 75% or $187,500 maximum exemption.

If homeowners are married, they would get $500,000 × 75% or $375,000 maximum exemption.

for income or investment. Section 1031 real estate exchanges can only be used by investors. Real estate dealers are not allowed to do tax deferred exchanges. Homeowners cannot do 1031 exchanges, but rather have a different system regarding gain. (See Special Interest Topic in this chapter for details.) U.S. property cannot be 1031 exchanged for foreign properties.

Under a properly structured 1031 real estate exchange, no tax is paid on the realized gain at the time of the transfer. Rather, the gain is carried over to the new property to be taxed when the new property is sold. Often the process is repeated, property after property, deferring gain until ultimately the owner dies. As of 2005, the decedent's heirs would receive the final property at a basis equal to market value at the date of death, and all previous deferred gains would be excused. Thus, a tax-deferred exchange can become a tax-free exchange upon death.

When structuring a 1031 exchange, the different properties may have unequal equities. To balance the difference in equities, one party must give some additional items to the other. If the difference in equities is balanced using items other than qualified like-kind real estate, the party who receives the unlike property is said to have received "boot." Boot is defined as any unlike property received in the exchange. Receipt of boot can trigger some tax in a real estate exchange. Thus, to have a completely tax-deferred exchange a person must avoid receiving boot.

Computation of boot and other details of 1031 tax-deferred exchanges are beyond the scope of this textbook. Readers are invited to discuss this subject with tax experts and knowledgeable real estate investment agents. The purpose here is to offer 1031 like-kind exchanges as another alternative to a regular real estate sale and payment of tax on the resulting gain.

REVIEWING YOUR UNDERSTANDING

1. List the steps needed to compute gain upon sale of income real estate.

2. What are the advantages and disadvantages of an installment sale?

3. Who can and who cannot do a 1031 tax-deferred real estate exchange?

CHAPTER SUMMARY

The major income tax advantages of owning income real estate include: the deductibility of mortgage interest, operating expenses, and depreciation while you own the property; capital gain treatment; use of installment sale reporting; and the ability to use a 1031 tax-deferred exchange when the property is transferred. These advantages are available to real estate investors. Real estate *dealers* cannot take depreciation and capital gains and are usually not allowed installment sale and 1031 exchange treatment.

Cost for income tax purposes is called basis. The amount of basis is determined by how title is acquired. Basis is used to determine the amount of depreciation allowed each year and to measure gain or loss upon resale. Once basis is established, it is allocated between land and improvements, after which the real estate improvements are depreciated for the time period allowed by law. Current rules (2005) allow 27½ years for residential rental and 39 years for nonresidential, using the straight-line method.

The Tax Reform Act of 1986 created the passive loss rules, which state that rental real estate is a passive activity and any passive real estate loss can offset only passive income. Passive losses can no longer offset active or portfolio income unless the $25,000 exception can be applied. The passive loss rules have had the impact of discouraging some people from investing in rental real estate. Some real estate professionals are exempt from these passive loss rules.

Once real estate owners decide to market their income properties, they basically have three choices of how to handle taxable gain. They could sell for cash, declare the gain, and pay the tax. They could carry some financing on behalf of the buyer and treat the gain in the seller carry note as an installment sale. Or, finally, the owners could decide to structure a like-kind 1031 tax-deferred exchange and transfer the gain into another income or investment property.

IMPORTANT TERMS AND CONCEPTS

Basis	*Straight-line: 27½ or 39 years*
Boot	*Tax-deferred exchange (1031)*
Depreciation	*Tax shelter*
Installment sale	*$25,000 exception to the passive*
Investor vs. dealer	*loss rules*
Passive loss rules	

REVIEWING YOUR UNDERSTANDING

1. Which of the following is a noncash income tax deduction?
   a. mortgage interest
   b. property taxes
   c. repairs
   d. depreciation

2. Which tax treatment does an investor receive that a dealer does not?
   a. mortgage interest deduction
   b. property tax deduction
   c. repair deduction
   d. depreciation

3. The initial basis to an owner who acquired title to real estate by gift is:
   a. donor's adjusted basis or market value, whichever is less
   b. market value at the date of gift
   c. purchase price, plus capitalized closing costs
   d. market value of new property less gain deferred from old property

4. The minimum depreciation write-off period for residential rental property is:
   a. 39 years
   b. 27½ years
   c. 7 years
   d. 5 years

5. For rental real estate investors, all of the following are depreciable *except*:
   a. carpets
   b. buildings
   c. land
   d. carport

6. Income or losses from rental real estate are considered to be:
   a. active
   b. portfolio
   c. passive
   d. tax sheltered

7. To use the full $25,000 exception to the passive loss rules, the rental property owner's modified adjusted gross income must not exceed:
   a. $125,000
   b. $100,000
   c. $75,000
   d. $25,000

8. When the seller of an income property carries financing for the buyer, the income tax reporting of the sale is known as:
   a. an installment sale
   b. a tax-deferred exchange (1031)
   c. an excluded gain
   d. a once-in-a-lifetime exemption

9. To qualify for a 1031 tax-deferred exchange, an investor must exchange:
   a. income or investment real estate for income or investment real estate
   b. real property for personal property
   c. a principal residence for a principal residence
   d. foreign rental property for U.S. rental property

10. The receipt of unlike taxable property in a 1031 exchange is called:
    a. leverage
    b. equity balance
    c. boot
    d. basis

11. Depreciation for income tax purposes is technically called:
    a. write-off
    b. cost recovery
    c. cash flow deduction
    d. tax loophole

12. The initial basis of real property acquired by purchase is best described as:
    a. basis of the seller, less closing costs
    b. market value date of purchase
    c. purchase price, plus capitalized buyer's closing costs
    d. loan amount, plus closing costs

13. Purchase price, including capitalized buyer closing cost, of a commercial property is $1 million, with land 40 percent and real estate improvements 60 percent. Ignoring the mid-month convention, what will be the total depreciation for 12 months?
    a. $15,385
    b. $36,364
    c. $21,819
    d. $25,641

14. Which of the following is considered passive income?
    a. wages
    b. profits from an owner-managed business
    c. dividends from stocks
    d. rents from investor-owned real estate

15. The general passive loss rule states that passive losses can only offset:
    a. passive income
    b. active income
    c. portfolio income
    d. all of the above

16. To use the $25,000 exception to the general passive loss rule, an investor must own at least what percent of the property?
    a. 1 percent
    b. 5 percent
    c. 10 percent
    d. 20 percent

17. Real estate passive losses that cannot be used in the current year:
    a. are lost forever
    b. can be carried forward to be used in future years
    c. can always be used when the investor's income drops below $25,000
    d. are carried back to offset income earned the previous year

18. Qualified real estate professionals are exempt from the passive loss rules on their rental properties.
    a. true
    b. false

19. Purchase price of income property is $300,000; buyer's capitalized closing cost, $3,000; capital improvements added, $15,000; and depreciation accumulated during term of ownership, $20,000. Based only on this information, what is the adjusted cost basis?
    a. $338,000
    b. $318,000
    c. $298,000
    d. $262,000

20. The property in Question 19 is resold for $400,000, seller's closing cost come to 8 percent, and carry-forward passive losses are $10,000. What is the gain or loss on the sale?
    a. <$8,000> loss
    b. $100,000 gain
    c. $85,000 gain
    d. $60,000 gain

21. To qualify as an installment sale, the seller must carry back a junior lien or second, not a first, deed of trust.
    a. true
    b. false

22. For the seller who carries a loan, one disadvantage of an installment sale is that:
    a. it could lower tax on gain in year of payoff
    b. in the event of default, seller may need to foreclose
    c. if inflation continues, the seller will pay the tax using cheaper dollars
    d. the seller will earn interest on gain and tax not yet reported

23. 1031 real estate exchanges cannot be used by:
    a. homeowners
    b. investors who own land
    c. investors who own commercial property
    d. investors who own farms

24. Foreign properties can be exchanged 1031 tax deferred for U.S. properties.
    a. true
    b. false

25. For a married couple to exclude up to $500,000 in gain upon the sale of their owner-occupied principal residence, they must:
    a. both be on title
    b. earn no more than $100,000 per year
    c. occupy the home for a minimum of one year
    d. file a joint income tax return for two years

CASE & POINT

Why Should Interest on Home Loans Be Deductible?

Whether homeowners should be allowed to deduct the interest they pay on their mortgages is currently under debate. After reading the following two viewpoints, see if you can separate the logical economic points from the emotional noneconomic points.

Viewpoint 1

Allowing homeowners to deduct mortgage interest is an economic rip-off. An income tax deduction should only be allowed for business, not personal expenses. A business expense deduction can be justified as a fair revenue neutral concept. When a company pays someone for a legitimate business expense it should be deductible to arrive at true taxable profit. Owning a home is not a business; it is a personal consumer item no different from owning a personal car or a television set. In the U.S. tax code, interest paid on money borrowed to purchase consumer products is not deductible, *except for homeowner interest!*

When homeowners are allowed to deduct mortgage interest, this lowers their income taxes. To make up for this lost revenue, the government increases other people's taxes. Not only is this tax shift unfair, but it discriminates against home renters, who cannot deduct their rental payments from their income. Renters tend to be lower-income people; thus, the home interest deductions of middle- and upper-income people are extracted at the expense of lower-income people.

To add insult to injury, homeowners can refinance their homes and pull out money to purchase consumer products, then turn around and deduct the interest on the refinance loan. In short, the homeowner borrows to acquire consumer goods, thereby shifting the nondeductible consumer interest into deductible homeowner interest. A renter cannot do this and therefore pays the full cost of consumer borrowing.

The argument that we need homeowner interest deductions to encourage people to purchase a home is bunk! Many other developed Western nations do not allow homeowners to deduct mortgage interest, and they have an equal or even greater percentage of home ownership than does the United States. Don't fool yourself: The only justification for an interest deduction for a home mortgage is to appease a special interest voting bloc consisting of homeowners and their PAC fund fat cats and allied real estate industries.

Viewpoint 2

The facts speak for themselves: Countries with a high percentage of private real estate ownership have a stable, law-abiding society. Citizens tend not to revolt and destroy a country if they own a piece of the land. For its own preservation, a country and its government should use all tools available, including the tax code, to make home ownership affordable to as many people as possible.

It is a basic economic principle that incentives change behavior. Giving tax incentives to own a home encourages more people to seek home ownership. Mortgage interest deductions for homeowners reduce the effective cost of owning a home. By reducing the cost of home ownership, a home becomes more affordable to more people. As homeowners pay off their mortgages, their equity increases and their interest deductions decrease. This increase in equity increases net worth, which in turn creates financial security and peace of mind. An increase in net worth reduces the need for government aid, which then diminishes the need to increase taxes.

Opponents of home interest deductions often state that they constitute discrimination against renters. One can counter by stating that by allowing interest deductions for homeowners, more renters can afford to become homeowners. If home interest deductions were abolished, fewer people could afford a home. This would result in less net worth and an increase in government aid, which would require an increase in everyone's taxes. If some renters cannot afford to purchase a home, the answer is to provide government loans so they can buy homes. *The answer should not be to make everyone a renter!*

It is slippery logic to state that home interest deductions are not needed to obtain a high percentage of home ownership and to cite the high ownership in other countries that do not allow home interest deductions. A comparison of the percentage of U.S. home ownership with other countries is not "apples with apples" but "apples with apricots." Different countries have different social security and welfare programs, cultural values, and tax structures. Any comparison just by percentage of home ownership is dishonest economics.

The concept of home ownership transcends a mere listing of who pays what tax. It goes to the greater issues of private property, the ability to accumulate a personal net worth, and the commitment to one's country and its social values.

CHAPTER 18
APPLIED REAL ESTATE ECONOMICS

PREVIEW

A complete investigation of a real estate investment includes a study of general economic trends in the real estate market, together with a detailed economic study of the value and investment return potential of the individual parcel. This chapter brings together these two elements to outline the real estate decision-making process. Section 18.1 explores the variables that a real estate investor should consider before making an investment decision. Section 18.2 uses flow charts to illustrate the steps in making a real estate investment decision. The Case & Point at the end of the chapter examines how to identify at what stage a real estate cycle is in. When you have completed this chapter, you will be able to:

1. Describe why real estate investing involves multiple choices.

2. List the five steps in the scientific method of analysis.

3. Summarize the steps in analyzing a parcel of improved real estate.

4. Summarize the steps in analyzing the alternatives for developing an unimproved parcel of land.

18.1 Real Estate Investment Variables

There are key factors that investors usually consider before making an investment decision. This section focuses on the investor's *expectations* for the investment and the process of selecting from *multiple choices*.

Expectations

As mentioned earlier, real estate is an expensive asset that is locked into a fixed location. The large initial investment frequently takes years to recoup. Because of these factors, real estate investments are heavily influenced by future changes. Therefore, real estate prices today are based on an investor's expectations or projection of earnings tomorrow and beyond.

The investor could simply assume that future earnings will be similar to today's. But this is not a reasonable assumption. In fact, the key element of the investment process is the *study of how possible changes may affect future earnings.*

What are the future changes that will influence real estate values? By definition, they are all based on economic, social, or political cycles or trends. Future real estate values, as always, will be influenced by changing economic events, by changes in social activities, and by the future political actions of governments.

Cycles and Trends

When investors seek to forecast changes in earnings, they must remember that *all* change involves either *cycles*—changes that recur regularly—or *trends*—long-term shifts in the same direction. Therefore, to forecast earnings one must forecast the economic, social, and political changes, the combination of cyclical and trend changes, and their influence on earnings. Because all future cycles and trends start in the past, this forecast must try to predict the movement of past cycles and trends into the future. Much of the material in Parts One and Two of this book is intended to discuss the major influences on such movements, so that investors can understand them and better forecast their future.

"What If"

There are numerous cycles and trends, perhaps millions. Investors should not be concerned with every change; only those that influence a particular real estate market need be of interest. To locate these important changes, analysts must play a game called "sensitivity analysis." This means asking what would be the effect, if any, of each perceived change. A sample group of questions follows.

What if:

> the tenant went bankrupt?
> the seller could not meet a promise of better than 90 percent occupancy?
> the largest industry in town closed its doors?
> the country went into a recession?
> the cost of gas and electricity doubled?
> zoning were changed to a land use of lower value?
> many lenders had problems with bad loans at the same time?
> auto gasoline were rationed?
> depreciation deductions were eliminated?
> Congress removed all real estate tax advantages?
> the city ordered a mandatory building code inspection?
> there were a major natural disaster?
> the most liberal or the most conservative local political group received a smashing majority vote at the next election?

The purpose of asking "what if" questions is not based on any particular expectation of their coming true. Rather, it is to explore how sensitive an investment is to change and which changes it is more sensitive to. No investment is completely protected; what an investor wants is an idea of what risks exist, so that he or she can more accurately judge a property's future profit potential.

Multiple Choices

Real estate investment analysis involves more than just assessing the likelihood of future benefits. It is also a process of selecting among alternative investments. Different investors have different objectives and need different investment characteristics. A salaried person with a high income may seek some form of tax shelter. An elderly person with a limited pension and no other investments needs to avoid risk of loss. A young person investing for retirement may seek a hedge against inflation.

Another important reason why real estate investment analysis involves selecting among multiple choices is that the best investment is not necessarily the one with the best characteristics; rather it is the one with *the best characteristics for the price.* If a real estate analyst had the information needed to make a foolproof forecast of all future investment returns, the analyst would conclude that a particular property should be purchased. Should the investor rush out and buy this property immediately? Not necessarily, because the market may have already bid this property up to an unreasonably high price level relative to its expected future returns. In the real world, an investor should search for a property that is expected to do well relative to its current price!

Still another aspect of multiple choices is that vacant land can be developed to many different uses. The legal use that develops the highest value for the land is known as the *highest and best use*. Thus, the investor faces a choice of possible uses for vacant land, creating different values for each use. Buildings also could be put to different uses, creating different values for each use.

Investing Involves Outthinking the Market

At any given moment, any number of investment properties may be for sale. Every potential buyer makes some sort of analysis, either consciously or unconsciously, regarding risks, returns, and the price he or she would be willing to pay. Years later, some of the investments will turn out to have provided much more in returns than their original prediction, whereas others will have become investment disasters. The purpose of investment analysis, and of choosing, is *to select investments that contain opportunities for future profits that the market is missing* or to avoid future problems that the market is ignoring. The goal of the average investor should be to do as well as or better than the market in general. This requires enough awareness of trends and issues to buy or sell before prices have completely changed in response to the new market awareness. Obviously, the earlier the awareness, the better off the investor.

The investor must recognize that he or she is in competition with all other investors to obtain profitable returns, be they investment dollars or amenities of home ownership. The competitive market gives greater returns to those who see advantages or problems and act on them! This could involve when and how to develop a vacant land parcel, or a possible change of use or alteration to a building.

Determining Investment Characteristics

Individual investments differ in location, type, size, rights, and financing. They also differ in how these characteristics affect the investment's future returns. Real estate investment textbooks contain many excellent discussions of the characteristics of investment types such as apartments, retail stores, and commercial office buildings.

Instead of describing the *current* investment characteristics for each type of real estate, this book has tried to focus attention on the future. Indeed, with the current revolutionary changes in the areas of energy, pollution, and work, it is certain that real estate investors in today's market had better consider those changes.

Limits on Choice in a Normal Market

The major limit on the investor's choice of properties is that in normal markets a lot of properties are for sale at any given time. As some of these may be "losers," only a few "good" properties may be left from which to choose. And these so-called good properties may have such high list prices as to discourage serious study.

Investment needs also limit the investor's choice, because different types of property differ in tax shelter, risk, and management. The investor's limited funds may restrict investments further and may require borrowing and pooling funds with other investors. Of course, in certain abnormal markets, there may be a flood of available properties, with plenty of cherry-picking by hard-driving buyers in a buyer's market.

Fancy Footwork

Most real estate investment seems complicated enough. From time to time, however, experts discover investment techniques that appear to increase investors' returns greatly. These usually involve income tax deductions to increase the tax shelter that the property offers. Past examples include rapid depreciation write-offs, prepaid interest, depreciation of separate building components, shortened economic life, and vineyard and orchard development cost deductions.

Some of the ideas suggested from time to time are perfectly legal; others may not be. There is a danger that the investor will allow these special tax benefits to override a careful study of the property itself. Every gimmick or new technique carries new risks (of legal error, an adverse court decision, a change of law, etc.) until the idea is widely used and politically accepted. These risks should be understood by the buyer and evaluated in the purchase decision.

This overview leads into Section 18.2, which concentrates on the steps in arriving at a real estate investment decision. Before you proceed, answer the questions below.

REVIEWING YOUR UNDERSTANDING

Real Estate Investment Variables

1. Explain the concept, "the present value of future benefits."

2. Why should an investor ask "what if?" questions before making a firm real estate decision?

18.2 Steps in Real Estate Decision Making[1]

Real estate decision making can be viewed as a series of steps that gather real estate information, analyze the information, and then arrive at a decision based on the analysis. The formal procedure is called *the scientific method*. The scientific method involves the following steps:

1. *Clearly identify and define the problem or purpose of the investigation.* This step is not as simple as it may sound. Unless a real estate investor knows exactly what he or she is attempting to decide, the investor will not acquire the information needed to make a sound decision. One clearly defined purpose might be to decide if now is the time to purchase a particular real estate property, which we shall call Property X.

2. *Collect relevant data.* With the problem or purpose clearly defined, the investor then gathers information that will be useful in arriving at a decision. It is equally important to avoid material that is extraneous and irrelevant to the problem at hand. An investor would attempt to gather as much economic, social, physical, and political data relevant to Property X as time and money allow.

3. *Analyze the data collected.* With the problem clearly defined and the relevant data collected, an investor must then correlate, classify, and analyze the data and arrive at a preliminary decision— often called a hypothesis. After analyzing the information, an investor may tentatively decide that Property X is the right property and that now is the time to buy.

---

[1]Dennis J. McKenzie, *Instructor's Guide for Real Estate Economics*, Sacramento: California Community Colleges, 2000.

4. *Formulate and test the tentative decision* (hypothesis). At this point in most scientific investigations, experiments are conducted to see if the tentative decision or hypothesis is correct. For real estate, it is difficult to experiment without having to make a firm commitment in advance. In other words, few sellers let an investor try the property before buying to see if the property produces the desired results. Although computer simulation is possible, frequently the only testing available is to determine how other similar parcels with similar owners are doing in the marketplace.

5. *Arrive at a final decision or conclusion.* Taking into consideration steps 1, 2, 3, and 4, an investor now makes a final decision by either accepting or rejecting the tentative decision (hypothesis). If an investor decides to accept the tentative decision (to buy Property X now), it should be recognized that there is a possibility that the investor is making a mistake. In other words, there is a chance that this is not the time to buy. So an investor should then estimate the probability of being wrong and decide if he or she is willing to take the risk. If it is decided that the property is an acceptable risk, the purchase takes place.

The scientific method is the rational way to approach real estate decisions. Unfortunately, too many people make real estate decisions based on emotions. The role of the real estate specialist is to bring rational behavior to a very emotional business. Figure 18.1 illustrates the steps in the scientific method.

Steps in Analyzing an Improved Property

Using the scientific method as a foundation, an outline of the steps in analyzing an improved parcel of real estate follows.

Because of the high purchase price, the first step for a real estate investor is to estimate if adequate financing is available. In some cases investors pay all cash, but usually financing is needed. As good as a particular real estate investment might be, an investor may have to abandon the project if adequate financing is not available.

After estimating whether financing is available, the next step is to analyze *national* cycles and trends. Questions that should be asked include: What is the state of the economy? What is government doing with fiscal and monetary policy? How will this influence national real estate activity? How will these national changes affect the property being analyzed?

Once national cycles and trends have been studied, an investor should look at *regional* economic changes. Important questions here

Figure 18.1 Steps in the scientific method.

include: Does the region follow national changes? Is the region insulated against national changes? Is it growing? Declining? Why? What influence will this have on the property being studied?

After regional cycles and trends have been studied, the next step is to look at *local* changes in the city or county where the property is located. Is the city following regional changes? To what degree? Does the city appear to be growing economically? Why? What are the directions of growth? What major transportation or development projects are pending? How will these factors influence the subject property?

Following the study of city or county changes, an investor should analyze the *neighborhood* where the property is located. Is it a growing, stagnant, or declining neighborhood? Why? What are the urban renewal plans? Changes in transportation routes? What influence does this have on the subject property?

Once national, regional, local community, and neighborhood changes have been studied, an investor is in a position to analyze the individual subject property. This step has two phases: appraisal and investment analysis. An appraisal estimates the market value of the property under consideration, and an investment analysis estimates if the property is "right" for the investor's purposes. The final step is to make a decision either to purchase or not. Figure 18.2 illustrates the steps in analyzing an improved property.

Steps in Analyzing Alternatives for Unimproved Real Estate Parcels

An in-depth analysis of the profitability of alternative uses for a parcel of land is frequently referred to as a *feasibility study*. The purpose of a feasibility study is to estimate if a proposed real estate project is economically sound—in other words, will it produce an acceptable profit? And, sometimes, which of several alternatives will produce the better profit? Although a complete feasibility study contains numerous other substeps, Figure 18.3 summarizes the steps in determining whether a particular real estate parcel has an economically feasible use.

From Figure 18.3, it can be seen that when analyzing the alternatives for unimproved parcels, one of the first steps is to check for government-approved uses and/or the prospect of obtaining a rezoning to achieve a higher and better use.

After the government-approved uses have been established, an investor checks the availability and cost of short-term construction financing and long-term take-out financing for each use.

After being assured of adequate financing, the next step is to estimate the physical barriers to the various alternative land uses, such as residential, commercial, industrial, or rural-recreational. In some cases, there may be more than one land use allowed by zoning, and the site must be studied to estimate its physical suitability for each legally possible use. When this is completed, a market study is conducted for each use, to estimate if a market exists for the proposed improvements and how strong the market is. At the root of all market studies are the fundamental principles of supply and demand. What is the current and future supply of improvements of this type? What is the current and future demand for improvements of this type? These two questions, and the balance between them, form the heart of a market study. If the study reveals no excess market demand potential for a particular use, then the analysis terminates. On the other hand,

Figure 18.2 Steps in analyzing an improved property.

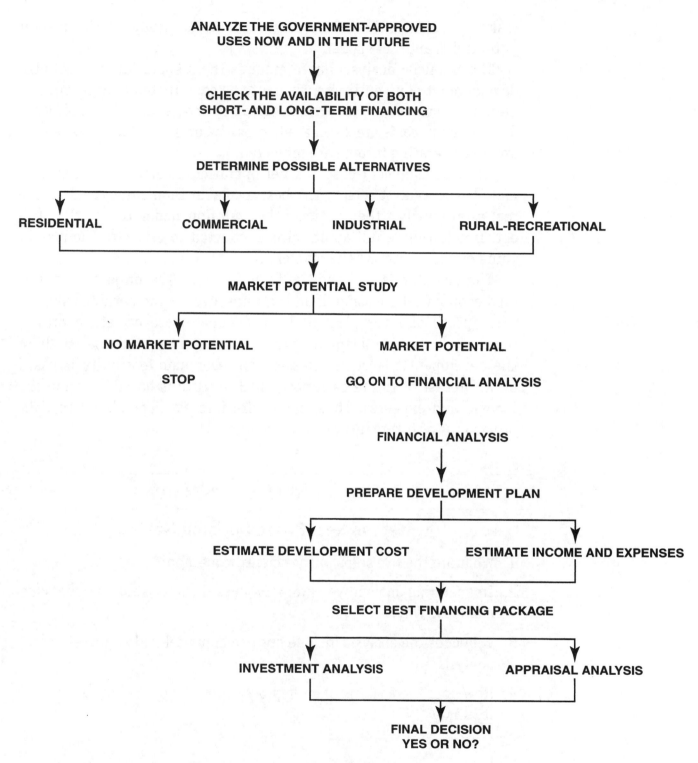

Figure 18.3 Steps in analyzing an unimproved property.

if the study reveals a good market potential, the real estate economist moves to the next major phase—financial analysis.

The purpose of financial analysis is to estimate whether the project is economically sound. Having a market potential is one thing, but being able to produce a real estate improvement at a cost that will make a profit at the prices estimated in the study of the market potential is another matter.

The financial analysis phase requires the preparation of a detailed development plan, outlining what is to be constructed and the timetable for construction. Then the development costs are estimated. Once development costs are estimated, gross income, operating expenses, and net operating income are projected.

After development cost and net operating income have been estimated, the analyst selects the best available financing package. The real estate analyst then projects the cash flow generated by the project. In addition, a full appraisal is conducted to estimate the market value of the project when completed.

The last step is to make the final decision. The project is considered economically feasible if all costs are covered and earnings provide a recapture of invested capital, an adequate rate of return on the investment, and an adequate profit for the entrepreneurial skills of the developer. It must be stressed that economic feasibility is based on a forecast of future earnings, which in turn is based on projected income and expenses. Thus, the entire forecast depends on *realistic projections* of future income and expenses.

REVIEWING YOUR UNDERSTANDING

Steps in Real Estate Decision Making

1. What are the five steps in the scientific method?

2. In analyzing an improved property, does the analyst study regional changes? Why?

3. Why does the analysis include both an appraisal and an investment analysis?

4. How does the analysis of an improved property differ from a feasibility study?

CHAPTER SUMMARY

Future earnings are the key element in investment profits, and forecasting these earnings is the focus of investment analysis. The analyst seeks to understand past and present social, political, and economic cycles and trends in order to anticipate future changes. Because not every future change will be important to the property being analyzed, the investor must consider the effect on the property of each possible change.

Investment analysis involves not only forecasting future benefits but also selecting among alternative investments. The investor must choose an investment that meets the desired investment characteristics (yield, tax aspects, risk, and so on). In addition, the investor must seek to find the investment that offers the best future returns for the current price. In practice, because a limited number of properties in a normal market are for sale at any one time, the analyst is trying to outthink the market.

Real estate decision making should involve careful study. The five steps of the scientific method provide an outline for such study. In analyzing improved property, key factors include financing availability; the impact of possible national, regional, local, and neighborhood changes; appraisals of market value; and analysis of investment characteristics and investment value.

For unimproved properties, added steps are the review of allowable uses, estimation of physically possible uses, estimation of market potentials, and preparation of a development plan.

IMPORTANT TERMS AND CONCEPTS

Change—cycles and trends	*Investment choices*
Expectation	*Limits on choice*
Feasibility study	*Profit potential*
Highest and best use	*Scientific method*
Investment characteristics	*Sensitivity analysis*

REVIEWING YOUR UNDERSTANDING

1. The city council's unanticipated rezoning to a lower density reduces the value of a property. This is an example of a(n):
   a. social force
   b. political force
   c. economic force
   d. physical force

2. A "what if" approach that anticipates the impact of various changes on an investment is:
   a. sensitivity analysis
   b. cash flow analysis
   c. economic analysis
   d. fail-safe analysis

3. The first step in the scientific method is:
   a. collect the data
   b. form the hypothesis
   c. analyze the data
   d. define the problem

4. A formal study of the profitability of various alternative uses for a vacant parcel of land is called a:
   a. "what if" analysis
   b. sensitivity analysis
   c. feasibility study
   d. critical path study

5. A real estate project is considered to be economically feasible only when:
   a. all operating costs are covered
   b. invested capital can be recovered
   c. 100 percent occupancy is anticipated
   d. there is residual profit for the entrepreneur and an adequate rate of return for investors

6. The main reason an investor should study real estate trends and cycles is to help estimate a property's:
   a. potential for bankruptcy
   b. demographic characteristics
   c. physical feasibility
   d. future earnings

7. Sensitivity analysis refers to a property's:
   a. reaction to change
   b. expense ratio
   c. position on the real estate cycles
   d. future earnings

8. A *cycle* differs from a *trend* in that a cycle:
   a. is a projection of the past into the future
   b. consists of recurring regular changes
   c. involves long-term shifts in the same direction
   d. cannot be forecast

9. Changing economic events, social attitudes, and political actions are important considerations for real estate analysts.
   a. true
   b. false

10. The real estate analyst studies past cycles and trends because history always repeats itself.
    a. true
    b. false

11. The investor asks "what if" questions in order to:
    a. explore how sensitive an investment is to change
    b. identify issues that should be studied
    c. identify which issues can be ignored
    d. all of the above

12. An appraisal estimates the market value of a property, whereas an investment analysis estimates if the property is "right" for the investor.
    a. true
    b. false

13. The best investment is the one with the:
    a. lowest price
    b. best location
    c. best building
    d. most profit potential for the price

14. *Highest and best use* refers to:
    a. the use with the least sensitivity to change
    b. the allowable use with the greatest physical density
    c. the legal use that generates the most land value
    d. the use with the strongest market demand

15. The *scientific method:*
    a. is a formal process for decision making
    b. depends on the availability of statistically valid data
    c. is the same as cash flow analysis for real estate investors
    d. shows how to examine the emotional aspects of real estate investing

CASE & POINT

Where Are We in the Real Estate Cycle?

One of the most difficult aspects of real estate investing in recent years has been interpreting where we are in the real estate cycle. This interpretation is critical, as a property should be worth more in the future if its cyclical influences are all positive and worth less if its cyclical influences are negative. It is a truism that "value is the present worth of future benefits." And the estimate of future benefits will depend on the estimate of future cyclical influences.

Note that the term used is *cyclical influences*, rather than the *business cycle*. First, every region or city has its own version of the business cycle and is at its own stage in that cycle. Each industry or occupation also has its own business cycle variation. Thus, each *user* of real estate, in each location, has an individual version of the business cycle. In addition, the supply and demand balance for each type of real estate in each location also has a distinctive cycle, only loosely related to the local business cycle. In real estate investment analysis, then, what counts is the *combination* of these various cycles and how this combination influences the particular property being studied.

The massive overconstruction of commercial building in the 1980s produced some of the worst supply and demand imbalances since the Great Depression of the 1930s. The dot.com collapse in the early 2000s produced massive commercial property vacancies in high-tech locations such as the San Francisco Bay Area.

The peaceful defeat of the former Soviet Union in the early 1990s produced sharp declines in areas dependent upon aero and defense industries. From 1990–1996 housing prices, in the defense industry dependent Southern California area, dropped in many cases 25% or more. During this same period, housing prices in Northern California dropped, but not as much as defense economy based Southern California. By the mid-2000s, housing prices in all areas of California were up by record amounts.

As with all markets, the main problem is in identifying *turning points* in the real estate market. In an "up market," the questions become: Will the escalation continue? If so, for how long? Or has the real estate market reached its top, with a decline imminent? Or will it bounce along at this high level, with only minor ups and downs? In a "down market," the questions become: Has the bottom been reached? If so, when will it start to turn up? Or will it continue to decline? If so, how far for how long? As always, it is easy to state what should have been done after the game has been played, as opposed to making the tough calls during the game.

CHAPTER 19
ANTICIPATING CHANGE

PREVIEW

It has been stressed how important future changes will be to the success of real estate investments and to the evaluation of any economic choice or decision. This chapter points out areas of possible future change that should be watched. In the process, it is hoped that readers will think about other possible changes. Section 19.1 studies the areas most directly connected to real estate. Section 19.2 discusses national issues, and Section 19.3 considers the most unpredictable changes. As this is not a book *about* the future, the coverage of these possible changes is brief. When you have completed this chapter, you will be able to:

1. List at least 10 potential areas of change.

2. Describe the nature of possible changes.

3. Show how each potential change can be monitored.

19.1 Real Estate Issues

Four areas of change are likely to have the most immediate impact on real estate in the years to come. These issues—land-use controls, the housing shortage and affordability, consumerism, and changes within the real estate industry itself—are more limited in scope than some of the larger-scale questions raised in subsequent portions of this chapter.

Land-Use Controls

Land-use controls change as society's perception of ideal land use evolves. The most important land-use issue of the moment appears to be the environment, especially pollution. Pollution control regulations by local, state, and federal governments are likely to have considerable influence on public and private land use in the next decade. Continuing serious air pollution in some urban areas is likely to lead to shifts in transportation methods that will have a direct impact on industrial, commercial, and residential real estate land uses. This in turn will have an impact on the market value of each property. And past regulation of land use to minimize water pollution is a pattern that is expected to continue throughout the nation.

After pollution controls, a second environmental issue of growing importance in studying property values is wildlife protection. Habitat protection is of growing importance in development planning. Future battles over water conservation to protect wildlife may sharply affect water cost and land values in some areas.

Finally, the extent of government control over private land will continue to be controversial. Where does legal land-use control under the police power end and public purchase under the eminent domain power start? In recent years, several courts have ruled that certain government land-use controls were illegal and were used to avoid the outright purchase of private land under the power of eminent domain. The continuing debate over the limits of government controls has the potential to significantly affect the value and future use of private parcels of real estate.

Housing Shortages and Affordability

Commentators have discussed the various problems of the housing industry for decades, and many cures have been tried. The four problems currently concerning housing specialists the most appear to be:

1. Environmentally related shortages of land and materials

2. The strong cyclical variation in the cost and supply of credit

3. Difficulty of keeping older units maintained

4. How to provide housing that elderly and low-income people can afford

Shortages of Land and Materials

Some cities and counties have stopped issuing building permits until new sources of water can be obtained or sewage treatment can be improved. Strict requirements for environmental impact reports have delayed many larger developments. Citizens have complained of the traffic and noise generated by new development and have forced building moratoriums, rezonings, and other actions that have also delayed development. In some cases, housing and commercial density has been sharply lowered, with many acres dedicated as permanent open space. Problems with air pollution and with expansion of necessary water and sewer supplies have produced a shortage of building sites from time to time in some locations.

Material shortages in the past have included cement, lumber, and bathtubs. Many shortages arose because manufacturers had to correct years of abuse in water and air pollution. Some products, such as asbestos and other hazardous materials, have pollution problems that are difficult to resolve. Correcting these problems has been costly for manufacturers, which in turn has raised prices to builders and, eventually, to consumers. Part of the problem relates to the extremely cyclical nature of homebuilding, with its booms and busts. Many material manufacturers cannot afford to maintain standby factories and skilled workers to meet builders' needs during boom times without going bankrupt during bust times.

The "Credit-Crunch" Cycle

Credit cost and availability are monetary policy tools that the Federal Reserve Board uses to help stabilize the U.S. economy. A problem is created when shifts in Federal Reserve policies create cyclical shifts in interest rates. These ups and downs in interest rates have a major impact on the real estate market. Mortgage market reforms, such as adjustable rate loans, more liquid secondary mortgage markets, and the influx of international capital, have helped to stabilize the U.S. mortgage market somewhat, but fluctuations in interest rates will still occur in the future. These interest rate swings cause swings in home sales volumes and, to a degree, prices. In turn, the swings impair the efficiency of real estate-related businesses, increasing the cost to consumers.

Maintaining Older Homes

As noted earlier, each year new homes constitute only a small percentage of addition to the existing stock. The average home has a long life, but as houses get older, they tend to show more wear and tear and are thus worth less. To a major degree, providing decent housing for poorer people means maintaining the existing stock of homes despite the wear and tear of the years.

Many ideas are being tried across the country, and the Housing and Urban Development Department and other federal agencies are seeking new concepts. Suggestions include rezoning, special rehabilitation funds, formation of neighborhood groups, privatization, and the use of housing vouchers.

Housing the Elderly and the Poor

Finally, there continue to be problems in providing specialized housing for elderly and large, low-income families. Ideas that have been tried have included:

1. Federally subsidized elderly housing projects.

2. Property tax credits for elderly people.

3. Still-unsuccessful experiments with publicly owned or subsidized housing for poverty-level households.

4. Increased emphasis on maintenance of older housing, including renovation grants or low-interest loans to elderly or low-income families.

5. A voucher system, whereby public housing projects are eliminated and the elderly and poor are given vouchers that allow the people to find their own housing in the private market.

6. Use of inclusionary zoning, as noted in Chapter 13, "Land-Use Controls."

The housing needs of the elderly have been better handled in recent years, but the typical poverty-level household (especially if very large or very poor) is probably housed little better than it was 10 years ago. Further changes in poverty housing programs seem likely. The tremendous projected growth in numbers of elderly over the next few decades coupled with immigration, both legal and illegal, will strain existing facilities; major growth in this specialized housing market is expected.

Consumerism

Newspaper headlines feature consumer rebellions, boycotts, class-action lawsuits, and mass appearances at regulatory or congressional hearings. People now are willing to express their objections to some of the goods and services they buy. So far, this has not been quite as noticeable with real estate as with cars, for example. Such a lag is to be expected, because people do not buy and sell real estate very often and find it complex and hard to understand. As consumers become more confident at expressing objections, however, their focus probably will include more real estate complaints.

Visible signs of this change can be seen in the increasing number of lawsuits against builders or sellers over structural and soil problems. The spread of real estate sale disclosure laws is another sign of this change. Another sign is the increasing use of broker errors and omissions insurance and home warranty insurance to cover house and equipment repairs in the year after sale. The increase in landlord-tenant conflict and changes in landlord-tenant law are added evidence of growing consumerism.

The Real Estate Industry

As any product or industry changes, the people who handle the product or are a part of the industry must change. The most obvious changes throughout the real estate industry are: (1) increased knowledge (via education or training), (2) increased specialization or a narrowing of the area of activity, and (3) an increase in the average size of a real estate firm or organization. The size of the typical real estate brokerage company has expanded by growth and merger and by joining franchise chains. Increased cooperation among real estate brokers seems to be a trend.

Future potential changes include a need for greater specialized knowledge on the part of individual brokers. One specialization, already evident, separates brokerage for a commission from consulting for a fee. Further specialization could go so far as to produce separate broker's licenses for home sales, investment property, and so forth. Some agents now primarily list property, separating themselves from those who represent buyers. Computer software and Internet marketing are playing increasingly important roles. With the increase in multiculturalism, there has been a trend for individual licensees and in some cases entire real estate offices to specialize along cultural lines. The use of clerical or semiprofessional assistants appears to be another trend.

The mechanisms for connecting properties with buyers may be the area for the most dramatic changes. The formation of regional, super regional, state-wide, national, and worldwide multiple listing services can expose properties to previously unheard of numbers of potential buyers. The entry of for-profit corporate-run listing services, competing directly with traditional, real estate association controlled, multiple listing services, will allow sellers to directly list their properties for sale, bypassing real estate agents. Finally, the possibility of "virtual" real estate companies on the web, could greatly reduce the need for "brick and mortar" building. In effect, a real estate company can have an "office" in every city, by having an agent in each town, working out of his or her home, and doing all broker-to-salesperson communications electronically.

REVIEWING YOUR UNDERSTANDING

Real Estate Issues

1. What appear to be the two major land-use problems? Give examples of each from your community.

2. How many examples can you give of connections between pollution and land use?

3. What four problems of housing are listed? How does each apply to your community?

4. What changes in consumer attitudes toward real estate have you noticed? List those that are favorable and those that are unfavorable.

19.2 National Changes

National changes are those that involve many areas of the general U.S. economy in addition to the real estate industry. People outside of real estate might not even consider these changes as affecting real estate. The issues mentioned here include demography, poverty, lifestyles, transportation, inflation, and finance and trade.

Demography

Demography is the study of influences on population, such as birth and death rates and migration. The most important demographic statistic for real estate is the rate of net population increase, or births in excess of deaths, plus net immigration, leading to the number of household formations. World trends, as well as trends in a particular area, are important because of immigration (in-migration), the effect on demand for agricultural and other exports, and competition for world resources.

Increasing population means greater demand for food and all other resources. To the degree that real estate is fixed in quantity, an increase in population means an increase in demand and in land prices. Large immigrations are also important, as demonstrated by the current growth in California and several other states.

Population Composition

Demographers also study how many people there are in each category of age, sex, race, education, and occupation. Demographers study the composition of the population in part because of the obvious changes that occur as people get older. The population of any area can be studied by starting with the age, sex, and household characteristics of the current population, adding the expected births, subtracting the anticipated deaths, and forecasting the net migration. Analysis of *current* populations is commonly done by all levels of government, and many states and countries obtain projections of future population.

The population of every city, state, and nation is changing, because of changes in composition and number as the people age. These changes in composition can be projected in detail. Such projections would draw conclusions about the projected future mix of household sizes, incomes, occupations, and ages, which would be very relevant to real estate. Housing markets, for example, often go through cycles of larger versus small housing units, and this cycle is related to swings in the proportion of younger households to middle-aged ones. Because of the unusually large number of Americans born between 1945 and 1965, the period of the so-called "baby boom," there is expected to be a major effect on housing demand as this group ages and retires. It is clear, therefore, that a number of future changes in housing demand have already been set in motion by these projected changes in population composition.

Poverty

The U.S. economy is able to provide a minimum standard of living. Yet we still have real poverty—too little money for safe and sanitary housing and a nutritious diet. The problem cannot simply be cured by increasing the incomes of the poor, because custom, behavior, attitudes, and failure in education can block effective use of money. There is an obvious frustration created by living in poverty and seeing televised and advertised luxuries. Avenues of advancement for the talented and motivated are needed as much as ever. However, what is needed, even more, are incentives to motivate people away from addictions and other self-destructive behavior.

These problems call for continuing with poverty programs, but it is *not* clear what type of programs. Current housing programs for the poor have been criticized as much as earlier ones. New proposals range from direct rent supplements via vouchers to guaranteed minimum incomes. The growing frustration of voters complicates the already confused situation. When analyzing a particular real estate market, the real estate economist should consider the effects of current housing programs, the impact of any curtailment, and the various major proposals for change.

Lifestyles

How people choose to live, within the limits set by their incomes, determines how they allocate their resources and the demand for goods and services that they bring to the economy. In the past, people had to work hard just to survive. In modern America, for most people, our society can provide an adequate *minimum* standard of living, with far less time spent on "work" than was true in the past.

To date, however, few people have reduced their workday; instead, many work relatively long hours and use the added income to buy a standard of living that, in this country, goes well above the minimum level. The effects on real estate are substantial. Examples include second homes, recreation resorts, bed and breakfast inns, expensive restaurants, acreage homesites, and new luxury homes.

There is now open discussion of alternatives to traditional full-time employment, and one sees increasing desire for time for non-income-producing pursuits, despite possibly lower incomes. It is too early to tell how widespread this movement toward nontraditional work patterns is, or whether these lifestyle changes will continue as people get older. Indeed, this trend is countered by the heightened emphasis on national and business competitiveness. However this plays out, the ultimate effect on the demand for real estate could be substantial.

Transportation

Transportation is a major source of pollution, as well as a major user of the nation's total energy. In addition, the different methods of transportation differ in their impact on city shape and density, as discussed in Chapter 7.

The automobile currently dominates American transportation, but it is clearly a major source of petroleum consumption as well as pollution. The problems of automobile pollution, petroleum price increases, and possible petroleum shortages suggest that, over the long term, the present auto will be altered, or its part in our society will be changed. The impact on real estate will be significant because of the impact the automobile has had in developing suburban areas. In some regions, the increased availability of public transit over the past several decades has unquestionably changed where people live and work. Will transportation problems be partially solved by the telecommunications revolution? Will this affect real estate trends and values?

Inflation

Very few books about the future written during the 1960s listed inflation as a serious problem in the United States, but by the 1970s, inflation was considered a major U.S. problem. Then in the 1980s, the rate of inflation in the United States dropped drastically. By the mid-2000s, inflation was squeezed to exceptionally low rates. Where will inflation head in the late 2000s? If it remains moderate, price levels will be determined by basic supply and demand interactions. But if rapid inflation again occurs, the dislocations of the 1970s could once more hit the U.S. economy, and this will have a destabilizing impact on the real estate market. There is strong concern in financial circles whenever inflation threatens the economy. This creates a political force against inflation. But past U.S. governments seem drawn, like a moth to a flame, by the attraction of offering benefits to voters without taxing them for it. Has government learned its lesson? Will pay-as-you-go become a permanent government philosophy? Does deficit reduction really matter?

Finance and International Trade

Because of the size, wealth in raw materials, and location of the United States, the role of foreign trade in the economy of this country has historically been rather small when compared to the economies of other industrialized countries. As a result, the American economy has in the past been able to resist the international economic fluctuations that have rocked other nations. However, the 1990s and 2000s have marked the end of this protected position.

The eroding position of America's balance of payments was the key. Our historic surplus of exports over imports has been reversed, and a lack of confidence abroad in the strength of the dollar has caused the value of the dollar to drop. The post-World War II agreements regulating international monetary exchange have been replaced by more flexible understandings that allow currencies to float in value. And the massive changes in petroleum prices have added another dimension of insecurity to an already shaken international financial picture.

Each of these crises has had effects on real estate. Interest rates, capital availability, import costs, and export jobs are now closely tied to international finance and trade issues. Each is also important to real estate values. Investors have a real concern about effective and prompt solutions to the international financial strains that occasionally emerge.

These international conflicts can lead to wars, and wars have massive repercussions on international resources and finances. Every current international economic issue—trade balances, resources, energy—has the danger of becoming entangled with past bitter rivalries and ethnic or religious conflicts to such a degree that war can erupt. The issues themselves have effects on real estate; wars multiply these effects. With the enactment of various trade agreements, such as the North American Free Trade Agreement (NAFTA) and the World Trade Organization (WTO), it is hoped that the opening of markets and the creation of interdependence will reduce some of the conflicts of the past. However, various groups and labor organizations have protested their formation.

REVIEWING YOUR UNDERSTANDING

National Issues

1. What is meant by population composition, and how does it affect real estate? Give an example from your community.

2. Show how attitudes toward the importance of work or leisure influence real estate use and value.

3. Can you give four reasons why poverty affects real estate?

4. How does transportation change affect the value of real estate? Why is future transportation change likely? What is the most recent transportation change in your community, and what were its real estate effects?

5. How do international issues affect real estate? Give four examples from your community. Is your region affected by trade agreements such as NAFTA and WTO?.

19.3 The Uncertain Future

The potential problems noted in this section are worldwide phenomena that penetrate to the core of culture and society. Although these issues may seem only remotely connected to real estate, they have a great long-range impact on land use and values. These will be among the major issues of the next generation. Here are some topics that are both uncertain and controversial.

Telemobility

The medium, or process, of our time—electronic technology—is reshaping and restructuring patterns of social interdependence and every aspect of our personal life.

> Everything is changing—you, your family, your neighborhood, your education, your job, your government, your relation to "the others." And they're changing dramatically.[1]

We don't really know whether the world will ultimately become a global village—McLuhan's thesis—or whether the impact of electronic media will make us a world of isolated individuals held together by a surface network of communications. But it is clear that the impact of electronics and digital technology on communications has changed the fundamental nature of our lives. Many things that our ancestors could *only* do face-to-face, including talking and shopping, we can now do from a distance. Instead of traveling in person, we can travel electrically; that is, we have *telemobility*. According to John Diebold, "It would be difficult to overstate the magnitude of change that will take place in the lives of all of us, in human history, as a result of the information revolution that has so unobtrusively taken place in our day."[2] Alvin Toffler, who created the expression "future shock" in 1965, describes the change that confronted the last quarter of our century as a firestorm: "Change sweeps through the highly industrialized countries with waves of ever accelerating speed and unprecedented impact. It spawns in its wake all sorts of curious social flora—from psychedelic churches and, 'free universities' to science cities in the Arctic and wife-swap clubs in California."[3]

Forty years ago, futurologists predicted a world of video telephones, computers and faxes in the home, and executives working

[1] Marshall McLuhan and Quentin Fiore, *The Medium Is the Message*. New York, Bantam Books, 1967, p. 8.
[2] John Diebold, *Beyond Automation*. New York, McGraw Hill, 1964.
[3] Alvin Toffler, *Future Shock*. New York, Bantam Books, 1971, p. 9.

Table 19.1 A Familiar Form of Compound Growth

If we place $1,000 in a savings certificate at 8 percent, with instructions to reinvest the interest, it will grow to:

1 year	$ 1,080
10 years	$ 2,159
50 years	$ 46,902
100 years	$2,199,761

from desks in their homes, perhaps meeting with colleagues once a week or so. They foresaw people shopping by catalog and television, paying bills by electronics, participating politically by cable TV, and entertaining themselves by video-recorders. Such a world—a world without office buildings, without massive customer facilities, without face-to-face contact—would have a *great impact* on real estate. Many of the futurologists' predictions have come true. What will the 21st century bring? Will working at home continue to grow as it has in the past decade? What does this say about home design? About central office rents? About downtown retail sales?

Growth

Population growth, although uneven among individual nations, has already been recognized as one of the world's most pressing current and future problems. Nearly always, this growth is "exponential," which means that population is growing by 2 percent each year, at a constant percentage increase, rather than by a constant number like, say, 2 million people each year. The problem with exponential growth is that it compounds, so that the increase in numbers grows larger each year. If it compounds long enough, the growth clearly becomes insupportably large, as the following 1967 quotation indicates.

> At the present time, starting someplace about 1946, the average annual rate of increase in the world's population is about 2 percent. Using the 1962 population as a base, and applying this rate of growth to it, shows that in 650 years—somewhat less than the time backwards to the Renaissance—there would be, in our world, one person standing on each square foot of land.[4]

Table 19.1 demonstrates the power of compounding. There are many examples in nature of such exponential growth, but they all end

---

[4] Don Fabun, *The Dynamics of Change*. Prentice Hall, Englewood Cliffs, New Jersey, 1967, pp. 1–10.

with the collapse of growth and a sharp drop in total numbers. The world obviously cannot physically hold enough people to accept a 2 percent yearly growth in population for 650 years, so some form of natural breakdown will reduce it. It seems clear that there is an upper limit to population growth.

Some argue that this time limit is much shorter than 650 years; that the world faces growing food shortages that can only be postponed at great expense and cannot be eliminated. Others point to the congestion of modern cities and other problems. They ask if human population may have other types of limits than just food, such as the chaos that may result from excessive social pressures. The growth problem raises some fundamental questions about our future and, in turn, about real estate and real estate investments.

Population Control

For religious and social reasons, population control is quite controversial. Yet more people appear involved with personal, social, or legal population control than ever before. It is obvious that this issue will be examined even more intensely in the future. The changes that could occur, whether legal or social, would undoubtedly affect general economic conditions, trends in particular industries, the economic base of cities, and real estate values, as well as the fundamental question of future world population levels.

Resources

Exponential population growth increases the need for agricultural products, petroleum, ores, timber, and every other commodity used by people. In fact, our *per-person* use of many commodities is also increasing exponentially. This means that production must increase even faster than population. An additional complication is that the better ores, fields, and wells are generally already in production. Thus, the increased production must come from either new technologies or more marginal areas, at higher costs.

Many believe that there are limits to future increases of resource production. They state that the limits arise from increased costs rather than from actually running out of the resources. As prices rise, it becomes more feasible to recapture or recycle the used resource than to hunt for new resources. Gold and platinum have long been in this category, more recently joined by silver and, increasingly, by aluminum and water. However, maximum recycling may only *postpone* the inevitable result of exponential growth, because some resources are lost in ways that cannot be recovered by recycling.

Pollution

All human activities produce some air, water, and noise pollution. As population doubles and production per person doubles again, pollution grows. Often the growth of pollutants is hidden, because the natural system can partly purify the water and the air and muffle sounds. Sometimes, quite suddenly, a pollution problem can appear when the natural cleansing system is overcome. Our society is now more aware of this and has begun to clean up the polluting by-products of many decades of production.

The cost of correcting pollution adds to the cost of operating plants and cities and affects the demand for the plant's products, or for various locations in the cities. Correcting for past pollution shifts the cost characteristics of nearly all products and nearly all locations, but not by the same amount for each. This causes a great sorting out, or readjustment, among competing locations and products. In this process, some locations and products will gain and some will lose.

The Los Angeles air basin was one of the first areas in the country to become troubled by automobile-created air pollution. The research and experience of Los Angeles has produced a wealth of information for everyone. Unfortunately, the L.A. region seems to be in a race. Population grows, and increasing auto ownership raises auto growth even faster. As long as the exponential growth in the number of automobiles continues, sharper and sharper cuts in the rate of pollution per automobile are necessary just to stay even. Because pollution control gets harder and more expensive the further you go, it must be concluded that either pollution will go up or the number of autos must not grow so fast. Every other polluting human activity is a similar problem, as long as the numbers continue to grow.

Energy

The United States is the world's predominant energy-driven society, substituting other energy sources for human labor. As a result, energy use per person has had its own exponential growth, on top of the growth of population and the growth of goods and services.

Unfortunately, the exponential increases in energy consume fuels, such as oil, natural gas, and coal, that cannot be renewed or recycled. The original solution pioneered in the 1950s and 1960s was nuclear energy. However, because of serious disasters worldwide, the development of nuclear plants in the United States came to a halt. Other alternatives—breeder reactors, fusion, geothermal energy, tides, winds, solar energy—require immense effort to be significant energy sources during our lifetimes. It is clear that energy demands of the next decade or so will continue to be borne mostly by oil, natural gas, and coal. However, energy conservation has had a significant initial impact. Similar future impacts will be harder to obtain.

Every aspect of economic production, resource allocation, and land-use determination is heavily influenced by energy availability and cost. The oil shortages that emerged with conflicts in the Mideast have major effects on real estate, as have increases in oil and natural gas prices.

Most countries of the world use much less energy per person than the United States does, but the growth rate of their use of energy per person is rising much faster. This means that worldwide competition for oil, gas, and coal is increasing rapidly. The result should be continued price increases, as well as pressure to develop new energy sources and reduce energy use.

From these changes in energy prices and use will come changes in real estate. Examples include additional emphasis on insulation and other aspects of energy conservation. Energy change will affect many businesses; local economies will then feel the effects, and, of course, real estate will be affected by these changes, possibly heavily.

REVIEWING YOUR UNDERSTANDING

The Uncertain Future

1. Define the concept *telemobility*. What is its significance to real estate? Can you give an actual example from your community?

2. Explain why the rate of net population increase is so important.

3. What is *exponential growth?*

CHAPTER SUMMARY

There cannot be a real summary of this chapter because no one can write a summary of the future! Others might see very different potential strengths and weaknesses. What is *your* view?

IMPORTANT TERMS AND CONCEPTS

Consumerism	*Inflation*
Exponential growth of	*Land-use controls*
Energy	*Lifestyles*
Pollution	*Limits to growth*
Population	*Telemobility*
Resource use	*Transportation*

ANSWERS TO REVIEWING YOUR UNDERSTANDING QUESTIONS

Chapter 2

1. b	6. a	11. b	16. c	21. b
2. d	7. c	12. a	17. d	22. b
3. b	8. a	13. d	18. a	23. d
4. c	9. d	14. b	19. a	24. a
5. a	10. b	15. a	20. c	25. d

Chapter 3

1. b	6. a	11. b	16. b	21. c
2. d	7. b	12. a	17. c	22. d
3. a	8. c	13. b	18. c	23. a
4. c	9. d	14. d	19. a	24. c
5. d	10. d	15. c	20. d	25. b

Chapter 4

1. d	6. b	11. c	16. d	21. a
2. a	7. a	12. a	17. c	22. a
3. c	8. b	13. b	18. b	23. b
4. c	9. c	14. b	19. d	24. d
5. c	10. a	15. a	20. b	25. d

Chapter 5

1. d	6. c	11. a	16. d	21. a
2. c	7. a	12. b	17. d	22. b
3. a	8. c	13. a	18. b	23. a
4. c	9. a	14. d	19. c	24. c
5. c	10. d	15. b	20. b	25. a

Chapter 6

1. b	6. d	11. b	16. c	21. a
2. c	7. d	12. b	17. b	22. b
3. a	8. a	13. c	18. a	23. b
4. d	9. d	14. b	19. b	24. a
5. a	10. d	15. a	20. b	25. c

Chapter 7

1. b	6. b	11. b	16. b	21. d
2. d	7. d	12. c	17. a	22. a
3. a	8. d	13. d	18. b	23. d
4. c	9. a	14. b	19. d	24. b
5. b	10. d	15. d	20. b	25. c

Chapter 8

1. a	6. c	11. b	16. b	21. b
2. d	7. b	12. b	17. b	22. b
3. c	8. c	13. b	18. c	23. b
4. d	9. c	14. b	19. a	24. d
5. d	10. d	15. a	20. c	25. a

Chapter 9

1. b	6. c	11. c	16. a	21. d
2. c	7. d	12. a	17. d	22. a
3. a	8. d	13. d	18. a	23. b
4. d	9. b	14. a	19. b	24. d
5. a	10. a	15. c	20. d	25. a

Chapter 10

1. b	6. a	11. a	16. b	21. b
2. c	7. d	12. c	17. b	22. c
3. d	8. c	13. a	18. c	23. c
4. b	9. b	14. a	19. a	24. a
5. a	10. a	15. d	20. b	25. c

Chapter 11

1. b	6. b	11. b	16. d	21. b
2. c	7. c	12. c	17. b	22. a
3. d	8. c	13. d	18. a	23. d
4. d	9. a	14. a	19. a	24. a
5. a	10. b	15. c	20. d	25. d

Chapter 12

1. d	6. b	11. a	16. d	21. b
2. c	7. d	12. a	17. c	22. a
3. a	8. b	13. c	18. b	23. d
4. a	9. d	14. b	19. c	24. a
5. b	10. c	15. c	20. b	25. d

Chapter 13

1. a	6. d	11. d	16. c	21. a
2. b	7. b	12. b	17. d	22. a
3. a	8. a	13. d	18. c	23. d
4. c	9. d	14. a	19. d	24. d
5. d	10. c	15. b	20. d	25. a

Chapter 14

1. c	6. d	11. c	16. a	21. a
2. a	7. b	12. d	17. a	22. d
3. d	8. a	13. a	18. a	23. a
4. c	9. d	14. b	19. a	24. c
5. b	10. a	15. b	20. d	25. a

Chapter 15

1. a	6. b	11. b	16. b	21. a
2. c	7. a	12. a	17. a	22. a
3. d	8. a	13. d	18. b	23. a
4. a	9. d	14. c	19. c	24. d
5. c	10. a	15. a	20. a	25. d

Chapter 16

1. d	6. d	11. c	16. b
2. c	7. d	12. c	17. a
3. c	8. b	13. b	18. b
4. a	9. a	14. b	19. c
5. b	10. a	15. a	

20. $15,860 Net Operating Income
21. Negative [$904] Before-Tax Cash Flow
22. $1,403 Net Spendable Income (After-Tax Cash Flow)
23. $$\frac{\text{Price } \$300,000}{\text{Gross Scheduled Income } \$ 22,800} = \begin{array}{c}13.16 \text{ Gross Rent} \\ \text{Multiplier}\end{array}$$

24. $$\frac{\text{Net Operating Income } \$15,860}{\text{Price } \$ 300,000} = \begin{array}{c}5.29\% \text{ Capitalization} \\ \text{Rate}\end{array}$$

25. $$\frac{\text{After-Tax Cash Flow } \$1,403}{\begin{array}{c}\text{Cash Invested } \$90,000 \\ \text{(down payment)}\end{array}} = \begin{array}{c}1.56\% \text{ After-Tax} \\ \text{Cash on Cash Rate}\end{array}$$

Appendix for Chapter 16

1. $6,780 Before-Tax Cash Flow
2. $5,083 Taxes Saved
3. $11,863 Net Spendable Income (After-Tax Cash Flow)
4. $$\frac{\text{Price } \$1,200,000}{\text{Gross Scheduled Income } \$120,000} = 10 \text{ Gross Rent Multiplier}$$

5. $$\frac{\text{Net Operating Income } \$85,980}{\text{Price } \$1,200,000} = 7.17\% \text{ Capitalization Rate}$$

6. $$\frac{\text{Before-Tax Cash Flow } \$6,780}{\text{Cash Invested } \$300,000} = \begin{array}{c}2.26\% \text{ Before-Tax Cash} \\ \text{on Cash Rate}\end{array}$$

7. $$\frac{\text{After-Tax Cash Flow } \$11,863}{\text{Cash Invested } \$300,000} = \begin{array}{c}3.95\% \text{ After-Tax Cash} \\ \text{On Cash Rate}\end{array}$$

8. $$\frac{\text{Net Operating Income } \$85,980}{\text{Market Capitalization Rate } .08} = \$1,074,750 \text{ Market Price}$$

9. $18,174 Net Spendable Income (After-Tax Cash Flow)

10. $$\frac{\text{Net Spendable Income } \$18,174}{\text{Cash Invested } \$268,687} = \begin{array}{c}6.76\% \text{ After-Tax Cash} \\ \text{on Cash Rate}\end{array}$$

Chapter 17

1. d	6. c	11. b
2. d	7. b	12. c
3. a	8. a	13. a ($1 mill. $\times$ 60% $\div$39 years = $15,385)
4. b	9. a	14. d
5. c	10. c	15. a

16. c
17. b
18. a
19. c $300,000 price + 3,000 costs + 15,000 imp. less
        $20,000 deposit = $298,000
20. d $400,000
        −32,000 seller closing costs
        −10,000 carry-forward passive loss
        −298,000 adjusted cost basis
        $ 60, 000 gain
21. b
22. b
23. a
24. b
25. d

Chapter 18

1. b	6. d	11. d
2. a	7. a	12. a
3. d	8. b	13. d
4. c	9. a	14. c
5. d	10. b	15. a

INDEX